Management
of Organizational
Behavior

Fourth Edition

Management of Organizational Behavior:

Utilizing Human Resources

PAUL HERSEY
Graduate School of Applied Behavioral Sciences
California American University
Escondido, California

KENNETH H. BLANCHARD
University of Massachusetts
Amherst, Massachusetts

PRENTICE-HALL, INC., *Englewood Cliffs, New Jersey* 07632

Library of Congress Cataloging in Publication Data

Hersey, Paul.
    Management of organizational behavior.

    Bibliography: p.
    Includes index.
    1. Organizational behavior.   2. Management.
3. Leadership.   I. Blanchard, Kenneth H.   II. Title.
HD58.7.H47 1982   658.3   81-12097
ISBN 0-13-549618-7   AACR2
ISBN 0-13-549600-4 (pbk.)

Editorial/production supervision and
   interior design by Sonia Meyer
Cover design by Mark Binn
Manufacturing Buyer: Ed O'Dougherty

Printed in the United States of America

20 19 18 17 16 15 14 13

ISBN 0-13-549618-7
ISBN 0-13-549600-4 {pbk.}

Prentice-Hall International, Inc., *London*
Prentice-Hall of Australia Pty. Limited, *Sydney*
Prentice-Hall of Canada, Ltd., *Toronto*
Prentice-Hall of India Private Limited, *New Delhi*
Prentice-Hall of Japan, Inc., *Tokyo*
Prentice-Hall of Southeast Asia Pte. Ltd., *Singapore*
Whitehall Books Limited, *Wellington, New Zealand*

to

RALPH E. HERSEY, SR., a retired telephone pioneer with over fifty patents for Bell Laboratories, whose work made direct distance dialing a reality. In looking back over his thirty-nine years of work with the telephone industry, he once commented that of all his contributions, the most rewarding aspect to him personally was that he became known as a *developer of people.*

and

the late REAR ADMIRAL THEODORE BLANCHARD, USNR, former Naval officer who was decorated with two Silver Stars, the Bronze Star, the Presidential Citation, and a Navy Unit Commendation for his courageous and competent World War II leadership in the Pacific. In talking with people who worked for him over the years, he was always described as an inspirational, dedicated and caring leader who always fought for his people and the "underdog," whether in peace or war time.

Contents

chapter 3

Motivating Environment 45

chapter 4

Leader Behavior 82

chapter 5

Determining Effectiveness   **106**

chapter 9

Developing Human Resources   193

chapter 10

Constructive Discipline 212

chapter 11

Building Effective Relationships 232

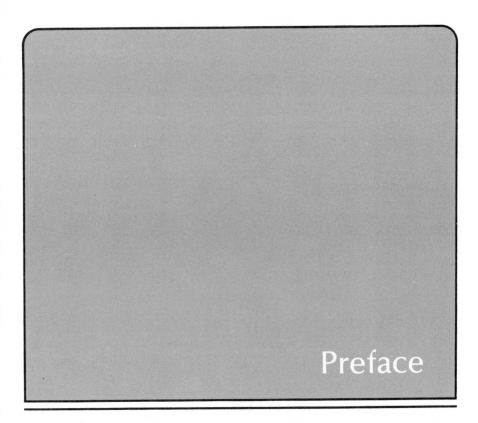

Preface

In the preface to our first edition we made the following statements, which we still believe:

> For a long time management theory has been characterized by a search for universals—a preoccupation with discovering essential elements of all organizations. The discovering of common elements is necessary, but they do not really provide practitioners with "principles" that can be applied with universal success.
>
> In the past decade there has appeared a relative maturity in this field as it begins to focus on "patterned variations"—situational differences. We assume that there are common elements in all organizations, but we also assume differences among them and in particular the managing of their human resources. As the inventory of empirical studies expands, making comparisons and contrasts possible, management theory will continue to emerge. Common elements will be isolated and important variables brought to light.
>
> We believe that management theory is important to all categories of organizations—business, government, military, medicine, education, "voluntary" organizations such as the church, and even the home. We thus have drawn our illustrations and cases from a variety of these organizations and incorporated concepts from many disciplines. Our purpose is to identify a framework which may be helpful in integrating independent approaches from these various disciplines to the understanding of human behavior and management theory.

The focus of this book is on behavior within organizations and not between organizations. Our belief is that an organization is a unique living organism whose basic component is the individual and this individual is our fundamental unit of study. Thus, our concentration is on the interaction of people, motivation, and leadership.

Though this book is an outgrowth of the insights of many earlier writers, we hope it will make some contribution to management theory.

The response to our first three editions has been widespread and diverse. Organizations in several fields have made use of the text in a variety of ways—not only in the United States, but in other countries throughout the world. Our goal of writing a concise and easy-to-read text—one that would make the behavioral sciences come alive for practitioners and students alike—appears to have been accomplished.

In this fourth edition we have clarified and updated much of the information presented in earlier editions. Passages in each chapter are enhanced with new and significant additions to make the contents practical and useful in today's world. Considerable rewriting is found in the sections dealing with the developmental cycle and the concept of constructive discipline.

Further, this fourth edition focuses in depth on the concept of power as it applies to leadership effectiveness. Since leadership at any level is basically an attempt to influence . . . and since power is properly defined as influence potential . . . the effective leader must understand from whence power is derived; what power bases are available; and how to use these power bases wisely. Chapter 8 discusses the Situational approach to using power in organizational settings.

We trust that this fourth edition will better represent a contribution to the current status of the behavioral sciences.

We owe much to colleagues and associates without whose guidance, encouragement, and inspiration the first edition of this book—much less the fourth—would never have been written. In particular, we are indebted to Harry Evarts, Ted Hellebrandt, Norman Martin, Don McCarty, Bob Melendes, Walter Pauk, Warren Ramshaw, and Franklin Williams.

We wish to make special mention of Chris Argyris, William J. Reddin and Edgar A. Schein. Their contributions to the field of applied behavioral science have been most valuable to us in the course of preparing this book, and we hereby express our appreciation to them.

Finally, we add a special thanks to Kevin Sullivan and Sonia Meyer for their skill and dedication in the editing and preparation of this edition, and to Suzanne and Margie, our wives, for their continued patience, support, and interest in the progress of our work.

Paul Hersey

Kenneth H. Blanchard

Management
of Organizational
Behavior

chapter 1

Management: A Behavioral Approach

The transformation of American society since the turn of the century has been breathtaking. We have progressed from a basically agrarian society to a dynamic, industrial society with a higher level of education and standard of living than was ever thought possible. In addition, our scientific and technical advancement staggers the imagination.

This progress has not been without its seamy side. At a time when we should be rejoicing in a golden age of plenty, we find ourselves wallowing in conflict—conflict between nations, conflict between races, conflict between management and workers, even conflict between neighbors. These problems that we face cannot be solved by scientific and technical skills alone; they will require social skills. Many of our most critical problems are not in the world of *things*, but in the world of *people*. Our greatest failure as human beings has been the inability to secure cooperation and understanding with others. Shortly after World War II, Elton Mayo recognized this problem when he reflected that "the consequences for society of the unbalance between the development of technical and of social skill have been disastrous."[1]

SUCCESSFUL VERSUS UNSUCCESSFUL SCIENCES

In seeking reasons for this unbalance, Mayo suggested that a significant part of the problem might be traced to the difference between what he called "the successful sciences" (chemistry, physics, and physiology) and "the unsuccessful sciences" (psychology, sociology, and political science). He labeled the former "successful" because in studying these sciences both theory and practice are provided. Pure knowledge is limited in value unless it can be applied in real situations. The implication of these profound conclusions is that in learning about chemistry or physics, students or practitioners are given direct experience in using their new technical skills in the laboratory, but on the other hand, according to Mayo, the unsuccessful sciences

> do not seem to equip students with a single social skill that is usable in ordinary human situations . . . no continuous and direct contact with the social facts is contrived for the student. He learns from books, spending endless hours in libraries; he reconsiders ancient formulae, uncontrolled by the steady development of experimental skill, the equivalent of the clinic or indeed of the laboratory.[2]

Change

Early contributions in the behavioral sciences, as Mayo suggests, seemed to provide knowledge without effecting changes in behavior. This book will focus on four levels of change in people: (1) knowledge changes, (2) attitudinal changes, (3) behavior changes, and (4) group or organizational performance changes.[3] The time relationship and the relative difficulty involved in making each of these levels of change when force or compliance is not a factor is illustrated in Figure 1-1.

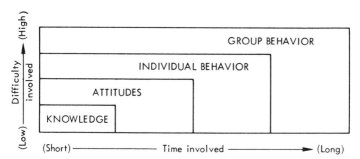

FIGURE 1-1. Time and difficulty involved in making various changes.

Changes in knowledge are the easiest to make, followed by changes in attitudes. Attitude structures differ from knowledge structures in that they are emotionally charged in a positive or a negative way. Changes in behavior are significantly more difficult and time consuming than either of the two previous levels. But the implementation of group or organizational performance change is perhaps the most difficult and time consuming. Our destiny may in fact be dependent upon how well the behavioral sciences are able to resolve conflict through understanding and implementing change.

A Problem of Investment

A major obstacle to the practical application of the behavioral sciences has been the small amount of money allocated by government, business, and other agencies for research in these areas. In the United States only one of every thirty dollars spent on research and development is channeled to behavioral science areas. The remainder is spent for research in the "hard sciences" to be used in developing "things." However, more must be done than spend money on research in the behavioral sciences. Funds are also needed to support the practical application of this research. This is especially important since managers, to be effective, regardless of the type of organization in which they operate, need to develop know-how in human skills in addition to their knowledge of the technical aspects of their jobs.

MANAGEMENT DEFINED

It is obvious after a review of the literature that there are almost as many definitions of management as there are writers in the field. A common thread that appears in these definitions is the manager's concern for accomplishing organizational goals or objectives.[4] We shall define management as *working with and through individuals and groups to accomplish organizational goals.*

This definition, it should be noted, makes no mention of business or industrial organizations. Management, as defined, applies to organizations whether they are businesses, educational institutions, hospitals, political organizations, or even families. To be successful, these organizations require their management personnel to have interpersonal skills. The achievement of organizational objectives through leadership is management. Thus, everyone is a manager in at least certain portions of his or her life.

Distinction Between Management and Leadership

Management and leadership are often thought of as one and the same thing. We feel, however, that there is an important distinction between the two concepts.

In essence, leadership is a broader concept than management. Management is thought of as a special kind of leadership in which the achievement of organizational goals is paramount. The key difference between the two concepts, therefore lies in the word *organization.* Leadership occurs any time one attempts to *influence the behavior* of an individual or group, regardless of the reason. It may be for one's own goals or those of others, and they may or may not be congruent with organizational goals.

MANAGEMENT PROCESS

The managerial functions of *planning, organizing, motivating,* and *controlling* are considered central to a discussion of management by many authors. These functions are relevant, regardless of the type of organization or level of management with which one is concerned. As Harold Koontz and Cyril O'Donnell have said:

"Acting in their managerial capacity, presidents, department heads, foremen, supervisors, college deans, bishops, and heads of governmental agencies all do the same thing. As managers they are all engaged in part in getting things done with and through people. As a manager, each must, at one time or another, carry out all the duties characteristic of managers."[5] Even a well-run household uses these managerial functions, although in many cases they are used intuitively.

Planning involves setting *goals* and *objectives* for the organization and developing "work maps" showing how these goals and objectives are to be accomplished. Once plans have been made, organizing becomes meaningful. This involves bringing together resources—people, capital, and equipment—in the most effective way to accomplish the goals. Organizing, therefore, involves an integration of resources.

Along with planning and organizing, motivating plays a large part in determining the level of performance of employees, which, in turn, influences how effectively the organizational goals will be met. Motivating is sometimes included as part of directing along with communicating and leading.

In his research on motivation, William James of Harvard found that hourly employees could maintain their jobs (that is, not be fired) by working at approximately 20 to 30 percent of their ability. His study also showed that employees work at close to 80 to 90 percent of their ability if highly motivated. Both the minimum level at which employees might work and yet keep their jobs and the level at which they could be expected to perform with proper motivation are illustrated in Figure 1-2.

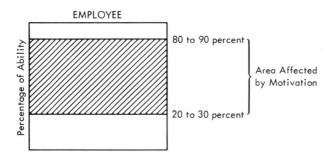

FIGURE 1-2   The potential influence of motivation on performance

This illustration shows us that if motivation is low, employees' performance will suffer as much as if ability were low. For this reason, motivating is an extremely important function of management.

Another function of management is controlling. This involves feedback of results and follow-up to compare accomplishments with plans and to make appropriate adjustments where outcomes have deviated from expectations.

Even though these management functions are stated separately, and as presented seem to have a specific sequence, one must remember that they are interrelated, as illustrated in Figure 1-3. While these functions are interrelated, at any one time, one or more may be of primary importance.

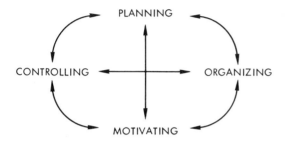

FIGURE 1-3 The process of management

SKILLS OF A MANAGER

It is generally agreed that there are at least three areas of skill necessary for carrying out the process of management: technical, human, and conceptual.

> *Technical skill*—Ability to use knowledge, methods, techniques, and equipment necessary for the performance of specific tasks acquired from experience, education, and training.
>
> *Human skill*—Ability and judgment in working with and through people, including an understanding of motivation and an application of effective leadership.
>
> *Conceptual skill*—Ability to understand the complexities of the overall organization and where one's own operation fits into the organization. This knowledge permits one to act according to the objectives of the total organization rather than only on the basis of the goals and needs of one's own immediate group.[6]

The appropriate mix of these skills varies as an individual advances in management from supervisory to top management positions. This is illustrated in Figure 1-4.

To be effective, less technical skill tends to be needed as one advances from lower to higher levels in the organization, but more and more conceptual skill is necessary. Supervisors at lower levels need considerable technical skill because they are often required to train and develop technicians and other employees in their sections. At the other extreme, executives in a business organization do not need to know how to perform all the specific tasks at the operational level. However, they should be able to see how all these functions are interrelated in accomplishing the goals of the total organization.

While the amount of technical and conceptual skills needed at these different levels of management varies, *the common denominator that appears to be crucial at all levels is human skill.*

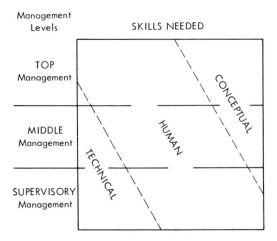

Management
Levels

SKILLS NEEDED

TOP
Management

MIDDLE
Management

SUPERVISORY
Management

CONCEPTUAL

HUMAN

TECHNICAL

FIGURE 1-4   Management skills necessary at various levels of an organization

Emphasis on Human Skills

The emphasis on human skills was considered important in the past, but it is of primary importance today. For example, one of the great entrepreneurs, John D. Rockefeller, stated: "I will pay more for the ability to deal with people than any other ability under the sun."[7] These words of Rockefeller are often echoed. According to a report by the American Management Association, an overwhelming majority of the two hundred managers who participated in a survey agreed that the most important single skill of an executive is his or her ability to get along with people.[8] In this survey, management rated this ability more vital than intelligence, decisiveness, knowledge, or job skills.

ORGANIZATIONS AS SOCIAL SYSTEMS

Although the emphasis in this text will be on human skill development, we must recognize that the organizations in which most managers operate are social systems comprised of many interrelated subsystems, only one of which is a human/social system. The others could include an administrative/structural subsystem, and informational/decision-making subsystem, and an economic/technological subsystem.[9]

The focus of the administrative/structural subsystem is on authority, structure, and responsibility within the organization: "who does what for whom" and "who tells whom to do what, when, and why." The informational/decision-making subsystem emphasizes key decisions and their informational needs to keep the system going. The main concern of the economic/technological subsystem is on the work to be done and the cost effectiveness of that work within the specific goals of the organization.

Although the focus of the human/social system is on the motivation and needs of the members of the organization and on the leadership provided or required (the major emphasis of this text), it should be emphasized that within a systems approach there is a clear understanding that changes in one subsystem effect changes in other parts of the total system. As illustrated in Figure 1-5, if the total system is healthy and functioning well, each of its parts or subsystems is effectively interacting with one another. Therefore, an organization over a sustained period of time cannot afford to overemphasize the importance of one subsystem at the expense of the others. At the same time, the internal management of the organization cannot ignore the needs and pressures from the external environment.

FIGURE 1-5   The interrelated subsystems of an organization

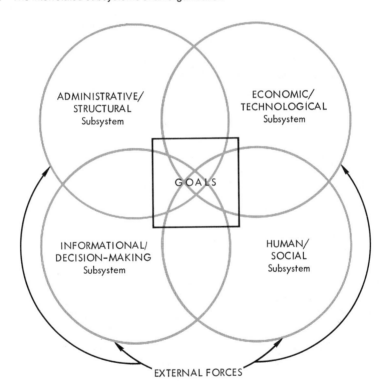

Managerial Roles in a Social System

According to Ichak Adizes,[10] four managerial roles must be performed if an organization is to be run effectively. These four roles are *producing, implementing, innovating,* and *integrating.* Each of these managerial roles is clearly related to one of the four social subsystems of an organization.

A manager in the role of *producing* is expected to achieve results equal to or better than the competition. "The principal qualification for an achiever is the possession of a functional knowledge of his field, whether marketing, engineering, accounting, or any other discipline."[11] The role of producing emphasizes activities in the economic/technological subsystem.

Being individually productive and having technical skills do not necessarily enable a manager to produce results in working with a group of people. As we stated earlier, a manager should have more than just technical skill. Managers should be more than individual producers. They should be able to administer the people with whom they work and to see that these people also produce results. In this *implementing* role managers schedule, coordinate, control, and discipline. If managers are implementers, they see to it that the system works as it has been designed to work. Implementing emphasizes the administrative/structural subsystem.

While producing and implementing are important, in a changing environment managers must use their judgment and have the discretion to change goals and change the systems by which they are implemented. In this role managers must be organizational entrepreneurs and innovators since, unlike administrators who are given plans to carry out and decisions to implement, entrepreneurs have to generate their own plan of action. They have to be self-starters. This *innovating* role stresses the informational/decision-making subsystem.

According to Adizes, the three roles of producing, implementing, and innovating in combination are insufficient for adequate managerial functioning. He contends, "Many an organization that had been managed by an excellent achiever-administrator-entrepreneur (usually their founder) nosedived when this key individual died or for some reason was replaced. For an organization to be continuously successful, an additional role must be performed . . . integrating."[12]

Integrating is the process by which individual strategies are merged into a group strategy; individual risks become group risks; individual goals are harmonized into group goals; ultimately, individual entrepreneurship emerges as group entrepreneurship. "When a group can operate on its own with a clear direction in mind and can choose its own direction over time without depending on any one individual for a successful operation, then we know that the integrating role has been performed adequately. It requires an individual who is sensitive to people's needs. Such an individual unifies the whole organization behind goals and strategies."[13] Integrating emphasizes the human/social system.

Adizes contends that whenever one of the four managerial roles is not performed in an organization, a certain style of mismanagement can be observed. And yet, Adizes argues that

> few managers fill perfectly all four of these roles and thus exhibit no mismanagement style since they are at once excellent technicians, administrators, entrepreneurs, and integrators. Thus, to discuss the role of THE manager, as is done in management literature, is a theoretical mistake. *No one manager can manage alone.* It takes several to perform the process adequately, several people to perform roles which seem to be in conflict but really are complementary. There should be indi-

viduals who possess the entrepreneurial and integrating qualities which can guide a united organization to new directions. There should be administrators who can translate these new actions into operative systems which should produce results. And there should be performers who can put the system into action and set an example for efficient operation.[14]

While all the roles seem to be necessary for running an effective organization, Adizes argues that if any one of the four roles can be truly indispensable for any executive, it is integration. If managers do not perform the other roles themselves, there may be others to supply them; but they have to be able to integrate in order to allow the other functions to work in a positive fashion. If this people-part of the managerial role is not fulfilled, the entrepreneur will become a "crisis maker," the administrator a "bureaucrat," and the producer a "loner."

INGREDIENTS FOR EFFECTIVE HUMAN SKILLS

If one accepts the fact that human skill development is important, one may ask what kind of expertise do managers and leaders need to be effective in their ability to have an impact on the behavior of other people. We feel that managers need three levels of expertise.

Understanding Past Behavior

First, managers need to understand why people behave as they do. If you are going to get things done through other people, you have to know why other people engage in behavior that is characteristic of them. So, understanding past behavior is the first area that managers need to examine.

What motivates people? What produces the patterns of behavior that are characteristic of individuals or groups? This is where most of the literature focuses. Most of what has been written in the behavioral sciences focuses on why people behave as they do. In both popular and scholarly texts and periodicals there are literally hundreds of different classifications that are useful in communicating the patterns of behavior that describe individuals and groups interacting with other people. We can say a person is schizophrenic or is paranoid or is a task leader or a team leader, and so on. All these are useful classifications for communicating to others why an individual or group is behaving in certain ways.

Predicting Future Behavior

Although understanding past behavior is important for developing effective human skills, it is not enough by itself. If you are supervising other people, it is essential that you understand why they did what they did yesterday, but perhaps even more important is being able to predict how they are going to behave today, tomorrow, next week, and next month under similar as well as changing environmental conditions. Therefore, the second level of expertise that managers need is predicting future behavior.

Directing, Changing, and Controlling Behavior

If you are going to be effective in your role as a manager or leader, you need to do more than just understand and predict behavior. You need to develop skills in directing, changing, and controlling behavior.

We recognize that when you talk about controlling behavior, many people today will respond with a question such as, "Do you mean that we are supposed to manipulate behavior?" Control and manipulation have gained negative connotations, particularly in the minds of young people today. Our response is that if in the home you are concerned about your children and the kinds of values they develop, and whether they do certain things and not do other things, you are concerned about controlling behavior. In your job as a manager, you are concerned about the people for whom you are responsible—their cohesiveness, commitment, and the kind of rapport they have with you. If you are concerned about their engaging in certain activities and not engaging in other activities, then you are concerned about controlling behavior. It really is not important what you call it; perhaps you can think of a better word—call it facilitating, training, having an impact, whatever. But remember, if you accept the role of manager or leader, you accept with it the responsibility of having an impact on the behavior of other people.

APPLIED BEHAVIORAL SCIENCES

If managers are able to understand, predict, and direct change and control behavior, they are essentially applied behavioral scientists.

What Is a Behavioral Scientist?

One way to answer is to say that a behavioral scientist attempts to bring together, from a variety of disciplines, those concepts, theories, and research that may be useful to people in making decisions about the behavior of individuals and groups. This means that a behavioral scientist integrates concepts and theories and the results of empirical studies from the areas of cultural anthropology, economics, political science, psychology, sociology, and social psychology. At the same time, a behavioral scientist also borrows from other areas such as engineering, physics, quantitative analysis and statistics. For example, force field analysis, developed by Kurt Lewin, which we will be talking about later in the text, is directly related to concepts in physics. So, perhaps the best way to look at the field is to say that a behavioral scientist attempts to integrate all of those areas or disciplines that can be useful to us as practitioners in better understanding, predicting, and having an impact on the behavior of individuals and groups.

The emphasis in this book will be on the applied behavioral sciences: those concepts from the behavioral sciences that can have an impact on making managers more effective, whether they be managers, supervisors, teachers, or parents. The hope is to apply behavioral science concepts in such a way as to move them from being strictly theoretical and descriptive to being more applied and pre-scriptive. In doing that, though, it should be remembered that applied behav-ioral science is not an exact science like physics, chemistry and biology. There are no principles or universal truths when it comes to management. People will never be 100 percent predictable. All that the behavioral sciences can give you are ways to increase your behavioral batting average. In other words, the behavioral sci-ences are probability sciences; there aren't any principles of management, only books called "Principles of Management."[15]

Learning to Apply Behavioral Science Theory

Learning to apply the behavioral sciences is much like learning anything; for example, how do you learn to hit a baseball? You learn to hit a baseball by getting up there and attempting to hit—by practice, by doing what you are attempting to learn. There is no way you are going to learn to hit a baseball by merely reading books, even those by people considered to be experts in the field, or by watching, in person or on slow motion film, great hitters. All that will do is give you more conceptual knowledge of hitting a baseball. And yet, the psy-chologist defines learning as a change in behavior—being able to do something different from what you were able to do before. So, in reading and watching others, all we can get is perhaps a change in our knowledge or a change in atti-tudes. But if we actually want to make something a learning situation, we have to "try on" or practice that which is learned to make it part of our relevant behavior.

Another thing to keep in mind in terms of learning is—how did you feel the first time you ever tried to hit a baseball? If you were like most people, you felt anxious, nervous, and uncomfortable. This is the way most of us feel any time we attempt to do something that is new—something significantly different from the things we are already comfortable doing within our behavioral patterns.

It's the same with learning to use behavioral science. Much of what you read in this text may have an impact on your knowledge and attitudes, but this book becomes relevant only if you are willing to "try on" some new behaviors. If you are, we think you should recognize that the first time you "try on" a new pattern of behavior in terms of attempting to implement behavioral science the-ory, you are going to feel ill at ease and uncomfortable. It is this "unfreezing" that we have to go through if we want to learn.

Another caution—the first time you are up at bat attempting to hit a base-ball, what is the probability that when the pitcher first delivers the ball, you are going to get a solid hit? The probability is low. It is not any different in learning behavioral science theory. The first time you attempt to behave differently based on theory, we can predict that you will probably be more effective using your old style of behavior rather than the new (although in the long run the new style may have a higher probability of success). This is why so often practitioners who go through a training experience in which they learn new knowledge as well as attitudes find that in "trying on" some new behavior for the first time, it doesn't work. As a result, they begin to respond negatively to the whole training experience, saying such things as, "How can we accept these things?" "They are not usable." "They do not work in the real world." It is this kind of attitude that has been a dilemma for managers attempting to make behavioral science theory a reality in terms of managing more effectively. All of us have to recognize that just like hitting a baseball, it takes practice. The first few times up, the probability of success is quite low. But the more we practice, the more we attempt to get relevant feedback, the more we can predict that the probability of success will increase.

The Design of This Text

In the chapters that follow we will attempt to help you better understand the field of applied behavioral sciences.

Chapters 2 and 3 on motivation are designed to provide information to help you understand and predict why people behave as they do. Chapters 4 through 13 on leadership, power, and developing human resources, focus on ways to facilitate and influence the behavior of other people.

Chapter 13 attempts to integrate all the concepts on understanding, predicting, and controlling behavior into a common framework that can be useful to practicing managers in terms of helping them become more effective in the human/social subsystem.

NOTES

[1] Elton Mayo, *The Social Problems of an Industrial Civilization* (Boston: Harvard Business School, 1945), p. 23.

[2] *Ibid.*, p. 20.

[3] R. J. House discusses similar concepts in *Management Development: Design, Implementation and Evaluation* (Ann Arbor: Bureau of Industrial Relations, University of Michigan, 1967).

[4] See as examples, Harold Koontz and Cyril O'Donnell, *Principles of Management,* 4th ed. (New York: McGraw-Hill Book Company, 1968); and William H. Newman, Charles E. Summer and E. Kirby Warren, *The Process of Management* (Englewood Cliffs, N.J.: Prentice-Hall, Inc., 1967).

[5] Koontz and O'Donnell, *Principles of Management,* p. 54.

[6] These descriptions were adapted from a classification developed by Robert L. Katz, "Skills of an Effective Administrator," *Harvard Business Review,* January-February 1955, pp. 33–42.

[7] John D. Rockefeller as quoted in Garret L. Bergen and William V. Haney, *Organizational Relations and Management Action* (New York: McGraw-Hill Book Company, 1966), p. 3.

[8] Data as reported in Bergen and Haney, *Organizational Relations and Management Action.*

[9] Paul Hersey and Douglas Scott identify these components of an internal social system in "A Systems Approach to Educational Organizations: Do We Manage or Administer?" *OCLEA* (a publication of the Ontario Council for Leadership in Educational Administration, Toronto, Canada), pp. 3–5. Much of the material for that article was adapted from lectures given by Boris Yavitz, Dean, School of Business Administration, Columbia University.

[10] Ichak Adizes, *How to Solve the Mismanagement Crisis* (Los Angeles: MDOR Institute, Inc., 1980). Also, see Adizes, "Mismanagement Styles," *California Management Review*, 19, No. 2, Winter 1976.

[11] Adizes, "Mismanagement Styles," p. 6.

[12] *Ibid.*

[13] *Ibid.*

[14] *Ibid.*, p. 18.

[15] See as examples, Koontz and O'Donnell, *Principles of Management*; D. E. McFarland, *Management: Principles and Practices,* 4th ed. (Macmillan, 1974); Robert J. Thierauf et al., *Management Principles and Practices: A Contingency and Questionnaire Approach* (Management and Administration Services, Wiley, 1977); Gerald Zaltman, *Management Principles for Agencies and Nonprofit Organizations,* (Am. Mgmt., 1979).

chapter 2

Motivation
and Behavior

The study of motivation and behavior is a search for answers to perplexing questions about human nature. Recognizing the importance of the human element in organizations, we will attempt in this chapter to develop a theoretical framework that may help managers to understand human behavior, not only to determine the "whys" of past behavior but to some extent to predict, to change, and even to control future behavior.

BEHAVIOR

Behavior is basically goal-oriented. In other words, our behavior is generally motivated by a desire to attain some goal. The specific goal is not always consciously known by the individual. All of us wonder many times, "Why did I do that?" The reason for our action is not always apparent to the conscious mind. The drives that motivate distinctive individual behavioral patterns ("personality") are to a considerable degree subconscious and therefore not easily susceptible to examination and evaluation.

Sigmund Freud was one of the first to recognize the importance of subconscious motivation. He believed that people are not always aware of everything they want, and hence much of their behavior is affected by subconscious motives or needs. In fact, Freud's research convinced him that an analogy could be drawn between the motivation of most people and the structure of an iceberg. A significant segment of human motivation appears below the surface where it is not always evident to the individual. Therefore, many times only a small portion of motivation is clearly visible or conscious to oneself.[1] This may be due to a lack of effort by individuals to gain self-insight. Yet, even with professional help—for example, psychotherapy—understanding oneself may be a difficult process yielding varying degrees of success.

The basic unit of behavior is an *activity*. In fact, all behavior is a series of activities. As human beings we are always doing something: walking, talking, eating, sleeping, working, and the like. In many instances we are doing more than one activity at a time, such as talking with someone as we walk or drive to work. At any given moment we may decide to change from one activity or combination of activities and begin to do something else. This raises some important questions. Why do people engage in one activity and not another? Why do they change activities? How can we as managers understand, predict, and even control what activity or activities a person may engage in at a given moment? To predict behavior, managers must know which motives or needs of people evoke a certain action at a particular time.

Motives

People differ not only in their ability to do but also in their will to do, or *motivation*. The motivation of people depends on the strength of their motives. *Motives* are sometimes defined as needs, wants, drives, or impulses within the individual. Motives are directed toward goals, which may be conscious or subconscious.

Motives are the "whys" of behavior. They arouse and maintain activity and determine the general direction of the behavior of an individual. In essence, motives, or needs, are the mainsprings of action. In our discussions we shall use these two terms—motives and needs—interchangeably. In this context, the term *need* should *not* be associated with urgency or any pressing desire for something. It simply means something within an individual that prompts that person to action.

Goals

Goals are *outside* an individual; they are sometimes referred to as "hoped for" rewards toward which motives are directed. These goals are often called *incentives* by psychologists. However, we prefer not to use this term since many people in our society tend to equate incentives with tangible financial rewards, such as increased pay, and yet most of us would agree that there are many intangible rewards, such as praise or power, which are just as important in evoking behavior. Managers who are successful in motivating employees are often providing an environment in which appropriate goals (incentives) are available for need satisfaction, as seen in Figure 2-1.

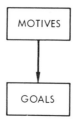

FIGURE 2-1   Motives are directed toward goals

Motive Strength

We have said that motives, or needs, are the reasons underlying behavior. All individuals have many hundreds of needs. All of these needs compete for their behavior. What, then, determines which of these motives a person will attempt to satisfy through activity? The need with the *greatest strength* at a particular moment leads to activity, as illustrated in Figure 2-2. Satisfied needs decrease in strength and normally do not motivate individuals to seek goals to satisfy them.

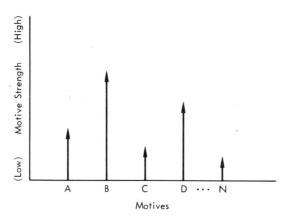

FIGURE 2-2   The most prepotent motive determines behavior (Motive B in this illustration)

In Figure 2-2 Motive B is the highest strength need, and therefore it is this need that determines behavior. What can happen to change this situation?

Changes in Motive Strength

A motive tends to decrease in strength if it is either satisfied or blocked from satisfaction.

Need Satisfaction. When a need is satisfied, according to Abraham Maslow, it is no longer a motivator of behavior.[2] High strength needs that are satisfied are sometimes referred to as "satisficed," that is, the need has been satisfied to the extent that some competing need is now more potent. If a high strength need is thirst, drinking tends to lower the strength of this need, and other needs may now become more important.

Blocking Need Satisfaction. The satisfaction of a need may be blocked. While a reduction in need strength sometimes follows, it does not always occur initially. Instead, there may be a tendency for the person to engage in *coping behavior.* This is an attempt to overcome the obstacle by trial-and-error problem solving. The person may try a variety of behaviors to find one that will accomplish the goal or will reduce tension created by blockage, as illustrated in Figure 2-3.

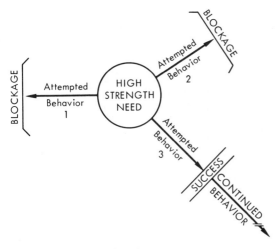

FIGURE 2-3 Coping behavior when blockage occurs in attempting to accomplish a *particular goal*

Initially this coping behavior may be quite rational. Perhaps the person may even make several attempts in direction 1 before going to 2, and the same in direction 2 before moving in direction 3 where some degree of success and goal attainment is finally perceived.

If people continue to strive for something without success, they may substitute goals that can satisfy the need. For example, if a boy has a strong desire to play varsity basketball in high school but is continually cut from the squad, he may be willing eventually to settle for playing in the city recreation league.

Cognitive Dissonance. Blocked motives and continually unsuccessful rational coping behavior may lead to forms of irrational coping behavior. Leon Festinger analyzes this phenomenon.[3] His theory of cognitive dissonance deals primarily with the relationships that exist between perceptions people have about themselves and their environment. When individual perceptions have nothing to do with each other, they are considered irrelevant to each other. If one supports the other, they are said to be in a consonant relationship. Dissonance is created when two perceptions that are relevant to each other are in conflict. This creates tension, which is psychologically uncomfortable and causes the individual to try to modify one of the incompatible knowledges so as to reduce the tension or dissonance. In a sense, that person engages in coping behavior to regain a condition of consonance or equilibrium. For example, Festinger has done research that shows that "heavy smokers are less likely to believe that there is a relationship between smoking and lung cancer than nonsmokers."[4] In other words, if they cannot give up smoking, they can at least remain skeptical about research that reports harmful effects. The same phenomenon is at work when a person goes out, fishes all day, doesn't catch anything, and remarks about the beautiful weather.

Frustration. The blocking or thwarting of goal attainment is referred to as *frustration*. This phenomenon is defined in terms of the condition of the individual, rather than in terms of the external environment. A person may be frustrated by an imaginary barrier and may fail to be frustrated by a real barrier.

As previously discussed, rational coping behavior can lead to alternative goal setting or decreasing need strength. Irrational behavior may occur in several forms when blockage to goal accomplishment continues and frustration develops. Frustration may increase to the extent that the individual engages in aggressive behavior. *Aggression* can lead to destructive behavior such as hostility and striking out. Freud was one of the first to demonstrate that hostility or rage can be exhibited by an individual in a variety of ways.[5] If possible, individuals will direct their hostility against the object or the person that they feel is the cause of frustration. The angry worker may try to hit her boss or may undermine his job and reputation through gossip and other malicious behavior. Often, however, people cannot attack the cause of their frustration directly, and they may look for a scapegoat as a target for their hostility. For example, a worker may fear his boss because the boss holds his fate in her hands. In this case, "the resentful worker may pick a quarrel with his wife, kick the cat, beat his children, or, more constructively, work off his feelings by chopping wood, by cursing and swearing, or engaging in violent exercises or horseplay of an aggressive nature."[6]

As Norman R. F. Maier has said, aggression is only one way in which frustration can be shown.[7] Other forms of frustrated behavior, such as rationalization, regression, fixation, and resignation, may develop if pressures continue and increase.

Rationalization simply means making excuses. For example, an individual might blame someone else for her inability to accomplish a given goal—"It was my boss' fault that I didn't get a raise." Or she talks herself out of the desirability of that particular goal—"I didn't want to do that anyway."

Regression is essentially not acting one's age. "Frustrated people tend to give up constructive attempts at solving their problems and regress to more primitive and childish behavior."[8] A person who cannot start his car and proceeds to kick it is demonstrating regressive behavior, and so is a manager who throws a temper tantrum when he is annoyed and frustrated. Barker, Dembo and Lewin have shown experimentally that when children are exposed to mild frustration their play may resemble that of a child two or more years younger.[9]

Fixation occurs when a person continues to exhibit the same behavior pattern over and over again, although experience has shown that it can accomplish nothing. Thus, "frustration can freeze old and habitual responses and prevent the use of new and more effectual ones."[10] Maier has shown that although habits are normally broken when they bring no satisfaction or lead to punishment, a fixation actually becomes stronger under these circumstances.[11] In fact, he argued that it is possible to change a habit into a fixation by too much punishment. This phenomenon is seen in children who blindly continue to behave objectionably after being severely punished. Thus, Maier concluded that punishment can have two effects on behavior. It may either eliminate the undesirable behavior or lead to fixation and other symptoms of frustration as well. It follows that punishment may be a dangerous management tool, since its effects are difficult to predict. According to J. A. C. Brown, common symptoms of fixation in industry are "the inability to accept change, the blind and stubborn refusal to accept new facts when experience has shown the old ones to be untenable, and the type of behavior exemplified by the manager who continues to increase penalties" even when this is only making conditions worse.[12]

Resignation or apathy occurs after prolonged frustration when people lose hope of accomplishing their goal(s) in a particular situation and want to withdraw from reality and the source of their frustration. This phenomenon is characteristic of people in boring, routine jobs where often they resign themselves to the fact that there is little hope for improvement within their environments.

A manager should remember that aggression, rationalization, regression, fixation, and resignation are all symptoms of frustration and may be indications that problems exist.

Increasing Motive Strength. Behavior may change if an existing need increases in strength to the extent that it is now the high strength motive. The strength of some needs tends to appear in a cyclical pattern. For example, the need for food tends to recur regardless of how well it has been satisfied at a given moment. One can increase or delay the speed of this cyclical pattern by affecting the environment. For example, a person's need for food may not be high strength unless the immediate environment is changed such that his or her senses are exposed to the sight and the aroma of tempting food.

People have a variety of needs at any given time. They may be hungry, thirsty, and tired, but the need with the highest strength will determine what they do. For example, they may eat, drink, and sleep, in that order, as shown in Figure 2-4.[13] All of these tend to be cyclical over time.

CATEGORIES OF ACTIVITIES

Activities resulting from high strength needs can generally be classified into two categories—goal-directed activity and goal activity. These concepts are important to practitioners because of their differing influence on need strength, which can be useful in understanding human behavior.

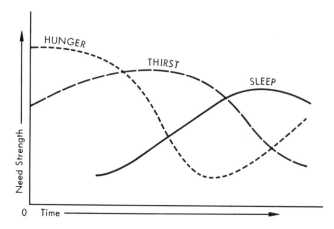

Figure 2-4 Multiple needs

Goal-directed activity, in essence, is motivated behavior directed at reaching a goal. If one's strongest need at a given moment is hunger, various activities such as looking for a place to eat, buying food, or preparing food would be considered goal-directed activities. On the other hand, *goal activity* is engaging in the goal itself. In the case of hunger, food is the goal and eating, therefore, is the goal activity.

An important distinction between these two classes of activities is their effect on the strength of the need. In goal-directed activity, the strength of the need tends to increase as one engages in the activity until goal behavior is reached or frustration sets in. As discussed earlier, frustration develops when one is continually blocked from reaching a goal. If the frustration becomes intense enough, the strength of the need for that goal may decrease until it is no longer potent enough to affect behavior—a person gives up.

The strength of the need tends to increase as one engages in goal-directed activity; however, once goal activity begins, the strength of the need tends to decrease as one engages in it. For example, as one eats more and more, the strength of the need for food declines for that particular time. At the point when another need becomes more potent than the present need, behavior changes.

On Thanksgiving Day, for example, as food is being prepared all morning (goal-directed activity), the need for food increases to the point of almost not being able to wait until the meal is on the table. As we begin to eat (goal activity), the strength of this need diminishes to the point where other needs become more important. As we leave the table, our need for food seems to be well satisfied. Our activity changes to that of watching football. This need for passive recreation has now become most potent, and we find ourselves in front of the television set. But gradually this need decreases, too. After several games, even though the competition is fierce, the need for passive recreation may also decline to the extent that other needs become more important—perhaps the need for fresh air and a walk or, better still, another piece of pumpkin pie. Several hours before we had sworn not to eat for a week, but now that pie looks very good. So once again hunger is the strongest need. Thus, it should be remembered that we never completely satiate a need. We satisfy it for only a period of time.

MOTIVATING SITUATION

The relationship between motives, goals, and activity can be shown in a simplified fashion, as illustrated in Figure 2-5.

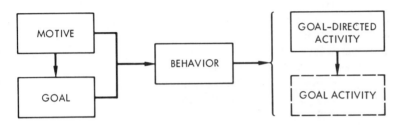

FIGURE 2-5 A motivating situation

This schematic illustration shows a *motivating situation* in which the motives of an individual are directed toward goal attainment. The strongest motive produces behavior that is either goal-directed or goal activity. Since not all goals are attainable, individuals do not always reach goal activity, regardless of the strength of the motive. Thus, goal activity is indicated by a dashed line.

An example of a tangible goal being used to influence behavior is illustrated in Figure 2-6.

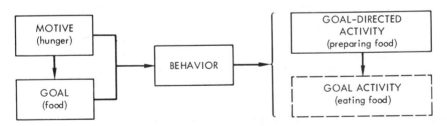

FIGURE 2-6 Use of a tangible incentive in a motivating situation

With a broad goal such as food, it should be recognized that the type of food that satisfies the hunger motive varies from situation to situation. If individuals are starving, they may eat anything; at other times they may realign their goals and only a steak will satisfy their hunger motive.

A similar illustration could be given for an intangible goal. If individuals have a need for recognition—a need to be viewed as contributing, productive people—praise is one incentive that will help satisfy this need. In a work situation, if their need for recognition is strong enough, being praised by their manager or supervisor may be an effective incentive in influencing people to continue to do good work.

In analyzing these two examples, it should be remembered that if you want to influence another person's behavior, you must first understand what motives or needs are most important to that person at that time. A goal, to be effective, must be appropriate to the need structure of the person involved.

A question that may be considered at this point is whether it is better to engage in goal-directed activity or in goal activity. Actually, maintenance at either level exclusively creates problems. If one stays at goal-directed activity too long, frustration will occur to the extent that the person may give up or other patterns of irrational behavior may be evoked. On the other hand, if one engages exclusively in goal activity and the goal is not challenging, a lack of interest and apathy will develop, with motivation again tending to decrease. A more appropriate and effective pattern might be a continuous cycling function between goal-directed activity and goal activity.

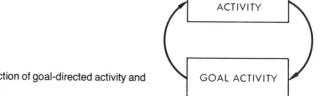

FIGURE 2-7   Cycling function of goal-directed activity and goal activity

A goal that is appropriate for a six-year-old may not be a meaningful goal for the same child at seven. Once the child becomes proficient in attaining a particular goal, it becomes appropriate for the parent to provide an opportunity for the child to evaluate and set new goals. In the same light, what is an appropriate goal for a new employee may not be meaningful for an employee who has been with a corporation six months or a year. There also may be distinctions between employees who have been with an organization for only a few years and those who have been with it for longer periods of time.

This cycling process between goal-directed activity and goal activity is a continuous challenge for the parent or the manager. As employees increase in their ability to accomplish goals, it is appropriate that the superior reevaluate and provide an environment allowing continual realignment of goals and an opportunity for growth and development. The learning and developing process is not a phenomenon that should be confined to only one stage of a person's life. In this process, the role of managers is not always that of setting goals for their followers. Instead, effectiveness may be increased by providing an environment in which subordinates can play a role in setting their own goals. Research indicates that commitment increases when people are involved in their own goal setting. If individuals are involved, they will tend to engage in much more goal-directed activity before they become frustrated and give up. On the other hand, if their boss sets the goals for them, they are likely to give up more easily because they perceive these as their boss' goals and not as their own.

Goals should be set high enough so that a person has to stretch to reach them but low enough so that they can be attained. Thus, goals must be realistic before a person will make a real effort to achieve them. As J. Sterling Livingston so aptly states:

> Subordinates will not be motivated to reach high levels of productivity unless they consider the boss' high expectations realistic and achievable. If they are encouraged to strive for unattainable goals, they eventually give up trying and settle for results that are lower than they are capable of achieving. The experience of a large electrical manufacturing company demonstrates this; the company discovered that production actually declined if production quotas were set too high, because the workers simply stopped trying to meet them. In other words, the practice of "dangling the carrot just beyond the donkey's reach," endorsed by many managers, is not a good motivational device.[14]

David C. McClelland and John W. Atkinson[15] have demonstrated in their research that the degree of motivation and effort rises until the probability of success reaches 50 percent, then begins to fall even though the probability of success continues to increase. This relationship could be depicted in the form of a bell-shaped curve as illustrated in Figure 2-8.

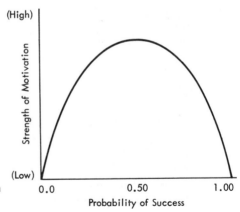

FIGURE 2-8   The relationship of motivation to probability of success[16]

As Figure 2-8 suggests, people are not highly motivated if a goal is seen as almost impossible or virtually certain to achieve.

Another problem with goals is that so often final goals are set and the person is judged only in terms of success in relation to those terminal goals. For example, a student is doing poorly in school and her parents want her to raise her marks to a *B* average. Suppose that after the first semester she gets only *C*'s. The result is usually that her parents reprimand her; if this continues to occur, there is a high probability that she may stop trying. Her grades, instead of improving, may get worse. An alternative for the parents is setting interim goals—realistic goals that move in the direction of the final goals as they are attained. Now with a change in the desired direction, even though only moderate, positive reinforcement may be used rather than reprimand.

EXPECTANCY AND AVAILABILITY

We have already discussed the strength of needs. Two important factors that affect need strength are expectancy and availability. Although these two concepts are interrelated, expectancy tends to affect motives, or needs, and availability tends to affect the perception of goals.

Expectancy is the perceived probability of satisfying a particular need of an individual based on past experience. Although expectancy is the technical term used by psychologists, it refers directly to the sum of the past experience. Experience can be either actual or vicarious. Vicarious experience comes from sources the person considers legitimate, such as parents, peer groups, teachers, and books or periodicals. To illustrate the effect that past experience can have on behavior, let us look at an example. Suppose a boy's father was a basketball star and the boy wants to follow in his footsteps. Initially his expectancy may be high, and therefore the strength of the need is high. If he is cut from the eighth-grade team, it is difficult to determine whether this failure will discourage the boy. Since a single failure is usually not enough to discourage a person (in fact, it sometimes results in increased activity), little change in his expectancy is anticipated. But if he continues to get cut from the team year after year, eventually this motive will no longer be as strong or of such high priority. In fact, after enough unsuccessful experiences, he may completely give up on his goal.

Availability reflects the perceived limitations of the environment. It is determined by how accessible the goals that can satisfy a given need are perceived by an individual. For example, if the electricity goes off in a storm, one cannot watch television or read. These goal activities are no longer possible because of the limitations of the environment. One may have a high desire to read, but if there is no suitable substitute for the type of illumination required, that person will soon be frustrated in any attempts to satisfy this desire and will settle for something else, like sleeping.

Consequently, availability is an environmental variable. Yet it should be stressed that it is not important whether the goals to satisfy a need are really available. It is the perception, or the interpretation of reality, that affects one's actual behavior. In other words, reality is what a person perceives.

An example of how perception can affect behavior was dramatically illustrated in an experiment with a fish. A pike was placed in an aquarium with many minnows swimming around it. After the fish became accustomed to the plentiful supply of food, a sheet of glass was placed between the pike and minnows. When the pike became hungry it tried to reach the minnows, but it continually hit its head on the glass. At first the strength of the need for food increased, and the pike tried harder than ever to get the minnows. But finally its repeated failure of goal attainment resulted in enough frustration that the fish no longer attempted to eat the minnows. In fact, when the glass partition was finally removed, the minnows again swam all around the pike, but no further goal-directed activity took place. Eventually, the pike died of starvation while in the midst of plenty of food. In both cases, the fish operated according to the way it perceived reality and not on the basis of reality itself.

The expanded diagram of a motivating situation including expectancy and availability is presented in Figure 2-9.

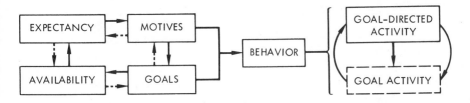

FIGURE 2-9 Expanded diagram of a motivating situation

Motives, needs within an individual, are directed toward goals that are aspirations in the environment. These are interpreted by the individual as being available or unavailable. This affects expectancy. If expectancy is high, motive strength will increase. This tends to be a cyclical pattern moving in the direction of the prominent arrows. But to some extent these are interacting variables indicated by the secondary arrows. For example, experience may affect the way we perceive our feelings of availability. The presence of goals in the environment may affect the given strength of motives, and so forth.

PERSONALITY DEVELOPMENT

As individuals mature, they develop habit patterns, or conditioned responses, to various stimuli. The sum of these habit patterns as perceived by others determines their *personality*.

habit *a*, habit *b*, habit *c*, . . . , habit *n* = *personality*

As individuals begin to behave in a similar fashion under similar conditions, this behavior is what others learn to recognize as them, as their personality. They expect and can even predict certain kinds of behavior from these people.

Changing Personality

Many psychologists contend that basic personality structures are developed quite early in life. In fact, some claim that few personality changes can be made after age seven or eight. Using a model similar to the one in Figure 2-9, we can

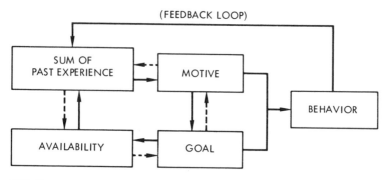

FIGURE 2-10 Feedback model

begin to understand why it tends to become more difficult to make changes in personality as people grow older.

Note that in this model we are using *sum of past experience* in place of the term *expectancy* used in the earlier model. These can be used interchangeably.

When an individual behaves in a motivating situation, that behavior becomes a new input to that person's inventory of past experience, as the feedback loop in Figure 2-10 indicates. The earlier in life that this input occurs, the greater its potential effect on future behavior. The reason is that, early in life, this behavior represents a larger portion of the total past experience of a young person than the same behavior input will later in life. In addition, the longer behavior is reinforced, the more patterned it becomes and the more difficult it is to change. That is why it is easier to make personality changes early in life. The older a person gets, the more time and new experiences are necessary to effect a change in behavior. An illustration might be helpful. Putting one new input, a drop of red coloring, into a half-pint bottle of clear liquid may be enough to change drastically the appearance of the total contents. Adding the same input, a drop of red coloring, to a gallon jug may make little, if any, noticeable change in its appearance to others. This example illustrates the relationship between the amount of past experience and the effect of any one new experience.

Although it is possible to change behavior in older people, it will be difficult to accomplish except over a long period of time under conducive conditions. It almost becomes a matter of economics—allocating limited resources in terms of unlimited human wants—how much we are willing to invest in implementing such a change. Not only may it be less expensive in terms of time necessary for training, but the potential payback period for younger people is much greater.

HIERARCHY OF NEEDS

We have argued that the behavior of individuals at a particular moment is usually determined by their strongest need. It would seem significant, therefore, for managers to have some understanding about the needs that are commonly most important to people.

An interesting framework that helps explain the strength of certain needs was developed by Abraham Maslow.[17] According to Maslow, there seems to be a hierarchy into which human needs arrange themselves, as illustrated in Figure 2-11.

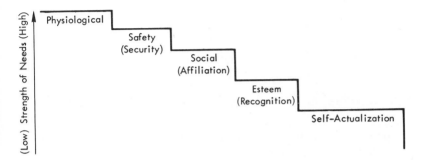

FIGURE 2-11 Maslow's hierarchy of needs

The *physiological* needs are shown at the top of the hierarchy because they tend to have the highest strength until they are somewhat satisfied. These are the basic human needs to sustain life itself—food, clothing, shelter. Until these basic needs are satisfied to the degree needed for the sufficient operation of the body, the majority of a person's activity will probably be at this level, and the others will provide little motivation.

But what happens to a person's motivation when these basic needs begin to be fulfilled? Rather than physiological needs, other levels of needs become important, and these motivate and dominate the behavior of the individual. And when these needs are somewhat satiated, other needs emerge, and so on down the hierarchy.

Once physiological needs become gratified, the *safety,* or *security,* needs become predominant, as illustrated in Figure 2-12. These needs are essentially the need to be free of the fear of physical danger and deprivation of the basic physiological needs. In other words, this is a need for self-preservation. In addition to the here and now, there is a concern for the future. Will people be able to maintain their property and/or job so they can provide food and shelter tomorrow and the next day? If an individual's safety or security is in danger, other things seem unimportant.

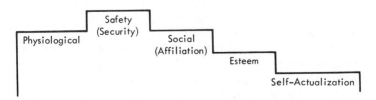

FIGURE 2-12 Safety need when dominant in the need structure

Once physiological and safety needs are fairly well satisfied, *social* or *affiliation* will emerge as dominant in the need structure, as illustrated in Figure 2-13. Since people are social beings, they have a need to belong and to be accepted by various groups. When social needs become dominant, a person will strive for meaningful relations with others.

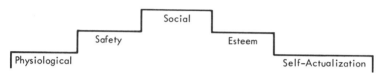

FIGURE 2-13   Social need when dominant in the need structure

After individuals begin to satisfy their need to belong, they generally want to be more than just a member of their group. They then feel the need for *esteem*— both self-esteem and recognition from others, as seen in Figure 2-14. Most people have a need for a high evaluation of themselves that is firmly based in reality— recognition and respect from others. Satisfaction of these esteem needs produces feelings of self-confidence, prestige, power, and control. People begin to feel that they are useful and have some effect on their environment. There are other occasions, though, when persons are unable to satisfy their need for esteem through constructive behavior. When this need is dominant an individual may resort to disruptive or immature behavior to satisfy the desire for attention—a child may throw a temper tantrum, employees may engage in work restriction or arguments with their coworkers or boss. Thus, recognition is not always obtained through mature or adaptive behavior. It is sometimes garnered by disruptive and irresponsible actions. In fact, some of the social problems we have today may have their roots in the frustration of esteem needs.

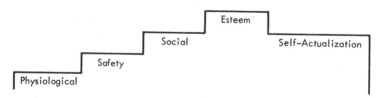

FIGURE 2-14   Esteem need when dominant in the need structure

Once esteem needs begin to be adequately satisfied, the *self-actualization* needs become more prepotent, as shown in Figure 2-15. Self-actualization is the need to maximize one's potential, whatever it may be. A musician must play music, a poet must write, a general must win battles, a professor must teach. As Maslow expressed it, "What a man *can* be, he *must* be." Thus, self-actualization is the desire to become what one is capable of becoming. Individuals satisfy this need in different ways. In one person it may be expressed in the desire to be an ideal mother; in another it may be expressed in managing an organization; in another it may be expressed athletically; in still another by playing the piano.

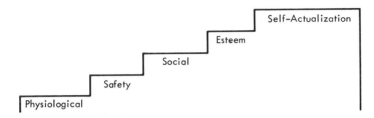

FIGURE 2-15 Self-actualization needs when dominant in the need structure

In combat, a soldier may put his life on the line and rush a machine-gun nest in an attempt to destroy it, knowing full well that his chances for survival are low. He is not doing it for affiliation or recognition, but rather for what he thinks is important. In this case, you may consider the soldier to have self-actualized—to be maximizing the potential of what is important to him at that time.

The way self-actualization is expressed can change over the life cycle. For example, a self-actualized athlete may eventually look for other areas in which to maximize potential as his or her physical attributes change over time or as his or her horizons broaden. In addition, the hierarchy does not necessarily follow the pattern described by Maslow. It was not his intent to say that this hierarchy applies universally. Maslow felt this was a *typical* pattern that operates most of the time. He realized, however, that there were numerous exceptions to this general tendency. For example, the Indian leader, Mahatma Gandhi, frequently sacrificed his physiological and safety needs for the satisfaction of other needs when India was striving for independence from Great Britain. In his historic fasts, Gandhi went weeks without nourishment to protest governmental injustices. He was operating at the self-actualization level while some of his other needs were unsatisfied.

In discussing the preponderance of one category of need over another, we have been careful to speak in such terms as "if one level of needs has been somewhat gratified, then other needs emerge as dominant." This was done because we did not want to give the impression that one level of needs has to be completely satisfied before the next level emerges as the most important. In reality, most people in our society tend to be partially satisfied at each level and partially unsatisfied, with greater satisfaction tending to occur at the physiological and safety levels than at the social, esteem, and self-actualization levels. For example, people in an emerging society, where much of the behavior engaged in tends to be directed toward satisfying physiological and safety needs, still operate to some extent at other levels. Therefore, Maslow's hierarchy of needs is not intended to be an all-or-none framework, but rather one that may be useful in predicting behavior on a high or a low probability basis. Figure 2-16 attempts to portray how people in an emerging nation may be categorized.

FIGURE 2-16 Need mix when physiological and safety needs are high strength

Many people in our society today might be characterized by very strong social or affiliation needs, relatively strong esteem and safety needs, with self-actualization and physiological needs somewhat less important, as shown in Figure 2-17.

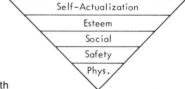

FIGURE 2-17 Need mix when social needs are high strength and self-actualization and physiological needs are less important

Some people, however, can be characterized as having satisfied to a large extent the physiological, safety, and social needs, and their behavior tends to be dominated by esteem and self-actualizing activities, as shown in Figure 2-18. This will tend to become more characteristic if standards of living and levels of education continue to rise.

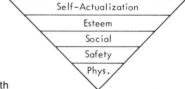

FIGURE 2-18 Need mix when esteem and self-actualization needs are high strength

These are intended only as examples. For different individuals, varying configurations may be appropriate. In reality, they would fluctuate tremendously from one individual or group to another.

Clare W. Graves[18] has developed a theory that seems to be compatible with Maslow's hierarchy of needs. Graves contends that human beings exist at different "levels of existence." "At any given level, an individual exhibits the behavior and values characteristic of people at that level; a person who is centralized at a lower level cannot even understand people who are at a higher level."[19] According to Graves, "most people have been confined to lower [subsistence] levels of existence where they were motivated by needs shared with other animals. Now, Western man appears ready to move up to a higher [being] level of existence, a distinctly human level. When this happens there will likely be a dramatic transformation of human institutions."[20]

MOTIVATIONAL RESEARCH

Having discussed Maslow's hierarchy of needs, we can now examine what researchers say about some of our motives and the incentives that tend to satisfy them.

Physiological Needs

The satisfaction of physiological needs (shelter, food, clothing) is usually associated in our society with *money*. It is obvious that most people are not interested in dollars as such, but only as a means to be used to satisfy other motives. Thus, it is what money can buy, not money itself, that satisfies one's physiological needs. To suggest that money as a tool is useful *only* to satisfy physiological needs would be shortsighted because money can play a role in the satisfaction of needs at every level. Extensive studies of the impact of money have found that money is so complicated an incentive that it is entangled with all kinds of needs besides physiological ones, and its importance is difficult to ascertain. Consequently, we will discuss the money motive in a separate section later in the chapter. It is clear, however, that the ability of a given amount of money to satisfy *seems* to diminish as one moves from physiological and safety needs to other needs on the hierarchy. In many cases, money can buy the satisfaction of physiological and safety needs and even social needs, if, for example, it provides entry into a desired group, such as a country club. But as one becomes concerned about esteem, recognition, and eventually self-actualization, money becomes a less appropriate tool to satisfy these needs and, therefore, less effective. The more individuals become involved with esteem and self-actualization needs, the more they will have to earn their satisfaction directly, and thus the less important money will be in their attainment.

Safety (Security) Needs

We mentioned earlier that motives are not always apparent to the individual. Although some motives appear above the surface, many are largely subconscious and are not obvious or easy to identify. According to Saul W. Gellerman, security needs appear in both forms.[21]

The conscious security needs are quite evident and very common among most people. We all have a desire to remain free from the hazards of life—accidents, wars, diseases, and economic instability. Therefore, individuals and organizations are interested in providing some assurance that these catastrophes will be avoided if possible. Gellerman suggests that many organizations tend to overemphasize the security motive by providing elaborate programs of fringe benefits, such as health, accident, and life insurance and retirement plans. Such emphasis on security may make people more docile and predictable, but it does not mean they will be more productive. In fact, if creativity or initiative is necessary in their jobs, an overemphasis on security can thwart desired behavior.

Although concern for security can affect major decisions, such as remaining in or leaving an organization, Gellerman indicates it is not likely to be an individual's dominant motive. Conscious security needs usually play a background role, often inhibiting or restraining impulses rather than initiating outward behavior. For example, if a particular course of action, such as disregarding a rule or expressing an unpopular position, might endanger one's job, then security considerations motivate a person *not* to take this course of action. Organizations can influence these security needs either positively—through pension plans, insurance programs, and the like—or negatively by arousing fears of being fired or laid off, demoted, or passed over. In both cases, the effect can be to make behavior too cautious and conservative.

Peter F. Drucker suggests that one's attitude toward security is important to consider in choosing a job.[22] He raises some interesting questions: Do you belong in a job calling primarily for faithfulness in the performance of routine work and promising security? Do you find real satisfaction in the precision, order, and system of a clearly laid-out job? Do you prefer the security not only of knowing what your work is today and what it is going to be tomorrow, but also security in your job, in your relationship to the people above, below, and next to you? Or do you belong in a job that offers a challenge to imagination and ingenuity—with the attendant penalty for failure? Are you one of those people who tend to grow impatient with anything that looks like a "routine" job? The answers to these questions are not always easy even though we all understand ourselves to some degree. But the answers are involved with how important the security motive is for that particular individual.

To reiterate, security needs can be conscious or subconscious. A strong subconscious orientation toward security is often developed early in childhood. Gellerman discusses several ways in which it can be implanted. A common way is through identification with security-minded parents who are willing to accept whatever fate comes along. This often occurs in depressed economic areas where the prospects for improvement are poor.[23]

The world seems uncertain and uncontrollable to people raised in a security-minded home. As a result, such people may not feel they are competent enough to be able to influence their environment.

The security-minded people we have been describing are often very likable. They are not competitive and, therefore, do not put people on the defensive. Others tend to expect little of them and thus are seldom critical of their work.

This, combined with the fact that they are pleasant to have around, often enables them to obtain a secure, nonthreatening position in an organization.

Subconscious security motives may also develop in children through interaction with overprotective parents. Such parents are constantly trying to shield their children from heartache, disappointment, or failure. The supportive attitude of these parents in many instances permits their children to have their own way. Conflict is avoided at all costs. As a result, these children are given a distorted picture of reality and gain little insight into what they can expect of other people and what others will expect of them. In some cases, they become unrealistic in their optimism about life. Even in the face of disaster, when they should be threatened, they seem to believe that all is well until too late.

When this type of security-minded people leave home after high school to seek their way in the world, they quickly wake up to reality. Often they find themselves unequipped to handle the hardships of life because they have *not* been permitted the opportunity to develop the capacity to handle frustration, tension, and anxiety. As a result, even a minor setback may throw them for a loss. Drucker suggests that getting fired from their first job might be the best thing that could happen to such young people. He feels that getting fired from the first job is the least painful and least damaging way to learn how to take a setback and that this is a lesson well worth learning. If people learn how to recover from seeming disaster when they are young, they will be better equipped to handle worse fate as they get older.

To many people, the security motive carries with it a negative connotation. A strong security need is frowned upon, for some reason, as if it were less respectable than other motives. This seems unjust, especially since nearly everyone has some conscious and subconscious security motives. Life is never so simple or clear-cut that one does not maintain some concern for security. In addition, many segments of our society often cater to these needs to the exclusion of such important needs as affiliation and self-actualization. We have already mentioned how industry concentrates on security needs by providing elaborate fringe benefits. Unions have a similar effect with their emphasis on seniority, and the government does much the same thing with welfare and other similar support programs.

Social (Affiliation) Needs

After the physiological and safety needs have become somewhat satisfied, the social needs may become predominant. Since people are social animals, most individuals like to interact and be with others in situations where they feel they belong and are accepted. While this is a common need, it tends to be stronger for some people than for others and stronger in certain situations. In other words, even such a commonplace social need as belongingness is, upon examination, quite complex.

In working toward a better understanding of our need to belong, Stanley Schachter of the University of Minnesota has made a significant contribution.[24] His efforts, in particular, have been directed toward studying the desire to socialize as an end in itself—that is, when people interact simply because they enjoy it. In some of these situations no apparent reward such as money or protection was gained from this affiliation.

Schachter found that it was not always simply good fellowship that motivated affiliation. In many instances, people seek affiliation because they desire to have their beliefs confirmed. People who have similar beliefs tend to seek each other out, especially if a strongly held belief has been shattered. In this case, they tend to assemble and try to reach some common understanding about what happened and what they should believe (even if it is the same as before). In this instance, the need for affiliation was prompted by a desire to make one's life *seem* a little more under control. When alone, the world seems "out of whack," but if one can find an environment in which others hold the same beliefs, it somehow makes order out of chaos. This attitude hints at some of the problems inherent in any change.

In pursuing this question further, it was found that when people are excited, confused, or unhappy, they do not seek out just anyone, they tend to want to be with others "in the same boat." Misery does not just love company, it loves other miserable company. These conclusions suggest that the strong informal work groups that Elton Mayo found developing in the factory system might have been a reaction to the boredom, insignificance, and lack of competence that the workers felt.[25] As a result, workers congregated because of mutual feelings of being beaten by the system.

In observing loners and rate-busters in similar factory situations, it became apparent that there is not some universal need for affiliation as an end in itself. It was found, however, that these exceptions to the affiliation tendency were special types of people. They tended not to join informal work groups because they felt either suspicious or contemptuous of them or else secure and competent enough to fend for themselves.

Management is often suspicious of informal groups that develop at work because of the potential power these groups have to lower productivity. Schachter found that such work-restricting groups were sometimes formed as a reaction to the insignificance and impotence that workers tend to feel when they have no control over their working environment. Such environments develop when the work is routine, tedious, and oversimplified. This situation is made worse when, at the same time, the workers are closely supervised and controlled but have no clear channels of communication with management.

In this type of environment workers who cannot tolerate this lack of control over their environment depend on the informal group for support of unfulfilled needs such as affiliation or achievement. Work restriction follows not from an inherent dislike for management, but as a means to preserve the identification of individuals within the group and the group itself. Rate-busters are not tolerated because they weaken the group and its power with management, and to weaken the group destroys the only dignity, security, and significance the workers feel they have.

Lowering productivity is not always the result of informal work groups. In fact, informal groups can be a tremendous asset to management if their internal organization is understood and fully utilized. The productivity of a work group seems to depend on how the group members see their own goals in relation to the goals of the organization. For example, if they perceive their own goals as being in conflict with the goals of the organization, then productivity will tend to be low. However, if these workers see their own goals as being the same as the goals of the organization or as being satisfied as a direct result of accomplishing organizational   goals, then productivity will tend to be high. Work restriction is therefore not a necessary aspect of informal work groups.

Esteem

The need for esteem or recognition appears in a number of forms. In this section we shall discuss two motives related to esteem—prestige and power.

Prestige. The prestige motive is becoming more evident in our society today, especially as we move toward a middle-class society. People with a concern for prestige want to "keep up with the Joneses"; in fact, given the choice, they would like to stay ahead of the Joneses. Vance Packard[26] and David Riesman[27] probably had the greatest impact in exposing prestige motivation. Packard wrote about the status seekers and their motives, while Riesman unveiled "other-directed" individuals who were part of "the lonely crowd."

What exactly is prestige? Gellerman describes it as "a sort of unwritten definition of the kinds of conduct that other people are expected to show in one's presence: what degree of respect or disrespect, formality or informality, reserve or frankness."[28] Prestige seems to have an effect on how comfortably or conveniently one can expect to get along in life.

Prestige is something intangible bestowed upon an individual by society. In fact, at birth children inherit the status of their parents. In some cases, this is enough to carry them through life on "a prestige-covered wave." For example, a Rockefeller or a Ford inherits instant prestige with that family background.

People seek prestige throughout their lives in various ways. Many tend to seek only the material symbols of status, while others strive for personal achievement or self-actualization, which might command prestige in itself. Regardless of the way it is expressed, there seems to be a widespread need for people to have their importance clarified and, in fact, set at a level that each feels is deserved. As discussed earlier, people normally want to have a high evaluation of themselves that is firmly based in reality as manifested by the recognition and respect accorded them by others.

The need for prestige is more or less self-limiting. People tend to seek prestige only to a preconceived level. When they feel they have gained this level, the strength of this need tends to decline and prestige becomes a matter of maintenance rather than of further advancement. Some people can become satisfied with their level of importance in their company and community. In their own evaluation, "they have arrived." Only the exceptional seek national or international recognition. Prestige motivation, therefore, often appears in young people who tend not to be satisfied yet with their status in life. Older people tend to have reached a level of prestige that satisfies them, or they become resigned to the fact that they can do little to improve their status.[29]

Power. The resource that enables a person to induce compliance from or influence others is *power*. It is a person's influence potential. There tend to be two kinds of power—position and personal. Individuals who are able to induce compliance from others because of their position in the organization have *position* power; individuals who derive their influence from their personality and behavior have *personal* power. Some people are endowed with both position and personal power. Others seem to have no power at all.

Alfred Adler, a one-time colleague of Freud, became very interested in this power motive.[30] By power Adler essentially meant the ability to manipulate or control the activities of others to suit one's own purposes. He found that this ability starts at an early age when children as babies realize that if they cry they influence their parents' behavior. Children's position as babies gives them considerable power over their parents.

According to Adler, this manipulative ability is inherently pleasurable. Children, for example, often have a hard time adjusting to the continuing reduction in their position power. In fact, they might spend a significant amount of time as adults trying to recapture the power they had as children. However, Adler did not feel that children seek power for its own sake as often as they do out of necessity. Power, for children, is often a life-and-death matter because they are helpless and need to count on their parents' availability. Parents are a child's lifeline. Thus, power acquires an importance in children that they somehow never lose, even though they are later able to fend for themselves.

After childhood, the power motive again becomes very potent in individuals who feel somehow inadequate in winning the respect and recognition of others. These people go out of their way to seek attention to overcome this weakness, which is often felt but not recognized. In this connection, Adler introduced two interesting and now well-known concepts in his discussion—*inferiority complex* and *compensation*.

A person with an inferiority complex has underlying fears of inadequacy, which may or may not have some basis in reality. In some cases, individuals compensate for this inferiority complex by exerting extreme efforts to achieve goals or objectives that (they feel) inadequacy would deny. In many cases, extreme effort seems to be an overcompensation for something not clearly perceived, although felt. Once accurately perceived, the frame of reference can be realigned with reality and can result in more realistic behavior.

Adler found another interesting thing. If children do not encounter too much tension as they mature, their need for power gradually transforms itself into a desire to perfect their social relationships. They want to be able to interact with others without fear or suspicion in an open and trusting atmosphere. Thus, individuals often move from the *task* aspect of power, wanting to structure and manipulate their environment and the people in it, to a concern for *relationships,* developing trust and respect for others. This transformation is often delayed with individuals who have had tension-filled childhoods and have not learned to trust. In these cases, the power motive would not only persist but might even become stronger. Thus, Adler, like Freud, felt that the personality of an individual is developed early in life and is often a result of the kind of past experiences the child had with adults in the world. We will discuss power in much greater detail in Chapter 8.

Self-actualization

Of all the needs discussed by Maslow, the one that social and behavioral scientists know least about is self-actualization. Perhaps this is because people satisfy this need in different ways. Thus, self-actualization is a difficult need to pin down and identify.

Although little research has been done on the concept of self-actualization, extensive research has been done on two motives that we feel are related to it— *competence* and *achievement.*

Competence. According to Robert W. White, one of the mainsprings of action in a human being is a desire for competence.[31] Competence implies control over environmental factors—both physical and social. People with this motive do not wish to wait passively for things to happen; they want to be able to manipulate their environment and make things happen.

The competence motive can be identified in young children as they move from the early stage of wanting to touch and handle everything in reach to the later stage of wanting not only to touch but to take things apart and put them back together again. Children begin to learn their way around their world. They become aware of what they can do and cannot do. This is not in terms of what they are allowed to do, but in terms of what they are able to do. During these early years, children develop a feeling of competence.

This feeling of competence is closely related to the concept of expectancy discussed earlier. Whether children have a strong or weak sense of competence depends on their successes and failures in the past. If their successes overshadow their failures, then their feeling of competence will tend to be high. They will have a positive outlook toward life, seeing almost every new situation as an interesting challenge that they can overcome. If, however, their failures carry the day, their outlook will be more negative and expectancy for satisfying various needs may become low. Since expectancy tends to influence motives, people with low feelings of competence will not often be motivated to seek new challenges or take risks. These people would rather let their environment control them than attempt to change it.

The sense of competence, while established early in life, is not necessarily permanent. White found that unexpected good or bad fortune may influence one's feelings of competence in a positive or negative way. Thus, the competence motive tends to be cumulative. For example, people can get off to a bad start and then develop a strong sense of competence because of new successes. There is, however, a point in time when a sense of competence seems to stabilize itself. When this occurs, the sense of competence almost becomes a self-fulfilling prophecy, influencing whether a given experience will be a success or a failure. After people reach a certain age, they seldom achieve more than they think they can, because they do not attempt things they think they cannot achieve.

According to White, the competence motive reveals itself in adults as a desire for job mastery and professional growth. The job is one arena where people can match their ability and skills against their environment in a contest that is challenging but not overwhelming. In jobs where such a contest is possible, the competence motive in an individual can be expressed freely, and significant personal rewards can be gained. But in routine, closely supervised jobs this contest is often impossible. Such situations make the worker dependent on the system and, therefore, completely frustrate people with high competence needs.

Achievement. Over the years behavioral scientists have observed that some people have an intense need to achieve; others, perhaps the majority, do not seem to be as concerned about achievement. This phenomenon has fascinated David C. McClelland. For over twenty years he and his associates at Harvard University have been studying this urge to achieve.[32]

McClelland's research has led him to believe that the need for achievement is a distinct human motive that can be distinguished from other needs. More important, the achievement motive can be isolated and assessed in any group.

What are some of the characteristics of people with a high need for achievement? McClelland illustrates some of these characteristics in describing a laboratory experiment. Participants were asked to throw rings over a peg from any distance they chose. Most people tended to throw at random—now close, now far away; but individuals with a high need for achievement seemed carefully to measure where they were most likely to get a sense of mastery—not too close to make the task ridiculously easy or too far away to make it impossible. They set moderately difficult but potentially achievable goals. In biology, this is known as the *overload principle.* In weight lifting, for example, strength cannot be increased by tasks that can be performed easily or that cannot be performed without injury to the organism. Strength can be increased by lifting weights that are difficult but realistic enough to stretch the muscles.

Do people with a high need for achievement behave like this all the time? No. Only if they can influence the outcome. Achievement-motivated people are not gamblers. They prefer to work on a problem rather than leave the outcome to chance.

With managers, setting moderately difficult but potentially achievable goals may be translated into an attitude toward risks. Many people tend to be extreme in their attitude toward risks, either favoring wild speculative gambling or minimizing their exposure to losses. Gamblers seem to choose the big risk because the outcome is beyond their power and, therefore, they can easily rationalize away their personal responsibility if they lose. The conservative individual chooses tiny risks where the gain is small but secure, perhaps because there is little danger of anything going wrong for which that person might be blamed. Achievement-motivated people take the middle ground, preferring a moderate degree of risk because they feel their efforts and abilities will probably influence the outcome. In business, this aggressive realism is the mark of the successful entrepreneur.

Another characteristic of achievement-motivated people is that they seem to be more concerned with personal achievement than with the rewards of success. They do not reject rewards, but the rewards are not as essential as the accomplishment itself. They get a bigger "kick" out of winning or solving a difficult problem than they get from any money or praise they receive. Money, to achievement-motivated people, is valuable primarily as a measurement of their performance. It provides them with a means of assessing their progress and comparing their achievements with those of other people. They normally do not seek money for status or economic security.

A desire by people with a high need for achievement to seek situations in which they get concrete feedback on how well they are doing is closely related to this concern for personal accomplishment. Consequently, achievement-motivated people are often found in sales jobs or as owners and managers of their own businesses. In addition to concrete feedback, the nature of the feedback is important to achievement-motivated people. They respond favorably to information about their work. They are not interested in comments about their personal characteristics, such as how cooperative or helpful they are. Affiliation-motivated people might want social or attitudinal feedback. Achievement-motivated people might want task-relevant feedback. They want to know the score.

Why do achievement-motivated people behave as they do? McClelland claims it is because they habitually spend time thinking about doing things better. In fact, he has found that wherever people start to think in achievement terms, things start to happen. Examples can be cited. College students with a high need for achievement will generally get better grades than equally bright students with weaker achievement needs. Achievement-motivated people tend to get more raises and are promoted faster because they are constantly trying to think of better ways of doing things. Companies with many such people grow faster and are more profitable. McClelland has even extended his analysis to countries where he related the presence of a large percentage of achievement-motivated individuals to the national economic growth.

McClelland has found that achievement-motivated people are more likely to be developed in families in which parents hold different expectations for their children than do other parents. More importantly, these parents expect their children to start showing some independence between the ages of six and eight, making choices and doing things without help, such as knowing the way around the neighborhood and taking care of themselves around the house. Other parents tend either to expect this too early, before children are ready, or to smother the development of the personality of these children. One extreme seems to foster passive, defeated attitudes as children feel unwanted at home and incompetent away from home. They are just not ready for that kind of independence so early. The other extreme yields either overprotected or overdisciplined children. These children become very dependent on their parents and find it difficult to break away and make their own decisions.

Given all we know about the need for achievement, can this motive be taught and developed in people? McClelland is convinced that this can be done. In fact, he has also developed training programs for business people that are designed to increase their achievement motivation. He is also in the process of developing similar programs for other segments of the population. These programs could have tremendous implications for training and developing human resources.

Achievement-motivated people can be the backbone of most organizations, but what can we say about their potential as managers? As we know, people with a high need for achievement get ahead because as individuals they are producers, they get things done. However, when they are promoted, when their success depends not only on their own work but on the activities of others, they may be less effective. Since they are highly task-oriented and work to their capacity, they tend to expect others to do the same. As a result, they sometimes lack the human skills and patience necessary for being effective managers of people who are competent but have a higher need for affiliation than they do. In this situation, their overemphasis on producing frustrates these people and prevents them from maximizing their own potential. Thus, while achievement-motivated people are needed in organizations, they do not always make the best managers unless they develop their human skills. As was pointed out in Chapter 1, being a good producer is not sufficient to make an effective manager.

Money Motive

As stated earlier, money is a very complicated motive that is entangled in such a way with all kinds of needs besides physiological needs that its importance is often difficult to ascertain. For example, in some cases, money can provide individuals with certain material things, such as fancy sports cars, from which they can gain a feeling of affiliation (join a sports car club), recognition (status symbol), and even self-actualization (become outstanding sports car drivers). Consequently, we delayed our discussion of the money motive until other basic concepts were clarified.

From extensive research on incentive pay schemes, William F. Whyte has found that money, the old reliable motivational tool, is not as almighty as it is supposed to be, particularly for production workers.[33] For each of these workers, another key factor, as Mayo discovered, is their work group. Using the ratio of high-producing rate-busters to low-producing restrictors as an index, Whyte estimates that only about 10 percent of the production workers in the United

States will ignore group pressure and produce as much as possible in response to an incentive plan. It seems that while workers are interested in advancing their own financial position, there are many other considerations, such as the opinions of their fellow workers, their comfort and enjoyment on the job, and their long-range security, which prevent them from making a direct, automatic, positive response to an incentive plan.

According to Gellerman, the most subtle and most important characteristic of money is its power as a symbol. Its most obvious symbolic power is its market value. It is what money can buy, not money itself, that gives it value. But money's symbolic power is not limited to its market value. Since money has no intrinsic meaning of its own, it can symbolize almost any need an individual wants it to represent. In other words, money can mean whatever people want it to mean.[34]

WHAT DO WORKERS WANT FROM THEIR JOBS?

In talking about motives it is important to remember that people have many needs, all of which are continually competing for their behavior. No one person has exactly the same mixture or strength of these needs. There are some people who are driven mainly by money, others who are concerned primarily with security, and so on. While we must recognize individual differences, this does not mean that, as managers, we cannot make some predictions about which motives seem to be currently more prominent among our employees than others. According to Maslow, these are prepotent motives—those that are still *not* satisfied. An important question for managers to answer is, what do workers really want from their jobs?

Some interesting research has been conducted among employees in American industry in an attempt to answer this question. In one such study[35] supervisors were asked to try to put themselves in a *worker's* shoes by ranking in order of importance a series of items that describe things workers may want from their jobs. It was emphasized that in ranking the items the supervisors should *not* think in terms of what they want but what they think a worker wants. In addition to the supervisors, the workers themselves were asked to rank these same items in terms of what *they* wanted most from their jobs. The results are given in Table 2-1. (1 = highest and 10 = lowest in importance).

As is evident from the results, supervisors in this 1948 study generally ranked good wages, job security, promotion, and good working conditions as the things workers want most from their jobs. On the other hand, workers felt that what they wanted most was full appreciation for work done, feeling "in" on things, and sympathetic understanding of personal problems—all incentives that seem to be related to affiliation and recognition motives. It is interesting to note that those things that workers indicated they wanted most from their jobs were rated by their foremen as least important. This study suggested very little sensi-

TABLE 2-1 What Do Workers Want from Their Jobs?

	Supervisors	Workers
Good working conditions	4	9
Feeling "in" on things	10	2
Tactful disciplining	7	10
Full appreciation for work done	8	1
Management loyalty to workers	6	8
Good wages	1	5
Promotion and growth with company	3	7
Sympathetic understanding of personal problems	9	3
Job security	2	4
Interesting work	5	6

tivity by supervisors as to what things were really most important to workers. Supervisors seemed to think that incentives directed to satisfy physiological and safety motives tended to be most important to their workers. Since these supervisors perceived their workers as having these motives, they acted, undoubtedly, as if these were their true motives. Therefore, these supervisors probably used the old reliable incentives—money, fringe benefits, and security—to motivate workers.

We have replicated this study periodically over the last several decades as part of management training programs and have found similar results in the perceptions of managers. The only real changes seem to be that workers, over the last five to ten years, were increasing in their desire for "promotion and growth with the company" and "interesting work" (both motivators in Herzberg's framework). We say *were* increasing because with the economic decline of the 1970s, "good wages" and "job security" once again were becoming high strength needs for workers. It is important that managers know the tremendous discrepancies that seemed to exist in the past between what they thought workers wanted from their jobs and what workers said they actually wanted. It is also important that they realize what effect an economic or other change has on these priorities.

One might generalize at this point that individuals act on the basis of their perceptions or interpretation of reality and *not* on the basis of reality itself. In fact, one of the reasons we study the behavioral sciences is that they give us ways to get our perceptions closer and closer to reality. The closer we get our perceptions to a given reality, the higher the probability that we can have some impact on that particular piece of reality. Therefore, by bringing their perceptions closer and closer to reality—what their people really want—managers can often increase their effectiveness in working with employees. Managers have to know their people to understand what motivates them; they cannot just make assumptions. Even if managers asked employees how they felt about something, this does not necessarily result in relevant feedback. The quality of communications that managers receive from their employees is often based on the rapport that has been established between their people and themselves over a long period of time.

It is becoming clearer that many managers do not realize or understand that what people want from their jobs in a growing economy is different from what they wanted a few decades ago. When employment is high in the United States, few people, with the exception of those in some of the urban ghettos and poverty belts, have to worry about where their next meal will come from or whether they will be protected from the elements or physical dangers. The satisfaction of physiological and safety needs has been the result of the tremendous rise in our standard of living, dramatic increases in pay and fringe benefits at all levels of work, and extensive aid from governmental programs—welfare, social security, medicare, and unemployment insurance. In addition, the union movement and labor laws have made significant strides in assuring safe working conditions and job security.

Our society during good times almost has a built-in guarantee of physiological and safety needs for large segments of the population. Since many physiological and safety needs are provided for during those times, it is understandable why people would become more concerned with social, recognition, and self-actualization motives. Managers must become aware of this fact and strive to create organizations that can provide the kind of environment to motivate and satisfy people at all need levels. In Chapter 3 we will describe some of the research that may be helpful to a manager in building a motivating environment that will increase organizational effectiveness.

NOTES

[1] Sigmund Freud, *The Ego and the Id* (London: Hogarth Press, 1927). See also *New Introductory Lectures on Psychoanalysis* (New York: W. W. Norton & Company, Inc., 1933).

[2] Abraham H. Maslow, *Motivation and Personality* (New York: Harper & Row Publishers, 1954).

[3] Leon Festinger, *A Theory of Cognitive Dissonance* (Stanford, Calif.: Stanford University Press, 1957).

[4] *Ibid.,* p. 155.

[5] Freud, *The Ego and the Id.*

[6] J. A. C. Brown, *The Social Psychology of Industry* (Baltimore: Penguin Books, Inc., 1954), p. 249.

[7] Norman R. F. Maier, *Frustration* (Ann Arbor: The University of Michigan Press, 1961).

[8] Brown, *The Social Psychology,* p. 252.

[9] H. Barker, T. Dembo and K. Lewin, *Frustration and Aggression* (Iowa City: University of Iowa Press, 1942).

[10] Brown, *The Social Psychology,* p. 253.

[11] Maier, *Frustration.*

[12] Brown, *The Social Psychology,* p. 254.

[13] Dewey E. Johnson, *Concepts of Air Force Leadership* (Washington, D.C.: Air Force ROTC, 1970), p. 209.

[14] J. Sterling Livingston, "Pygmalion in Management," *Harvard Business Review,* July-August 1969, pp. 81–89.

[15] See John W. Atkinson, "Motivational Determinants of Risk-Taking Behavior, *Psychological Review*, 64, No. 6, 1957, 365.

[16] This figure was adapted from Livingston, "Pygmalion in Management," p. 85.

[17] Maslow, *Motivation and Personality*.

[18] Clare W. Graves, "Human Nature Prepares for a Momentous Leap," *The Futurist*, April 1974, pp. 72–87.

[19] *Ibid.*, p. 72.

[20] *Ibid.*

[21] Saul W. Gellerman, *Motivation and Productivity* (New York: American Management Association, 1963). See also Gellerman, *Management by Motivation* (New York: American Management Association, 1968).

[22] Peter F. Drucker, "How to Be an Employee," *Psychology Today*, March 1968, a reprint from *Fortune* magazine.

[23] Gellerman, *Motivation and Productivity*, pp. 154–55.

[24] Stanley Schachter, *The Psychology of Affiliation* (Stanford, Calif.: Stanford University Press, 1959).

[25] Elton Mayo, *The Social Problems of an Industrial Civilization* (Boston: Harvard Business School, 1945); see also Mayo, *The Human Problems of an Industrial Civilization* (New York: The Macmillan Company, 1933).

[26] Vance Packard, *The Status Seekers* (New York: David McKay Co., Inc., 1959).

[27] David Reisman, *The Lonely Crowd* (New Haven, Conn.: Yale University Press, 1950).

[28] Gellerman, *Motivation and Productivity*, p. 151.

[29] *Ibid.*, pp. 150–54.

[30] Alfred Adler, *Social Interest* (London: Faber & Faber Ltd., 1938). See also H. L. Ansbacher and R. R. Ansbacher, eds., *The Individual Psychology of Alfred Adler* (New York: Basic Books, Inc., Publishers, 1956).

[31] Robert W. White, "Motivation Reconsidered: The Concept of Competence," *Psychological Review*, LXVI, No. 5 (1959).

[32] David C. McClelland, J. W. Atkinson, R. A. Clark and E. L. Lowell, *The Achievement Motive* (New York: Appleton-Century-Crofts, 1953); and *The Achieving Society* (Princeton, N.J.: D. Van Nostrand Co., Inc., 1961).

[33] William F. Whyte, ed., *Money and Motivation* (New York: Harper & Row, Publishers, 1955).

[34] Gellerman, *Motivation and Productivity*, pp. 160–69.

[35] Lawrence Lindahl, "What Makes a Good Job," *Personnel*, Vol. 25, January 1949.

chapter 3

Motivating Environment

In 1924 efficiency experts at the Hawthorne, Illinois, plant of the Western Electric Company designed a research program to study the effects of illumination on productivity. At first, nothing about this program seemed exceptional enough to arouse any unusual interest. After all, efficiency experts had long been trying to find the ideal mix of physical conditions, working hours, and working methods that stimulate workers to produce at maximum capacity. Yet by the time these studies were completed (over a decade later), there was little doubt that the work at Hawthorne would stand the test of time as one of the most exciting and important research projects ever done in an industrial setting. For it was at Western Electric's Hawthorne plant that the Human Relations Movement began to gather momentum, and one of its early advocates, Elton Mayo of the Harvard Graduate School of Business Administration, gained recognition.[1]

HAWTHORNE STUDIES

Elton Mayo

In the initial study at Hawthorne, efficiency experts assumed that increases in illumination would result in higher output. Two groups of employees were selected: an *experimental* or *test group*, which worked under varying degrees of light, and a *control group,* which worked under normal illumination conditions in the plant. As lighting power was increased, the output of the test group went up as anticipated. Unexpectedly, however, the output of the control group went up also—without any increase in light.

Determined to explain these and other surprising test results, the efficiency experts decided to expand their research at Hawthorne. They felt that in addition to technical and physical changes, some of the behavioral considerations should be explored, so Mayo and his associates were called in to help.

Mayo and his team started their experiments with a group of women who assembled telephone relays, and, like the efficiency experts, the Harvard staff uncovered astonishing results. For over a year and a half during this experiment, Mayo's researchers improved the working conditions of the women by implementing such innovations as scheduled rest periods, company lunches, and shorter work weeks. Baffled by the results, the researchers suddenly decided to take everything away from the women, returning the working conditions to the exact way they had been at the beginning of the experiment. This radical change was expected to have a tremendous negative psychological impact on the women and reduce their output. Instead, their output jumped to a new *all-time high.* Why?

The answers to this question were *not* found in the production aspects of the experiment (changes in plant and physical working conditions), but in the *human* aspects. As a result of the attention lavished upon them by experimenters, the women were made to feel they were an important part of the company. They no longer viewed themselves as isolated individuals, working together only in the sense that they were physically close to each other. Instead, they had become participating members of a congenial, cohesive work group. The relationships that developed elicited feelings of affiliation, competence, and achievement. These needs, which had long gone unsatisfied at work, were now being fulfilled. The women worked harder and more effectively than they had worked previously.

Realizing that they had uncovered an interesting phenomenon, the Harvard team extended their research by interviewing over twenty thousand employees from every department in the company. Interviews were designed to help researchers find out what the workers thought about their jobs, their working conditions, their supervisors, their company, and anything that bothered them, and how these feelings might be related to their productivity. After several interview sessions, Mayo's group found that a structured question-and-answer-type interview was useless for eliciting the information they wanted. Instead, the workers wanted to talk freely about what *they* thought was important. So the predetermined questions were discarded, and the interviewer allowed the workers to ramble as they chose.

The interviews proved valuable in a number of ways. First of all, they were therapeutic; the workers got an opportunity to get a lot off their chests. Many felt this was the best thing the company had ever done. The result was a wholesale change in attitude. Since many of their suggestions were being implemented, the workers began to feel that management viewed them as important, both as individuals and as a group; they were now participating in the operation and future of the company and not just performing unchallenging, unappreciated tasks.

Second, the implications of the Hawthorne studies signaled the need for management to study and understand relationships among people. In these studies, as well as in the many that followed, the most significant factor affecting organizational productivity was found to be the interpersonal relationships that are developed on the job, not just pay and working conditions. Mayo found that when informal groups identified with management, as they did at Hawthorne through the interview program, productivity rose. The increased productivity seemed to reflect the workers' feelings of competence—a sense of mastery over the job and work environment. Mayo also discovered that when the group felt that their own goals were in opposition to those of management, as often happened in situations where the workers were closely supervised and had no significant control over their job or environment, productivity remained at low levels or was even lowered.

These findings were important because they helped answer many of the questions that had puzzled management about why some groups seemed to be high producers while others hovered at a minimal level of output. The findings also encouraged management to involve workers in planning, organizing, and controlling their own work in an effort to secure their positive cooperation.

Mayo saw the development of informal groups as an indictment of an entire society, which treated human beings as insensitive machines that were concerned only with economic self-interest. As a result, workers had been taught to look at work merely as an impersonal exchange of money for labor. Work in American industry meant humiliation—the performance of routine, tedious, and oversimplified tasks in an environment over which one had no control. This environment denied satisfaction of esteem and self-actualization needs on the job. Instead, only physiological and safety needs were satisfied. The lack of avenues for satisfying other needs led to tension, anxiety, and frustration in people. Such feelings of helplessness were called *anomie* by Mayo. This condition was characterized by workers' feeling unimportant, confused, and unattached—victims of their own environment.

While anomie was a creation of the total society, Mayo felt its most extreme application was found in industrial settings where management held certain negative assumptions about the nature of people. According to Mayo, too many managers assumed that society consisted of a horde of unorganized individuals whose only concern was self-preservation or self-interest. It was assumed that people were primarily dominated by physiological and safety needs, wanting to make as much money as they could for as little work as possible. Thus, management organized work on the basic assumption that workers, on the whole, were a contemptible lot. Mayo called this assumption the Rabble Hypothesis. He deplored the authoritarian, task-oriented management practices that it created.

THEORY X AND THEORY Y

Douglas McGregor

The work of Mayo and particularly his exposure of the Rabble Hypothesis may have paved the way for the development of the now classic "Theory X–Theory Y" by Douglas McGregor.[2] According to McGregor, traditional organization with its centralized decision making, superior-subordinate pyramid, and external control of work is based upon assumptions about human nature and human motivation. These assumptions are very similar to the view of people defined by Mayo in the Rabble Hypothesis. Theory X assumes that most people prefer to be directed, are not interested in assuming responsibility, and want safety above all. Accompanying this philosophy is the belief that people are motivated by money, fringe benefits, and the threat of punishment.

Managers who accept Theory X assumptions attempt to structure, control, and closely supervise their employees. These managers feel that external control is clearly appropriate for dealing with unreliable, irresponsible, and immature people.

After describing Theory X, McGregor questioned whether this view of human nature is correct and if management practices based upon it are appropriate in many situations today: Are not people in a democratic society, with its increasing level of education and standard of living, capable of more mature behavior? Drawing heavily on Maslow's hierarchy of needs, McGregor concluded that Theory X assumptions about human nature, when universally applied, are often inaccurate and that management approaches that develop from these assumptions may fail to motivate many individuals to work toward organizational goals. Management by direction and control may not succeed, according to McGregor, because it is a questionable method for motivating people whose physiological and safety needs are reasonably satisfied and whose social, esteem, and self-actualization needs are becoming predominant.

McGregor felt that management needed practices based on a more accurate understanding of human nature and motivation. As a result of his feeling, McGregor developed an alternate theory of human behavior called Theory Y. This theory assumes that people are *not*, by nature, lazy and unreliable. It postulates that people *can be* basically self-directed and creative at work if properly motivated. Therefore, it should be an essential task of management to unleash this potential in individuals. The properly motivated people can achieve their own goals *best* by directing *their own* efforts toward accomplishing organizational goals.

The impression that one might get from the discussion of Theory X–Theory Y is that managers who accept Theory X assumptions about human nature usually direct, control, and closely supervise people while Theory Y managers are supportive and facilitating. We want to caution against drawing that kind of

TABLE 3-1 List of Assumptions About Human Nature That Underline McGregor's Theory X and Theory Y

Theory X	Theory Y
1. Work is inherently distasteful to most people.	1. Work is as natural as play, if the conditions are favorable.
2. Most people are not ambitious, have little desire for responsibility, and prefer to be directed.	2. Self-control is often indispensable in achieving organizational goals.
3. Most people have little capacity for creativity in solving organizational problems.	3. The capacity for creativity in solving organizational problems is widely distributed in the population.
4. Motivation occurs only at the physiological and safety levels.	4. Motivation occurs at the social, esteem, and self-actualization levels, as well as physiological and security levels.
5. Most people must be closely controlled and often coerced to achieve organizational objectives.	5. People can be self-directed and creative at work if properly motivated.

conclusion because it could lead to the trap of thinking that Theory X is "bad" and Theory Y is "good" and that everyone is mature, independent, and self-motivated rather than, as McGregor implies, that most people have the *potential* to be mature and self-motivated. This assumption of the potential self-motivation of people necessitates a recognition of the difference between attitude and behavior. Theory X and Theory Y are attitudes or predispositions toward people. Thus, although the "best" assumptions for a manager to have may be Theory Y, it may not be appropriate to behave consistent with those assumptions all the time. Managers may have Theory Y assumptions about human nature, but they may find it necessary to behave in a very directive, controlling manner (as if they had Theory X assumptions) with some people in the short run to help them "grow up" in a developmental sense, until they are truly Theory Y people.

Chris Argyris recognizes the difference between attitude and behavior when he identifies and discusses behavior patterns A and B in addition to Theory X and Y.[3] Pattern A represents the interpersonal behavior, group dynamics, and organizational norms that Argyris has found in his research to be associated with Theory X; pattern B represents the same phenomena found to be associated with Theory Y. In pattern A, individuals do not own up to feelings, are not open, reject experimenting, and do not help others to engage in these behaviors. Their behavior tends to be characterized by close supervision and a high degree of structure. On the other hand, pattern B finds individuals owning up to feelings, open, experimenting, and helping others to engage in these behaviors. Their behavior tends to be more supportive and facilitating. The result is norms of trust, concern, and individuality.

As Argyris emphasizes, "although XA and YB are *usually* associated with each other in everyday life, they do not have to be. Under certain conditions, pattern A could go with Theory Y or pattern B with Theory X."[4] Thus, XA and

YB are the most frequent combinations, but some managers at times may be XB or YA. Although XB managers have negative assumptions about people, they seem to be behaving in supportive and facilitating ways. We have found that this XB combination tends to occur for two reasons. These managers (although they think most people are lazy and unreliable) engage in supportive and facilitating behaviors either because they have been told or learned from experience that such behavior will increase productivity or they work for people who have created a supportive environment and if they want to maintain their jobs they are expected to behave accordingly. On the other hand, YA managers (although they think people are generally self-motivated and mature) control and closely supervise people either because they work for controlling people who demand similar behavior from them or they find it necessary to behave in a directive, controlling manner for a period of time. When they use pattern A behavior, these managers usually are attempting to help people develop the skills and abilities necessary for self-direction and thus creating an environment in which they can become YB managers.

The latter type of Y manager attempts to help employees mature by exposing them to progressively less external control, allowing them to assume more and more self-control. Employees are able to achieve the satisfaction of social, esteem, and self-actualization needs within this kind of environment, often neglected on the job. To the extent that the job does not provide need satisfaction at every level, today's employee will usually look elsewhere for significant need satisfaction. This helps explain some of the current problems management is facing in such areas as turnover and absenteeism. McGregor argues that this does not have to be the case.

Management is interested in work, and McGregor feels that work is as natural and can be as satisfying for people as play. After all, both work and play are physical and mental activities; consequently, there is no inherent difference between work and play. In reality, however, particularly under Theory X management, a distinct difference in need satisfaction is discernible. Whereas play is internally controlled by the individuals (they decide what they want to do), work is externally controlled by others (people have no control over their jobs). Thus, management and its assumptions about the nature of people have built in a difference between work and play that seems unnatural. As a result, people are stifled at work and hence look for excuses to spend more and more time away from the job in order to satisfy their esteem and self-actualization needs (provided they have enough money to satisfy their physiological and safety neeeds). Because of their conditioning to Theory X types of management, most employees consider work a *necessary evil* rather than a source of personal challenge and satisfaction.

Does work really have to be a necessary evil? No—especially in organizations where cohesive work groups have developed and where the goals parallel organizational goals. In such organizations there is high productivity, and people come to work gladly because work is inherently satisfying.

HUMAN GROUP

George C. Homans

Management is often suspicious of strong informal work groups because of their potential power to control the behavior of their members and, as a result, the level of productivity. Where do these groups get their power to control behavior? George C. Homans has developed a model of social systems that may be useful to the practitioner trying to answer this question.[5]

There are three elements in a social system. *Activities* are the tasks that people perform. *Interactions* are the behaviors that occur between people in performing these tasks. And *sentiments* are the attitudes that develop between individuals and within groups. Homans argues that while these concepts are separate, they are closely related. In fact, as Figure 3-1 illustrates, they are mutually dependent upon each other.

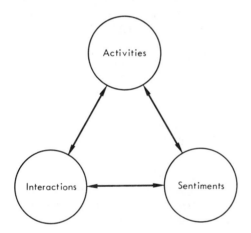

FIGURE 3-1 The mutual dependence of activities, interactions, and sentiments

A change in any of these three elements will produce some change in the other two.

In an organization, certain activities, interactions, and sentiments are essential, or required from its members, if it is to survive. In other words, jobs (activities) have to be done that require people to work together (interactions). These jobs must be sufficiently satisfying (sentiments) for people to continue doing them. As people interact on their jobs, they develop sentiments toward each other. As people increase interaction with each other, more positive sentiments will tend to develop toward each other. The more positive the sentiment, the more people will tend to interact with each other. It can become a spiraling process until some equilibrium is reached. As this spiraling process continues, there is a tendency for the group members to become more alike in their activities and sentiments—in what they do and how they feel about things. As this happens, the group tends to develop expectations or norms that specify how people in the group "might" tend to behave under specific circumstances. For example, a group of workers might have a norm that "you should not talk to the boss, or help him, any more than necessary." If the group is cohesive enough, that is, the group is attractive to its members and they are reluctant to leave it, then it will have little trouble in getting members to conform. People who deviate significantly from group norms usually incur sanctions from the group. "The group has at its disposal a variety of penalties, ranging from gentle kidding to harsh ostracism, for pressuring deviant members into line."[6] Group members may react in several ways. They may decide to go ahead and continue to deviate from group norms. If the resulting pressure from their peers becomes too great, they may leave the group.

The influence group pressures can have in achieving conformity in the perceptions and behavior of people is well documented. For example, S. E. Asch conducted a classic experiment in which groups of eight college men were each asked to match the length of a line with one of three unequal lines.[7] Seven members of each group were privately told to give the same incorrect answer. The uninstructed member was the last one asked to give his answer and was thus confronted with the dilemma of either reporting what he saw as being correct or reporting what all the others had said in order to be congruent with the group. Asch reported that "one-third of all the estimates were errors identical with or in the direction of the distorted estimates of the majority."[8] If pressure can cause distorted behavior in this kind of exercise, imagine what peer group pressure can induce with more subjective judgments.

It should be reiterated that strong informal work groups do not have to be a detriment to organizations. In fact, as Mayo discovered at Hawthorne, these groups can become powerful driving forces in accomplishing organizational goals if they see their own goals as being satisfied by working for organizational goals.

INCREASING INTERPERSONAL COMPETENCE

Chris Argyris

Even though management based on the assumptions of Theory X is perhaps no longer widely appropriate in the opinion of McGregor and others, it is still widely practiced. Consequently, a large majority of the people in the United States today are treated as immature human beings in their working environments. In attempting to analyze this situation, Chris Argyris,[9] now of Harvard University, has compared bureaucratic/pyramidal values (the organizational counterpart to Theory X assumptions about people) that still dominate most organizations with a more humanistic/democratic value system (the organizational counterpart to Theory Y assumptions about people) as illustrated in Table 3-2.[10]

TABLE 3-2 Two Different Value Systems as Seen by Chris Argyris

Bureaucratic/Pyramidal Value System	Humanistic/Democratic Value System
1. Important human relationships—the crucial ones—are those related to achieving the organization's objectives, *i.e.,* getting the job done.	1. The important human relationships are not only those related to achieving the organization's objectives but those related to maintaining the organization's internal system and adapting to the environment as well.
2. Effectiveness in human relationship increases as behavior becomes more rational, logical, and clearly communicated; but effectiveness decreases as behavior becomes more emotional.	2. Human relationships increase in effectiveness as *all* the relevant behavior (rational and interpersonal) becomes conscious, discussible, and controllable.
3. Human relationships are most effectively motivated by carefully defined direction, authority, and control, as well as appropriate rewards and penalties that emphasize rational behavior and achievement of the objective.	3. In addition to direction, controls, and rewards and penalties, human relationships are most effectively influenced through authentic relationships, internal commitment, psychological success, and the process of confirmation.

According to Argyris, following bureaucratic or pyramidal values leads to poor, shallow, and mistrustful relationships. Because these relationships do not permit the natural and free expression of feelings, they are phony or nonauthentic and result in decreased interpersonal competence. "Without interpersonal competence or a 'psychologically safe' environment, the organization is a breeding ground for mistrust, intergroup conflict, rigidity, and so on, which in turn lead to a decrease in organizational success in problem solving."[11]

If, on the other hand, humanistic or democratic values are adhered to in an organization, Argyris claims that trusting, authentic relationships will develop among people and will result in increased interpersonal competence, intergroup cooperation, flexibility, and the like and should result in increases in organizational effectiveness. In this kind of environment people are treated as human beings, both organizational members and the organization itself are given an opportunity to develop to the fullest potential, and there is an attempt to make work exciting and challenging. Implicit in "living" these values is "treating each human being as a person with a complex set of needs, *all* of which are important in his work and in his life . . . and providing opportunities for people in organizations to influence the way in which they relate to work, the organization, and the environment."[12]

Immaturity–Maturity Theory

The fact that bureaucratic/pyramidal values still dominate most organizations, according to Argyris, has produced many of our current organizational problems. While at Yale, he examined industrial organizations to determine what effect management practices have had on individual behavior and personal growth within the work environment.[13]

According to Argyris, seven changes should take place in the personality of individuals if they are to develop into mature people over the years.

First, individuals move from a passive state as infants to a state of increasing activity as adults. Second, individuals develop from a state of dependency upon others as infants to a state of relative independence as adults. Third, individuals behave in only a few ways as infants, but as adults they are capable of behaving in many ways. Fourth, individuals have erratic, casual, and shallow interests as infants but develop deeper and stronger interests as adults. Fifth, the time perspective of children is very short, involving only the present, but as they mature, their time perspective increases to include the past and the future. Sixth, individuals as infants are subordinate to everyone, but they move to equal or superior positions with others as adults. Seventh, as children, individuals lack an awareness of a "self," but as adults they are not only aware of, but they are able to control "self." Argyris postulates that these changes reside on a continuum and that the "healthy" personality develops along the continuum from "immaturity" to "maturity" (See Table 3-3).

TABLE 3-3   Immaturity–Maturity Continuum

Immaturity ————————————▶ *Maturity*
Passive ———————————————————— Active
Dependence ——————————————————— Independence
Behave in a few ways ———————————— Capable of behaving in many ways
Erratic shallow interests ———————————— Deeper and stronger interests
Short time perspective ———————————— Long time perspective (past and future)
Subordinate position ———————————— Equal or superordinate position
Lack of awareness of self ———————————Awareness and control over self

These changes are only general tendencies, but they give some light on the matter of maturity. Norms of the individual's culture and personality inhibit and limit maximum expression and growth of the adult, yet the tendency is to move toward the "maturity" end of the continuum with age. Argyris would be the first to admit that few, if any, develop to full maturity.

In examining the widespread worker apathy and lack of effort in industry, Argyris questions whether these problems are simply the result of individual laziness. He suggests that this is *not* the case. Argyris contends that, in many cases, when people join the force, they are kept from maturing by the management practices utilized in their organizations. In these organizations, they are given minimal control over their environment and are encouraged to be passive, dependent, and subordinate; therefore, they behave immaturely. The worker in many organizations is expected to act in immature ways rather than as a mature adult. This does not occur only in industrial settings. In fact, one can even see it happening in many school systems, where most high school students are subject to more rules and restrictions and generally treated less maturely than their younger counterparts in elementary school.

According to Argyris, keeping people immature is built into the very nature of the formal organization. He argues that because organizations are usually created to achieve goals or objectives that can best be met collectively, the formal organization is often the architect's conception of how these objectives may be achieved. In this sense the individual is fitted to the job. The design comes first. This design is based upon four concepts of scientific management: task specialization, chain of command, unity of direction, and span of control. Management tries to increase and enhance organizational and administrative efficiency and productivity by making workers "interchangeable parts."

Basic to these concepts is that power and authority should rest in the hands of a few at the top of the organization, and thus those at the lower end of the chain of command are strictly controlled by their superiors or the system itself. Task specialization often results in the oversimplification of the job so that it becomes repetitive, routine, and unchallenging. This implies directive, task-oriented leadership where decisions about the work are made by the superior, with the workers only carrying out those decisions. This type of leadership evokes managerial controls such as budgets, some incentive systems, time and motion studies, and standard operating procedures, which can restrict the initiative and creativity of workers.

Theory into Practice

Argyris feels that these concepts of formal organization lead to assumptions about human nature that are incompatible with the proper development of maturity in human personality. He sees a definite incongruity between the needs of a mature personality and the formal organizations as they now exist. Since he implies that the classical theory of management (based on Theory X assumptions) usually prevails, management creates childlike roles for workers that frustrate natural development.

An example of how work is often designed at this extremely low level was dramatically illustrated by the successful use of mentally retarded workers in such jobs. Argyris cites two instances, one in a knitting mill and the other in a radio manufacturing corporation, in which mentally retarded people were successfully employed on unskilled jobs. In both cases, the managers praised these workers for their excellent performance. In fact, a manager in the radio corporation reported that these workers:

> . . . proved to be exceptionally well-behaved, particularly obedient, and strictly honest and trustworthy. They carried out work required of them to such a degree of efficiency that *we were surprised they were classed as subnormals for their age.* Their attendance was good, and their behavior was, if anything, certainly better than that of any other employee of the same age.[14]

Disturbed by what he finds in many organizations, Argyris, as did McGregor, challenges management to provide a work climate in which everyone has a chance to grow and mature as individuals, as members of a group by satisfying their own needs, while working for the success of the organization. Implicit here is the belief that people can be basically self-directed and creative at work if properly motivated, and, therefore, management based on the assumptions of Theory Y will be more profitable for the individual and the organization.

More and more companies are starting to listen to the challenge that Argyris is directing at management. For example, the president of a large company asked Argyris to show him how to better motivate his workers. Together they went into one of his production plants where a product similar to a radio was being assembled. There were twelve women involved in assembling the product, each doing a small segment of the job as designed by an industrial engineer. The group also had a foreman, an inspector, and a packer.

Argyris proposed a one-year experiment during which each of the women would assemble the total product in a manner of her own choice. At the same time, each woman would inspect, sign her name to the product, pack it, and handle any correspondence involving complaints about it. The women were assured that they would receive no cut in pay if production dropped but would receive more pay if production increased.

Once the experiment began, production dropped 70 percent during the first month. By the end of six weeks it was even worse. The women were upset— morale was down. This continued until the eighth week, when production started to rise. By the end of the fifteenth week production was higher than it had ever been before. And this was without an inspector, a packer, or an industrial engineer. More important than increased productivity, costs due to errors and waste decreased 94 percent; letters of complaint dropped 96 percent.

Experiments like this are being duplicated in numerous other situations.[15] It is being found over and over again that broadening individual responsibility is beneficial to both the workers and the company. Giving people the opportunity to grow and mature on the job helps them satisfy more than just physiological and safety needs, which in turn motivates them and allows them to use more of their potential in accomplishing organizational goals. Although all workers do *not* want to accept more responsibility or deal with the added problems responsibility inevitably brings, Argyris contends that the number of employees whose motivation can be improved by increasing and upgrading their responsibility is much larger than most managers would suspect.

MOTIVATION-HYGIENE THEORY

Frederick Herzberg

We have noted that needs such as esteem and self-actualization seem to become more important as people mature. One of the most interesting series of studies that concentrates heavily on these areas has been directed by Frederick

Herzberg, now of the University of Utah.[16] Out of these studies has developed a theory of work motivation that has broad implications for management and its efforts toward effective utilization of human resources.

Herzberg, in developing his motivation-hygiene theory, seemed to sense that scholars like McGregor and Argyris were touching on something important. Knowledge about human nature, motives, and needs could be invaluable to organizations and individuals.

> To industry, the payoff for a study of job attitudes would be increased productivity, decreased absenteeism, and smoother working relations. To the individual, an understanding of the forces that lead to improved morale would bring greater happiness and greater self-realization.[17]

Herzberg set out to collect data on job attitudes from which assumptions about human behavior could be made. The motivation-hygiene theory resulted from the analysis of an initial study by Herzberg and his colleagues at the Psychological Service of Pittsburgh. This study involved extensive interviews with some two hundred engineers and accountants from eleven industries in the Pittsburgh area. In the interviews, they were asked about what kinds of things on their job made them unhappy or dissatisfied and what things made them happy or satisfied.

In analyzing the data from these interviews, Herzberg concluded that people have two different categories of needs that are essentially independent of each other and affect behavior in different ways. He found that when people felt dissatisfied with their jobs, they were concerned about the environment in which they were working. On the other hand, when people felt good about their jobs, this had to do with the work itself. Herzberg called the first category of needs *hygiene* or *maintenance* factors: hygiene because they describe people's environment and serve the primary function of preventing job dissatisfaction; maintenance because they are never completely satisfied—they have to continue to be maintained. He called the second category of needs *motivators* since they seemed to be effective in motivating people to superior performance.

Hygiene Factors

Company policies and administration, supervision, working conditions, interpersonal relations, money, status, and security may be thought of as maintenance factors. These are not an intrinsic part of a job, but they are related to the conditions under which a job is performed. Herzberg related his original use of the word hygiene to its medical meaning (preventive and environmental). He found that hygiene factors produced no growth in worker output capacity; they only prevented losses in worker performance due to work restriction. This is why more recently Herzberg has been calling these maintenance factors.

Motivators

Satisfying factors that involve feelings of achievement, professional growth, and recognition that one can experience in a job that offers challenge and scope are referred to as motivators. Herzberg used this term because these factors seem capable of having a positive effect on job satisfaction, often resulting in an increase in one's total output capacity.

TABLE 3-4   Motivation and Hygiene Factors

MOTIVATORS	HYGIENE FACTORS
The Job Itself	Environment
Achievement	Policies and administration
Recognition for accomplishment	Supervision
Challenging work	Working conditions
Increased responsibility	Interpersonal relations
Growth and development	Money, status, security

In recent years motivation-hygiene research has been extended well beyond scientists and accountants to include every level of an organization, from top management all the way down to hourly employees. For example, in an extensive study at Texas Instruments, Scott Meyers concluded that Herzberg's motivation-hygiene theory "is easily translatable to supervisory action at all levels of responsibility. It is a framework on which supervisors can evaluate and put into perspective the constant barrage of 'helpful hints' to which they are subjected, and hence serves to increase their feelings of competence, self-confidence, and autonomy."[18]

Perhaps an example will further differentiate between hygiene factors and motivators and help explain the reason for classifying needs as Herzberg has done.

Let us assume that a man is highly motivated and is working at 90 percent of capacity. He has a good working relationship with his supervisor, is well satisfied with his pay and working conditions, and is part of a congenial work group. Suppose his supervisor is suddenly transferred and replaced by a person he is unable to work with, or suppose he finds out that someone whose work he feels is inferior to his own is receiving more pay. How will these factors affect this individual's behavior? Since we know performance or productivity depends on both ability and motivation, these unsatisfied hygiene needs (supervision and money) may lead to restriction of output. This decline in productivity may be intentional or he may not be consciously aware that he is holding back. In either case, productivity will be lowered as illustrated in Figure 3-2.

In our illustration even if the worker's former supervisor returns and his salary is adjusted well above his expectations his productivity will probably increase only to its original level.

Conversely, let us take the same person and assume that dissatisfaction has

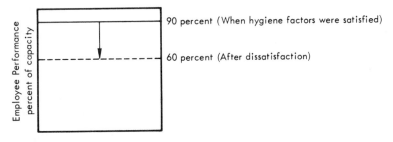

90 percent (When hygiene factors were satisfied)

60 percent (After dissatisfaction)

FIGURE 3-2 Effect of dissatisfying hygienes

not occurred; he is working at 90 percent capacity. Suppose he is given an opportunity to mature and satisfy his motivational needs in an environment where he is free to exercise some initiative and creativity, to make decisions, to handle problems, and to take responsibility. What effect will this situation have on this individual? If he is able to fulfill his supervisor's expectations in performing these new responsibilities, he may still work at 90 percent capacity, but as a person he may have matured and grown in his ability and may be capable now of more productivity, as illustrated in Figure 3-3.

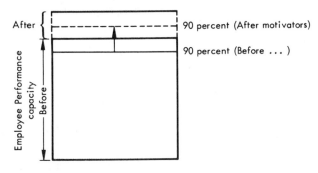

90 percent (After motivators)

90 percent (Before ...)

FIGURE 3-3 Effect of satisfying motivators

Hygiene factors, when satisfied, tend to eliminate dissatisfaction and work restriction, but they do little to motivate an individual to superior performance or increased capacity. Satisfaction of the motivators, however, will permit an individual to grow and develop in a mature way, often implementing an increase in ability. Thus, hygiene factors affect an individual's willingness or motivation and motivators impact an individual's ability.

The Relationship of Herzberg to Maslow

In terms of Hersey and Blanchard's motivating situation framework discussed in Chapter 2, Maslow is helpful in identifying needs or motives and Herzberg provides us with insights into the goals and incentives that tend to satisfy these needs, as illustrated in Figure 3-4.

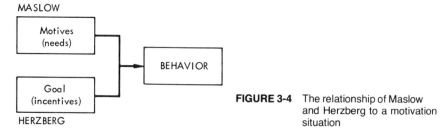

MASLOW

FIGURE 3-4   The relationship of Maslow and Herzberg to a motivation situation

HERZBERG

Thus, in a motivating situation, if you know what are the high strength needs (Maslow) of the individuals you want to influence, then you should be able to determine what goals (Herzberg) you could provide in the environment to motivate those individuals. At the same time, if you know what goals these people want to satisfy, you can predict what their high strength needs are. That is possible because it has been found that money and benefits tend to satisfy needs at the physiological and security levels; interpersonal relations and supervision are examples of hygiene factors that tend to satisfy social needs; increased responsibility, challenging work, and growth and development are motivators that tend to satisfy needs at the esteem and self-actualization levels. Figure 3-5 shows the relationship we feel exists between the Maslow and Herzberg frameworks.

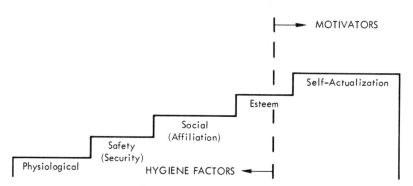

FIGURE 3-5   The relationships between the motivation-hygiene theory and Maslow's hierarchy of needs

We feel that the physiological, safety, social, and part of the esteem needs are all hygiene factors. The esteem needs are divided because there are some distinct differences between status per se and recognition. Status tends to be a function of the position one occupies. One may have gained this position through family ties or social pressures, and thus this position may not be a reflection of personal achievement or earned recognition. Recognition is gained through competence and achievement. It is earned and granted by others. Consequently, status is classified with physiological, safety, and social needs as a hygiene factor, while recognition is classified with esteem as a motivator.

It appears to us that McClelland's[19]concept of achievement motivation is also related to Herzberg's motivation-hygiene theory. People with high achievement motivation tend to be interested in the motivators (the job itself). Achievement-motivated people want task-relevant feedback. They want to know how well they are doing on their job. On the other hand, people with low achievement motivation are more concerned about the environment. They want to know how people feel about them rather than how well they are doing.

JOB ENRICHMENT

Prior to Herzberg's work, many other behavioral scientists were concerned with worker motivation. For several years there was an emphasis on what was termed "job enlargement" or "job rotation." This was purported to be an answer to the overspecialization that had characterized many industrial organizations. The assumption was that workers could gain more satisfaction at work if their jobs were enlarged, that is, if the number or variety of operations in which they engaged was increased.

Herzberg makes some astute observations about this trend. He claims that doing a snippet of this and a snippet of that does not necessarily result in motivation. Washing dishes, then silverware, and then pots and pans does no more to satisfy and provide an opportunity to grow than washing only dishes. What we really need to do with work, Herzberg suggests, is to *enrich* the job. By job enrichment is meant the deliberate upgrading of responsibility, scope, and challenge in work.

Example of Job Enrichment

An example of job enrichment may be illustrated by the experience an industrial relations superintendent had with a group of janitors. When the superintendent was transferred to a new plant, he soon found, much to his amazement, that in addition to his duties, fifteen janitors in plant maintenance reported directly to him. There was no foreman over these men. Browsing through the files one day, the superintendent noticed there was a history of complaints about housekeeping around the plant. After talking to others and observing for himself, it took the superintendent little time to confirm the reports. The janitors seemed to be lazy, unreliable, and generally unmotivated. They were walking examples of Theory X assumptions about human nature.

Determined to do something about the behavior of the janitors, the superintendent called a group meeting of all fifteen men. He opened the meeting by saying that he understood there were a number of housekeeping problems in the plant but confessed that he did not know what to do about them. Since he felt they, as janitors, were experts in the housekeeping area, he asked if together they would help him solve these problems. "Does anyone have a suggestion?" he asked. There was a deadly silence. The superintendent sat down and said nothing; the janitors said nothing. This lasted for almost twenty minutes. Finally one janitor spoke up and related a problem he was having in his area and made a suggestion. Soon others joined in, and suddenly the janitors were involved in a lively discussion while the superintendent listened and jotted down their ideas. At the conclusion of the meeting the suggestions were summarized with tacit acceptance by all, including the superintendent.

After the meeting, the superintendent referred any housekeeping problems to the janitors, individually or as a group. For example, when any cleaning equipment or material salesmen came to the plant the superintendent did not talk to them—the janitors did. In fact, the janitors were given an office where they could talk to salesmen. In addition, regular meetings continued to be held in which problems and ideas were discussed.

All of this had a tremendous influence on the behavior of these men. They developed a cohesive productive team that took pride in its work. Even their appearance changed. Once a grubby lot, now they appeared at work in clean, pressed work clothes. All over the plant, people were amazed how clean and well kept everything had become. The superintendent was continually stopped by supervisors in the plant and asked, "What have you done to those lazy, good-for-nothing janitors, given them pep pills?" Even the superintendent could not believe his eyes. It was not uncommon to see one or two janitors running floor tests to see which wax or cleaner did the best job. Since they had to make all the decisions including committing funds for their supplies, they wanted to know which were the best. Such activities, while taking time, did not detract from their work. In fact, these men worked harder and more efficiently than ever before in their lives.

This example illustrates that even at low levels in an organization, people can respond in responsible and productive ways to a work environment in which they are given an opportunity to grow and mature. People begin to satisfy their esteem and self-actualization needs by participating in the planning, organizing, motivating, and controlling of their own tasks.

A Problem of Placement

It should be pointed out that the problem of motivation is not always a question of enriching jobs. As Chris Argyris dramatically showed in his successful use of mentally retarded workers on the assembly line, some organizations have a tendency to hire people with ability far in excess of the demands of the work.

An example of overhiring happened in the start-up operation of a large plant. As in the case of most new plants, one of the first work groups to be assembled was security. The supervisor of plant security set, as hiring criteria, a high school education and three years of police or plant protection experience as minimal requirements for applicants. Being the first large industrial plant in a relatively agricultural area, the company was able to hire people not at the minimum level but well over these standards.

When these people began their jobs—which consisted simply of checking badges on the way in and lunch pails on the way out—boredom, apathy, and lack of motivation soon characterized their performance. This resulted in a high rate of turnover. When the problem was reevaluated, the reverse of the hiring procedures was found to be appropriate. Those applicants with a high school education were considered overqualified. Those with police or security experience were also considered overqualified. Rather than experienced workers, applicants with fourth- and fifth-grade educations, and thus lower job expectations, were hired for these positions. Their performance was found to be much superior, and the turnover, absenteeism, and tardiness rates were cut to a minimum. Why? For these workers, a new uniform, a badge, and some power were important, but they also found the job as one incorporating opportunities for more responsibility and challenging work.

MANAGEMENT SYSTEMS

Rensis Likert

Most managers, if asked what they would do if they suddenly lost half of their plant, equipment, or capital resources, are quick to answer. Insurance or borrowing are often avenues open to refurbish plant, equipment, or capital. Yet when these same managers are asked what they would do if they suddenly lost half of their human resources—managers, supervisors, and hourly employees— they are at a loss for words. There is no insurance against outflows of human resources. Recruiting, training, and developing large numbers of new personnel into a working team takes years. In a competitive environment this is almost an impossible task. Organizations are only beginning to realize that their most important assets are human resources and that the managing of these resources is one of their most crucial tasks.

Rensis Likert and his colleagues of the Institute for Social Research at the University of Michigan emphasized the need to consider both human resources and capital resources as assets requiring proper management.[20] As a result of behavioral research studies of numerous organizations, Likert implemented organizational change programs in various industrial settings. It appears these programs were intended to help organizations move from Theory X to Theory Y assumptions, from fostering immature behavior to encouraging and developing mature behavior, from emphasizing only hygiene factors to recognizing and helping workers to satisfy the motivators.

Likert in his studies found that the prevailing management styles of organization can be depicted on a continuum from System 1 through System 4. These systems might be described as follows.

System 1—Management is seen as having no confidence or trust in subordinates, since they are seldom involved in any aspect of the decision-making process. The bulk of the decisions and the goal setting of the organization are made at the top and issued down the chain of command. Subordinates are forced to work with fear, threats, punishment, and occasional rewards and need satisfaction at the physiological and safety levels. The little superior-subordinate interaction that does take place is usually with fear and mistrust. Although the control process is highly concentrated in top management, an informal organization generally develops in opposition to the goals of the formal organization.

System 2—Management is seen as having condescending confidence and trust in subordinates, such as master has toward servant. The bulk of the decisions and goal setting of the organization are made at the top, but many decisions are made within a prescribed framework at lower levels. Rewards and some actual or potential punishment are used to motivate workers. Any superior-subordinate interaction takes place with some condescension by superiors and fear and caution by subordinates. Although the control process is still concentrated in top management, some is delegated to middle and lower levels. An informal organization usually develops, but it does not always resist formal organizational goals.

System 3—Management is seen as having substantial but not complete confidence and trust in subordinates. Broad policy and general decisions are kept at the top, but subordinates are permitted to make more specific decisions at lower levels. Communication flows both up and down the hierarchy. Rewards, occasional punishment, and some involvement are used to motivate workers. There is a moderate amount of superior-subordinate interaction, often with a fair amount of confidence and trust. Significant aspects of the control process are delegated downward with a feeling of responsibility at both higher and lower levels. An informal organization may develop, but it may either support or partially resist goals of the organization.

System 4—Management is seen as having complete confidence and trust in subordinates. Decision making is widely dispersed throughout the organization, although well integrated. Communication flows not only up and down the hierarchy but among peers. Workers are motivated by participation and involvement in developing economic rewards, setting goals, improving methods, and appraising progress toward goals. There is extensive, friendly superior-subordinate interaction with a high degree of confidence and trust. There is widespread responsibility for the control process, with the lower units fully involved. The informal and formal organizations are often one and the same. Thus, all social forces support efforts to achieve stated organizational goals.[21]

In summary, System 1 is a task-oriented, highly structured authoritarian management style; System 4 is a relationships-oriented management style based on teamwork, mutual trust, and confidence. Systems 2 and 3 are intermediate stages between two extremes, which approximate closely Theory X and Theory Y assumptions.

To expedite the analysis of a company's present behavior, Likert's group developed an instrument that enables members to rate their organization in terms of its management system. This instrument is designed to gather data about a number of operating characteristics of an organization. These characteristics include leadership, motivation, communication, decision making, interaction and influence, goal setting, and the control process used by the organization. Sample items from this instrument are presented in Table 3-5. The complete instrument includes over twenty such items.[22] Various forms of this instrument have been adapted to be situation specific. For example, a version for school systems is now available with forms for the school board, superintendent, central staff, principals, teachers, parents, and students.

In testing this instrument, Likert asked hundreds of managers from many different organizations to indicate where the *most* productive department, division, or organization they have known would fall between System 1 and System 4. Then these same managers were asked to repeat this process and indicate the position of the *least* productive department, division, or organization they have known. While the ratings of the most and the least productive departments varied among managers, almost without exception each manager rated the high-producing unit closer to System 4 than the low-producing department. In summary, Likert has found that the closer the management style of an organization approaches System 4, the more likely it is to have a continuous record of high productivity. Similarly, the closer this style reflects System 1, the more likely it is to have a sustained record of low productivity.

Likert has also used this instrument not only to measure what individuals believe are the present characteristics of their organization but also to find out what they would like these characteristics to be. Data generated from this use of the instrument with managers of well-known companies have indicated a large discrepancy between the management system they feel their company is now using and the management system they feel would be most appropriate. System 4 is seen as being most appropriate, but few see their companies presently utilizing this approach. These implications have led to attempts by some organizations to adapt their management system to approximate more closely System 4. Changes of this kind are not easy. They involve a massive reeducation of all concerned, from the top management to the hourly workers.

Theory into Practice

One instance of a successful change in the management style of an organization occurred with a leading firm in the pajama industry.[23] After being unprofitable for several years, this company was purchased by another corporation. At the time of the transaction, the purchased company was using a management style falling between System 1 and System 2. Some major changes were soon

TABLE 3-5 Examples of Items from Likert's Table of Organizational and Performance Characteristics of Different Management Systems

Organizational Variable	System 1	System 2	System 3	System 4
Leadership processes used				
Extent to which superiors have confidence and trust in *subordinates*	Have no confidence and trust in subordinates	Have condescending confidence and trust, such as master has to servant	Substantial but not complete confidence and trust; still wishes to keep control of decisions	Complete confidence and trust in all matters
Character of motivational forces				
Manner in which motives are used	Fear, threats, punishment, and occasional rewards	Rewards and some actual or potential punishment	Rewards, occasional punishment, and some involvement	Economic rewards based on compensation system developed through participation; group participation and involvement in setting goals, improving methods, appraising progress toward goals, etc.
Character of interaction-influence process				
Amount and character of interaction	Little interaction and always with fear and distrust	Little interaction and usually with some condescension by superiors; fear and caution by subordinates	Moderate interaction, often with fair amount of confidence and trust	Extensive, friendly interaction with high degree of confidence and trust

implemented by the new owners. The changes that were put into effect included extensive modifications in how the work was organized, improved maintenance of machinery, and a training program involving managers and workers at every level. Managers and supervisors were exposed in depth to the philosophy and understanding of management approaching System 4. All of these changes were supported by the top management of the purchasing company.

Although productivity dropped in the first several months after the initiation of the change program, productivity increased by almost 30 percent within two years. Although it is not possible to calculate exactly how much of the increased productivity resulted from the change in management system, it was obvious to the researchers that the impact was considerable. In addition to increases in productivity, manufacturing costs decreased 20 percent, turnover was cut almost in half, and morale rose considerably (reflecting a more friendly attitude of workers toward the organization). The company's image in the community was enhanced, and for the first time in years the company began to show a profit.

TRANSACTIONAL ANALYSIS

Eric Berne

As is evident from Likert's work, the suggestion is that System 4 is the management style with the greatest chance of success in producing long-term productivity. One of the reasons (we shall discuss more later) that he cannot guarantee this impact is because the response of people to a management intervention is not always predictable. If it is true that we cannot always anticipate the action of people to a management intervention, how can we better predict the kind of responses our interventions may evoke from people? *Transactional analysis* (TA) may help us in this area.

TA is a method of analyzing and understanding behavior that was developed by Eric Berne[24] and in more recent years has been popularized in the writings of Thomas Harris,[25] Muriel James and Dorothy Jongeward,[26] and Abe Wagner.[27] In particular, Jongeward[28] and Wagner[29] have shown how the concepts of TA can be applied to organizations and related to the work of other theorists, such as McGregor and Likert. Their work has been very helpful to us in writing this section on transactional analysis.

TA, as we view it, is an outgrowth of earlier Freudian psychology. Sigmund Freud[30] was the first to suggest that there are three sources within the human personality that stimulate, monitor, and control behavior. The Freudian *id, ego,* and *superego* are important concepts, but their definitions are difficult for practitioners to understand or apply without extensive training in psychotherapy. Thus, one of the major contributions of TA theorists is that they have, in a sense, borrowed from Freud but have put some of his concepts into a language that everyone can understand and, without being trained psychiatrists, can use for diagnostic purposes in understanding why people behave as they do.

Ego States

According to TA, a *transaction* is a stimulus plus a response. For example, if you say to one of your staff, "You really did a fine job on that project, Don," that's a stimulus; if he says, "Thanks," that's a response. Thus, transactions take place between people. They can also take place between the "people" in our heads. If we have a sudden impulse to say something to someone, we may mentally hear a voice telling us not to say it and then a second voice agreeing. These people in our heads are called *ego states*.

The personality of a person is the collection of behavior patterns developed over time that other people begin to recognize as that person. These behavior patterns are evoked in differing degrees from three ego states—Parent, Adult, and Child. These terms are capitalized so as not to be confused with their lower-cased counterparts. Thus, a parent (mother or father) has Parent, Adult, and Child ego states; and a child (son or daughter) also has Parent, Adult, and Child ego states. These ego states have nothing to do with chronological age, only psychological age.

As Berne states, "Although we cannot directly observe these ego states, we can observe behavior and from this infer which of the three ego states is operating at that moment."[31] The three ego states are usually diagrammed as shown in Figure 3-6.

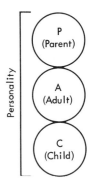

FIGURE 3-6 The Parent, Adult, and Child (P-A-C) subsystems

The *Parent* ego state is a result of the "messages" (conditioning) people receive from their parents, older sisters and brothers, school teachers, Sunday school teachers, and other authority figures during their early childhood. These messages can be thought of as recorded on "little cassette tapes" in people's heads. They're in place, stored up, and ready to go—all you have to do is push the right button and you get the message almost like dialing a number on the telephone. Push another button and you get a different message. After the message is given, the tape is rewound and ready to go again. For instance, if a father's son was eating his dinner and was playing with his food, a very common Parent tape like the following might be played: "Stop playing with your food, Garth, and clean up your plate. People are starving all over the world, so you're going to eat everything." Now where did the father learn to say that? He probably learned it from his mother and father, who learned it from their parents. And now he's playing it on his kids. This is a Parent tape. Many of us were taught when we were young that it's good to clean our plate and bad to leave food on our plate. In fact, if we are honest with ourselves, many of us probably still feel guilty today if we leave food on our plate.

Thus, a person is operating from a Parent ego state when he or she mentally plays back "old tapes" from childhood. These recordings say such things as "it's right!" "it's wrong!" "it's bad!" "it's good!" "you should!" "you shouldn't!" Thus, our Parent ego state is the *evaluative* part of us that evokes value-laden behavior. But remember, this value-laden behavior is not necessarily "real value"—it's "learned value." In our example with Garth not cleaning his plate, it might be more appropriate for his father to say, "Don't feel you have to eat everything on your plate if you're really not hungry"—particularly if Garth is a little overweight. Thus, cleaning up one's plate is a "learned value" because, in a real sense, whether or not Garth eats all the food on his plate won't impact starving children around the world; it will only impact the size of the garbage.

There are two kinds of Parent ego states: *Nurturing Parent* and *Critical Parent*. The Nurturing Parent is that part of a person that is understanding and caring about other people. While behavior coming from the Nurturing Parent may set limits on and provide direction for people's behavior, it will not put these people down and make them feel not okay as individuals. The Critical Parent makes people feel that they, not just their behavior, are not okay. Thus, Critical Parent behavior attacks peoples' personalities as well as their behavior. When people are in their Critical Parent ego state, they are very evaluative and judgmental. They are always ready to respond with a "should" or "ought" to almost anything people tell them. People with a heavy Critical Parent ego state "should" on other people as well as "should" on themselves.

The *Adult* ego state evokes behavior that could be described simply as logical, reasonable, rational, and unemotional. Behavior from the Adult ego state is characterized by problem-solving analysis and rational decision making. People operating from the Adult ego state are taking the emotional content of their Child ego state and the value-laden content of their Parent ego state and checking them out in the reality of the external world. These people are examining alternatives, probabilities, and values prior to engaging in behavior.

As suggested, the *Child* ego state is associated with behaviors that appear when a person is responding emotionally. A person's Child contains the "natural" impulses and attitudes learned from child experiences. There are several forms of the Child ego state that various authors discuss.[32] In our work we use two kinds of Child ego states: *Happy Child* and *Destructive Child*.

People behaving from their Happy Child are doing things because they want to, but their behavior is not disruptive to others or destructive to the environment. People in their Destructive Child are also doing things because they feel like it, but their behavior is either disruptive to others or destructive to themselves or their environment. In understanding the difference between these two types of Child ego state, it helps to remember that behavior by itself is not happy or destructive. Whether a person's behavior is coming from the Happy Child or Destructive Child depends on the transaction or feedback from others. For example, if George is a draftsman and is singing while he works, he may be in his Happy Child. But if one of his coworkers, Helen, tells him she's having trouble working because of his singing, and he keeps on singing, he has moved from Happy Child to Destructive Child.

One form of the Destructive Child ego state is the *Rebellious Child.* When people are in this ego state, they aren't going to listen to anyone who tells them what to do. They either rebel openly by being very negative or rebel subtly by forgetting, being confused, or putting off doing something that someone wants them to do. Persons behaving from Rebellious Child will not do anything an authority figure asks them to do even if it makes sense.

Another Destructive Child ego state is *Compliant Child.* When people are in this ego state, they do what others want. Complying with the wishes of others is okay if the person really wants to, or if it makes sense to do it. When that is the case, Compliant Child would be classified as a form of Happy Child because the behavior would not be considered disruptive to others or destructive to themselves or their environment. However, Compliant Child can hurt the development of people who comply unquestionably all the time, even when it makes no sense to them. These people tend to remain dependent rather than become independent. When this occurs, Compliant Child becomes a form of Destructive Child.

It is healthy for people to have a functioning Child ego state that is spontaneous, emotional, and sometimes dependent. However, as managers, we want to discourage too much development of our people's Compliant or Rebellious forms of Destructive Child. In later chapters we will talk about when and how people develop a Rebellious or Compliant Child ego state and how to discourage behaviors evoked from these two forms of the Child ego state.

Behavior coming from the Adult ego state is very different from behavior evoked from the Child ego state. Child ego state behavior is behavior that's often almost a stimulus-response relationship. Something happens and the person responds almost immediately. What happens is not processed intellectually. It almost goes in one ear, picks up speed, and goes out the other ear. With Adult ego state behavior, when something happens, there is not an immediate response. A response follows only conscious evaluation and thought.

A Healthy Personality

All people behave from these three ego states at different times. A healthy person has a personality that maintains a balance among all three, particularly, according to Abe Wagner,[33] Nurturing *Parent, Adult* and Happy *Child.* This means that these people are able, at times, to let the Adult ego state take over and think very rationally and engage in problem solving. At other times, these people are able to free the Child ego state and let their hair down, have fun, and be spontaneous and emotional. At still other times, healthy people are able to defer to the Parent ego state and learn from experience; they do not have to reinvent the wheel every time. They develop values that aid in the speed and effectiveness of decision making.

While a balance among all three ego states seems to be most healthy, some people seem dominated at times by one or two ego states. This is especially a problem when the Adult ego state is not in the "executive position" and a person's personality is being dominated by the Critical Parent or the Destructive Child. When this occurs in people, it poses problems for their managers in the world of work.

More specifically, Child-dominated people who are mainly coming from Destructive Child do not engage in much rational problem solving. They learned in their early years that they could get things by screaming, hollering, and being emotional. It's very difficult to reason with them in many situations. Rather than solve their own problems, these people want their managers or some other person to tell them what to do, where to do it, and how to do it or what's right, what's wrong, what's good, and what's bad.

Parent-dominated people, who are mainly coming from Critical Parent, also do not engage in much rational problem solving because they already know what's right and what's wrong. They seem to have an answer for everything. These people we would characterize with the comment, "Look! Don't confuse me with the facts. I've already made up my mind." It really doesn't matter how much real information anyone brings to these people—they've already decided "it's good," "it's bad," "you should," or "you shouldn't."

Even Adult-dominated people can be troublesome, because they can be very boring people with whom to work. They are often "workaholics." They don't seem to act like other people. They are never able to let down their hair and have fun. Thus, a balance between the three ego states makes for a healthy person with whom to work.

Life Position

In the process of growing up, people make basic assumptions about their own self-worth, as well as about the worth of significant people in their environment, that may or may not be generalized to other people later in life. Harris[34] calls the combination of an assumption about oneself and another person a *life position*. Life positions tend to be more permanent than ego states. They are learned throughout life by way of reinforcements for, and responses to, expressed needs. These assumptions are described in terms of "okayness." Thus, individuals assume that they are either OK or not OK, or that as people they do or do not possess value or worth. Further, other individuals are assumed to be either OK or not OK.

Four possible relationships result from these life positions: (1) neither person has value ("I'm not OK, you're not OK"); (2) you have value, but I do not have value ("I'm not OK, you're OK"); (3) I have value, but you do not ("I'm OK, you're not OK"); and (4) we both have value ("I'm OK, you're OK").

"I'm not OK, you're not OK" people tend to feel bad about themselves and see the whole world as miserable. People with this life position usually give up. They don't trust other people and have no confidence in themselves.

People with an *"I'm not OK, you're OK"* life position often come from their Compliant Child ego state. They feel that others are more capable and generally have fewer problems than they themselves do. They tend to think that they always get the short end of the stick. This is the most common life position for people who have a high deference for authority. They see their world as "I don't have any control or much power, but those people (folks with authority or position power) seem to have all the power and rewards and punishments."

People who feel *"I'm OK, you're not OK"* often come from their Critical Parent ego state. They tend to be down on other people for at least two reasons. First, they often regard other people as sources of criticism. They feel that if they're not exactly perfect or right, people will be excessively critical of them. Second, they want to break away or rebel from some authority figure and become more independent, but they're either not sure how to go about this or they have had unpleasant experiences in attempting it in the past.

This is a life position in which the person has had a few "zaps" along the road and feels, "I've got a lot of self-confidence and autonomy but I sure don't want to be open, honest, and sharing with others in my environment or I'll get punished." With this life position, listening often tends to stop even when someone is still trying to communicate with this person. Harris found in his work that people with an *"I'm OK, you're not OK"* life position, while acting self-confident and under control, really were hiding "not OK" feelings about themselves. The way they play out their "not OK" feelings often is expressed in the need for power and control.

"I'm OK, you're OK" is suggested as the healthy life position. People with these feelings express confidence in themselves as well as trust and confidence in other people in their environment. Their behavior tends to come from their Nurturing Parent, Adult, and Happy Child ego states, while seldom being evoked from their Destructive Child or Critical Parent.

Transactions Between People

TA may be used to explain why people behave in specific patterns, patterns that frequently seem to be repeated throughout their lives (life scripts). In this form of analysis, the basic observational unit is called a *transaction*. Transactions are exchanges between people that consist of no less than one stimulus and one response. This analysis enables people to identify patterns of transactions between themselves and others. Ultimately, this can help us determine which ego state is most heavily influencing our behavior and the behavior of other people with whom we interact.

Two types of transactions may be useful for managers to know: *open* (com-

plementary) and *blocked* (crossed).[35] There are many combinations of open transactions; however, the basic principle to remember is that the ego state that is
addressed is the one that responds. Therefore, the response to the stimulus is the
expected or predictable one. When this occurs, communication can continue.
(This in no way suggests effective communication or indicates any openness between individuals, for, in fact, the content of the communication may be a distortion of true data.) Open transactions are Adult to Adult, Child to Child,
Parent to Child, and Parent to Parent. Not all open transactions are beneficial.
What we want to strive for in our relationships are OK open transactions—
Happy Child to Happy Child, Nurturing Parent to Happy Child, Adult to
Adult, and Nurturing Parent to Nurturing Parent. Not OK open transactions
involve any of the less healthy ego states, for example, Critical Parent, Rebellious
Child, or Compliant Child (when complying does not make sense to the person's
Adult ego state). Examples of both OK and not OK open transactions are shown
in Figure 3-7.

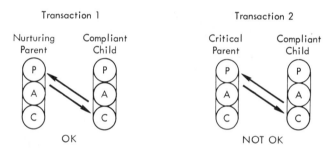

FIGURE 3-7 Two types of open transactions

As illustrated in Transaction 1, if a manager says to one of her staff members
from her Nurturing Parent, "I want you to be more careful in writing your
reports because I found a number of typographical and grammatical errors in this
report," and her staff member responds from his Compliant Child, "OK, Mrs.
Jones, I didn't notice all those mistakes," then we have a completed communication in which information has been easily shared and everyone still feels OK
about themselves. If, however, as illustrated in Transaction 2, this manager was
coming from her Critical Parent and said something like, "How can you be so
stupid? The last report you gave me had all kinds of typographical and grammatical errors. I don't see how you can possibly do your job if you don't know how to
write a decent report," and her staff member responded from Compliant Child
back to his manager's Critical Parent by meekly saying, "I'm sorry, I'll try not to
make those mistakes next time," we have a completed communication in which
information is shared with a minimum effort. But the staff member feels put
down by his boss and does not feel OK.

A blocked transaction is one that results in the closing, at least temporarily,
of communications. Unlike open transactions, the response is either inappropriate or unexpected, as well as being out of context with what the sender of the

stimulus had originally intended. This occurs when a person responds with an ego state different from the one the other person was addressing. In other words, it occurs when the stimulus from one ego state to another ego state is responded to as if the source were some other ego state, such that the sender feels misunderstood, confused, or even threatened. When this occurs, sharing and listening stop, at least temporarily. For example, if Alan asks a coworker a question from his Adult ego state like "What time is it, John?" he would expect John to respond from his Adult ego state and share information with him, that is, tell him what time it is. If, however, John responds from his Critical Parent and answers, "Don't ask so many questions," then a blocked transaction has taken place, as illustrated in Figure 3-8.

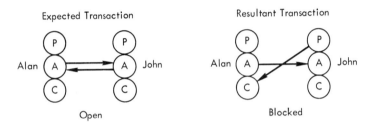

FIGURE 3-8 A blocked transaction

The example in Figure 3-8 illustrates that in a blocked transaction the lines of communication get crossed and stop effective communication (although talking may continue).

Blocked transactions can either be helpful or destructive to the development of people. The preceding example was a destructive transaction because the Critical Parent response to Alan's Adult question leaves Alan with not OK feelings. Destructive blocked transactions occur between people when either responds to the other from the Critical Parent or the Rebellious or Compliant Destructive Child.

When people argue or fight, a destructive blocked transaction is usually involved. For example, if a manager makes a statement in a Critical Parent manner ("I don't think you should hire that fellow for your staff assistant. He'll be nothing but trouble.") directed toward his staff member's Compliant (happy) Child and his staff member responds from his Rebellious (destructive) Child ("You have no right to tell me who I can hire for my staff assistant.") to his boss' Child, the lines of communication get blocked and the manager and his subordinate stop listening (although talking or yelling may continue). Now the interaction becomes a win–lose power struggle. Manager and staff member seem to be talking past each other, each matching his "oughts and shoulds" with the other's "oughts and shoulds." If, in this example, the boss wins—and bosses usually do—the win has a cost. It forces the staff member to become Destructive (compliant) Child and teaches him to either go "underground" with his feelings in the future, plot how to get out from under the command of his boss, or become compliant and do what others say because "I'm not OK."

In some situations, we may find blocked transactions useful in helping people to switch out of the less healthy Rebellious Child, Compliant Child, and Critical Parent ego states into their Adult, Nurturing Parent, or Happy Child. This will become clear as we integrate concepts from TA with other theories in later chapters.

By analyzing open and blocked transactions, it is possible to determine the various strengths of the three ego states. This in turn provides an indication of which life position the individual has selected. We can thus gather data on individuals in a way that will help to predict future patterns of behavior.

Ulterior transactions, like blocked transactions, are generally not desired. "An ulterior transaction happens when someone appears to be sending one kind of message but is secretly sending another. Thus, the real message is disguised."[36] An example of an ulterior transaction is when Alice says to her boss, "I'd be happy to add up all those figures, Mr. Johnson. It looks like it would be a real challenge."

In this example of an ulterior transaction (see Figure 3-9), Alice is not talking straight about her needs but is sending her message in a disguised way. She appears to be giving Mr. Johnson factual information in an adult to adult transaction. Actually, she is probably annoyed about all of the routine, boring tasks that she's continually asked to do. Perhaps she would like to ask Mr. Johnson directly if there's a way that she could expand her responsibilities and take on some more exciting tasks. "It should be challenging to add up all those figures" may be a plea for more challenging work from Alice's Child to Mr. Johnson's Parent.

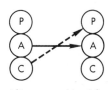

Alice   Mr. Johnson   **FIGURE 3-9** Ulterior transaction

Strokes

It is important to recognize one more thing about transactions. "Strokes" are being exchanged *whenever* two people are transacting. According to Jongeward and Seyer,[37] in TA language,

> The term "stroke" refers to giving some kind of recognition to a person. This may or may *not* involve physical touching. As we grow from infancy into child and adulthood, we do not entirely lose our need for stroking. Part of our original need

for physical stroking seems to be satisfied with symbolic stroking. We no longer need constant cuddling, but we need attention. When we receive a stroke, we choose to feel either good or bad. If we choose to feel good, we think of the stroke as a "warm fuzzy" or "positive" stroke. On the flip side, if we choose to feel bad, we can think of it as a "cold prickly" or "negative" stroke.

If it is true that people have a basic need for strokes, they will work hard to get them. For example, ignored people will engage in all sorts of creative activities to get strokes. Often such people quickly learn at work that they can get strokes from their boss by

- fighting with coworkers.
- doing sloppy work.
- injuring themselves.

A person who carries out one of these actions is likely to get a cold prickly (negative) stroke. But given a choice between no strokes or negative strokes, most people will opt for negative strokes. To such a person, any kind of stroke is better than no stroke at all; a cold prickly is better than nothing. The same is true for children who live in a stroke-deprived home. We will talk more about this in Chapter 9.

Psychological Game Analysis

When people don't get enough strokes at work, they will try a variety of things, some harmful, to make up their "stroke deficit." To do that, they may play *psychological games*.[38] A psychological game is a set of transactions with the following characteristics:

- Transactions tend to be repeated.
- They make sense on a superficial or social level.
- One or more of the transactions is ulterior.
- A set of transactions ends with a predictable payoff—a negative feeling. Payoffs usually reinforce the decision made in childhood about oneself or about others. They reflect feelings of not okayness, as we shall see.

Let's look at an example of a psychological game called *Yes, But:*

Doug: "I need your help again, Ken. I just don't seem to be very excited about my job. I really can't remember a job that really 'turned me on.' "

Ken: "Why don't you go to a career planning center and take some of those tests to find out what you might really be interested in?"

Doug: "Yes, I've thought of doing that, but they cost quite a bit of money and our budget is a little tight right now."

Ken: "Why don't you talk to your boss and see if there's any opportunity to enlarge or expand your job?"

Doug: "Yes, that's possible, but he's awfully busy and is hard to get to see."

Ken: "I know! Why don't you try to get a teaching job? You could go over and see . . . ?"

Doug: "Yes, but teaching jobs are really hard to find these days."

Ken: (Silent)

Let's examine how each of the characteristics of a psychological game is present in this example.[39]

- *Repeated transactions:* Doug and Ken have played this game before. Note Doug's opening line, "I need your help *again,* Ken."
- *Transactions make sense:* Outwardly it seems that Doug is honestly asking Ken for help. Ken's suggestions are reasonable and Doug's replies also seem to make sense.
- *Ulterior transactions:* Notice that Doug consistently rejects all of Ken's advice. At one level, Doug seems to be giving reasons why Ken's advice won't work. But he is also simultaneously sending an ulterior message that says, "Nobody's going to tell me what to do." Doug may still be rebelling against the advice his parent figures gave him when he was young. He operates from a belief that authority figures are not OK.
- *Predictable payoff:* According to TA theory,

    The game of *Yes, But* is often played by people whose parents either dominated them or didn't give them reasonable answers. So they tend to take a stand against parental figures. They play *Yes, But* to prove to themselves that nobody can tell them anything they don't already know. The feeling of power they get becomes a payoff for playing the game, which they seek over and over again. They prove once more that "Parents can't tell me anything."[40]

SCRIPT ANALYSIS

As we have pointed out, the life positions (I'm OK, you're OK, etc.) that people act out tend to vary according to the situation. The life position that people take and the games that they learn to play are part of what TA calls a "script."

> In everyday language, a script is the text of a play, motion picture, or radio or TV program. In TA, a person's life is compared to a play and the script is the text of that play. A person's psychological script is a life plan—a drama he or she writes and then feels compelled to live out. These plans may be positive, negative, or circular—endless repetition headed nowhere.[41]

All people have a script. People develop their scripts based on their experiences as a child. The most important influence on how one's script develops is through interactions with our parents or other authority figures. These interactions in turn lead us to make certain decisions, formulate our life positions, play psychological games, and start the drama of our script.

Jongeward and Seyer[42] cite an excellent example of script development and its impact on later life:

> As Edwin was growing up, he was frequently put down and compared to his older brother, Sid. He constantly heard things like:
>
> - "Well, Edwin, you only got 60% on this test, but gee, that's pretty good for you, considering your ability."
> - "Edwin! You spilled the soda all over my new chair. What's wrong with you? Why are you always doing such dumb things? Don't you have a brain in your head?"
> - "Edwin is not as bright as Sid, you know, so don't expect much from him."
> - "What a stupid thing to do, Edwin. Sid would never have done a thing like that."
>
> Given this background, what psychological position do you think Edwin usually took as a child? Edwin most likely took an I'm not OK position on many occasions as a child. He often felt not OK about himself because of all the negative things he heard from his parents. He probably felt his parents (and others) were not OK because of the cruel way they spoke to him.
>
> Assuming that Edwin believed what he heard about himself, imagine him as a high school student. Do you think he likes school? Do you think he was a good student? Given his predominant psychological position, Edwin would probably dislike school and be a poor student. (Occasionally, however, a person like Edwin takes an "I'll show you" stance and knocks himself out trying to be perfect at everything, yet rarely satisfied with how he's doing.)
>
> Now imagine Edwin on the job later in life. He is talking to one of his coworkers about a report he is working on. Which one of these things would he be most likely to say? (a) "I feel concerned about the progress I've made on this project" or (b) "I'm just a bungling idiot. I misplaced that report again! I'll never learn, will I?" Undoubtedly, he would have taken (b).
>
> Do you think it is clear that Edwin was born with inferior mental capacity? Edwin might have a good brain and the potential to become a brilliant executive. But he has come to believe that he *is* stupid. Consequently, Edwin may have unconsciously (and compulsively) arranged things to strengthen this script.

We must remember that all of us have scripts. And, like Edwin, without being aware of it, we often arrange our environment so that our script prevails. Sometimes managers have to deal with the scripts that people bring with them to the world of work. In later chapters we will be discussing some concepts that may be useful to managers in helping people write new scripts.

SUMMARY AND CONCLUSION

We have tried through the material presented to examine what is known today about understanding and motivating employees. The attempt has been to review theoretical literature, empirical research, and case examples with the intention of integrating these sources into frameworks that may be useful to managers for analyzing and understanding behavior. In reflecting upon the theories we have discussed, we can easily isolate two polar positions. At one extreme (and most people still think the most common extreme) are organizations that are dominated by Theory X assumptions about human nature, bureaucratic/pyramidal values, and Pattern A behavior. As a result, these organizations tend to be managed by Critical Parent managers with I'm OK, you're not OK life positions, who think people are only motivated by physiological and safety needs and satisfied hygiene factors. The subordinates in these organizations tend to be passive, dependent and childlike with "I'm not OK, you're not OK" or "I'm not OK, you're OK" feelings.

At the other extreme are the "ideal" organizations with their Theory Y assumptions about human nature, humanistic/democratic values, and pattern B behavior. As a result, these organizations tend to be managed by people with a good balance of Parent-Adult-Child (P.A.C.), "I'm OK   you're OK" feelings and a sense that people are also motivated by affiliation, esteem, and self-actualization needs as job-related "motivators." The style(s) of these managers fosters similar feelings among subordinates and evokes Adult problem-solving behavior. Although the differences between these two extremes and the suggested movement are obvious, as Argyris argues, the journey from XA to YB is not an "easy road to haul." To prepare for this journey, analyzing and understanding are necessary, but real skills are also needed in directing, changing, and controlling behavior. Beginning with Chapter 4, a framework for applying leader behavior may help get us "on the road."

NOTES

[1] For detailed descriptions of this research, see F. J. Roethlisberger and W. J. Dickson, *Management and the Worker* (Cambridge: Harvard University Press, 1939); T. N. Whitehead, *The Industrial Worker*, 2 vols. (Cambridge: Harvard University Press, 1938); Elton Mayo, *The Human Problems of an Industrial Civilization* (New York: The Macmillan Company, 1933).

[2] Douglas McGregor, *The Human Side of Enterprise* (New York: McGraw-Hill Book Company, 1960). See also McGregor, *Leadership and Motivation* (Boston: MIT Press, 1966).

[3] Chris Argyris, *Management and Organizational Development: The Path from XA to YB* (New York: McGraw-Hill Book Company, 1971).

[4] *Ibid.*, p. 12.

[5] George C. Homans, *The Human Group* (New York: Harcourt, Brace & World, Inc., 1950).

[6] Anthony G. Athos and Robert E. Coffey, *Behavior in Organizations: A Multidimensional View* (Englewood Cliffs, N.J.: Prentice-Hall, Inc., 1968), p. 101.

[7] S. E. Asch, "Effects of Group Pressure upon the Modification and Distortion of Judgments," in *Groups, Leadership and Men,* ed. Harold Guetzkow (New York: Russell and Russell, Publishers, 1963), pp. 177–90. Also in Dorwin Cartwright and Alvin Zander, *Group Dynamics,* 2nd ed. (Evanston, Ill.: Row, Peterson & Company, 1960), pp. 189–200.

[8] *Ibid.*

[9] Chris Argyris, *Interpersonal Competence and Organizational Effectiveness* (Homewood, Ill.: Irwin Dorsey Press, 1962).

[10] This table was taken with minor changes from Warren G. Bennis, *Organizational Development: Its Nature, Origins and Prospects* (Reading, Mass.: Addison-Wesley Publishing Company, 1969), p. 13.

[11] Bennis, *Organizational Development*, p. 13.

[12] *Ibid.*

[13] Chris Argyris, *Personality and Organization* (New York: Harper & Row, Publishers, 1957); *Interpersonal Competence and Organizational Effectiveness* (Homewood, Ill.: Irwin Dorsey Press, 1962); and *Integrating the Individual and the Organization* (New York: John Wiley & Sons, Inc., 1964).

[14] N. Breman, *The Making of a Moron* (New York: Sheed & Ward, 1953).

[15] For other examples of successful interventions, see Argyris, *Intervention Theory and Method: A Behavioral Science View* (Reading, Mass.: Addison-Wesley Publishing Company, 1970).

[16] Frederick Herzberg, Bernard Mausner and Barbara Snyderman, *The Motivation to Work* (New York: John Wiley & Sons, Inc., 1959); and Herzberg, *Work and the Nature of Man* (New York: World Publishing Co., 1966).

[17] Herzberg, Mausner and Snyderman, *The Motivation to Work*, p. ix.

[18] Scott M. Meyers, "Who Are Your Motivated Workers," in David R. Hampton, *Behavioral Concepts in Management* (Belmont, Calif.: Dickenson Publishing Co., Inc., 1968), p. 64. Originally published in *Harvard Business Review*, January–February 1964, pp. 73–88.

[19] David C. McClelland, J. W. Atkinson, R. A. Clark and E. L. Lowell, *The Achievement Motive* (New York: Appleton-Century-Crofts, 1953); and *The Achieving Society* (Princeton, N.J.: D. Van Nostrand Co., Inc., 1961).

[20] Rensis Likert, *The Human Organization* (New York: McGraw-Hill Book Company, 1967); see also Likert, *New Patterns of Management* (New York: McGraw-Hill Book Company, 1961).

[21] Descriptions adapted from Likert, *The Human Organization*, pp. 4–10.

[22] *Ibid.*

[23] A. J. Marrow, D. G. Bowers and S. E. Seashore, eds., *Strategies of Organizational Change* (New York: Harper & Row, Publishers, 1967).

[24] Eric Berne, *Games People Play* (New York: Grove Press, Inc., 1964).

[25] Thomas Harris, *I'm OK—You're OK: A Practical Guide to Transactional Analysis* (New York: Harper & Row, 1969).

[26] Muriel James and Dorothy Jongeward, *Born to Win* (Reading, Mass: Addison-Wesley Publishing Company, 1971).

[27] Abe Wagner, *The Transactional Manager: How to Solve Your People Problems with T.A.*, (Englewood Cliffs, N.J. Prentice-Hall, Inc., 1981).

[28] Dorothy Jongeward, *Everybody Wins: Transactional Analysis Applied to Organizations* (Reading, Mass.: Addison-Wesley Publishing Company, 1973).

[29] Wagner, *The Transactional Manager*.

[30] Sigmund Freud, *The Ego and the Id* (London: Hogarth Press, 1927).

[31] Eric Berne, *Principles of Group Treatment* (New York: Oxford University Press, 1964), p. 281.

[32] The most popular classification of child ego states is Natural Child, Adaptive Child, and Little Professor.

[33] Abe Wagner was very helpful in the writing of this particular section.

[34] Harris, *I'm OK—You're OK*.

[35] The work of Dorothy Jongeward and Abe Wagner was very helpful in this section. See Dorothy Jongeward and Phillip C. Seyer, *Choosing Success: Transactional Analysis on the Job* (New York: John Wiley & Sons, Inc., 1978), and Wagner, *The Transactional Manager*.

[36] Jongeward and Seyer, *Choosing Success,* p. 21.
[37] *Ibid.,* p. 26.
[38] *Ibid.,* pp. 28–29.
[39] This information was adapted from Jongeward and Seyer, *Choosing Success,* p. 28.
[40] Jongeward and Seyer, *Choosing Success,* p. 28.
[41] *Ibid.,* p. 34.
[42] Ibid., pp. 35–36.

chapter **4**

Leader
Behavior

The successful organization has one major attribute that sets it apart from unsuccessful organizations: dynamic and effective leadership. Peter F. Drucker points out that managers (business leaders) are the basic and scarcest resource of any business enterprise.[1] Statistics from recent years make this point more evident: "Of every one hundred new business establishments started, approximately fifty, or one half, go out of business within two years. By the end of five years, only one-third of the original one hundred will still be in business."[2] Most of the failures can be attributed to ineffective leadership.

On all sides there is a continual search for persons who have the necessary ability to lead effectively. This shortage of effective leadership is not confined to business but is evident in the lack of able administrators in government, education, foundations, churches, and every other form of organization. Thus, when we decry the scarcity of leadership talent in our society, we are not talking about a lack of people to fill administrative bodies. What we are agonizing over is a scarcity of people who are willing to assume significant leadership roles in our society and can get the job done effectively. ` (Hersey 82)`

LEADERSHIP DEFINED

According to George R. Terry, "Leadership is the activity of influencing people to strive willingly for group objectives."[3] Robert Tannenbaum, Irving R. Weschler, and Fred Massarik define leadership as "interpersonal influence exercised in a situation and directed, through the communication process, toward the attainment of a specialized goal or goals."[4] Harold Koontz and Cyril O'Donnell state that "leadership is *influencing* people to follow in the achievement of a common goal."[5] `` (Hersey, 83)

— A review of other writers reveals that most management writers agree that leadership is *the process of influencing the activities of an individual or a group in efforts toward goal achievement in a given situation.* From this definition of leadership, it follows that the leadership process is a function of the *leader,* the *follower,* and other *situational* variables, $L = f(l, f, s)$.

It is important to note that this definition makes no mention of any particular type of organization. In any situation in which someone is trying to influence the behavior of another individual or group, leadership is occurring. Thus, everyone attempts leadership at one time or another, whether his or her activities are centered on a business, educational institution, hospital, political organization, or family.

It should also be remembered that when this definition mentions leader and follower, one should not assume that we are talking only about a hierarchical relationship such as suggested by superior (boss)/subordinate. Any time an individual is attempting to influence the behavior of someone else, that individual is the *potential leader* and the person he or she is attempting to influence is the *potential follower,* no matter whether that person is the boss, a colleague (associate), a subordinate, a friend, or a relative. —

TRAIT VERSUS SITUATIONAL APPROACH TO THE STUDY OF LEADERSHIP

For many years the most common approach to the study of leadership concentrated on leadership traits per se, suggesting that there were certain characteristics, such as physical energy or friendliness, that were essential for effective leadership. These inherent personal qualities, like intelligence, were felt to be transferable from one situation to another. Since all individuals did not have these qualities, only those who had them would be considered potential leaders. Consequently, this approach seemed to question the value of training individuals to assume leadership positions. It implied that if we could discover how to identify and measure these leadership qualities (which are inborn in the individual), we should be able to screen leaders from nonleaders. Leadership training would then be helpful only to those with inherent leadership traits.

A review of the research literature using this trait approach to leadership has revealed few significant or consistent findings.[6] As Eugene E. Jennings concluded, "Fifty years of study have failed to produce one personality trait or set of qualities that can be used to discriminate leaders and nonleaders."[7] Empirical studies suggest that leadership is a dynamic process, varying from situation to situation with changes in leaders, followers, and situations. Current literature seems to support this situational or leader behavior approach to the study of leadership.[8]

The focus in the situational approach to leadership is on observed behavior, not on any hypothetical inborn or acquired ability or potential for leadership. The emphasis is on the behavior of leaders and their group members (followers) and various situations. With this emphasis on behavior and environment, more encouragement is given to the possibility of training individuals in adapting styles of leader behavior to varying situations. Therefore, it is believed that most people can increase their effectiveness in leadership roles through education, training, and development. From observations of the frequency (or infrequency) of certain leader behavior in numerous types of situations, theoretical models can be developed to help leaders make some predictions about the most appropriate leader behavior for their present situation. For these reasons, in this chapter we will talk in terms of leader behavior rather than leadership traits, thus emphasizing the situational approach to leadership.

LEADERSHIP PROCESS

We have defined leadership as the process of influencing the activities of an individual or a group in efforts toward goal achievement in a given situation. In essence, leadership involves accomplishing goals with and through people. Therefore, a leader must be concerned about tasks and human relationships. Although using different terminology, Chester I. Barnard identified these same leadership concerns in his classic work, *The Functions of the Executive,* in the late 1930s.[9] These leadership concerns seem to be a reflection of two of the earliest schools of thought in organizational theory—scientific management and human relations.

Scientific Management Movement

Frederick Winslow Taylor

In the early 1900s one of the most widely read theorists on administration was Frederick Winslow Taylor. The basis for his *scientific management* was technological in nature. It was felt that the best way to increase output was to improve the techniques or methods used by workers. Consequently, he has been interpreted as considering people as instruments or machines to be manipulated by their leaders. Accepting this assumption, other theorists of the scientific management movement proposed that an organization as rationally planned and executed as possible be developed to create more efficiency in administration and consequently increase production. Management was to be divorced from human affairs and emotions. The result was that the workers had to adjust to the management and not the management to the people.

To accomplish this plan, Taylor initiated time and motion studies to analyze work tasks to improve performance in every aspect of the organization. Once jobs had been reorganized with efficiency in mind, the economic self-interest of the workers could be satisfied through various incentive work plans (piece rates, and such).

The function of the leader under scientific management or classical theory was obviously to set up and enforce performance criteria to meet organizational goals. The main focus of a leader was on the needs of the organization and not on the needs of the individual.[10]

Human Relations Movement

Elton Mayo

In the 1920s and early 1930s the trend started by Taylor was to be replaced at center stage by the *human relations* movement, initiated by Elton Mayo and his associates. These theorists argued that in addition to finding the best technological methods to improve output, it was beneficial to management to look into human affairs. It was claimed that the real power centers within an organization were the interpersonal relations that developed within the working unit. The study of these human relations was the most important consideration for management and the analysis of organization. The organization was to be developed around the workers and had to take into consideration human feelings and attitudes.[11]

The function of the leader under human relations theory was to facilitate cooperative goal attainment among followers while providing opportunities for their personal growth and development. The main focus, contrary to scientific management theory, was on individual needs and not on the needs of the organization.

In essence, then, the scientific management movement emphasized a concern for task (output), while the human relations movement stressed a concern for relationships (people). The recognition of these two concerns has characterized the writings on leadership ever since the conflict between the scientific management and the human relations schools of thought became apparent.

Authoritarian-Democratic Leader Behavior

Robert Tannenbaum and Warren H. Schmidt

Past writers have felt that concern for task tends to be represented by authoritarian leader behavior, while a concern for relationships is represented by democratic leader behavior. This feeling was popular because it was generally agreed that leaders influence their followers by either of two ways: (1) they can tell their followers what to do and how to do it or (2) they can share their leadership responsibilities with their followers by involving them in the planning and execution of the task. The former is the traditional authoritarian style, which emphasizes task concerns. The latter is the more nondirective democratic style, which stresses the concern for human relationships.

The differences in the two styles of leader behavior are based on the assumptions leaders make about the source of their power or authority and human nature. The authoritarian style of leader behavior is often based on the assumption that the power of leaders is derived from the position they occupy and that people are innately lazy and unreliable (Theory X). The democratic style assumes that the power of leaders is granted by the group they are to lead and that people can be basically self-directed and creative at work if properly motivated (Theory Y). As a result, in the authoritarian style, all policies are determined by the leader; in the democratic style, policies are open for group discussion and decision.

There are, of course, a wide variety of styles of leader behavior between these two extremes. Robert Tannenbaum and Warren H. Schmidt depicted a broad range of styles as a continuum moving from authoritarian or boss-centered leader behavior at one end to democratic or subordinate-centered leader behavior at the other end,[12] as illustrated in Figure 4-1. Tannenbaum and Schmidt now refer to these two extremes as manager power and influence and nonmanager power and influence.[13]

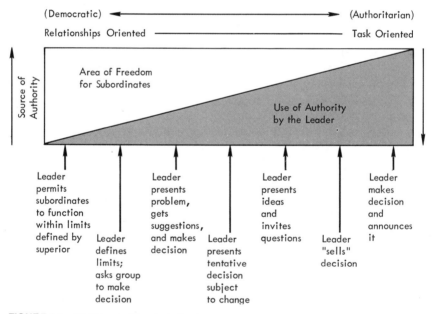

FIGURE 4-1 Continuum of leader behavior

Leaders whose behavior is observed to be at the authoritarian end of the continuum tend to be task-oriented and use their power to influence their followers; leaders whose behavior appears to be at the democratic end tend to be group-oriented and thus give their followers considerable freedom in their work. Often this continuum is extended beyond democratic leader behavior to include a *laissez-faire* style.[14] This style of behavior permits the members of the group to do whatever they want to do. No policies or procedures are established. Everyone is let alone. No one attempts to influence anyone else. As is evident, this is not included in the continuum of leader behavior illustrated in Figure 4-1. This was done because it was felt that in reality, a *laissez-faire* atmosphere represents an absence of formal leadership. The formal leadership role has been abdicated and, therefore, any leadership that is being exhibited is informal and emergent.

The recognition of two leadership styles, one emphasizing task and the other stressing relationships, has been given support in several leadership studies.

Michigan Leadership Studies

In the early studies of the Survey Research Center at the University of Michigan, there was an attempt to approach the study of leadership by locating clusters of characteristics that seemed to be related to each other and various indicators of effectiveness. The studies identified two concepts, which they called *employee orientation* and *production orientation.*

Leaders who are described as employee-oriented stress the relationships aspect of their job. They feel that every employee is important and take interest in everyone, accepting their individuality and personal needs. Production orientation emphasizes production and the technical aspects of the job; employees are seen as tools to accomplish the goals of the organization. These two orientations parallel the authoritarian (task) and democratic (relationship) concepts of the leader behavior continuum.[15]

Group Dynamics Studies

Dorwin Cartwright and Alvin Zander, summarizing the findings of numerous studies at the Research Center for Group Dynamics, claim that group objectives fall into one of two categories: (1) the achievement of some specific group goal or (2) the maintenance or strengthening of the group itself.[16]

According to Cartwright and Zander, the type of behavior involved in goal achievement is illustrated by these examples: the manager "initiates action . . . keeps members' attention on the goal . . . clarifies the issue and develops a procedural plan."[17]

On the other hand, characteristic behaviors for group maintenance are: the manager "keeps interpersonal relations pleasant . . . arbitrates disputes . . . provides encouragement . . . gives the minority a chance to be heard . . . stimulates self-direction . . . and increases the interdependence among members."[18]

Goal achievement seems to coincide with the task concepts discussed earlier (authoritarian and production orientation), while group maintenance parallels the relationship concepts (democratic and employee orientation).

Research findings in recent years indicate that leadership styles vary considerably from leader to leader. Some leaders emphasize the task and can be described as authoritarian leaders; others stress interpersonal relationships and may be viewed as democratic leaders. Still others seem to be both task-oriented and relationship-oriented. There are even some individuals in leadership positions who are not concerned about either. No dominant style appears. Instead, various combinations are evident. Thus, task and relationship are not either/or leadership styles as the preceding continuum suggests. They are separate and distinct dimensions that can be plotted on two separate axes rather than on a single continuum.

Ohio State Leadership Studies

The leadership studies initiated in 1945 by the Bureau of Business Research at Ohio State University attempted to identify various dimensions of leader behavior.[19] The staff, defining leadership as the behavior of an individual when directing the activities of a group toward a goal attainment, eventually narrowed the description of leader behavior to two dimensions: *Initiating Structure* and *Consideration.* Initiating Structure refers to "the leader's behavior in delineating the relationship between himself and members of the work group and in endeavoring to establish well-defined patterns of organization, channels of communication, and methods of procedure." On the other hand, Consideration refers to "behavior indicative of friendship, mutual trust, respect, and warmth in the relationship between the leader and the members of his staff."[20]

To gather data about the behavior of leaders, the Ohio State staff developed the Leader Behavior Description Questionnaire (LBDQ), an instrument designed to describe *how* leaders carry out their activities.[21] The LBDQ contains fifteen items pertaining to Consideration and an equal number for Initiating Structure. Respondents judge the frequency with which their leader engages in each form of behavior by checking one of five descriptions— always, often, occasionally, seldom, or never—as it relates to each particular item of the LBDQ. Thus, Consideration and Initiating Structure are dimensions of observed behavior as perceived by others. Examples of items used in the LBDQ for both these dimensions are given below.

Consideration	Initiating Structure
The leader finds time to listen to group members.	The leader assigns group members to particular tasks.
The leader is willing to make changes.	The leader asks the group members to follow standard rules and regulations.
The leader is friendly and approachable.	The leader lets group members know what is expected of them.

Although the major emphasis in the Ohio State Leadership Studies was on *observed behavior,* the staff did develop the Leader Opinion Questionnaire (LOQ) to gather data about the self-perceptions that leaders have about their own leadership style. The LBDQ was completed by leaders' subordinate(s), superior(s), or associates (peers), but the LOQ was scored by the leaders themselves.

In studying leader behavior, the Ohio State staff found that Initiating Structure and Consideration were separate and distinct dimensions. A high score on one dimension does not necessitate a low score on the other. The behavior of a leader could be described as any mix of both dimensions. Thus, it was during these studies that leader behavior was first plotted on two separate axes rather than on a single continuum. Four quadrants were developed to show various combinations of Initiating Structure (task behavior) and Consideration (relationship behavior), as illustrated in Figure 4-2.

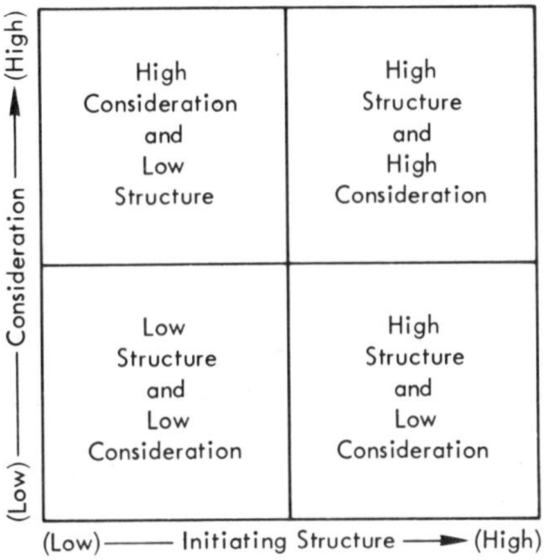

FIGURE 4-2 The Ohio State leadership quadrants

Managerial Grid

Robert R. Blake and Jane S. Mouton

In discussing the Ohio State, Michigan, and Group Dynamics leadership studies, we have been concentrating on two theoretical concepts, one emphasizing *task* accomplishment and the other stressing the development of personal *relationships*. Robert R. Blake and Jane S. Mouton have popularized these concepts in their Managerial Grid and have used them extensively in organization and management development programs.[22]

In the Managerial Grid, five different types of leadership based on concern for production (task) and concern for people (relationship) are located in four quadrants (see Figure 4-3) similar to those identified by the Ohio State studies.

Concern for production is illustrated on the horizontal axis. Production becomes more important to the leader as his rating advances on the horizontal scale. A leader with a rating of nine on the horizontal axis has a maximum concern for production.

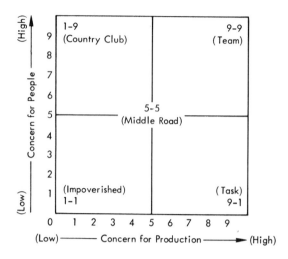

FIGURE 4-3 The Managerial Grid leadership styles

Concern for people is illustrated on the vertical axis. People become more important to the leader as his or her rating progresses up the vertical axis. A leader with a rating of nine on the vertical axis has maximum concern for people. The five leadership styles are described as follows:

> *Impoverished.* Exertion of minimum effort to get required work done is appropriate to sustain organization membership.
>
> *Country Club.* Thoughtful attention to needs of people for satisfying relationships leads to a comfortable friendly organization atmosphere and work tempo.
>
> *Task.* Efficiency in operations results from arranging conditions of work in such a way that human elements interfere to a minimum degree.
>
> *Middle-of-the-Road.* Adequate organization performance is possible through balancing the necessity to get out work while maintaining morale of people at a satisfactory level.
>
> *Team.* Work accomplishment is from committed people; interdependence through a "common stake" in organization purpose leads to relationships of trust and respect.[23]

In essence, we feel the Managerial Grid has given popular terminology to five points within the four quadrants of the Ohio State studies. However, we want to point out one significant difference between the two frameworks. "Concern for" is a predisposition about something or an attitudinal dimension. Therefore, the Managerial Grid tends to be an attitudinal model that measures the values and feelings of a manager, while the Ohio State framework attempts to include behavioral concepts (items), as well as attitudinal items. The Center for Leadership Studies model that will be presented later on is purely a behavioral model since it emphasizes only activities that managers engage in. A diagram combining the two frameworks could be illustrated as shown in Figure 4-4.

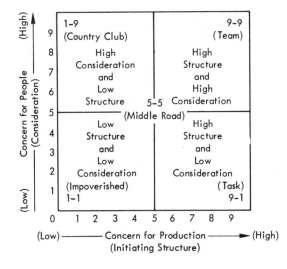

FIGURE 4-4 Merging of the Ohio State and the Managerial Grid theories of leadership

Is There a Best Style of Leadership?

After identifying the two central concerns of any leadership situation, task and relationship, the researchers discussed earlier have recognized the potential conflict in satisfying both concerns. Consequently, an attempt has been made to find a middle ground that will encompass both concerns. Chester Barnard recognized this fact when he purposely included both concerns as necessary factors for the survival of an organization.[24]

According to Warren G. Bennis, theorists like Barnard who express concern for both task and relationship are called "revisionists."

> The revisionists are now concerned with external, economic factors, with productivity, with formal status, and so on, but not to the exclusion of the human elements that the traditional theorists so neglected. So what we are observing now is the pendulum swinging just a little farther to the middle from its once extreme position to balance and modulate with more refinement in the human organization requirements.[25]

Andrew W. Halpin, using the Leader Behavior Description Questionnaire in a study of school superintendents, found that the administrators he interviewed had a tendency to view Consideration and Initiating Structure as either/or forms of leader behavior. "Some administrators act as if they were forced to emphasize one form of behavior at the expense of the other."[26] Halpin stressed that this conflict between Initiating Structure and Consideration should not necessarily exist. He points out that according to his findings, "effective or desirable leadership behavior is characterized by high scores on both Initiating Structure and Consideration. Conversely, ineffective or undesirable leadership behavior is marked by low scores on both dimensions."[27]

From these observations, Halpin concludes that a successful leader "must contribute to both major group objectives: goal achievement and group maintenance (in Cartwright and Zander's terms); or in Barnard's terms, he must facilitate cooperative group action that is both effective and efficient."[28] Thus, the Ohio State Leadership Studies seem to conclude that the high Initiating Structure and high Consideration style is theoretically the ideal or "best" leader behavior and that the style low on both dimensions is theoretically the "worst."

The Managerial Grid also implies that the most desirable leader behavior is "team management" (maximum concern for production and people). In fact, Blake and Mouton have developed training programs that attempt to change managers toward a 9-9 management style.[29]

Using the earlier Michigan studies as a starting place, Rensis Likert did some extensive research to discover the general pattern of management used by high producing managers in contrast to that used by the other managers. He found that "supervisors with the best records of performance focus their primary attention on the human aspects of their subordinates' problems and on endeavoring to build effective work groups with high performance goals."[30] These supervisors were called "employee-centered." Other supervisors who kept constant pressure on production were called "job-centered" and were found more often to have low-producing sections.[31] Figure 4-5 presents the findings from one study.

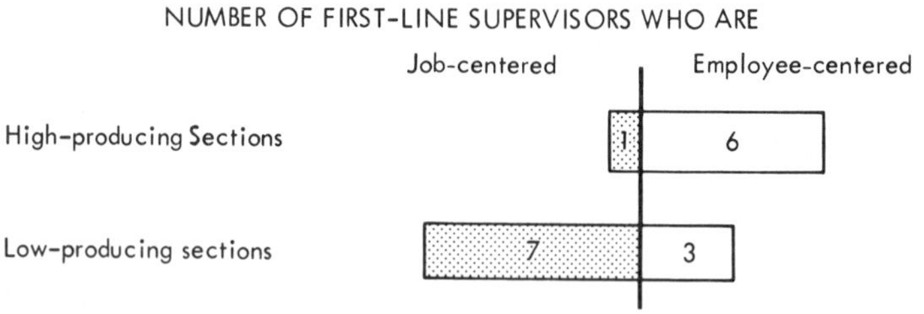

NUMBER OF FIRST-LINE SUPERVISORS WHO ARE

	Job-centered	Employee-centered
High–producing Sections	1	6
Low–producing sections	7	3

FIGURE 4-5 Employee-centered supervisors are higher producers than job-centered supervisors

Likert also discovered that high-producing supervisors "make clear to their subordinates what the objectives are and what needs to be accomplished and then give them freedom to do the job."[32] Thus, he found that general rather than close supervision tended to be associated with high productivity. This relationship, found in a study of clerical workers,[33] is illustrated in Figure 4-6.

The implication throughout Likert's writings is that the ideal and most productive leader behavior for industry is employee-centered or democratic. Yet, his own findings raise questions as to whether there can be an ideal or single

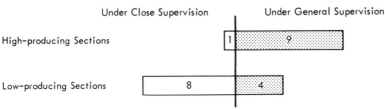

Under Close Supervision   Under General Supervision

High-producing Sections   1   9

Low-producing Sections   8   4

FIGURE 4-6 Low-production section heads are more closely supervised than high-production heads

normatively good style of leader behavior that can apply in all leadership situations. As the preceding figures revealed, one of the eight job-centered supervisors and one of the nine supervisors using close supervision had high-producing sections; also, three of the nine employee-centered supervisors and four of the thirteen supervisors who used general supervision had low-producing sections. In other words, in almost 35 percent of the low-producing sections, the suggested ideal type of leader behavior produced undesirable results and almost 15 percent of the high-producing sections were supervised by the suggested "undesirable" style.

Similar findings and interpretations were made by Halpin and Winer in a study of the relationship between the aircraft commander's leadership pattern and the proficiency rating of his crew.[34] Using the LBDQ, they found that eight of ten commanders with high proficiency ratings were described as using above average Consideration and Initiating Structure and that six of seven commanders with low ratings were seen as below average in Consideration and Initiating Structure. As Likert did, Halpin and Winer reported only that the leaders above average in both Consideration and Initiating Structure are likely to be effective and did not discuss the two high proficiency, low Consideration, low Initiating Structure commanders and the one low producing, high Initiating Structure, high Consideration commander.

Further evidence suggesting that a single ideal or normative style of leader behavior is unrealistic was provided when a study was done in an industrial setting in Nigeria.[35] The results were almost the exact opposite of Likert's findings. In that country the tendency was for job-centered supervisors who provide close supervision to have high-producing sections and for employee-centered supervisors who provide general supervision to have low-producing sections. Thus, a single normative leadership style does not take into consideration cultural differences, particularly customs and traditions as well as the level of education, the standard of living, or industrial experience. These are examples of cultural differences in the followers and the situation that are important in determining the appropriate leadership style to be used. Therefore, based on the definition of leadership process as a function of the leader, the followers, and other situational variables, the desire to have *a single ideal type of leader behavior seems unrealistic.*

ADAPTIVE LEADER BEHAVIOR

This desire to have an ideal type of leader behavior is common. Many managers appear to want to be told how to act. It is also clear from the preceding discussion that some writers in the field of leadership suggest a normative style. Most of these writers have supported either an integrated leadership style (high concern for both task and relationship) or a permissive, democratic, human relations approach. These styles might be appropriate in some industrial or educational settings, but they may be inappropriate in others. Effective leader behavior in other institutions, such as the military, hospitals, prisons and churches, is also dependent on the specific situation or environment that is uniquely characteristic of each. The formula[36] for effective leadership should then read: $E = f(l, f, s)$. The E stands for effectiveness. Effective leaders are able to adapt their style of leader behavior to the needs of the followers and the situation. Since these are not constants, the use of an appropriate style of leader behavior is a challenge to the effective leader. "The manager must be much like the musician who changes his techniques and approaches to obtain the shadings of total performance desired."[37] The concept of *adaptive leader behavior* might be stated as follows:

> The more managers adapt their style of leader behavior to meet the particular situation and the needs of their followers, the more effective they will tend to be in reaching personal and organizational goals.[38]

Leadership Contingency Model

Fred E. Fiedler

The concept of adaptive leader behavior questions the existence of a "best" style of leadership; it is not a matter of the best style but of the most effective style for a particular situation. The suggestion is that a number of leader behavior styles may be effective or ineffective depending on the important elements of the situation.

According to a Leadership Contingency Model developed by Fred E. Fiedler, three major situational variables seem to determine whether a given situation is favorable to leaders: (1) their personal relations with the members of their group (leader-member relations); (2) the degree of structure in the task that their group has been assigned to perform (task structure); and (3) the power and authority that their position provides (position power).[39] Leader-member relations seem to parallel the relationship concepts discussed earlier, while task structure and position power, which measure very closely related aspects of a situation, seem to be associated with task concepts. Fiedler defines the *favorableness of a situation* as "the degree to which the situation enables the leader to exert his influence over his group."[40]

In this model, eight possible combinations of these three situational variables can occur. As a leadership situation varies from high to low on these variables, it will fall into one of the eight combinations (situations). The most favorable situation for leaders to influence their group is one in which they are well liked by the members (good leader-member relations), have a powerful position (high position power), and are directing a well-defined job (high task structure); for example, a well-liked general making inspection in an army camp. On the other hand, the most unfavorable situation for leaders is one in which they are disliked, have little position power, and face an unstructured task, such as an unpopular head of a voluntary hospital fund-raising committee.

Having developed this model for classifying group situations, Fiedler has attempted to determine what the most effective leadership style—task-oriented or relationship-oriented—seems to be for each of the eight situations. In a reexamination of old leadership studies and an analysis of new studies, Fiedler has concluded that:

1. *Task-oriented* leaders tend to perform best in group situations that are either very favorable or very unfavorable to the leader.
2. *Relationship-oriented* leaders tend to perform best in situations that are intermediate in favorableness.

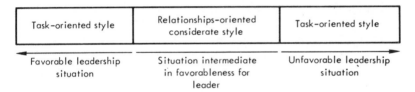

FIGURE 4-7   Leadership styles appropriate for various group situations[41]

Although Fiedler's model is useful to a leader, he seems to be reverting to a single continuum of leader behavior, suggesting that there are only two basic leader behavior styles, task-oriented and relationship-oriented. Most evidence indicates that leader behavior must be plotted on two separate axes rather than on a single continuum. Thus, a leader who is high on task behavior is not necessarily high or low on relationship behavior. Any combination of the two dimensions may occur.

THE TRI-DIMENSIONAL LEADER EFFECTIVENESS MODEL

Paul Hersey and Kenneth H. Blanchard

In the leadership models developed by Paul Hersey and Kenneth H. Blanchard at the Center for Leadership Studies, the terms *task behavior* and *relationship behavior* are used to describe concepts similar to Consideration and Initiating Structure of the Ohio State studies. The four basic leader behavior quadrants are labeled: high task and low relationship; high task and high relationship; high relationship and low task; and low relationship and low task (see Figure 4-8).

These four basic styles depict essentially different leadership styles. The *leadership style* of an individual is the behavior pattern that person exhibits when

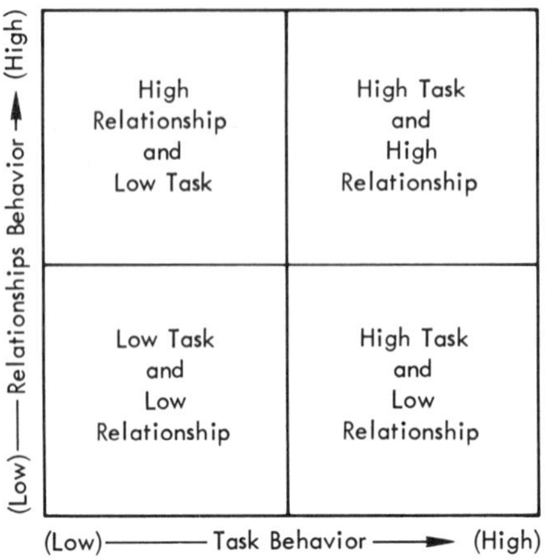

High Relationship and Low Task	High Task and High Relationship
Low Task and Low Relationship	High Task and Low Relationship

Relationships Behavior →→ (High) / (Low)

(Low) ——— Task Behavior ——→ (High)

FIGURE 4-8 Basic leader behavior styles

attempting to influence the activities of others as perceived by those others. This may be very different from how the leader perceives his or her own behavior, which we shall define as *self-perception* rather than style. A person's leadership style involves some combination of task behavior and relationship behavior. The two types of behavior, task and relationship, which are central to the concept of leadership style, are defined as follows:

> *Task behavior*—The extent to which leaders are likely to organize and define the roles of the members of their group (followers); to explain what activities each is to do and when, where, and how tasks are to be accomplished; characterized by endeavoring to establish well-defined patterns of organization, channels of communication, and ways of getting jobs accomplished.
>
> *Relationship behavior*—The extent to which leaders are likely to maintain personal relationships between themselves and members of their group (followers) by opening up channels of communication, providing socioemotional support, "psychological strokes," and facilitating behaviors. [42]

Effectiveness Dimension

Recognizing that the effectiveness of leaders depends on how their leadership style interrelates with the situation in which they operate, an effectiveness dimension should be added to the two-dimensional model. This is illustrated in Figure 4-9.

In his 3-D Management Style Theory, William J. Reddin was the first to add an effectiveness dimension to the task concern and relationship concern dimensions of earlier attitudinal models such as the Managerial Grid. [43] Reddin, whose pioneer work influenced us greatly in the development of our Tri-Dimensional Leader Effectiveness Model presented in this text, felt that a useful theoretical model "must allow that a variety of styles may be effective or ineffective depending on the situation." [44]

By adding an effectiveness dimension to the task behavior and relationship behavior dimensions of the earlier Ohio State leadership model, we are attempt-

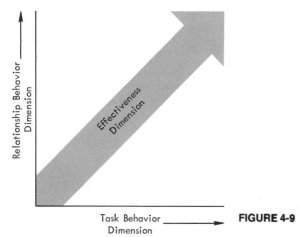

Relationship Behavior
Dimension

Effectiveness
Dimension

Task Behavior
Dimension

FIGURE 4-9 Adding an effectiveness
dimension

ing in the Tri-Dimensional Leader Effectiveness Model to integrate the concepts of leader style with situational demands of a specific environment. When the style of a leader is appropriate to a given situation, it is termed *effective;* when the style is inappropriate to a given situation, it is termed *ineffective.*

If the effectiveness of a leader behavior style depends on the situation in which it is used, it follows that any of the basic styles may be effective or ineffective depending on the situation. The difference between the effective and ineffective styles is often not the actual behavior of the leader but the appropriateness of this behavior to the environment in which it is used. In reality, the third dimension is the environment. It is the interaction of the basic style with the environment that results in a degree of effectiveness or ineffectiveness. We call the third dimension *effectiveness* because in most organizational settings various performance criteria are used to measure the degree of effectiveness or ineffectiveness of a manager or leader. But the authors feel it is important to keep in mind that the third dimension is the environment in which the leader is operating. One might think of the leader's basic style as a particular stimulus, and it is the response to this stimulus that can be considered effective or ineffective. This is an important point because theorists and practitioners who argue that there is one best style of leadership are making value judgments about the stimulus, while those taking a situational approach to leadership are evaluating the response or the results rather than the stimulus. This concept is illustrated in the diagram of the Tri-Dimensional Leader Effectiveness Model presented in Figure 4-10.

Although effectiveness appears to be an either/or situation in this model, in reality it should be represented as a continuum. Any given style in a particular situation could fall somewhere on this continuum from extremely effective to extremely ineffective. Effectiveness, therefore, is a matter of degree, and there could be an infinite number of faces on the effectiveness dimension rather than only three. To illustrate this fact, the effectiveness dimension has been divided into quartiles ranging on the effective side from + 1 to +4 and on the ineffective side from − 1 to −4.

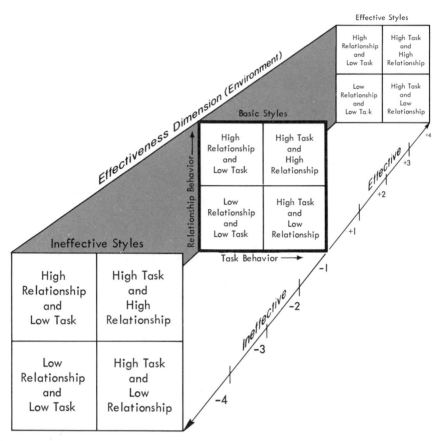

FIGURE 4-10 Tri-dimensional leader effectiveness model

The four effective and the four ineffective styles are, in essence, how appropriate a leader's basic style is to a given situation as seen by his or her followers, superiors, or associates. Table 4-1 describes briefly one of many different ways each style might be perceived as effective or ineffective by others. [45]

A model such as the Tri-Dimensional Leader Effectiveness Model is distinctive because it does not depict a single ideal leader behavior style that is suggested as being appropriate in all situations. For example, the high task and high relationship style is appropriate only in certain situations. In basically crisis-oriented organizations such as the military or the fire department, there is considerable evidence that the most appropriate style would be high task and low relationship, since under combat, fire, or emergency conditions success often depends on immediate response to orders. Time demands do not permit talking things over or explaining decisions. But once the crisis is over, other styles might become appropriate. For example, although the fire chief may have to initiate a high level of structure at the scene of a fire, upon returning to the firehouse it may be appropriate for the chief to engage in other styles while his staff are participating in ancillary functions, such as maintaining the equipment or studying new firefighting techniques.

TABLE 4-1. How the basic leader behavior styles may be seen by others when they are effective or ineffective

Basic Styles	Effective	Ineffective
High Task and Low Relationship Behavior	Seen as having well-defined methods for accomplishing goals that are helpful to the followers.	Seen as imposing methods on others; sometimes seen as unpleasant and interested only in short-run output.
High Task and High Relationship Behavior	Seen as satisfying the needs of the group for setting goals and organizing work, but also providing high levels of socioemotional support.	Seen as initiating more structure than is needed by the group and often appears not to be genuine in interpersonal relationships.
High Relationship and Low Task Behavior	Seen as having implicit trust in people and as being primarily concerned with facilitating their goal accomplishment.	Seen as primarily interested in harmony; sometimes seen as unwilling to accomplish a task if it risks disrupting a relationship or losing "good person" image.
Low Relationship and Low Task Behavior	Seen as appropriately delegating to subordinates decisions about how the work should be done and providing little socioemotional support where little is needed by the group.	Seen as providing little structure or socioemotional support when needed by members of the group.

Instrumentation

To gather data at the Center for Leadership Studies about the behavior of leaders in terms of the Tri-Dimensional Leader Effectiveness Model, the Leader Effectiveness and Adaptability Description (LEAD)[46] instruments were developed. The LEAD-Self contains twelve leadership situations in which respondents are asked to select from four alternative actions—a high task/low relationship behavior, a high task/high relationship behavior, a high relationship/low task behavior, and a low relationship/low task behavior—the style they felt would most closely describe their own behavior in that type of situation. An example of a situation–action combination used in the LEAD-Self is given below:

Situation	Alternative Actions
Your subordinates are no longer responding to your friendly conversation and obvious concern for their welfare. Their performance is declining rapidly.	a. Emphasize the use of uniform procedures and the necessity for task accomplishment
	b. Make yourself available for discussion, but don't push your involvement.
	c. Talk with subordinates and then set goals
	d. Intentionally do not intervene.

The LEAD-Self was designed to measure self-perception of three aspects of leader behavior: (1) style; (2) style range; and (3) style adaptability. Style and style range are determined by four ipsative style scores, and the style adaptability (effectiveness score) is determined by one normative score. The LEAD-Self was originally designed to serve as a training instrument, and the length of the scale (twelve items) and time requirement (ten minutes) clearly reflect the intended function. Since there has been such wide acceptance of the LEAD instruments in a variety of organizational settings, many researchers have requested technological information about the scale, and some data and a LEAD manual have been developed by John F. Greene.[47]

Since the major thrust of our work at the Center for Leadership Studies is on observed behavior, we have developed the LEAD-Other to gather leadership style information for ongoing interventions into organizations. The LEAD-Self is scored by leaders themselves, but the LEAD-Other is completed by leaders' subordinate(s), superior(s), or associates (peers). We will discuss both these instruments in more detail in Chapter 11.

What About Consistency?

You might queston why it is inappropriate to use the same leadership style all the time. "After all, we've been told that consistency is good." This advice might have been given in the past, but in our terms *consistency* is *not* using the same style all the time. Instead, consistency is using the same style for all similar situations and varying the style appropriately as the situation changes. Therefore, if a manager uses a supportive high relationship/low task style with a staff member when that person is performing well and also when that staff member is performing poorly, that manager would be inconsistent, not consistent. Managers are consistent if they direct their subordinates and even sometimes discipline them when they are performing poorly, but support and reward them when they are performing well. Managers are inconsistent if they smile and respond supportively when their subordinates are not doing their job as well as when they are.

To be *really* consistent (in our terms), managers must behave the same way in similar situations for all parties concerned. Thus, a consistent manager would not discipline one subordinate when he or she makes a costly mistake but not another staff member, and vice versa. It is also important for managers to treat their subordinates the same way in similar circumstances even when it is *inconvenient*—when they don't have time or when they don't feel like it.

Some managers are consistent only when it is convenient. They may praise and support their people when they feel like it and redirect and supervise their activities when they have time. This leads to problems. Parents are probably the worst in this regard. For example, suppose Wendy and Walt get upset when their children argue with each other and are willing to clamp down on them when it happens. However, there are exceptions to their consistency in this area. If they are rushing off to a dinner party, they will generally not deal with the childrens' fighting. Or if they are in the supermarket with the kids, they will frequently permit behavior they would normally.not allow, because they are uncomfortable disciplining the children in public. Since children are continually testing the boundaries or limits of their behavior (they want to know what they can do and cannot do), Walt and Wendy's kids soon learn that they should not fight with each other except when "Mom and Dad are in a hurry to go out or when we're in a store." Thus, unless parents and managers are willing to be consistent, even when it is inconvenient, they may actually be encouraging misbehavior.

Attitude Versus Behavior

One of the ideas behind the old definition of consistency was the belief that your behavior as a manager *must* be consistent with your attitudes. This particularly was a problem with some people who were heavily involved with the human relations or sensitivity training movement. They believed that if you care about people and have positive assumptions about them, you should also treat them in high relationship ways, and seldom in directive or controlling ways.

We feel that much of this problem stemmed from the failure of some theorists and practitioners to distinguish between an attitudinal model and a behavioral model. For example, in examining the dimensions of the Managerial Grid (concern for production and concern for people) and Reddin's 3-D Management Style Theory (task orientation and relationship orientation), one can see that these appear to be *attitudinal* dimensions. Concern or orientation is a feeling or an emotion toward something. The same can be said about McGregor's Theory X and Theory Y assumptions about human nature. Theory X describes negative feelings about the nature of people, and Theory Y describes positive feelings. These are all models that describe attitudes and feelings.

On the other hand, the dimensions of the Tri-Dimensional Leader Effectiveness model (task behavior and relationship behavior) are dimensions of *observed* behavior. Thus, the Leader Effectiveness model describes *how* people behave, while the Managerial Grid, the 3-D Management Style Theory and Theory X–Theory Y describe *attitudes* or *predispositions* toward production and people. [48]

Although attitudinal models and the Leader Effectiveness model examine different aspects of leadership, they are not incompatible. A conflict only develops when behavioral assumptions are drawn from analysis of the attitudinal dimension of models such as the Managerial Grid and theories like Theory X–Theory Y. First of all, it is very difficult to predict behavior from attitudes and values. In fact, it has been found that you can actually do better the other way around. You can do a much better job of predicting values or attitudes from behavior. If you want to know what's in a person's heart, look at what that person does. Look at the person's behavior.

For example, assume that a person has a very high concern for conditions in the ghetto—for poverty. Does that tell you what that person's going to do about it? No. You may have one person who has a high concern for conditions in the ghetto and poverty who engages in the following behavior: "Don't even talk to me about it. I don't want to go on that side of town." In other words, the person engages in avoidance or withdrawal behavior (low relationship behavior and low task behavior). You may have another person who has a very high concern for conditions in the ghetto and poverty, who goes down into the ghetto and begins to tell people what to do, how to do it, when to do it, and where to do it (high task behavior and low relationship behavior). You may have another person who has high concern for conditions in the ghetto and poverty who would go down to the ghetto areas saying, "Gee, I'm sorry you have problems. Do you want to talk to me about it? Let's discuss it. Gosh, I'm sympathetic" (high relationship behavior and low task behavior). Finally, you might get someone else who has a high concern for conditions in the ghetto and poverty who would try to provide both high amounts of task behavior and relationship behavior.

What we're suggesting is that the same values set can evoke a variety of behaviors. You cannot easily predict behaviors from values. A look at one of the simplest models in the behavior sciences may help to emphasize our point of view. The model is the S–O–R (a stimulus directed toward an organism produces some response). The trap that many of the humanistic trainers fall into is to suggest that we assess the effectiveness of management by looking at the stimulus or the leadership style. In other words, they say there are good styles and bad styles. What we are saying is that if you are going to assess performance, you don't evaluate the stimulus, you assess the results—the response. It's here that we need to make assessments in terms of performance. This is exactly what we suggest. There is no best leadership style or stimulus. Any leadership style can be effective or ineffective depending on the response that style gets in a particular situation. As you will see in the next chapter, when we are talking about response, we're not just talking about output or productivity. We also have to look at the impact the leaders have on the human resources. It's not enough to have a tremendous amount of productivity for the next six months and then have your people get upset and leave and join your competitors in other organizations. You've also got to be concerned about what impact you are having on the human resources, on developing their competency and their commitment. So when we talk about response or results, we're talking about output and impact on the human resources.

There is another reason to be careful about making behavioral assumptions from attitudinal measures. Although high *concern* for both production and people (9-9 attitude) and positive Theory Y assumptions about human nature are basic ingredients for effective managers, it may be appropriate for managers to engage in a variety of behaviors as they face different problems in their environment. Therefore, the high task/high relationship style often associated with the Managerial Grid 9-9 Team style or the participative high relationship/low task behavior that is often argued as consistent with Theory Y may not always be appropriate. For example, if a manager's subordinates are emotionally mature and can take responsibility for themselves, the appropriate style of leadership for working with them may be low task and low relationship. In this case, the manager delegates to those subordinates the responsibility of planning, organizing and controlling their own operation. The manager plays a background role, providing socioemotional support only when necessary. In using this style appropriately, the manager would not be "impoverished" (low concern for both people and production) or Theory X. In fact, delegating to competent and confident people is the best way a manager can demonstrate his 9-9 attitude and Theory Y assumptions about human nature. The same is true for using a directive high task/low relationship style. Sometimes the best way you can show your concern for people and production (9-9) is to direct, control and closely supervise their behavior when they are insecure and don't have the skills yet to perform their job.

In summary, empirical studies tend to show that there is no normative (best) style of leadership. Effective leaders adapt their leader behavior to meet the needs of their followers and the particular environment. If their followers are different, they must be treated differently. Therefore, effectiveness depends on the *leader,* the *follower*(s), and other *situational* variables: $E = f(l, f, s)$. Therefore, anyone who is interested in his or her own success as a leader must give serious thought to these behavioral and environmental considerations.

We have now discussed a number of approaches to the study of leader behavior, concluding with the Tri-Dimensional Leader Effectiveness model. In Chapter 5 we will discuss the effectiveness dimension in this model.

NOTES

[1] Peter F. Drucker, *The Practice of Management* (New York: Harper & Row, Publishers, 1954).

[2] George R. Terry, *Principles of Management,* 3rd ed. (Homewood, Ill.: Richard D. Irwin, Inc., 1960), p. 5.

[3] Terry, *Principles of Management,* p. 493.

[4] Robert Tannenbaum, Irving R. Weschler and Fred Massarik, *Leadership and Organization: A Behavioral Science Approach* (New York: McGraw-Hill Book Company, 1959).

[5] Harold Koontz and Cyril O'Donnell, *Principles of Management,* 2nd ed. (New York: McGraw-Hill Book Company, 1959), p. 435.

[6] Cecil A. Gibb, "Leadership," in *Handbook of Social Psychology,* Gardner Lindzey, ed. (Cambridge, Mass.: Addison-Wesley Publishing Company, Inc., 1954). See also Roger M. Stogdill, "Personal Factors Associated with Leadership: A Survey of Literature," *Journal of Psychology,* 25 (1948), pp. 35–71.

[7] Eugene E. Jennings, "The Anatomy of Leadership," *Management of Personnel Quarterly,* I, No. 1 (Autumn 1961).

[8] John K. Hemphill, *Situational Factors in Leadership,* Monograph No. 32 (Columbus, Ohio: Bureau of Educational Research, The Ohio State University, 1949).

[9] Chester I. Barnard, *The Functions of the Executive* (Cambridge: Harvard University Press, 1938).

[10] Frederick W. Taylor, *The Principles of Scientific Management* (New York: Harper & Brothers, 1911).

[11] Elton Mayo, *The Social Problems of an Industrial Civilization* (Boston: Harvard Business School, 1945), p. 23.

[12] This figure was adapted from Exhibit 1 in Robert Tannenbaum and Warren H. Schmidt, "How to Choose a Leadership Pattern," *Harvard Business Review,* March-April 1957, pp. 95–101.

[13] Robert Tannenbaum and Warren H. Schmidt, "How to Choose a Leadership Pattern," *Harvard Business Review*, May-June 1973. This is an update of their original 1957 acticle.

[14] K. Lewin, R. Lippitt and R. White identified *laissez-faire* as a third form of leadership style. See Lewin, Lippitt and White, "Leader Behavior and Member Reaction in Three 'Social Climates,' " in *Group Dynamics: Research and Theory*, 2nd ed., Dorwin Cartwright and Alvin Zander, eds. (Evanston. Ill.: Row, Peterson & Company, 1960).

[15] D. Katz, N. Macoby and Nancy C. Morse, *Productivity, Supervision, and Morale in an Office Situation* (Ann Arbor, Mich.: Survey Research Center, 1950); D. Katz, N. Macoby, G. Gurin and Lucretia G. Floor, *Productivity, Supervision and Morale among Railroad Workers* (Ann Arbor, Mich.: Survey Research Center, 1951).

[16] Dorwin Cartwright and Alvin Zander, eds., *Group Dynamics: Research and Theory*, 2nd ed. (Evanston, Ill.: Row, Peterson & Company, 1960).

[17] *Ibid.*, p. 496.

[18] *Ibid.*

[19] Roger M. Stogdill and Alvin E. Coons, eds., *Leader Behavior: Its Description and Measurement*, Research Monograph No. 88 (Columbus, Ohio: Bureau of Business Research, The Ohio State University, 1957)

[20] Andrew W. Halpin, *The Leadership Behavior of School Superintendents* (Chicago: Midwest Administration Center, The University of Chicago, 1959), p. 4.

[21] *Ibid.*, pp. 6–9.

[22] Robert R. Blake and Jane S. Mouton, *The Managerial Grid* (Houston, Tex.: Gulf Publishing, 1964).

[23] Robert R. Blake et al., "Breakthrough in Organization Development," *Harvard Business Review*, November-December 1964, p. 136.

[24] Barnard, *The Functions of the Executive.*

[25] Warren G. Bennis, "Leadership Theory and Administrative Behavior: The Problems of Authority," *Administrative Science Quarterly*, IV, No. 3 (December 1959), p. 274.

[26] Halpin, *The Leadership Behavior of School Superintendents*, p. 79.

[27] *Ibid.*

[28] *Ibid.*, p. 6.

[29] Blake et al., "Breakthrough," p. 135.

[30] Rensis Likert, *New Patterns of Management* (New York: McGraw-Hill Book Company, 1961), p. 7.

[31] *Ibid.*

[32] *Ibid.*, p. 9.

[33] *Ibid.*

[34] Andrew W. Halpin and Ben J. Winer, *The Leadership Behavior of Airplane Commanders* (Columbus, Ohio: The Ohio State University Research Foundation, 1952).

[35] Paul Hersey, an unpublished research project, 1965.

[36] Robert Tannenbaum and Warren H. Schmidt discuss the factors in this formula in Tannenbaum and Schmidt, "How to Choose a Leadership Pattern," *Harvard Business Review*, May-June 1973, Vol. 51, No. 3, pp. 162–171.

[37] Koontz and O'Donnell, *Principles of Management.*

[38] Paul Hersey, *Management Concepts and Behavior: Programmed Instruction for Managers* (Little Rock, Ark.: Marvern Publishing Co., 1967), p. 15.

[39] Fred E. Fiedler, *A Theory of Leadership Effectiveness* (New York: McGraw-Hill Book Company, 1967).

[40] *Ibid.*, p. 13.

[41] Adapted from Fiedler, *A Theory of Leadership Effectiveness*, p. 14.

[42] Since our model is an outgrowth of the Ohio State Leadership Studies, these definitions have been adapted from their definitions of "Initiating Structure" (task) and "Consideration" (relationship) Stogdill and Coons, *Leader Behavior: Its Description and Measurement*, pp. 42–43.

[43] William J. Reddin, "The 3-D Management Style Theory," *Training and Development Journal*, April 1967, pp. 8–17; see also *Managerial Effectiveness* (New York: McGraw-Hill Book Company, 1970).

[44] Reddin, "The 3-D Management Style Theory," p. 13.

[45] Parts of this table were adapted from the managerial style descriptions of William J. Reddin, *The 3-D Management Style Theory*, Theory Paper #2—Managerial Styles (Fredericton, N.B., Canada: Social Science Systems, 1967), pp. 5–6.

[46] The first publication on the LEAD (formerly known as the Leader Adaptability and Style Inventory [LASI]) appeared as Paul Hersey and Kenneth H. Blanchard, "So You Want to Know Your Leadership Style?" *Training and Development Journal*, February 1974. LEAD instruments are distributed through Center for Leadership Studies, Escondido, Calif.

[47] The LEAD-Self Manual, written by John F. Greene, contains a discussion of the Situational Leadership Model, format of the scale, characteristics of ipsative measures, standardization procedures, item derivation and selection, estimates of reliability, logical validity, empirical validity, types of scores, and normative information. Administration and scoring procedures are also included. The LEAD-Self was standardized on the responses of two hundred sixty-four managers constituting a North American sample. The managers ranged in age from twenty-one to sixty-four; 30 percent were at the entry level of management; 55 percent were middle managers; 14 percent were at the high level of management. The twelve-item validities for the adaptability score ranged from .11 to .52, and ten of the twelve coefficients (83 percent) were .25 or higher. Eleven coefficients were significant beyond the .01 level and one was significant at the .05 level. Each response option met the operationally defined criterion of less than 80 percent with respect to selection frequency. The stability of the LEAD-Self was moderately strong. In two administrations across a six-week interval, 75 percent of the managers maintained their dominant style and 71 percent maintained their alternate style. The contingency coefficients were both .71 and each was significant (p .01). The correlation for the adaptability scores was .69 (p .01). The LEAD-Self scores remained relatively stable across time, and the user may rely on the results as consistent measures.

The logical validity of the scale was clearly established. Face validity was based on a review of the items, and content validity emanated from the procedures used to create the original set of items.

Several empirical validity studies were conducted. As hypothesized, correlations with the demographic/organismic variables of sex, age, years of experience, degree and management level were generally low, indicating the relative independence of the scales with respect to these variables. Satisfactory results were reported supporting the four style dimensions of the scale using a modified approach to factor structure. In forty-six of the forty-eight item options (96 percent), the expected relationship was found. In another study, a significant correlation of .67 was found between the adaptability scores of the managers and the independent ratings of their supervisors. Based on these findings, the LEAD-Self is deemed to be an empirically sound instrument. Copies of the LEAD-Self manual may be obtained through the Center for Leadership Studies, Escondido, California.

[48] Fiedler in his Contingency Model of Leadership Effectiveness (Fiedler, *A Theory of Leadership Effectiveness*) also tends to make behavioral assumptions from data gathered from an attitudinal measure of leadership style. A leader is asked to evaluate his least preferred coworker (LPC) on a series of semantic differential type scales. Leaders are classified as high or low LPC depending on the favorableness with which they rate their LPC.

chapter 5

Determining Effectiveness

The most important aspect of the Tri-Dimensional Leader Effectiveness Model is that it adds *effectiveness* to the task and relationship dimensions of earlier leadership models. For this reason, it seems appropriate to examine closely the concept of effectiveness.

MANAGEMENT EFFECTIVENESS
VERSUS LEADERSHIP EFFECTIVENESS

In discussing effectiveness, it is important once again to distinguish between *management* and *leadership*. As we discussed in Chapter 1, leadership is a broader concept than management. Management is thought of as a special kind of leadership in which the accomplishment of organizational goals is paramount. Any time that you are attempting to influence the behavior of someone else you are engaging in leadership; therefore, it is obvious that all your leadership behavior is not directed toward accomplishing organizational goals. In fact, many times when you are trying to influence someone else you are not even part of an organization. For example, when you are trying to get some friends to go somewhere with you, you are not engaging in management, but you certainly are attempting leadership. If they agree to go, you are an effective leader but not an effective manager. Even within an organizational setting, managers may attempt to engage in leadership rather than management since they are trying to accomplish personal goals, not organizational ones. For example, a vice-president may have a strong personal goal to become the company president. In attempting to achieve this goal, this executive may not be concerned with organizational goals at all, but only with undermining the plans of the president and other executives who may be contenders for the job. The vice-president may accomplish this personal goal and, in that sense, be a successful leader. However, this individual cannot be considered an effective manager because his or her actions are probably disruptive to the effective operation of the firm. *Parkinson's Law*[1] suggests a clear example of personal goals being placed before organizational goals. His law states that in bureaucracies managers often tend to try to build up their own departments by adding unnecessary personnel, more equipment, or expanded facilities. Although this tendency may increase the prestige and importance of these managers, it often leads to "an organizational environment which not only is inefficient but stifling and frustrating to the individuals who must cope with [it]."[2] Thus, in discussing effectiveness we must recognize the differences between *individual goals, organizational goals, leadership,* and *management.*

SOURCES OF POWER

One of the characteristics of leadership is that leaders exercise power. Amitai Etzioni discusses the difference between *position power* and *personal power.* His distinction springs from his concept of power as the ability to induce or influence behavior. He claims that power is derived from an organizational office, personal influence, or both. Individuals who are able to induce other individuals to do a certain job because of their position in the organization are considered to have position power; individuals who derive their power from their followers are considered to have personal power. Some individuals can have both position and personal power.[3]

Where do managers get the position power that is available to them? Although Etzioni would argue that it comes from the organizational office of a manager, we feel it comes from above and, therefore, is not inherent in the office. Managers occupying positions in an organization may have more or less position power than their predecessor or someone else in a similar position in the same organization. It is not a matter of the office having power, but rather the extent to which those people to whom managers report are willing to delegate authority and responsibility down to them. So position power tends to flow down in an organization. This is not to say that leaders do not have any impact on how much position power they accrue. They certainly do. The confidence and trust they develop with the people above them will often determine the willingness of superior(s) to delegate down to them. And remember, it is not just a downward delegation; their boss can take it back. We have all seen this occur on occasions, when managers still have the same responsibilities, but all of a sudden their authority (reward system and sanctions) to get the job done in the way they once did is taken away.

Personal power is the extent to which followers respect, feel good about, and are committed to their leader, and see their goals as being satisfied by the goals of their leader. In other words, personal power is the extent to which people are willing to follow a leader. As a result, personal power in an organizational setting comes from below—the followers. Thus, we must be careful when we say that some leaders are charismatic or have personal power that flows from them. If that were true, we would have to be able to say that managers with personal power could take over any department and have the same commitment and rapport they had in their last department. We know that is not true. Although managers certainly can influence the amount of personal power they have by the way they treat their people, it is a volatile kind of power. It can be taken away rapidly by followers. Make a few dramatic mistakes and see how many people are willing to follow. Personal power is a day-to-day phenomenon—it can be earned and it can be taken away.

Etzioni postulates that the best situation for leaders is when they have both personal and position power. But in some cases it is not possible to build a relationship on both. Then the question becomes whether it is more important to have personal power or position power. Happiness and human relations have been culturally reinforced over the past several decades. With this emphasis, most people would pick personal power as being the most important. But there may be another side of the coin.

In his sixteenth-century treatise *The Prince,* Machiavelli presents an interesting viewpoint when he raises the question of whether it is better to have a relationship based on love (personal power) or fear (position power).[4] Machiavelli, as Etzioni, contends that it is best to be both loved and feared. If, however, one cannot have both, he suggests that a relationship based on love alone tends to be volatile, short-lived, and easily terminated when there is no fear of retaliation. On the other hand, Machiavelli contends that a relationship based on fear tends to be longer lasting in that the individual must be willing to incur the sanction (pay the price) before terminating the relationship. This is a difficult concept for many people to accept, and yet one of the most difficult roles for leaders— whether they be a boss, teacher, or parent—is disciplining someone about whom they care. Yet to be effective, leaders sometimes have to sacrifice short-term friendship for long-term respect if they are interested in the growth and development of the people with whom they are working. Machiavelli warns, however, that one should be careful that fear does not lead to hatred. For hatred often evokes overt behavior in terms of retaliation, undermining, and attempts to overthrow.

We will be discussing power and its impact on leadership in much more detail in Chapter 8.

SUCCESSFUL LEADERSHIP
VERSUS EFFECTIVE LEADERSHIP

If an individual attempts to have some effect on the behavior of another, we call this stimulus *attempted* leadership. The response to this leadership attempt can be successful or unsuccessful. Since a basic responsibility of managers in any type of organization is to get work done with and through people, their success is measured by the output or productivity of the group they lead. With this thought in mind, Bernard M. Bass suggests a clear distinction between *successful* and *effective* leadership or management.[5]

Suppose manager A attempts to influence individual B to do a certain job. A's attempt will be considered successful or unsuccessful depending on the extent to which B accomplishes the job. It is not really an either/or situation. A's success could be depicted on a continuum (Figure 5-1) ranging from very successful to very unsuccessful with gray areas in between which would be difficult to ascertain as either.

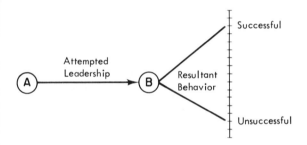

FIGURE 5-1 Successful and unsuccessful leadership continuum

Let us assume that A's leadership is successful. In other words, B's response to A's leadership stimulus falls on the successful side of the continuum. This still does not tell the whole story of effectiveness.

If A's leader style is not compatible with the expectations of B, and if B is antagonized and does the job only because of A's position power, then we can say that A has been successful but not effective. B has responded as A intended because A has control of rewards and punishment, and not because B sees his own needs being accomplished by satisfying the goals of the manager or the organization.

On the other hand, if A's attempted leadership leads to a successful response, and B does the job because he wants to do it and finds it rewarding, then we consider A as having not only position power but also personal power. B respects A and is willing to cooperate with her, realizing that A's request is consistent with some personal goals. In fact, B sees these personal goals as being accomplished by this activity. This is what is meant by effective leadership, keeping in mind that effectiveness also appears as a continuum which can range from very effective to very ineffective, as illustrated in Figure 5-2.

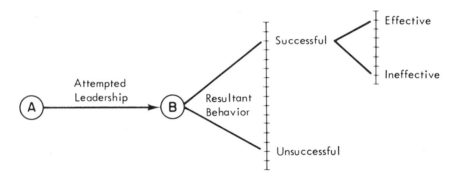

FIGURE 5-2 Successful and effective leadership continuums

Success has to do with how the individual or the group behaves. On the other hand, effectiveness describes the internal state or predisposition of an individual or a group and thus is attitudinal in nature. If individuals are interested only in success, they tend to emphasize their position power and use close supervision. However, if they are effective, they will also depend on personal power and be characterized by more general supervision. Position power tends to be delegated down though the organization, while personal power is generated upward from below through follower acceptance.

In the management of organizations, the difference between successful and effective often explains why many supervisors can get a satisfactory level of output only when they are right there, looking over the worker's shoulder. But as soon as they leave, output declines and often such things as horseplay and scrap loss increase. We have seen this phenomenon occur in schools with some teachers who, if they left the room during an exam, upon returning would find the kids exchanging papers and answers without any regard for rules. Other teachers could leave the room and the kids would behave no differently than if they were there. In fact, if someone started to cheat, a student might even stop the violator and say, "We don't do that *in this class!*"

The phenomenon described applies not only to educational and business organizations but also to less formal organizations like the family. If parents are successful and effective, have both position and personal power, their children accept family goals as their own. Consequently, if the husband and wife leave for the weekend, the children behave no differently than if their parents were there. If, however, the parents continually use close supervision and the children view their own goals as being stifled by their parents' goals, the parents have only position power. They maintain order because of the rewards and the punishments they control. If these parents went away on a trip leaving the children behind, upon returning they might be greeted by havoc and chaos.

In summary, managers could be successful but ineffective, having only a shortlived influence over the behavior of others. On the other hand, if managers are both successful and effective, their influence tends to lead to long-run productivity and organizational development.

It should be pointed out that this *successful versus effective framework is a way of evaluating the response to a specific behavioral event and not of evaluating performance over time.* Long-term evaluation is not a result of a single leadership event, but a summation of many different leadership events. The evaluation of a leader or an organization over time will be discussed in the following section.

WHAT DETERMINES ORGANIZATIONAL EFFECTIVENESS?

In discussing effectiveness we have concentrated on evaluating the results of individual leaders or managers. These results are significant, but perhaps the most important aspect of effectiveness is its relationship to an entire organization. Here we are concerned not only with the outcome of a given leadership attempt but with the effectiveness of the organizational unit over a period of time. Rensis Likert identifies three variables—causal, intervening, and end-result—which are useful in discussing effectiveness over time.[6]

Causal Variables

Causal variables are those factors that influence the course of developments within an organization and its results or accomplishments. These independent variables can be altered by the organization and its management; they are not beyond the control of the organization, like general business conditions. Leadership strategies, skills, and behavior, management's decisions, and the policies and structure of the organization are examples of causal variables.

Intervening Variables

Leadership strategies, skills, and behavior, and other causal variables affect the human resources or intervening variables in an organization. According to Likert,[7] intervening variables represent the current condition of the internal state of the organization. They are reflected in the commitment to objectives, motivation, and morale of members and their skills in leadership, communications, conflict resolution, decision making and problem solving.

Output or End-Result Variables

Output or end-result variables are the dependent variables that reflect the achievements of the organization. In evaluating effectiveness, perhaps more than 90 percent of managers in organizations look at measures of output alone. Thus, the effectiveness of business managers is often determined by net profits; the effectiveness of college professors may be determined by the number of articles and books they have published; and the effectiveness of basketball coaches may be determined by their won-lost record.

Many researchers talk about effectiveness by emphasizing similar output variables. Fred E. Fiedler, for example, in his studies evaluated "leader effectiveness in terms of group performance on the group's primary assigned task."[8] William J. Reddin, in discussing management styles, thinks in similar terms about effectiveness. He argues that the effectiveness of a manager should be measured "objectively by his profit center performance"—maximum output, market share, or other similar criteria.[9]

We might visualize the relationship between the three classes of variables as stimuli (causal variables) acting upon the organism (intervening variables) and creating certain responses (output variables), as illustrated in Figure 5-3.[10]

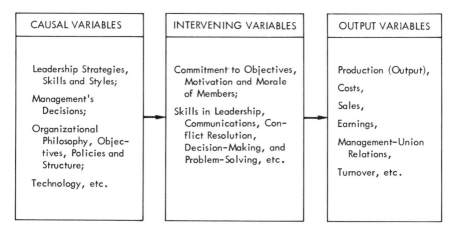

FIGURE 5-3   Relationship between causal, intervening, and output variables

The level or condition of the intervening variables is produced largely by the causal variables and in turn has influence upon the end-result variables. Attempts by members of the organization to improve the intervening variables by endeavoring to alter these variables directly will be much less successful usually than efforts directed toward modifying them through altering the causal variables. Similarly, efforts to improve the end-result variables by attempting to modify the intervening variables usually will be less effective than changing the causal variables.[11]

Long-Term Goals Versus Short-Term Goals

Intervening variables are concerned with building and developing the organization, and they tend to be long-term goals. This is the one part of effectiveness that many managers overlook because it emphasizes long-term potential as well as short-term performance. This oversight is understandable because most managers tend to be promoted on the basis of short-term output variables, such as increased production and earnings, without concern for the long-run potential and organizational development. This creates a dilemma.

Organizational Dilemma

One of the major problems in industry today is that there is a shortage of effective managers. Therefore, it is not uncommon for managers to be promoted in six months or a year if they are "producers." Since the basis on which top management promotes is often short-run output, managers attempt to achieve high levels of productivity and often overemphasize tasks, placing extreme pressure on everyone, even when it is inappropriate.

We have all probably had some experience with coming into an office or a home and raising the roof with people. The immediate or short-run effect is probably increased activity. We also know that if this style is inappropriate for those concerned, and if it continues over a long period of time, the morale and climate of the organization will deteriorate. Some indications of deterioration of these intervening variables at work may be turnover, absenteeism, increased accidents, scrap loss, and numerous grievances. Not only the number of grievances but the nature of grievances is important. Are grievances really significant problems or do they reflect pent-up emotions due to anxieties and frustration? Are they settled at the complaint stage between the employee and the supervisor or are they pushed up the hierarchy to be settled at higher levels or by arbitration? The organizational dilemma is that in many instances a manager who places pressure on everyone and produces in the short run is promoted out of this situation before the disruptive aspects of the intervening variables catch up.

There tends to be a time lag between declining intervening variables and significant restriction of output by employees under such management climate. Employees tend to feel things will get better. Thus, when high-pressure managers are promoted rapidly, they often stay "one step ahead of the wolf."

The real problem is faced by the next manager. Although productivity records are high, this manager has inherited many problems. Merely the introduction of a new manager may be enough to collapse the slowly deteriorating intervening variables. A tremendous drop in morale and motivation leading almost immediately to significant decrease in output can occur. Change by its very nature is frightening; to a group whose intervening variables are declining, it can be devastating. Regardless of this new manager's style, the present expectations of the followers may be so distorted that much time and patience will be needed to close the now apparent "credibility gap" between the goals of the organization and the personal goals of the group. No matter how effective this manager may be in the long run, superiors in reviewing a productivity drop may give the manager only a few months to improve performance. But as Likert's studies indicate, rebuilding a group's intervening variables in a small organization may take one to three years, and in a large organization it may extend to seven years.

This dilemma is not restricted to business organizations. It is very common in school systems where superintendents and other top administrators can get promoted to better, higher paying jobs in other systems if they are innovative and implement a number of new programs in their systems. One such superintendent brought a small town national prominence by putting every new and innovative idea being discussed in education into one of his schools. In this process, there was almost no involvement or participation by the teachers or building administrator(s) in the decision making that went into these programs. After two years, the superintendent, because of his innovative reputation, was asked to move to a larger system where he received a $15,000-a-year raise. A new superintendent was appointed in his "old" system, but almost before the new superintendent unpacked turmoil hit the system with tremendous teacher turnover, a faculty union, and a defeated bond issue. As things became unglued, people were heard saying that they wished the old superintendent was back. "If he were here, this wouldn't have happened!" And yet, in reality, it was his very style that deteriorated the intervening variables and set up the trouble that followed the entrance of the new superintendent. Examples in other types of organizations are also available.

In one of Fiedler's studies he examined the leadership on basketball teams. The criterion he used in evaluating the effectiveness of these leaders was percentage of games won and lost. Most people also tend to evaluate coaches on won-and-lost records. Let's look at an example.

Charlie, a high school coach, has had several good seasons. He knows if he has one more such season he will have a job offer with a better salary at a more prestigious school. Under these conditions, he may decide to concentrate on the short-run potential of the team. He may play only his seniors and he may have an impressive record at the end of the season. Short-run output goals have been maximized, but the intervening variables of the team have not been properly used. If Charlie leaves this school and accepts another job, a new coach will find himself with a tremendous rebuilding job. But because developing the freshmen and sophomores and rebuilding a good team take time and much work, the team could have a few poor seasons in the interim. When the alumni and fans see the team losing, they soon forget that old adage "It's not whether you win or lose, it's how you play the game." They immediately consider the new coach a bum. After all, "We had some great seasons with good old Charlie." It is difficult for them to realize that the previous coach concentrated only on short-run winning at the expense of building for the future. The problem is that the effectiveness of a new coach is judged immediately on the same games-won basis as his or her predecessor. The new coach may be doing an excellent job of rebuilding and may have a winning season in two or three years, but the probability of that coach's being given the opportunity to build a future winner is low. Problems don't occur just when leaders concentrate on output without taking into consideration the condition of the human resources. For example, in the classic World War II movie about the Air Force, *Twelve O'Clock High,* Frank Savage (played by Gregory Peck) is asked suddenly to take over a bomber group from a commanding officer whom everyone loves and respects but whose overidentification with his men and concern about his human resources have resulted in an outfit that is not producing and is hurting the war effort.

Thus, it should be clear that we do not think this is an either/or process. It is often a matter of determining how much to concentrate on each—output and intervening variables. In our basketball example, suppose a women's team has good potential, having a large number of experienced senior players, but as the season progresses it does not look as if it is going to be an extremely good year. There comes a point in this season when the coach must make a basic decision. Will she continue to play her experienced seniors and hope to win a majority of her final games, or should she forget about concentrating on winning the last games and play her sophomores and juniors to give them experience, in hopes of developing and building a winning team for future years? The choice is between short- and long-term goals. If the accepted goal is building the team for the future, then the coach should be evaluated on these terms and not entirely on her present won-lost record.

Although intervening variables do not appear on won-lost records, balance sheets, sales reports, or accounting ledgers, we feel that these long-term considerations are just as important to an organization as short-term output variables. Therefore, although difficult to measure, intervening variables should not be overlooked in determining organizational effectiveness. One of the instruments used by Likert to measure these variables was discussed in Chapter 3.

In summary, we feel that effectiveness is actually determined by whatever the manager and the organization decide are their goals and objectives, but they should remember that *effectiveness is a function of:*

1. output variables (productivity/performance).
2. intervening variables (the condition of the human resources).
3. short-range goals.
4. long-range goals.

FORCE FIELD ANALYSIS

Kurt Lewin

Force field analysis, a technique developed by Kurt Lewin for diagnosing situations, may be useful in looking at the variables involved in determining effectiveness.[12]

Lewin assumes that in any situation there are both driving and restraining forces that influence any change that may occur. *Driving forces* are those forces affecting a situation that are pushing in a particular direction; they tend to initiate a change and keep it going. In terms of improving productivity in a work group, pressure from a supervisor, incentive earnings, and competition may be examples of driving forces. *Restraining forces* are forces acting to restrain or decrease the driving forces. Apathy, hostility, and poor maintenance of equipment may be examples of restraining forces against increased production. Equilibrium is reached when the sum of the driving forces equals the sum of the restraining forces. In our example, equilibrium represents the present level of productivity, as shown in Figure 5-4.

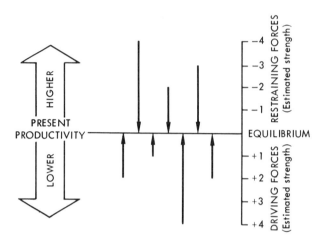

FIGURE 5-4   Driving and restraining forces in equilibrium

This equilibrium, or present level of productivity, can be raised or lowered by changes in the relationship between the driving and the restraining forces. For illustration, let us look again at the dilemma of the new manager who takes over a work group in which productivity is high but whose predecessor drained the human resources (intervening variables). The former manager had upset the equilibrium by increasing the driving forces (that is, being autocratic and keeping continual pressure on subordinates) and thus achieving increases in output in the short run. By doing this, however, new restraining forces developed, such as increased hostility and antagonism, and at the time of the former manager's departure the restraining forces were beginning to increase and the results manifested themselves in turnover, absenteeism, and other restraining forces, which lowered productivity shortly after the new manager arrived. Now a new equilibrium at a significantly lower productivity is faced by the new manager.

Now just assume that our new manager decides not to increase the driving forces but to reduce the restraining forces. The manager may do this by taking time away from the usual production operation and engaging in problem solving and training and development. In the short run, output will tend to be lowered still further. However, if commitment to objectives and technical know-how of the group are increased in the long run, they may become new driving forces, and that, along with the elimination of the hostility and the apathy that were restraining forces, will now tend to move the balance to a higher level of output.

Managers are often in a position in which they must consider not only output but also intervening variables and not only short-term but also long-term goals. A framework that is useful in diagnosing these interrelationships is available through force field analysis.

INTEGRATION OF GOALS AND EFFECTIVENESS

The extent that individuals and groups perceive their own goals as being satisfied by the accomplishment of organizational goals is the degree of integration of goals. When organizational goals are shared by all, this is what McGregor calls a true "integration of goals."[13]

To illustrate this concept, we can divide an organization into two groups, management and subordinates. The respective goals of these two groups and the resultant attainment of the goals of the organization to which they belong are illustrated in Figure 5-5.[14]

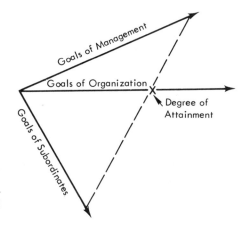

FIGURE 5-5 Directions of goals of management, subordinates, and the organization— *moderate* organizational accomplishment

In this instance, the goals of management are somewhat compatible with the goals of the organization but are not exactly the same. On the other hand, the goals of the subordinates are almost at odds with those of the organization. The result of the interaction between the goals of management and the goals of subordinates is a compromise, and actual performance is a combination of both. It is at this approximate point that the degree of attainment of the goals of the organization can be pictured. This situation can be much worse when there is little accomplishment of organizational goals, as illustrated in Figure 5-6.

In this situation, there seems to be a general disregard for the welfare of the organization. Both managers and workers see their own goals conflicting with those of the organization. Consequently, both morale and performance will tend to be low and organizational accomplishment will be negligible. In some cases, the organizational goals can be so opposed that no positive progress is obtained.

FIGURE 5-6 Little organizational
accomplishment

The result often is substantial losses, or draining off of assets (see Figure 5-7). In
fact, organizations are going out of business every day for these very reasons.

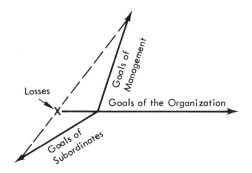

FIGURE 5-7 No positive organizational
accomplishment

The hope in an organization is to create a climate in which one of two things
occurs. The individuals in the organization (both managers and subordinates)
either perceive their goals as being the same as the goals of the organization or,
although different, see their own goals being satisfied as a direct result of working
for the goals of the organization. Consequently, the closer we can get the individual's goals and objectives to the organization's goals, the greater will be the
organizational performance, as illustrated in Figure 5-8.

FIGURE 5-8 An integration of the goals
of management, subordi-
nates, and the organiza-
tion—*high* organizational
accomplishment

One of the ways in which effective leaders bridge the gap between the individual's and the organization's goals is by creating a loyalty to themselves among their followers. They do this by being an influential spokesperson for followers with higher management.[15] These leaders have no difficulty in communicating organizational goals to followers and these people do not find it difficult to associate the acceptance of these goals with accomplishment of their own need satisfaction.

PARTICIPATION AND EFFECTIVENESS

In an organizational setting, it is urged that the criteria for an individual or a group's performance should be mutually decided in advance. In making these decisions, managers and their subordinates should consider output and intervening variables, short- and long-range goals. This process has two advantages. First, it will permit subordinates to participate in determining the basis on which their efforts will be judged. Second, involving subordinates in the planning process will increase their commitment to the goals and objectives established. Research evidence seems to support this contention.

One of the classic studies in this area was done by Coch and French in an American factory.[16] They found that when managers and employees discussed proposed technological changes, productivity increased and resistance to change decreased once these procedures were initiated. Other studies have shown similar results.[17] These studies suggest that involving employees in decision making tends to be effective in our society. Once again, we must remember that the success of using participative management depends on the situation. Although this approach tends to be effective in some industrial settings in America, it may not be appropriate in other countries.

This argument was illustrated clearly when French, Israel, and As attempted to replicate the original Coch and French experiment in a Norwegian factory.[18] In this setting, they found no significant difference in productivity between work groups in which participative management was used and those in which it was *not* used. In other words, increased participation in decision making did not have the same positive influence on factory workers in Norway as it did in America. Similar to Hersey's replication of one of Likert's studies in Nigeria, this Norwegian study suggests that cultural differences in the followers and the situation may be important in determining the appropriate leadership style.

Management by Objectives

We realize that it is not an easy task to integrate the goals and objectives of all individuals with the goals of the organization. Yet it is not an impossible task. A participative approach to this problem, which has been used successfully in some organizations in our culture, is a process called *Management by Objectives* (MBO). The concepts behind MBO were introduced by Peter Drucker[19] in the early 1950s and have become popularized throughout the world, particularly through the efforts of George Odiorne[20] and John Humble.[21] Through their work and the efforts of others,[22] managers in all kinds of organizational settings, whether they be industrial, educational, governmental, or military, are attempting to run their organizations with the MBO process as a basic underlying management concept.

Management by objectives is basically:

> A process whereby the superior and the subordinate managers of an enterprise jointly identify its common goals, define each individual's major areas of responsibility in terms of the results expected of him, and use these measures as guides for operating the unit and assessing the contribution of each of its members.[23]

This process in some cases has been successfully carried beyond the managerial level to include hourly employees. A number of companies, including Non-Linear Systems and Union Carbide, have had significant success in broadening individual responsibility and involvement in work planning at the lowest organizational levels.[24] The concept rests on a philosophy of management that emphasizes an integration between external control (by managers) and self-control (by subordinates). It can apply to any manager or individual no matter what level or function, and to any organization, regardless of size.

The smooth functioning of this system is an agreement between a manager and subordinate about that subordinate's own or group performance goals during a stated time period. These goals can emphasize either output variables or intervening variables, or some combination of both. The important thing is that goals are jointly established and agreed upon in advance. This is then followed by a review of the subordinate's performance in relation to accepted goals at the end of the time period. Both superior and subordinate participate in this review and in any other evaluation that takes place. It has been found that objectives that are formulated with each person participating seem to gain more acceptance than those imposed by an authority figure in the organization. Consultation and participation in this area tend to establish personal risk for the attainment of the formulated objective by those who actually perform the task.

Prior to setting individual objectives, the common goals of the entire organization should be clarified, and, at this time, any appropriate changes in the organizational structure should be made: changes in titles, duties, relationships, authority, responsibility, span of control, and so forth.

Throughout the time period what is to be accomplished by the entire organization should be compared with what is being accomplished; necessary adjustments should be made and inappropriate goals discarded. At the end of the time period a final mutual review of objectives and performance takes place. If there is a discrepancy between the two, efforts are initiated to determine what steps can be taken to overcome these problems. This sets the stage for the determination of objectives for the next time period.

The entire cycle of management by objectives is represented graphically in Figure 5-9.[25]

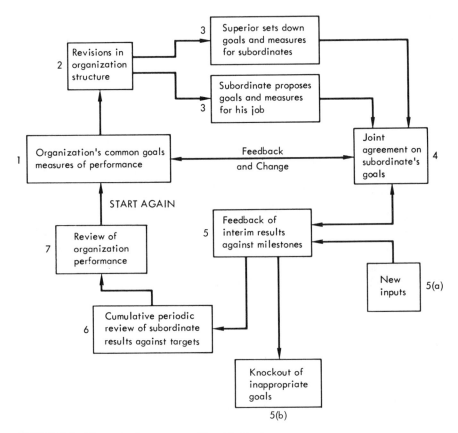

FIGURE 5-9 The cycle of management by objectives

Management by objectives may become a powerful tool in gaining mutual commitment and high productivity for an organization in which management realizes this type of involvement of subordinates is appropriate in its situation.

STYLE AND EFFECTIVENESS

Examples of research that support the argument that all the basic leader behavior styles may be effective or ineffective depending on the situation are readily available.

A. K. Korman gathered some of the most convincing evidence that dispels the idea of a single best style of leader behavior.[26] Korman attempted to review all studies that examined the relationships between the Ohio State behavior dimensions of Initiating Structure (task) and Consideration (relationship) and various measures of effectiveness, including group productivity, salary, performance under stress, administrative reputation, work group grievances, absenteeism, and turnover. In all, over twenty-five studies were reviewed. In every case the

..ง dimensions were measured by either the Leadership Opinion Questionnaire or the Leader Behavior Description Questionnaire. The former is used to assess how leaders think they should behave in a given situation; the latter measures follower perceptions of leader behavior. Korman concluded that:

> Despite the fact that "Consideration" and "Initiating Structure" have become almost bywords in American industrial psychology, it seems apparent that very little is now known as to how these variables may predict work group performance and the conditions which affect such predictions. At the current time, we cannot even say whether they have any predictive significance at all.[27]

Thus, Korman found that Consideration and Initiating Structure had no significant predictive value in terms of effectiveness. This suggests that since situations differ, so must leader style.

Fred Fiedler, in testing his contingency model of leadership in over fifty studies covering a span of sixteen years (1951–67), concluded that both directive, task-oriented leaders and nondirective, human relations-oriented leaders are successful under some conditions. As Fiedler argues:

> While one can never say that something is impossible, and while someone may well discover the all-purpose leadership style or behavior at some future time, our own data and those which have come out of sound research by other investigators do not promise such miraculous cures.[28]

A number of other investigators besides Korman and Fiedler have also shown that *different leadership situations require different leader styles.*[29] In summary, the evidence is clear that there is no single, all-purpose leader behavior style that is effective in all situations.

While our basic conclusion in this chapter is that the type of leader behavior needed depends on the situation, this conclusion leaves many questions unanswered for a specific individual in a leadership role. Such individuals may be personally interested in how leadership depends on the situation and how they can find some practical value in theory. To accommodate this type of concern, in Chapter 6 we will discuss the environmental variables that may help a leader or a manager to make effective decisions in problematic leadership situations.

NOTES

[1] C. Northcote Parkinson, *Parkinson's Law* (Boston: Houghton Mifflin, 1957).

[2] Fred J. Carvell, *Human Relations in Business* (Toronto: The MacMillan Company, 1970), p. 182.

[3] Amitai Etzioni, *A Comparative Analysis of Complex Organizations* (New York: The Free Press, 1961).

[4] Niccolo Machiavelli, "Of Cruelty and Clemency, Whether It Is Better to Be Loved or Feared," *The Prince and the Discourses* (New York: Random House, Inc., 1950), Chap. XVII.

[5] Suggested by Bernard M. Bass in *Leadership, Psychology, and Organizational Behavior* (New York: Harper & Brothers, 1960).

[6] Rensis Likert, *The Human Organization* (New York: McGraw-Hill Book Company, 1967), pp. 26–29.

[7] Rensis Likert, *New Patterns of Management* (New York: McGraw-Hill Book Company, 1961), p. 2.

[8] Fred E. Fiedler, *A Theory of Leadership Effectiveness* (New York: McGraw-Hill Book Company, 1967), p. 9.

[9] William J. Reddin, "The 3-D Management Style Theory," *Training and Development Journal,* April 1967. This is one of the critical differences between Reddin's 3-D Management Style Theory and the Tri-Dimensional Leader Effectiveness Model. Reddin in his model seems to consider only output variables in determining effectiveness, while in the Tri-Dimensional Leader Effectiveness Model both intervening variables and output variables are considered.

[10] Adapted from Likert, *The Human Organization,* pp. 47–77.

[11] *Ibid.,* p. 77.

[12] Kurt Lewin, "Frontiers in Group Dynamics: Concept, Method, and Reality in Social Science; Social Equilibria and Social Change," *Human Relations,* I, No. 1 (June 1947), pp. 5–41.

[13] Douglas McGregor, *The Human Side of Enterprise* (New York: McGraw-Hill Book Company, 1960). See also McGregor, *Leadership and Motivation* (Boston: MIT Press, 1966).

[14] In reality, the schematics presented in the following pages are simplifications of vector analyses and therefore would be more accurately portrayed as parallelograms.

[15] Saul W. Gellerman, *Motivation and Productivity* (New York: American Management Association, 1963), p. 265. See also Gellerman, *Management by Motivation* (New York: American Management Association, 1968).

[16] L. Coch and J. R. P. French, "Overcoming Resistance to Change," in Dorwin Cartwright and Alvin Zander, eds., *Group Dynamics: Research and Theory,* 2nd ed. (Evanston, Ill.: Row, Peterson & Company, 1960).

[17] See Kurt Lewin, "Group Decision and Social Change," in G. Swanson, T. Newcomb, and E. Hartley, eds., *Readings in Social Psychology* (New York: Henry Holt, 1952), pp. 459–73; K. Lewin, R. Lippitt, and R. White, "Leader Behavior and Member Reaction in Three 'Social Climates,' " in Cartwright and Zander, *Group Dynamics: Research and Theory*; and N. Morse and E. Reimer, "The Experimental Change of a Major Organizational Variable," *Journal of Abnormal Social Psychology,* 52 (1956), pp. 120–29.

[18] John R. P. French, Jr., Joachim Israel, and Dagfinn Ås, "An Experiment on Participation in a Norwegian Factory," *Human Relations,* 13 (1960), pp. 3–19.

[19] Peter F. Drucker, *The Practice of Management* (New York: Harper and Row, 1964).

[20] George S. Odiorne, *Management by Objectives: A System of Managerial Leadership* (New York: Pitman Publishing Corp., 1965).

[21] John W. Humble, *Management by Objectives* (London: Industrial Education and Research Foundation, 1967).

[22] See also J. D. Batten, *Beyond Management by Objectives* (New York: American Management Association, 1966); Ernest C. Miller, *Objectives and Standards Approach to Planning and Control,* AMA Research Study '74 (New York: American Management Association, 1966); and William J. Reddin, *Effective Management by Objectives: The 3-D Method of MBO* (New York: McGraw-Hill Book Company, 1971).

[23] Odiorne, *Management by Objectives.*

[24] Chris Argyris, *Integrating the Individual and the Organization* (New York: John Wiley & Sons, Inc., 1964); Abraham Maslow, *Eupsychian Management* (Homewood, Ill.: Richard D. Irwin, Inc., and Dorsey Press, 1965).

[25] Odiorne, *Management by Objectives*, p. 78.

[26] A. K. Korman, " 'Consideration,' 'Initiating Structure,' and Organizational Criteria—A Review," *Personnel Psychology: A Journal of Applied Research*, XIX, No. 4 (Winter 1966), pp. 349–61.

[27] *Ibid.*, p. 360.

[28] Fiedler, *A Theory of Leadership Effectiveness*, p. 247.

[29] See C. A. Gibb, "Leadership," in *Handbook of Social Psychology*, Gardner Lindzey, ed. (Cambridge, Mass.: Addison-Wesley Publishing Company, Inc., 1964); A. P. Hare, *Handbook of Small Group Research* (New York: John Wiley & Sons, Inc., 1965); and D. C. Pelz, "Leadership within a Hierarchial Organization," *Journal of Social Issues*, 7 (1961), pp. 49–55.

chapter 6

Diagnosing
the Environment

The Tri-Dimensional Leader Effectiveness Model is built on the concept that effectiveness results from a leader using a behavioral style that is appropriate to the demands of the environment. The key for managers or leaders is learning to diagnose their environment.

ENVIRONMENTAL VARIABLES

The environment in an organization consists of the leader, that leader's follower(s), superior(s), associates, organization, and job demands.[1] This list is not all-inclusive, but it contains some of the interacting components that tend to be important to a leader.[2] As illustrated in Figure 6-1, the environment a leader faces may have some other situational variables that are unique to it as well as an external environment that has an impact on it.

Except for job demands, each of these environmental variables can be viewed as having two major components—style and expectations. Thus, our list of variables is expanded to include the following:

Leader's style	Leader's expectations
Followers' styles	Followers' expectations
Superiors' styles	Superiors' expectations
Associates' styles	Associates' expectations
Organization's style	Organization's expectations

Job demands

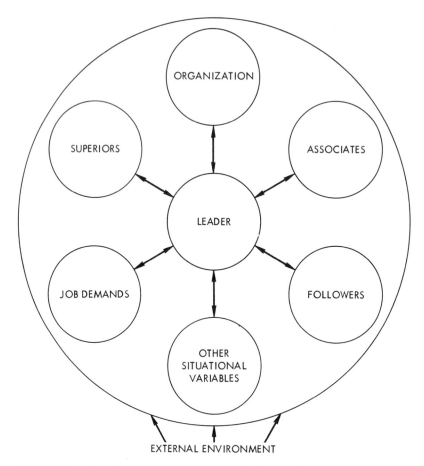

FIGURE 6-1   Interacting components of an organizational setting

Style Defined

As discussed in Chapter 4, the style of leaders is the consistent behavior patterns that they use when they are working with and through other people as perceived by those people. These patterns emerge in people as they begin to respond in the same fashion under similar conditions; they develop habits of action that become somewhat predictable to those who work with them.

Some writers, including the authors of this text, have used style and personality interchangeably. In Chapter 9 we will distinguish between these two terms.

Expectations Defined

Expectations are the perceptions of appropriate behavior for one's own role or position or one's perceptions of the roles of others within the organization. In other words, the expectations of individuals define for them what they should do under various circumstances in their particular job and how they think others—their superiors, peers, and subordinates—should behave in relation to their positions. To say that a person has *shared expectations* with another person means that each of the individuals involved perceives accurately and accepts his or her own role and the role of the other. If expectations are to be compatible, it is important to share common goals and objectives. While two individuals may have differing personalities because their roles require different styles of behavior, it is imperative for an organization's effectiveness that they perceive and accept the institution's goals and objectives as their own.

The task of diagnosing a leader environment is very complex when we realize that the leader is the pivotal point around which all of the other environmental variables interact, as shown in Figure 6-1. In a sense, all these variables are communicating role expectations to the leader.

STYLE AND EXPECTATIONS

Behavior of managers in an organization, as Jacob W. Getzels suggests, results from the interaction of style and expectations.[3] Some managerial positions or roles are structured greatly by expectations; that is, they allow people occupying that position very little room to express their individual style. The behavior of an army sergeant, for example, may be said to conform almost completely to role expectations. Little innovative behavior is tolerated. In supervising highly structured, routine jobs based on Theory X assumptions about human nature, the behavior required by a manager is almost predetermined, that is, close supervision, "firm but fair," and so on.

On the other hand, some managerial positions have fewer formal expectations, allowing for more individual latitude in expressing one's style of operating. The behavior of a research and development manager, for example, is derived extensively from that person's style, as innovation and creativity are encouraged. It seems that as a manager moves from supervising a structured job to working with people on a more structured job, style tends to play a more important role than expectations.

The difference between these two positions in terms of style and expectations is illustrated in Figure 6-2.[4]

While the mix varies from job to job, behavior in an organization remains a function of both style and expectations and involves some combination of task and relationship orientation.

Leader's Style and Expectations

One of the most important elements of a leadership situation is the style of the leader(s). Leaders develop their style over a period of time from experience, education, and training. Tannenbaum and Schmidt suggest there are at least four internal forces that influence a manager's leadership style: the manager's value

managers leadership style

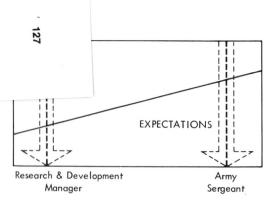

EXPECTATIONS

Research & Development
Manager

Army
Sergeant

FIGURE 6-2 Style and expectations as related to two different positions or roles

system, confidence in subordinates, leadership inclinations, and feelings of security in an uncertain situation.[5]

A manager's value system consists of the answers to such questions as how strongly does a manager feel that individuals should have a share in making the decisions that affect them or how convinced is the manager that the person who is paid to assume responsibility should personally carry the burden of decision making? The strength of a manager's convictions on questions like these will tend to affect that manager's leadership style, particularly in terms of the amount of direction or support that manager is willing to provide for staff members.

Confidence in subordinates is often influenced by the manager's Theory X or Theory Y assumptions about human nature. In other words, the amount of control or freedom a manager gives to staff members depends on whether that manager believes that people are basically lazy, unreliable, or irresponsible or that people can be creative and self-motivated in an environment if properly motivated. In addition, a manager's confidence in subordinates also depends on feelings about the knowledge and competence of staff members in a particular area of responsibility.

A manager's own inclinations have an impact on leadership style; thus, some managers are much more comfortable being directive (controlling and supervising). Other managers operate more comfortably in a team management situation in which they are providing some direction and/or facilitating the interactions of subordinates. Still other managers are at ease in delegating and letting staff members run with the ball on specific problems and issues.

Feelings of security in an uncertain situation have a definite impact on the manager's willingness to release control over decision making to other people in an uncertain environment. What might be involved here is the manager's tolerance for ambiguity. Another factor that might be influenced is the leader's life position in terms of his feelings of OKness about himself, as well as OKness about others in the environment.

While it is important to recognize that managers have different leadership styles, it is important to remember that style is not how leaders *think* they behave in a situation but how others (most importantly, their followers) perceive their behavior. This is often a difficult concept for leaders to understand. For example, if a leader's followers think that she is a hard-nosed, task-oriented leader, this is very valuable information for her to know. In fact, it makes little difference whether *she* thinks she is a relationship-oriented, democratic leader, because her followers will behave according to how *they* perceive her behavior. In this case, the followers will treat the leader as if she were a hard-nosed, task-oriented leader. Thus, leaders have to learn how they are coming across to others. Yet this kind of information is difficult to obtain. People are often reluctant to be honest with one another on this subject, especially in a superior-subordinate relationship.

One method that has been developed to help individuals learn how others perceive their behavior is sensitivity or T-group training. This method was developed at Bethel, Maine, in 1947, by Leland P. Bradford, Kenneth D. Benne and others.[6] It is based on the assumption that a number of individuals meeting in an unstructured situation in an open climate will develop working relations with each other and will learn a great deal about themselves as perceived by the other group members.

> The training process relies primarily and almost exclusively on the behavior experienced by the participants; i.e., the *group itself* becomes the focus of inquiry . . . In short, the participants learn to analyze and become more sensitive to the processes of human interaction and acquire concepts to order and control these phenomena.[7]

An example follows of one of Chris Argyris's experiences with a T-group in which the president and nine vice-presidents of a large industrial organization went into a retreat for a week to discuss their problems.

> At the outset, after defining the objectives of this educational experience, the seminar leader said, in effect, "Okay. Let's go." There was a very loud silence and someone said, "What do you want us to do?"
>
> (Silence.)
>
> "Where's the agenda?"
>
> (Silence.)
>
> "Look, here, what's going on? Aren't you going to lead this?"
>
> (Silence.)
>
> "I didn't come up here to feel my stomach move. What's up?"
>
> (Silence.)
>
> "Fellows, if he doesn't speak in five minutes, I'm getting out of here."
>
> "Gentlemen," said the treasurer, "We've paid for the day, so let's remain at least till five."
>
> "You know, there's something funny going on here."
>
> "What's funny about it?"
>
> "Well, up until a few minutes ago we trusted this man enough that all of us were willing to leave the company for a week. Now we dislike him. Why? He hasn't done anything."

"That's right. And it's his job to do something. He's the leader and he ought d."

"But I'm learning something already about how we react under these conditions. I honestly feel uncomfortable and somewhat fearful. Does anybody else?"

"That's interesting that you mention fear, because I think that we run the company by fear."

The president turned slightly red and became annoyed: "I don't think that we run this company by fear and I don't think you should have said that."

A loud silence followed. The vice-president thought for a moment, took a breath, looked the president straight in the eye and said, "I still think we run this company by fear and I agree with you. I should not have said it."

The group laughed and the tension was broken.

"I'm sorry," the president said. "I wanted all you fellows with me here so that we can try to develop a higher sense of openness and trust. The first one that really levels with us, I let him have it. I'm sorry—but it isn't easy to hear about management by fear . . ."

"And it's not easy to tell you."

"Why not? Haven't I told you that my door is open?"

And the group plunged into the issue of how they judge the openness of a person—by the way he speaks or by the way he behaves?[8]

Argyris reported that:

The group explored their views about each other—the way each individual tended unintentionally to inhibit the other (the vice-presidents learned that they inhibited each other as much as the president did but for years had felt it was his fault); their levels of aspiration, their goals in their company life and in their total life; their ways of getting around each other, ranging from not being honest with one another to creating organizational fires which had to be put out by someone else; their skill at polarizing issues when deep disagreements occurred so that the decisions could be bucked right up to the president, who would have to take the responsibility and the blame; their techniques in the game of one-upmanship . . .[9]

The result was highly satisfying. Once these top executives returned home, they found that they could reduce the number of meetings, the time spent at meetings, the defensive politicking and the windmilling at the lower levels. In time they also found that they could truly delegate more responsibility, get more valid information up from the ranks and make decisions more freely.

Although the main objective of T-group training was originally personal growth or self-insight, the process is now being used extensively to implement organization improvement or change.[10] It should be remembered, however, that this approach is still relatively new and is still being developed. It has some critics as well as advocates among organizations that have experimented with these techniques.

A central problem according to some is that sensitivity training is designed to change individuals, not necessarily to change the environment they work in.

When individuals attempt to use what they have learned, they often find their coworkers unwilling to accept it or, even worse, what they have learned may not be appropriate for their back home situation. In an article from *The Wall Street Journal* entitled "The Truth Hurts," an example was cited in which this very thing happened:

> A division manager at one big company was described by a source familiar with his case as "a ferocious guy—brilliant but a thoroughgoing autocrat—who everyone agreed was just what the division needed, because it was a tough, competitive business." Deciding to smooth over his rough edges, the company sent him to sensitivity training, where he found out exactly what people thought of him. "So he stopped being a beast," says the source, "and his effectiveness fell apart." The reason he'd been so good was that he didn't realize what a beast he was. Eventually, they put in a new manager.

All leaders have expectations about the way they should behave in a certain situation. How they actually behave often depends on these expectations. The resulting behavior, however, is sometimes modified by the impact of how they interpret the expectations of other persons in their environment, such as their boss or subordinates.

Followers' Styles and Expectations

The styles of followers (subordinates) are an important consideration for leaders in appraising their situation. In fact, as Fillmore Sanford has indicated, there is some justification for regarding the followers "as the most crucial factor in any leadership event."[11] Followers in any situation are vital, not only because individually they accept or reject the leader but because as a group they actually determine whatever personal power that leader will have.

This element is important at all levels of management. Victor H. Vroom has uncovered evidence that the effectiveness of a leader is dependent to a great extent on the style of the individual workers.[12]

> Place a group with strong independence drives under a supervisor who needs to keep his men under his thumb, and the result is very likely to be trouble. Similarly, if you take docile men who are accustomed to obedience and respect for their supervisors and place them under a supervisor who tries to make them manage their own work, they are likely to wonder uneasily whether he really knows what he is doing.[13]

It has been argued that a manager can permit subordinates greater freedom if the following essential conditions exist:[14]

- If the subordinates have relatively high needs for independence.
- If the subordinates have a readiness to assume responsibility for decision making.
- If they have a relatively high tolerance for ambiguity.
- If they are interested in the problem and feel it is important.

- If they understand and identify with the goals of the organization.
- If they have the necessary knowledge and experience to deal with the problem.
- If they have learned to expect to share in decision making.

Therefore, even though managers would prefer to change their followers' styles, they may find that they must adapt, at least temporarily, to the followers' present behavior. For example, a supervisor who wants her subordinates to take more responsibility and to operate under general rather than close supervision cannot expect this kind of change to take place overnight. Her current behavior, at least to some extent, must be compatible with the present expectations of the group, with planned change taking place over a long-term period. We have seen numerous examples of the need for this kind of diagnosis in schools where humanistic teachers have tried to turn over significant responsibility to students without recognizing that many of these students expect teachers to tell them what to do. This rapid change in style often produces irresponsibility rather than more student initiative.

Leaders should know the expectations that followers have about the way they should behave in certain situations. This is especially important if leaders are new in their position. Their predecessor's leader behavior style is then a powerful influence. If this style is different from the one they plan to use, this may create an immediate problem.[15] Leaders must either change their style to coincide with followers' expectations or change follower expectations. Since the style of leaders often has been developed over a long period of time, it can be difficult for them to make any drastic changes in the short run. It may, therefore, be more effective if leaders concentrate on changing the expectations of their followers. In other words, in some cases they may be able to convince their followers that their style, although not what they as followers would normally expect, if accepted, will be adequate.

Superiors' Styles and Expectations

Another element of the environment is the leadership style of one's boss. Just about everyone has a boss of one kind or another. Most managers give considerable attention to supervising subordinates, but some do not pay enough attention to being a subordinate themselves. Yet meeting the superior's expectations is often an important factor affecting one's style, particularly if one's boss is located in close proximity. If a boss is very task-oriented, for example, she might expect her subordinate(s) to operate in the same manner. Relationship-oriented behavior might be evaluated as inappropriate, without even considering results. This has become evident when first-line supervisors are sent to training programs to improve their human relations skills. Upon returning to the company, they try to implement some of these new ideas in working with their people. Yet, because the superior has not accepted these concepts, he or she becomes impatient with the first-line supervisor's newfound concern for people:

"Joe, cut out all that talking with the men and get the work done." With such reactions, it would not take this supervisor long to revert to his old style, and in the future, it will be much more difficult to implement any change in his behavior.

It is important for managers to know their boss' expectations, particularly if they want to advance in the organization. If they are predisposed toward promotion, they may tend to adhere to the customs and mores (styles and expectations) of the group to which they aspire to join rather than those of their peer group.[16] Consequently, their superiors' expectations have become more important to them than those of the other groups with which they interact—their followers or associates.

The importance of the expectations of one's boss and the effect it can have on leadership style was vividly illustrated by Robert H. Guest in a case analysis of organizational change.[17] He examined a large assembly plant of an automobile company, Plant Y, and contrasted the situation under two different leaders.

Under Stewart, the plant manager, working relationships at Plant Y were dominated by hostility and mistrust. His high task style was characterized by continual attempts to increase the driving forces pushing for productivity. As a result, the prevailing atmosphere was that of one emergency following on the heels of another, and the governing motivation for employee activity was fear— fear of being chewed out right on the assembly line, fear of being held responsible for happenings in which one had no clear authority, fear of losing one's job. Consequently, of the six plants in this division of the corporation, Plant Y had the poorest performance record, and it was getting worse.

Stewart was replaced by Cooley, who seemed like an extremely effective leader. Over the next three years dramatic changes took place. In various cost and performance measures used to rate the six plants, Plant Y was now truly the leader; and the atmosphere of interpersonal cooperation and personal satisfaction had improved impressively over the situation under Stewart. These changes, moreover, were effected through an insignificant number of dismissals and reassignments. Using a much higher relationships style, Cooley succeeded in turning Plant Y around.

On the surface, the big difference was style of leadership. Cooley was a good leader. Stewart was not. But Guest points out clearly in his analysis that leadership style was only one of two important factors. "The other was that while Stewart received daily orders from division headquarters to correct specific situations, Cooley was left alone. Cooley was allowed to lead; Stewart was told how to lead."[18] In other words, when productivity in Plant Y began to decline during changeover from wartime to peacetime operations, Stewart's superiors expected him to get productivity back on the upswing by taking control of the reins, and they put tremendous pressure on him to do just that. Guest suggests that these expectations forced Stewart to operate in a very crisis-oriented, autocratic way. However, when Cooley was given charge as plant manager, a hands-off policy was initiated by his superiors. The fact that the expectations of top management had changed enough to put a moratorium on random, troublesome outside stimuli from headquarters gave Cooley an opportunity to operate in a completely different style.

Associates' Styles and Expectations

A leader's associates or peers are those individuals who have similar positions within the organization. For example, the associates of a vice-president for production are the other vice-presidents in the company; the associates of a teacher would be other teachers. Yet not all associates are significant for leaders; only those they interact with regularly are going to have impact on their style and effectiveness.

The styles and expectations of one's associates are important when a leader has frequent interaction with them, for example, a situation that involves trading and bargaining for resources, such as budget money.[19]

In discussing superiors, we mentioned the manager who has a strong drive to advance in an organization. Some people, however, are satisfied with their present positions. For these people, the expectations of their associates may be more important in influencing their behavior than those of their superiors. College professors tend to be good examples. Often they are more concerned about their peer group, other professors, or colleagues in their area of expertise than they are in being promoted to administrative positions. As a result, college presidents and deans often have little position power with professors.

Organization's Style and Expectations

The style and expectations of an organization are determined by the history and tradition of the organization as well as by the organizational goals and objectives that reflect the style and expectations of present top management.

Over a period of time, an organization, much like an individual, becomes characterized by certain modes of behavior that are perceived as its style. The development of an organizational style, or corporate image, has been referred to as the process of institutionalization.[20] In this process, the organization is infused with a system of values that reflects its history and the people who have played vital roles in its formation and growth. Thus, it is difficult to understand Ford Motor Company without knowing the impact that Henry Ford had on its formation. Some organizations, for example, hold to the notion that the desirable executive is one who is dynamic, imaginative, decisive, and persuasive. Other organizations put more emphasis on the importance of the executive's ability to work effectively with people—his human relation skills.[21]

Members of the organization soon become conscious of the value system operating within the institution and guide their actions from many expectations derived from these values. The organization's expectations are most often expressed in forms of policy, operating procedures, and controls, as well as in informal customs and mores developed over time.

Organizational Goals. The goals of an organization usually consist of some combination of output and intervening variables. As we discussed earlier, output variables are those short-run goals that can easily be measured, such as net profits, annual earnings, and won-lost record. On the other hand, intervening variables consist of those long-run goals reflecting the internal condition of the organization that *cannot* easily be measured, such as its capacity for effective interaction, communication, and decision making. These organizational goals can be expressed in terms of task and relationship, as illustrated in Figure 6-3.

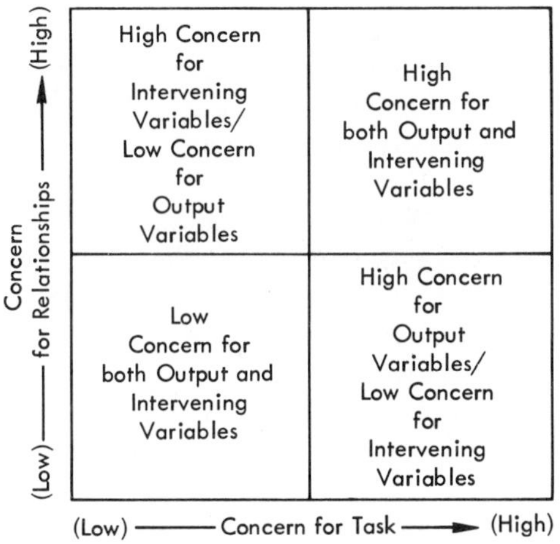

(High)	High Concern for Intervening Variables/ Low Concern for Output Variables	High Concern for both Output and Intervening Variables
Concern for Relationships (Low)	Low Concern for both Output and Intervening Variables	High Concern for Output Variables/ Low Concern for Intervening Variables
	(Low) — Concern for Task ——▶ (High)	

FIGURE 6-3 Organizational goals as expressed in terms of task and relationship

OTHER SITUATIONAL VARIABLES

Job Demands

Another important element of a leadership situation is the demands of the job that the leader's group has been assigned to perform. Fiedler[22] called this situation variable *task structure*—the degree of structure in the task that the group has been asked to do. He found that a task that has specific instructions on what leaders and their followers should do requires a different leadership style than an unstructured task with no prescribed operating procedures. Research findings indicate that highly structured jobs that need directions seem to require high task behavior, while *unstructured* jobs that do not need directions seem to favor relationship-oriented behavior.

Robert J. House,[23] in his Path-Goal Theory of Leadership, suggests a different relationship between leadership style and task structure. He proposes that if followers are performing highly structured tasks, the most effective leader behavior style is one that is high on supportive (relationship) behavior and low on instrumental (task) behavior. This proposition is based on the assumption that highly structured tasks are inherently less satisfying and a source of frustration and stress for followers. Leader relationship behavior should help reduce the frustration and mitigate the dissatisfying nature of highly structured tasks. Further, it is assumed that if followers' tasks are highly structured, the required activities are clear to followers, and leader task behavior (providing direction and instruction) is less important.

If followers are performing relatively unstructured tasks, the Path-Goal Theory proposes that a leadership style high on task behavior and low on relationship behavior will be most effective. It is assumed that required activities and performance expectations are unclear and leader task behavior is needed to provide direction and role structuring. Unstructured tasks, however, are assumed to be more challenging, more intrinsically satisfying, and less frustrating and stressful. Under these conditions, leader relationship behavior is less important.

Research by John E. Stinson and Thomas W. Johnson[24] has suggested that the relationship between leader behavior and task structure is somewhat more complex than was proposed by House. Stinson and Johnson found that although leader relationship behavior is more important if followers are performing highly structured tasks, the amount of task behavior the leader should use depends on the nature of the followers as well as the type of task the followers are performing.

Specifically, they propose that high leader task behavior is most effective if:

1. Followers' tasks are highly structured *and* followers have strong needs for achievement and independence and a high level of education and/or experience (that is, followers are overqualified for the job).
2. Followers' tasks are unstructured *and* followers have weak needs for achievement and independence and a low level of task relevant education and/or experience (that is, followers are underqualified for the job).

Low task behavior by the leader is most effective if:

1. Followers' tasks are highly structured *and* followers share weak needs for achievement and independence but an adequate level of task relevant education and/or experience.
2. Followers' tasks are unstructured *and* followers have strong needs for achievement and independence and a high level of education and/or experience.

Figure 6-4 shows the high probability leader behavior style for different combinations of task structure and follower capacity. Follower capacity refers to the degree of achievement motivation, need for independence, and task relevant education and experience.

As Figure 6-4 suggests, a high task/low relationship tends to be an effective leadership style if a manager is supervising an unstructured task being performed by followers with low capacity; high task/high relationship style seems to be

TASK STRUCTURE		
	Low	High
Follower Capacity — High	Low Relationship Low Task	High Task High Relationship
Follower Capacity — Low	High Task Low Relationship	High Relationship Low Task

FIGURE 6-4 The relationship between leadership style and different combinations of task structure and follower capacity

appropriate for high capacity followers performing a structured task; high relationship/low task behavior tends to be effective with low capacity followers performing a highly structured task; and finally, low relationship/low task behavior seems appropriate for high capacity followers performing an unstructured task.

The *amount of interaction* the job requires of subordinates is an important consideration for managers in analyzing their work environment. Victor H. Vroom and Floyd C. Mann studied this aspect of a job in a large trucking company.[25] They investigated two groups of workers. One group was involved in the package and handling operation and the other consisted of truck drivers and their dispatchers. The nature of the work in the package and handling operation required that the men work closely together in small groups. Cooperation and teamwork were required not only among the workers but also between the workers and their superiors. In this situation, the workers preferred and worked better under employee-centered supervisors. The truck drivers, on the other hand, usually worked alone, having little contact with other people. These men did not depend on others for accomplishing their task, except for the dispatchers from whom they needed accurate information. Since the truck drivers generally worked alone, they were not concerned about harmony but were concerned about the structure of the job in terms of where and when they were to deliver or pick up. In this situation, they preferred task-oriented supervisors.

Another important aspect of job demands that managers should consider is the type of control system being used. In our work, we have identified three types of control systems, as shown in Figure 6-5.

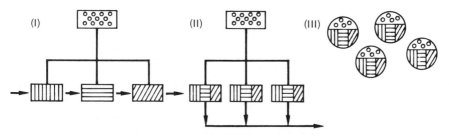

FIGURE 6-5 Three fundamental types of control systems

137

As illustrated, Type I shows the simplest and most structured of the control systems. The boss controls the activities of three separate functions and the horizontal arrows show the work moving in an assembly-line fashion to completion.

Type II depicts an organization in which work has been "enlarged." The boss still controls the activities of three people, but now all three functions are combined in each job and the three employees see end-product result (vertical arrows).

Type III is the least structured organization model ("enriched"), with each employee having the advantage of Type II plus decision-making responsibility, reserved only for the boss in Types I and II.

In an example of producing booklets, under a Type I control system employee A is responsible for typing, B for mimeographing, and C for proofreading. The boss is responsible for coordination, end result, and customer relations.

In Type II, job enlargement takes place, and the boss is now responsible for directing the activities of three people who type, mimeograph, and proofread their own work. Here, some motivational or job satisfaction considerations come into play. The boss gets satisfaction by relating directly to the customer (or persons needing booklets). The employees' satisfaction comes closer to being served in Type II since they can now see a new dimension of their work, and psychologically they come closer to understanding the customer.

In Type III, all four members of the group act as separate decision-making and functional units, having advantage reserved for only the manager in Types I and II, that of direct contact with the customer and control of work.

Time

Another important element in the environment of a leader is the *time available for decision making.* If a manager's office burst into flames, he could not seek opinions and suggestions from his followers or use other methods of involvement to determine the best way to leave the building. The leader must make an immediate decision and point the way. Therefore, short-time demands, such as in an emergency, tend to require task-oriented behavior. On the other hand, if time is not a major factor in the situation, there is more opportunity for the leader to select from a broader range of leadership style, depending on the other situational variables.

One could probably enumerate many more variables. For example, even the physical stature of a leader can affect the kind of style that leader can use. Take the example of the foreman in the steel mill who is six feet six inches tall and weighs over two hundred fifty pounds. He may be able to use a different style than a foreman five feet four inches tall weighing ninety-eight pounds, since their subordinates' expectations about their behavior will probably be influenced by their physical appearance. Sex may be similar. For example, some men may respond and interact very differently with a female boss, associate, or subordinate than a male, and vice versa. This undoubtedly is influenced by the amount of past experience one has in working with members of the opposite sex. But it certainly may be a situational variable worth examining in a leadership environment.

The kinds of environmental variables we have been discussing tend to be important whether one is concerned about an educational, a business, or an informal organization. But specific organizations may have additional variables that are unique to themselves that must be evaluated before determining effectiveness.

External Environment

Years ago managers didn't worry much about the external environment because it didn't seem to affect them or their decisions. Today this is no longer true. Organizations are continually influenced by external variables. Reality dictates that organizations do not exist in a vacuum but are continually affected in numerous ways by changes in the society.

In the last several decades we have been bombarded by numerous movements that have challenged many of our society's core beliefs and practices. Consider the implications for organizations of such recent social developments as the youth revolution and its distrust and contempt for the "establishment"; the Civil Rights Movement and the opening of wider opportunities in organizations for all minority groups; the ecology and consumer movements and their demands on organizations from the outside; and the increasing widespread concern for the quality of working life and its relationship to worker productivity, participation and satisfaction.[26]

> These and other societal changes make effective leadership in the future a more challenging task, requiring even greater sensitivity and flexibility than was ever needed before. Today's manager is more likely to deal with employees who resent being treated as subordinates, who may be highly critical of any organizational system, who expect to be consulted and to exert influence, and who often stand on the edge of alienation from the institution that needs their loyalty and commitment. In addition, he is frequently confronted by a highly turbulent, unpredictable environment.[27]

DEVELOPING STRATEGIES

Changing Style

One of the most difficult changes to make is a complete change in the style of a person, and yet industry invests many millions of dollars annually for training and development programs that concentrate on changing the style of its leaders. As Fiedler suggests:

> A person's leadership style reflects the individual's basic motivational and need structure. At best it takes one, two, or three years of intensive psychotherapy to effect lasting changes in personality structure. It is difficult to see how we can change in more than a few cases an equally important set of core values in a few

hours of lectures and role playing or even in the course of a more intensive training program of one or two weeks.[28]

Fiedler's point is well taken. It is indeed difficult to effect changes in the styles of managers overnight. While not completely hopeless, it is a slow and expensive process that requires creative planning and patience. In fact, Likert found that it takes from three to seven years, depending on the size and complexity of the organization, to implement a new management theory effectively.

> Haste is self-defeating because of the anxieties and stresses it creates. There is no substitute for ample time to enable the members of an organization to reach the level of skillful and easy, habitual use of the new leadership.[29]

What generally happens in present training and development programs is that managers are encouraged to adopt certain normative behavior styles. In our culture, these styles are usually high relationship/low task or high task/high relationship styles. Although we agree that there is a growing tendency for these two styles to be more effective than the high task/low relationship or low-relationship/low task styles, we recognize that this is not universally the case even in our own culture. In fact, it is often not the case even within a single work group. Most people might respond favorably to the high relationship styles, but a few might react in a negative manner, taking advantage of what they consider a soft touch. As a result, certain individuals will have to be handled in a different way. Perhaps they will respond only to the proverbial kick in the pants or close supervision (a high task/low relationship style). Thus, it is unrealistic to think that any of these styles can be successfully applied everywhere. In addition to considering application, it is questionable whether every leader can adapt to one normative style.

Most training and development programs do not recognize these two considerations. Consequently, a foreman who has been operating as a task-oriented, authoritarian leader for many years is encouraged to change his style—get in the step with the times. Upon returning from the training program, the foreman will probably try to utilize some of the new relationship-oriented techniques he has been taught. The problem is that the style he has used for a long time is not compatible with the new concepts. As long as things are running smoothly, he has no difficulty using them. However, the minute an important issue or a crisis develops, he tends to revert to his old basic style and becomes inconsistent, vacillating between the new relationship-oriented style he has just been taught and his old task-oriented style, which has the force of habit behind it. We have seen similar problems occur for some women who, when exposed to assertive training, have to try to reconcile these new learnings with the socioemotional role they have been conditioned to accept in male-dominated organizations.

This idea was supported in a study that the General Electric Company conducted at one of its turbine and generator plants.[30] In this study the leadership styles of about ninety foremen were analyzed and rated as "democratic," "authoritarian," or "mixed." In discussing the findings, Saul W. Gellerman reported that

> The lowest morale in the plant was found among those men whose foremen were rated *between* the democratic and authoritarian extremes. The GE research team felt that these foremen may have varied inconsistently in their tactics, permissive at one moment and hardfisted the next, in a way that left their men frustrated and unable to anticipate how they could be treated. The naturally autocratic supervisor who is exposed to human relations training may behave in exactly such a manner . . . a pattern which will probably make him even harder to work for than he was before being "enlightened."[31]

In summary, changing the style of managers is a difficult process, and one that takes considerable time. Expecting miracles overnight will only lead to frustration and uneasiness for both managers and their subordinates. Consequently, we recommend that change in overall management style in an organization should be planned and implemented on a long-term basis so that expectations can be realistic for all involved.

Changes in Expectations Versus Changes in Style

Using the feedback model discussed in Chapter 2, we can begin to explain why it is so difficult to make changes in leader style in a short period of time.

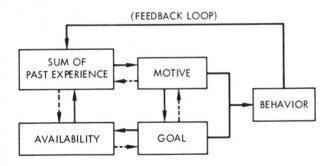

FIGURE 6-6 Feedback model

As discussed earlier, when a person behaves in a motivating situation, that behavior becomes a new input to the individual's inventory of past experience. The earlier in life that this input occurs, the greater its potential effect on future behavior. At that time, this behavior represents a larger portion of the individual's total past experience than the same behavior input will later in life. In addition, the longer a behavior is reinforced, the more patterned it becomes and the more difficult it is to change. That is why it is easier to make personality changes early in life. As a person gets older, more time and new experiences are necessary to effect a change in behavior.

As discussed in Chapter 1, changes in behavior are much more difficult and time-consuming than changes in knowledge and attitudes if force is not a factor. Since changes in expectations, in reality, are changes in knowledge and attitudes, these can be implemented more rapidly than changes in style. In fact, changes in expectations may be accomplished merely by having leaders sit down and clarify what their behavior will be with the individuals involved. Once they understand their leader's style, followers can more easily adjust their expectations to it. This is easier than attempting the tedious task of changing the basic style of a leader.

Team Building: Selection of Key Subordinates

It is important to point out that it is not always necessary for superiors and subordinates within an organization to have similar styles. People do not have to have the same personalities to be compatible. What is necessary is that they share perceptions of each other's roles and have common goals and objectives. It is often more appropriate for a manager to recruit key subordinates who can compensate for areas in which they have shortcomings than to surround themselves with aides who are all alike. And yet there are large companies today that have created problems for themselves by a testing and selection process that eliminates personalities not congruent with the norm. The usual process is to measure the values and styles of the top management and then select new peopole who are compatible with those patterns. The assumption is that if those people got to the top, their values and styles must be what are needed to be successful in the organization. When these norms become part of the screening process, what the organization is saying is that there is a best style, at least for this organization.

One of the reasons that hiring "likes" became popular is that they led to a more harmonious organization. For example, if we have the same set of values and like to behave in similar ways, are we going to tend to get along? Yes, because we will tend to be compatible. There will probably not be much conflict or confrontation. On the surface, this kind of screening appears to be very positive. Yet we have found that this approach can lead to organizational or management inbreeding, which tends to stifle creativity and innovation. To be effective in the long run, we feel that organizations need an open dialogue in which there is a certain amount of conflict, confrontation, and differing points of view to encourage new ideas and patterns of behavior so that the organization will not lose its ability to adjust to external competition. Organizations that have had these problems almost have been forced to break their prior policy of promoting only from within and have had to hire some key people from the outside who can encourage open dialogue.

What is often needed in organizations is more emphasis on team building in which people are hired who complement rather than replicate a manager's style. For example, Henry Ford, who was considered a paternalistic leader, placed in key positions in the organization men who supplemented him rather than duplicated his style. Henry Bennett, for one, acted as a hatchet man, clearing deadwood from the organization (high task). Another subordinate acted as a confidant to Henry (high relationship). While these styles differed considerably, Ford's success during that time was based on compatibility of expectations; each understood the other's role and was committed to common goals and objectives.

Other examples could be cited. This kind of team building is common in sports like football. Assistant coaches not only may have differential task roles, that is, line coach, backfield coach, and so forth, but may have different behavioral roles with the players; the same with principals and vice-principals, and so on.

Changing Situational Variables

Recognizing some of the limitations of training and development programs that concentrate only on changing leadership styles, Fiedler has suggested that "it would seem more promising at this time to teach the individual to recognize the conditions under which he can perform best and to modify the situation to suit his leadership style."[32] This philosophy, which he calls "organizational engineering," is based on the following assumption: "It is almost always easier to change a man's work environment than it is to change his personality or his style of relating to others."[33] Although we basically agree with Fiedler's assumption, we want to make it clear that we feel changes in both are difficult but possible. In many cases, the best strategy might be to attempt to make some changes in both the style of leaders and the expectations of the other variables of their situation rather than concentrate on one or the other.

Fiedler is helpful, however, in suggesting ways in which a leadership situation can be modified to fit the leader's style. These suggestions are based on his Leadership Contingency Model, which we discussed in Chapter 4. As you will recall, Fiedler feels there are three major situational variables that seem to determine whether a given situation is favorable or unfavorable to leaders: (1) *leader-member relations*—their personal relations with the members of their group, (2) *position power*—the power and authority that their position provides, and (3) *task structure*—the degree of structure (routine versus challenging) in the task that the group has been assigned to perform. The changes in each of these variables that Fiedler recommends can be expressed in task or relationship terms; each change tends to favor either a task-oriented or a relationships-oriented leader, as illustrated in Table 6-1.

With changes like these, Fiedler suggests that the situational variables confronting leaders can be modified to fit their style. He recognized, however, as we have been arguing, that the success of organizational engineering depends on training individuals to be able to diagnose their own leadership style and the other situational variables. Only when they have accurately interpreted these variables can they determine whether any changes are necessary. If changes are needed, leaders do not necessarily have to initiate any in their own particular situation. They might prefer to transfer to a situation that better fits their style. In this new environment, no immediate changes may be necessary.

TABLE 6-1   Changes in the leadership situation expressed in terms of task and relationship[34]

Variable Being Changed	Change Made — Style Favors	
	Task	*Relationship*
Leader-member Relations	Leaders could be given: 1. Followers who are quite different from them in a number of ways. 2. Followers who are notorious for their conflict.	Leaders could be given: 1. Followers who are very similar to them in attitude, opinion, technical background, race, etc. 2. Followers who generally get along well with their superiors.
Position Power of the Leader	Leaders could be given: 1. High rank and corresponding recognition, i.e., a vice-presidency. 2. Followers who are two or three ranks below them. 3. Followers who are dependent upon their leader for guidance and instruction. 4. Final authority in making all the decisions for the group. 5. All information about organizational plans, thus making them expert in their group.	Leaders could be given: 1. Little rank (office) or official recognition. 2. Followers who are equal to them in rank. 3. Followers who are experts in their field and are independent of their leader. 4. No authority in making decisions for the group. 5. No more information about organizational plans than their followers get, placing the followers on an equal "footing" with the leaders.
Task Structure	Leaders could be given: 1. A structured production task that has specific instructions on what they and their followers should do.	Leaders could be given: 1. An unstructured policy-making task that has no prescribed operating procedures.

DIAGNOSING THE ENVIRONMENT—A CASE

Any of the situational elements we have discussed may be analyzed in terms of task and relationship. Let us take the case of Steve, a general foreman who has been offered a promotion to superintendent in another plant. In his present position, which he has held for fifteen years, Steve has been extremely effective as a task-oriented manager responsible for the operation of several assembly line processes.

Steve's first impulse is immediately to accept this promotion in status and salary and move his family to the new location. But, instead, he feels it is important first to visit the plant and to talk with some of the people with whom he will be working. In talking with these people, Steve may gain some insight into some of the important dimensions of this new position. An analysis of all these variables in terms of task and relationship could be summarized together as illustrated in Figure 6-7.[35]

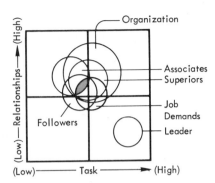

FIGURE 6-7 An example of all the environmental variables being analyzed together in terms of task and relationship

If Steve, using diagnostic skills, makes this type of analysis, he has gone a long way toward gathering the necessary information he needs for effectively determining his appropriate actions.

The circle designated for the leader represents Steve's leadership style, which has been reinforced over the past fifteen years. The other circles represent the expectations of all the other environmental variables in terms of what is considered appropriate behavior for a foreman. In this plant, all of the situational variables seem to demand a high task/high relationship or high relationship/low task superintendent. Unfortunately, Steve's style does not seem appropriate for any of the situational variables, for he tends to be a high task/low relationship manager. Thus, if he accepts the job and makes no changes, there is a high probability that Steve will be ineffective. At this point, he has to make a decision. Several alternatives are available to him.

1. He can attempt to change his style of behavior, thus permitting him to work effectively with the various situational variables in the new environment.

2. He can attempt to change some or all of the situational elements. For example, he can attempt to change the behavior and the expectations of his followers through training and development programs and/or coaching and counseling.

3. He can attempt to make *some* changes in both his own range of behavior and some or all of the situational elements, thus attempting in the long run to have the two move toward each other rather than concentrating only on changing one or the other.

4. He can reject the job and seek another superintendent's position in an environment in which his range of behavior is more compatible with the demands of the other situational elements.

5. He can remain in his present position where he knows he has been effective and will probably continue to be.

Reddin,[36] in doing a similar analysis, would attempt to find an area where the expectations of the organization, superiors, associates, followers, and job demands intersected. It is within this area that he would suggest that a leader would probably have to behave to maximize effectiveness. While that averaging process perhaps could be used for a case like Steve's in which the expectations of all the other situational variables are grouped closely together, it would not be useful in other situations.

When the expectations of various key variables do not intersect, it is not possible to use a generalized style but will require that leaders use different styles with each of the important situational variables in their environment. Thus, Dorothy, a sales manager, may have to treat her boss differently from the way she treats any of her subordinates or associates. Even among the salespeople who report to her, she will probably have to treat some very differently from others.

Although these examples have been written from the point of view of an individual, this type of analysis is just as important from an organization's point of view. It is vital that the people placed in key positions throughout the organization have the prerequisites for carrying out the organizational goals effectively. Management must realize that it does not follow that a person will be effective in one position merely because he or she has been effective in another situation. It is assumptions like these about which Laurence J. Peter writes. The Peter Principle is stated as follows: "In a hierarchy every employee tends to rise to his level of incompetence."[37]

Anti-Peter Principle Vaccine

The dilemma expressed by Peter is not necessarily a self-fulfilling prophecy or principle. There are several ways an organization can develop an immunity to the problem. One method is appropriate training and development before upward mobility takes place. This training may often include, prior to movement, the delegation of some responsibility, so that the person has had an opportunity for some real experience that approximates the new position. Another part of the solution is careful selection of people whose personality and expectations are appropriate for the new job, instead of having upward mobility depend only on good performance at the preceding level.

HOW CAN MANAGERS LEARN TO DEAL WITH ALL THESE ENVIRONMENTAL VARIABLES?

It is our feeling that it would be an impossible task if managers attempted to look at all the interacting influence variables discussed in this chapter every time they had to make a leadership decision. As a result, in the next chapter we are going to zero in on what we think is the key to two environmental variables—the relationship between the leader and the follower.

Why do we say that the relationship between the leader and the follower is the key for diagnosing a situation? The main reason is that our work at the Center for Leadership Studies confirms Sanford's[38] work. We have found that if the follower decides not to follow, it really doesn't matter what the boss thinks, what the nature of the work is, how much time is involved, or what the other situational variables are.

NOTES

[1] These environmental variables have been adapted from a list of situational elements discussed by William J. Reddin in *The 3-D Management Style Theory*, Theory Paper #5—Diagnostic Skill (Fredericton, N.B., Canada: Social Science Systems, 1967), p. 2.

[2] Robert Tannenbaum and Warren H. Schmidt indicate that the appropriate leadership style that should be used in a given situation is the function of factors in the leader, the follower, and the situation. What constitutes the situation can vary in different environmental settings. See Tannenbaum and Schmidt, "How to Choose a Leadership Pattern," *Harvard Business Review*, March-April 1957.

[3] The introductory section here was adapted from a model that discusses the interaction of personality and expectations. See Jacob W. Getzels and Egon G. Guba, "Social Behavior and the Administrative Process," *The School Review*, LXV, No. 4 (Winter 1957), pp. 423–41. See also Getzels, "Administration as a Social Process," in Andrew W. Halpin, ed., *Administrative Theory in Education* (Chicago: Midwest Administration Center, University of Chicago, 1958).

[4] Adapted from Getzels, p. 158.

[5] Tannenbaum and Schmidt, "How to Choose a Leadership Pattern."

[6] Leland P. Bradford, Jack R. Gibb and Kenneth D. Benne, *T-Group Theory and Laboratory Method* (New York: John Wiley & Sons, Inc., 1964).

[7] Warren G. Bennis, *Changing Organizations* (New York: McGraw-Hill Book Company, 1966), p. 120.

[8] Chris Argyris, "We Must Make Work Worthwhile," *Life*, 62, No. 18, (May 5, 1968), pp. 67–68.

[9] *Ibid.*

[10] See Chris Argyris, "T-Groups for Organization Effectiveness," *Harvard Business Review*, 42 (1964), pp. 60–74; Edgar H. Schein and Warren G. Bennis, *Personal and Organizational Change through Group Methods* (New York: John Wiley & Sons, Inc., 1965); Robert R. Blake et al., "Breakthrough in Organization Development," *Harvard Business Review*, November-December 1964; and Chris Argyris, *Interpersonal Competence and Organizational Effectiveness* (Homewood, Ill.: Dorsey Press, 1962).

[11] Fillmore H. Sanford, *Authoritarianism and Leadership* (Philadelphia: Institute for Research in Human Relations, 1950).

[12] Victor H. Vroom, *Some Personality Determinants of the Effects of Participation* (Englewood Cliffs, N.J.: Prentice-Hall, Inc., 1960).

[13] Saul W. Gellerman, *Motivation and Productivity* (New York: American Management Association, 1963).

[14] Tannenbaum and Schmidt, "How to Choose a Leadership Pattern."

[15] Reddin, *The 3-D Management Style Theory*, Theory Paper #5—Diagnostic Skill, p. 4.

[16] William E. Henry, "The Business Executive: The Psychodynamics of a Social Role," *The American Journal of Sociology*, LIV, No. 4 (January 1949), pp. 286–91.

[17] Robert H. Guest, *Organizational Change: The Effect of Successful Leadership* (Homewood, Ill.: Dorsey Press and Richard D. Irwin, Inc., 1964).

[18] Charles Perrow, *Organizational Analysis: A Sociological View* (Belmont, Calif.: Wadsworth Publishing Co., Inc., 1970), p. 12.

[19] Reddin, *The 3-D Management Style Theory*, Theory Paper #5—Diagnostic Skill, p. 4.

[20] Waino W. Suojanen, *The Dynamics of Management* (New York: Holt, Rinehart & Winston, Inc., 1966).

[21] Tannenbaum and Schmidt, "How to Choose a Leadership Pattern."

[22] Fred E. Fiedler, *A Theory of Leadership Effectiveness* (New York: McGraw-Hill Book Company, 1967).

[23] Robert J. House, "A Path-Goal Theory of Leader Effectiveness," *Administrative Science Quarterly,* 16 (1971), pp. 321–38. See also House and G. Dressler, "The Path-Goal Theory of Leadership: Some Post Hoc and A Priori Tests," in J. G. Hunt and L. L. Larson, eds., *Contingency Approaches to Leadership* (Carbondale, Ill.: Southern Illinois University Press, 1974), pp. 29–55.

[24] John E. Stinson and Thomas W. Johnson, "The Path-Goal Theory of Leadership: A Partial Test and Suggested Refinement," *Academy of Management Journal,* 18, No. 2 (June 1975), pp. 242–52.

[25] Victor H. Vroom and Floyd C. Mann, "Leader Authoritarianism and Employee Attitudes," *Personnel Psychology,* XIII, No. 2 (1960).

[26] Robert Tannenbaum and Warren H. Schmidt, "How to Choose a Leadership Pattern," *Harvard Business Review,* May-June 1973.

[27] *Ibid.*

[28] Fiedler, *A Theory of Leadership Effectiveness,* p. 248.

[29] Rensis Likert, *New Patterns of Management* (New York: McGraw-Hill Book Company, 1961), p. 248.

[30] *Leadership Style and Employee Morale* (New York: General Electric Company, Public and Employee Relations Services, 1959).

[31] Gellerman, *Motivation and Productivity,* p. 43.

[32] Fiedler, *A Theory of Leadership Effectiveness,* p. 255.

[33] *Ibid.*

[34] This table was adapted from Fiedler's discussion in *A Theory of Leadership Effectiveness,* pp. 255–56.

[35] Adapted from Reddin, Theory Paper #6—Style Flex, p. 6.

[36] Reddin, Theory Paper #6—Style Flex.

[37] Laurence J. Peter and Raymond Hull, *The Peter Principle: Why Things Go Wrong* (New York: William Morrow & Co., Inc., 1969).

[38] Fillmore H. Sanford, *Authoritarianism and Leadership* (Philadelphia: Institute for Research in Human Relations, 1950).

chapter 7

Situational
Leadership

The importance of a leader's *diagnostic ability* cannot be overemphasized. Edgar H. Schein expresses it well when he contends that *"the successful manager must be a good diagnostician and must value a spirit of inquiry.* If the abilities and motives of the people under him are so variable, he must have the sensitivity and diagnostic ability to be able to sense and appreciate the differences."[1] In other words, managers must be able to identify clues in an environment. Yet even with good diagnostic skills, leaders may still not be effective unless they can *adapt* their leadership style to meet the demands of their environment. "He must have the personal flexibility and range of skills necessary to vary his own behavior. If the needs and motives of his subordinates are different, they must be treated differently."[2]

It is easier said than done to tell practicing managers that they should use behavioral science theory and research to develop the necessary diagnostic skills to maximize effectiveness. First, much of the research currently published in the field of applied behavioral sciences is not even understood by practitioners, and often appears in final form to be more an attempt to impress other researchers than to help managers to be more effective. Second, even if practitioners could understand the research, many would argue that it is impractical to consider every situational variable in every decision, as advised by the management theorists and behavioral scientists. As a result, one of the major focuses of our work at the Center for Leadership Studies has been the development of a conceptual framework that attempts to pinpoint the *key situational variables*. This approach uses as its basic data the perceptions and observations made by managers—parents in the home or supervisors on the job—on a day-to-day basis in their own environments, rather than data gathered only by professional researchers and consultants through instrumentation, systematic observation, and interviews. Situational Leadership,[3] which will be presented in this chapter, is the result of those efforts.

SITUATIONAL LEADERSHIP

Paul Hersey and Kenneth H. Blanchard

The need for a significant Situational Model in the leadership area has been recognized in the literature for some time.

A. K. Korman, in his extensive review of studies examining the Ohio State concepts of Initiating Structure and Consideration, concluded that:

> What is needed . . . in future concurrent (and predictive) studies is not just recognition of this factor of "situational determinants" but, rather, a systematic conceptualization of situational variance as it might relate to leadership behavior [Initiating Structure and Consideration].[4]

In discussing this conclusion, Korman suggests the possibility of a curvilinear relationship rather than a simple linear relationship between Initiating Structure (task behavior) and Consideration (relationship behavior) and other variables. Situational Leadership, which is an outgrowth of our Tri-Dimensional Leader Effectiveness Model, has identified such a curvilinear relationship.

Situational Leadership is based on an interplay among (1) the amount of guidance and direction (task behavior) a leader gives; (2) the amount of socioemotional support (relationship behavior) a leader provides; and (3) the readiness ("maturity") level that followers exhibit in performing a specific task, function or objective. This concept was developed to help people attempting leadership, regardless of their role, to be more effective in their daily interactions with others. It provides leaders with some understanding of the relationship between an effective style of leadership and the level of maturity of their followers.

Thus, while all the situational variables (leader, follower(s), superior(s), associates, organization, job demands, and time) are important, the emphasis in Situational Leadership will be on the behavior of a leader in relation to followers. As Fillmore H. Sanford has indicated, there is some justification for regarding the followers "as the most crucial factor in any leadership event." [5] Followers in any situation are vital, not only because individually they accept or reject the leader, but because as a group they actually determine whatever personal power the leader may have.

It was emphasized in Chapter 4 that when discussing leader/follower relationships, we are not necessarily talking about a hierarchical relationship, that is, superior/subordinate. The same caution will hold during our discussion of Situational Leadership. *Thus, any reference to leader(s) or follower(s) in this theory should imply potential leader and potential follower.* As a result, although our examples may suggest a hierarchical relationship, the concepts presented in Situational Leadership should have application no matter whether you are attempting to influence the behavior of a subordinate, your boss, an associate, a friend, or a relative.

Maturity of the Followers or Group

Maturity is defined in Situational Leadership as the ability and willingness of people to take responsibility for directing their own behavior. *These variables of maturity should be considered only in relation to a specific task to be performed.* That is to say, an individual or a group is not mature or immature in any *total* sense. All persons tend to be more or less mature in relation to a specific task, function, or objective that a leader is attempting to accomplish through their efforts. Thus, a saleswoman may be very responsible in securing new sales but very casual about completing the paperwork necessary to close on a sale. As a result, it is appropriate for her manager to leave her alone in terms of closing on sales but to supervise her closely in terms of her paper work until she can start to do well in that area too.

In addition to assessing the level of maturity of individuals within a group, a leader may have to assess the maturity level of the group as a group, particularly if the group interacts frequently together in the same work area, as happens with students in the classroom. Thus, a teacher may find that a class as a group may be at one level of maturity in a particular area, but a student within that group may be at a different level. When the teacher is one-to-one with that student, he or she may have to behave very differently than when working with the class as a group. In reality, the teacher may find a number of students at various maturity levels. For example, the teacher may have one student who is not doing his work regularly; when he turns work in, it is poorly organized and not very academic. With that student, the teacher may have to initiate some structure and supervise closely. Another student, however, may be doing good work but is insecure and shy. With that student, the teacher may not have to engage in much task behavior in terms of schoolwork but may need to be supportive, to engage in two-way communication, and help facilitate the student's interaction with others in the class. Still another student may be psychologically mature as well as competent in her schoolwork, and thus can be left on her own. So leaders have to understand that they may have to behave differently one-on-one with members of their group from the way they do with the group as a whole.

Basic Concept of Situational Leadership

According to Situational Leadership, there is no one best way to influence people. Which leadership style a person should use with individuals or groups depends on the maturity level of the people the leader is attempting to influence, as illustrated in Figure 7-1.

STYLE OF LEADER

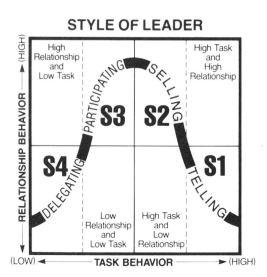

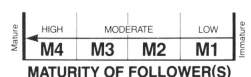

MATURITY OF FOLLOWER(S)

FIGURE 7-1 Situational leadership

Style of Leader Versus Maturity of Follower(s)

The attempt in Figure 7-1 is to portray the relationship between task-relevant maturity and the appropriate leadership styles to be used as followers move from immaturity to maturity. As indicated, the reader should keep in mind that the figure represents two different phenomena. The appropriate leadership style (*style of leader*) for given levels of follower maturity is portrayed by the prescriptive curve going through the four leadership quadrants. This bell-shaped curve is called a *prescriptive curve* because it shows the appropriate leadership style directly above the corresponding level of maturity.

Each of the four leadership styles—"telling," "selling," "participating," and "delegating"—identified in Figure 7-1, is a combination of task and relationship behavior. As discussed in Chapter 4, task behavior is the extent to which a leader provides direction for people: telling them what to do, when to do it, where to do it, and how to do it. It means setting goals for them and defining their roles.

Relationship behavior is the extent to which a leader engages in two-way communication with people: providing support, encouragement, "psychological strokes," and facilitating behaviors. It means actively listening to people and supporting their efforts.

The maturity of followers is a question of degree. As can be seen in Figure 7-1, some bench marks of maturity are provided for determining appropriate leadership style by dividing the maturity continuum below the leadership model into four levels: low (M1), low to moderate (M2), moderate to high (M3), and high (M4).

The appropriate leadership style for each of the four maturity levels includes the right combination of task behavior (direction) and relationship behavior (support).

"Telling" is for low maturity. People who are both *unable and unwilling* (M1) to take responsibility to do something are not competent or confident. In many cases, their unwillingness is a result of their *insecurity* regarding the necessary task. Thus, a directive "telling" style (S1) that provides clear, specific directions and supervision has the highest probability of being effective with individuals at this maturity level. This style is called "telling" because it is characterized by the leader's defining roles and telling people what, how, when, and where to do various tasks. It emphasizes directive behavior. Too much supportive behavior with people at this maturity level may be seen as permissive, easy and, most importantly, as rewarding of poor performance. This style involves high task behavior and low relationship behavior.

"Selling" is for low to moderate maturity. People who are *unable but willing* (M2) to take responsibility are confident but lack skills at this time. Thus, a "selling" style (S2) that provides directive behavior, because of their lack of ability, but also supportive behavior to reinforce their willingness and enthusiasm appears to be most appropriate with individuals at this maturity level. This style is called "selling" because most of the direction is still provided by the leader. Yet, through two-way communication and explanation, the leader tries to get the followers psychologically to "buy into" desired behaviors. Followers at this maturity level will usually go along with a decision if they understand the reason for the decision and if their leader also offers some help and direction. This style involves high task behavior and high relationship behavior.

"Participating" is for moderate to high maturity. People at this maturity level are *able* but *unwilling* (M3) to do what the leader wants. Their unwillingness is often a function of their lack of confidence or *insecurity*. If, however, they are competent but unwilling, their reluctance to perform is more of a motivational problem than a security problem. In either case, the leader needs to open the door (two-way communication and active listening) to support the follower's efforts to use the ability he already has. Thus, a supportive, nondirective, "participating" style (S3) has the highest probability of being effective with individuals at this maturity level. This style is called "participating" because the leader and follower share in decision making, with the main role of the leader being facilitating and communicating. This style involves high relatonship behavior and low task behavior.

"Delegating" is for high maturity. People at this maturity level are both *able and willing, or confident,* to take responsibility. Thus, a low-profile "delegat-

ing" style (S4), which provides little direction or support, has the highest probability of being effective with individuals at this maturity level. Even though the leader may still identify the problem, the responsibility for carrying out plans is given to these mature followers. They are permitted to run the show and decide on the how, when, and where. At the same time, they are psychologically mature and therefore do not need above average amounts of two-way communication or supportive behavior. This style involves low relationship behavior and low task behavior.

It should be clear that the appropriate leadership style for all four of the maturity designations—low maturity (M1), low to moderate maturity (M2), moderate to high maturity (M3), and high maturity (M4)—correspond to the following leadership style designations: *telling* (S1), *selling* (S2), *participating* (S3), and *delegating* (S4). That is, low maturity needs a *telling* style, low to moderate needs a *selling* style, and so on. These combinations are shown in Table 7-1.

TABLE 7-1 Leadership styles appropriate for various maturity levels

MATURITY LEVEL	APPROPRIATE STYLE
M1 *Low Maturity* Unable and unwilling or insecure	S1 *Telling* High task and low relationship behavior
M2 *Low to* *Moderate Maturity* Unable but willing or confident	S2 *Selling* High task and high relationship behavior
M3 *Moderate to* *High Maturity* Able but unwilling or insecure	S3 *Participating* High relationship and low task behavior
M4 *High Maturity* Able/competent and willing/confident	S4 *Delegating* Low relationship and low task behavior

In using the shorthand designations (S1, S2, S3, S4) and labels ("telling," "selling," "participating," and "delegating") for leadership styles that are identified in Figure 7-1 and Table 7-1, one must keep in mind that they should only be used when referring to behaviors represented by the effective face of the Tri-Dimensional Leader Effectiveness Model. However, when discussing basic or ineffective styles, we shall refer to them only by quadrant number: Q1, Q2, Q3, or Q4. For example, when a low relationship/low task style is used appropriately with the corresponding maturity level M4, it will be referred to as S4 or "delegating." But when that same style is used inappropriately with any of the other three maturity levels, it will only be called Q4 and might be better described as abdication or withdrawal rather than "delegating."

Situational Leadership not only suggests the high probability leadership style for various maturity levels, but it also indicates the probability of success of the other style configurations if a leader is unable to use the desired style. The probability of success of each style for the four maturity levels, depending on how far the style is from the high probability style along the prescriptive curve in the style of leader portion of the model, is as follows:

M1   S1 high, S2 2nd, Q3 3rd, Q4 low probability

M2   S2 high, S1 2nd, S3 2nd, Q4 low probability

M3   S3 high, S2 2nd, S4 2nd, Q1 low probability

M4   S4 high, S3 2nd, Q2 3rd, Q1 low probability

In indicating the probability of success of each style above, in some cases the "S" designation was used for a style, and in other cases the "Q" designation was used. As discussed, the shorthand designations (S1, S2, S3, S4) and labels ("telling," "selling," "participating," and "delegating") should only be used when referring to behaviors represented by the effective face of the Tri-Dimensional Leader Effectiveness Model. Thus, the high probability style and the 2nd (secondary) styles were indicated by an "S" designation, while the 3rd and low probability styles were indicated by a "Q" designation. In most cases, there are at least two leadership styles in the effective range. At the same time, there are usually one or two leadership styles that are clearly in the less effective range.

APPLICATION OF SITUATIONAL LEADERSHIP

The key to using Situational Leadership is to assess the maturity level of the follower(s) and to behave as the model prescribes. Implicit in Situational Leadership is the idea that a leader should help followers grow in maturity as far as they are able and willing to go. This development of followers should be done by adjusting leadership behavior through the four styles along the prescriptive curve in Figure 7-1.

Situational Leadership contends that strong direction (task behavior) with immature followers is appropriate if they are to become productive. Similarly, it suggests that an increase in maturity on the part of people who are somewhat immature should be rewarded by increased positive reinforcement and socioemotional support (relationship behavior). Finally, as followers reach high levels of maturity, the leader should respond by not only continuing to decrease control over their activities but also continuing to decrease relationship behavior as well.

With very mature people, the need for socioemotional support is no longer as important as the need for autonomy. At this stage, one of the ways leaders can prove their confidence and trust in highly mature people is to leave them more and more on their own. It is not that there is less mutual trust and friendship between leader and follower; in fact, there is more, but it takes less supportive behavior on the leader's part to prove this to mature followers.

Regardless of the level of maturity of an individual or group, change may occur. Whenever a follower's performance begins to slip—for whatever reason—and ability or motivation decreases, the leader should reassess the maturity level of this follower and move backward through the prescriptive curve, providing appropriate socioemotional support and direction.

These developmental and regressive processes will be discussed in depth in Chapters 9 and 10. At this point, though, it is important to emphasize that Situational Leadership focuses on the appropriateness or effectiveness of leadership styles according to the task-relevant maturity of the followers.

Determining Appropriate Style

To determine what leadership style you should use with a person in a given situation, you must do several things.

First, you must decide what areas of an individual or group's activities you would like to influence. In the world of work, those areas would vary according to a person's responsibilities. For example, a salesperson might have responsibility in sales, administration (paperwork), service and team development. Therefore, before managers can begin to determine the appropriate leadership style to use with an individual, they must decide what aspect of that person's job they want to influence.

Once this decision has been made, the second step is to determine the ability and motivation (maturity level) of the individual or group in each of the selected areas.

The third and final step is deciding which of the four leadership styles (see Table 7-1) would be appropriate with this individual in each of these areas. Let us look at an example. Suppose a manager has determined that a subordinate's maturity level, in terms of administrative paper work, is low (M1); that is, the staff member is unable and unwilling to take responsibility in this area. Using Table 7-1, he would know that when working with this subordinate he should use a directive "telling" (S1) style (high task/low relationship behavior).

In this example, low relationship behavior does not mean that the manager is unfriendly to the subordinate. We merely suggest that the manager, in supervising the subordinate's handling of administrative paper work, should spend more time directing the person in what to do and how, when, and where to do it than providing socioemotional support and reinforcement. Increased relationship behavior should occur only when the subordinate begins to demonstrate the ability to handle necessary administrative paperwork. At this point, a movement from "telling" to "selling" would be appropriate.

Components of Maturity

It has been argued that the key to effective leadership is to identify the *maturity level* of the individual or group you are attempting to influence and then bring to bear the appropriate leadership style. If that is true, how can managers get a better handle on what maturity actually means?

In examining the components of maturity, several comments should be made. First, according to David C. McClelland's research,[6] achievement-motivated people have certain characteristics in common, including the capacity to set high but obtainable goals, the concern for personal achievement rather than the rewards of success, and the desire for task-relevant feedback (how well am I doing?) rather than for attitudinal feedback (how well do you like me?). Of these characteristics we are most interested, in terms of task-relevant maturity, in the capacity to set high but attainable goals.

Second, in terms of education and/or experience, we are contending that there is no conceptual difference between the two. One can gain task-relevant maturity through education or experience or some combination of both. The only difference between the two is that when we are talking about education, we are referring to formal classroom experiences, and experience involves what is learned on one's own or on the job.

Third, in our recent work, we have argued that education and/or experience affects ability and that achievement-motivation affects willingness. As a result, in discussing maturity in terms of ability and willingness, we are suggesting that the concept of maturity consists of two dimensions: *job maturity* (ability) and *psychological maturity* (willingness).

Job maturity is related to the ability to do something. It has to do with knowledge and skill. Individuals who have high job maturity in a particular area have the knowledge, ability, and experience to perform certain tasks without direction from others. A person high in job maturity might say: "My talent really lies in that aspect of my job. I can work on my own in that area without much help from my boss."

Psychological maturity is related to the willingness or motivation to do something. It has to do with confidence and commitment. Individuals who have high psychological maturity in a particular area or responsibility think that responsibility is important and have self-confidence and good feelings about themselves in that aspect of their job. They do not need extensive encouragement to get them to do things in that area. A comment from a person high in psychological maturity might be: "I really enjoy that aspect of my job. My boss doesn't have to get after me or provide any encouragement for me to do work in that area."

Another way of looking at maturity is in terms of the immaturity–maturity continuum of Chris Argyris, where he contends that as people mature over time they move from a passive state to a state of increasing activity, from dependency on others to relative independence, and the like.[7] Age may be a factor, but it is not directly related to maturity as used in Situational Leadership. Our concern is more for psychological than for chronological age.

It should be remembered that although maturity is a useful concept for making diagnostic judgments, other situational variables—the boss' style (if he or she is in your specific location), a crisis or time bind, the nature of the work—can be of equal or greater importance. Yet, the maturity concept is a solid bench mark for choosing the appropriate style with an individual or group at a particular time.

Instruments to Measure Maturity

To help managers and their followers make valid judgments about follower maturity, Hambleton, Blanchard and Hersey have developed two different maturity instruments: the *Manager's Rating Form* and the *Self-Rating Form*. [8]

Both maturity instruments measure *ability* (*job maturity*) and *willingness* (*psychological maturity*) by using five rating scales. Examples of these rating scales from the *Manager's Rating Form* are given in Figure 7-2.

The five job maturity scales and five psychological maturity scales were selected after pilot research from a pool of about thirty potential indicators of both dimensions. As is clear from Figure 7-2, corresponding to each scale, "behavioral indicators" of the end points were produced. Also, eight-point rating scales are used in the instrument. Low to high designations correspond to the four maturity levels (M1 to M4) associated with Situational Leadership.

In more recent work, Hersey, Blanchard and Keilty developed a Maturity Style Match rating form that measures maturity using only one scale for each dimension—one measuring *ability* and the other measuring *willingness*. [9] In this instrument, a person's ability (knowledge and skill) is thought of as a matter of degree. That is, an individual's ability does not change drastically from one moment to the next. At any given moment, an individual has a little, some, quite a bit, or a great deal of ability.

Willingness (confidence and motivation), however, is different. A person's motivation can, and often does, fluctuate from one moment to another. Therefore, a person is seldom, on occasion, often, or usually willing to take responsibility in a particular area.

The availability of both a *Manager's Rating Form* and a *Staff Member Form* of the *Maturity Style Match* is necessary to initiate a program combining *Situational Leadership* with *Contracting for Leadership Style*. [10] We will discuss that process in some detail in Chapter 11.

Components of Leadership Style

Once managers have identified the maturity level of the individual or group they are attempting to influence, the key to effective leadership is then to bring to bear the *appropriate leadership style*. If that is true, how can managers get a better handle on the behaviors that comprise each of the four leadership styles?

Instruments to measure leader behavior. To help managers and their staff members make better judgments about leadership style, Hersey, Blanchard,

JOB MATURITY SCALES

This person ·········· in performing this objective

Scales	High M4 8	7	6 M3	5	Moderate 4 M2	3	2	Low M1 1
1. Past Job Experience	Has experience relevant to job 8	7	6	5	4	Does not have relevant experience 3	2	1
2. Job Knowledge	Possesses necessary job knowledge 8	7	6	5	4	Does not have necessary job knowledge 3	2	1
3. Understanding of Job Requirements	Thoroughly understands what needs to be done 8	7	6	Has little understanding of what needs to be done 5	4	3	2	1

PSYCHOLOGICAL MATURITY SCALES

This person ·········· in performing this objective

Scales	High M4 8	7	6 M3	5	Moderate 4 M2	3	2	Low M1 1
1. Willingness to Take Responsibility	Is very eager 8	7	6	5	4	3	Is very reluctant 2	1
2. Achievement Motivation	Has a high desire to achieve 8	7	6	5	4	3	Has little desire to achieve 2	1
3. Commitment	Is very dedicated 8	7	6	5	4	3	Is uncaring 2	1

FIGURE 7-2 A portion of the manager's rating form of maturity

159

and Hambleton have developed two different leadership scales: the *Manager's Rating Form* and the *Staff Member Form*.[11]

Both leadership instruments measure task and relationship behavior on five behavioral dimensions. The five task behavior dimensions and five relationship behavior dimensions are listed in Table 7-2.

TABLE 7-2   Task behavior and relationship behavior dimensions and their behavior indicators

TASK-BEHAVIOR DIMENSIONS	BEHAVIORAL INDICATOR
	The extent to which a leader . . .
Goal setting	Specifies the goals people are to accomplish.
Organizing	Organizes the work situation for people.
Setting Time Lines	Sets time lines for people.
Directing	Provides specific directions.
Controlling	Specifies and requires regular reporting on progress.

RELATIONSHIP-BEHAVIOR DIMENSIONS	BEHAVIORAL INDICATOR
	The extent to which a leader . . .
Giving Support	Provides support and encouragement.
Communicating	Involves people in "give-and-take" discussions about work activities.
Facilitating Interactions	Facilitates people's interactions with others.
Active Listening	Seeks out and listens to people's opinions and concerns.
Providing Feedback	Provides feedback on people's accomplishments.

After the five dimensions were established for both leader behaviors, behavioral indicators of the extreme of each of these dimensions were identified to help managers and their staff members differentiate between high and low amounts of each leader behavior. For example, with the task behavior dimension "organizing" on the *Staff Member Form,* the end points of a rating scale were chosen to be "organizes the work situation for me" and "lets me organize the work situation." For the relationship behavior dimension "providing feedback," the end points of the rating scale were chosen to be "frequently provides feedback on my accomplishments" and "leaves it up to me to evaluate accomplishments."

In the *Maturity Style Match* instrument discussed earlier, each of the four basic leadership styles are described, rather than the separate behavioral dimensions that make up each style. The descriptions of the four leader behaviors are given below:

Telling (S1) — Provide specific instructions
and closely supervise performance.

Selling (S2) — Explain decisions and provide
opportunity for clarification.

Participating (S3) — Share ideas and facilitate in
making decisions.

Delegating (S4) — Turn over responsibility for
decisions and implementation.

The advantage of using the *Maturity Style Match* is that it permits managers and their staff members to rate leadership style and maturity on the same instrument. Figure 7-3 shows that integration. This figure provides a good summary of the key components involved in Situational Leadership.

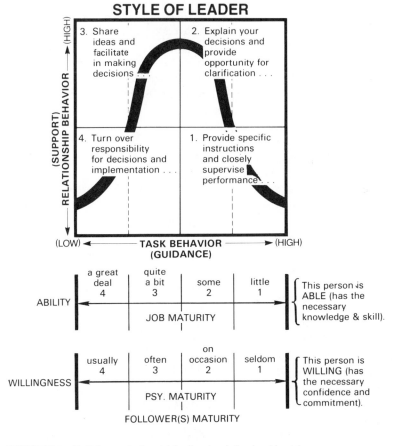

FIGURE 7-3 Defining maturity and the four basic leadership styles

SITUATIONAL LEADERSHIP AND VARIOUS ORGANIZATIONAL SETTINGS

We have found that Situational Leadership has application in every kind of organizational setting, whether it be business and industry, education, government, military, or even the family. The concepts apply in any situation in which people are trying to influence the behavior of other people.

The only problem we have found in working in various organizational settings is that some of the language has to be adapted to fit specific vocabularies. For example, we found that in training nonworking spouses, when we talked about task and relationship behavior, that did not ring any bells for them. We soon realized that in working in such family settings, it was much easier for parents and children to identify with "directive" behavior than with task behavior and to identify with "supportive" behavior than with relationship behavior.

On the other hand, when working with trainers and facilitators who have had a lot of personal growth experience and, therefore, are high on human relation quotients, even directive behavior will often tend to be a negative stimulus. Therefore, in working with these people we have found the word "guidance" is a good substitute for "directive behavior." We want to emphasize that in utilizing various labels for the two basic leader behaviors—task behavior and relationship behavior—we are not changing the definitions at all. Task behavior is essentially the extent to which a leader engages in one-way communication by explaining what each staff member is to do as well as when, where, and how tasks are to be accomplished. Relationship behavior, even when we call it supportive behavior, is still the extent to which a leader engages in two-way communication by providing socioemotional support, "psychological strokes," and facilitating behaviors.

The reason it is important to modify the use of various words is that a key concept in all behavior sciences is communication. If you're going to help people grow and develop, you have to learn to put frameworks, concepts and research results into terminology that is acceptable to the groups you are attempting to influence. This has to be done if you want to have the highest probability of gaining acceptance and, therefore, affecting their growth.

Parent-Child Relationships

We have found tremendous application of Situational Leadership to the family and the parent-child relationship. Our book, The Family Game,[12] is devoted completely to applying Situational Leadership to the family setting.

We hypothesize that when working with children (while they will need "different strokes even for the same folks"), there is a general pattern and movement in leadership style over their developmental years. Thus, when working with children who are low in maturity on a particular task, a directive parent style has the highest probability of success. This is especially true during the first few years of children's lives when children are unable to control much of their own environment. This whole development process will be discussed in more depth in Chapter 9.

Ineffective Parent Styles

One of the useful aspects of Situational Leadership is that one can begin to predict not only the leadership styles with the highest probability of effectiveness but also which styles tend to be ineffective in what circumstances. For instance, we can take four examples of parents who tend to use a single leadership style during the child's entire developmental period (see Figure 7-4).

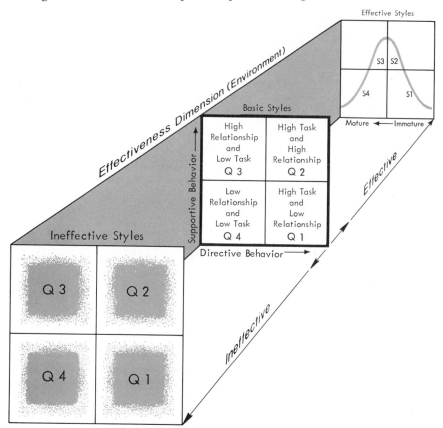

FIGURE 7-4 Consequences of using a *single* parent-child style over time

First, let us look at the parent who uses a high directive/low supportive style (Q1) with their children throughout the developmental years, i.e., "As long as you're living in this house, you'll be home at ten o'clock and abide by the rules I've set." Two predictions might be made. The first one is that the children might pack their bags and leave home at the earliest opportunity. If this does not occur, they may succumb to their parents' authority and become very passive, dependent individuals throughout their lives, always needing someone to tell them what to do and when to do it.

A high probability result of a parent using exclusively a style of high directive/high supportive behavior (Q2) might be called the "Mama's boy" or "Daddy's little girl" syndrome. Even when the children get older, they may chronologically be adults, but they are still psychologically dependent on their parent(s) to make decisions for them. Since most of the direction for their behavior and socioemotional support has been provided by their parent(s), these young people are unable to provide it for themselves.

What happens when parents are unfailingly supportive and never structure or direct any of their children's activities? The response to this high supportive/low directive style (Q3) may be called a "spoiled brat" syndrome, for the children develop into individuals who have little regard for rules and little consideration for the rights of others.

A low directive/low supportive behavior style (Q4) seems to be characteristic of two of the socioeconomic classifications described by Lloyd Warner, the *upper-upper* level and the *lower-lower* level.[13] In both cases, the children may become products of their environment rather than products of the parents' style. In the upper-upper level, this responsibility may be delegated to a private school; in the lower-lower level, children are often left on their own and learn appropriately or inappropriately from their peers how to cope with the day-to-day contingencies of their environment.

As we mentioned in Chapter 4, some people might question why it is inappropriate to use the same leadership style all the time— "after all, we've been told that consistency is good." This advice might have been given in the past, but, as we argue, according to Situational Leadership, consistency is *not* using the same style all the time. Instead, consistency is using the same style for all similar situations but varying the style appropriately as the situation changes. Parents are consistent if they tend to discipline their children when they are behaving inappropriately and reward them when they are behaving appropriately. Parents are inconsistent if they smile and engage in other supportive behavior when their children are bad as well as when they are good.

This discussion of consistency urges parents to remember that children are often at different levels of maturity in various aspects of their lives. Thus, parental style must vary as children's activities change.

Management of Research and Development Personnel

In working with highly trained and emotionally mature people, an effective leader behavior style in many cases is low relationship/low task behavior.[14] This was dramatically demonstrated in a military setting. Normally, in basically crisis-oriented organizations, such as the military or the fire department, the most appropriate style tends to be high task (S1), since under combat or fire conditions success often depends on immediate response to orders. Time demands do not permit talking things over or explaining decisions. For success, behavior must be almost automatic. Although a high task style may be effective for a combat officer, it is often ineffective in working with research and development personnel within the military. This was pointed out when line officers trained at West Point were sent to command outposts in the DEW line, part of the American advanced-warning system. The scientific and technical personnel involved, living in close quarters in an Arctic region, did not respond favorably to the high levels of task behavior of the combat-trained officers. The levels of education, research experience, and maturity of these people were such that they did not need their commanding officer to initiate a great deal of structure in their work. In fact, they tended to resent it. Other experiences with scientific and research-oriented personnel indicate that many of these people also desire or need a limited amount of socioemotional support too.

Educational Setting

Educational settings provide us with numerous examples of Situational Leadership in operation.[15]

Teacher-Student Relationship. In an educational setting, Situational Leadership is being used in studying the teacher-student relationship.

For example, Paul Hersey and two colleagues in Brazil, Arrigo L. Angelini and Sofia Caracushansky,[16] conducted a study applying Situational Leadership to teaching. In the study, an attempt was made to compare the learning effectiveness scores between: (1) students who attended a course in which a conventional teacher-students relationship prevailed (control subgroups) and (2) students who attended a course in which Situational Leadership was applied by the same teacher (experimental subgroups). In the control group classes, lectures prevailed, but group discussions, audiovisual aids, and other participative resources were also used. In the experimental classes, the maturity level of students (willingness and ability to direct their own learning and provide their own reinforcement) was developed over time by a systematic shift in teaching style. The teacher's style started at S1 (high task/low relationship—teacher in front of the class lecturing), then moved to S2 (high task/high relationship behavior—group discussions in a circular design with the teacher directing the conversation), then to S3 (high relationship/low task—group discussions with the teacher participating as a supportive but nondirective group member), and finally to S4 (low relationship/low task—the group continuing to discuss with the teacher only involved when asked by the class). The development of student maturity was a slow process at first, with gradual decreases in teacher direction and increases in teacher encouragement. As the students demonstrated their ability not only to assume more and more responsibility for directing their own learning but also to provide their own reinforcement (self-gratification), decreases in teacher socioemotional support accompanied continual decreases in teacher direction.

In two experiments with this design, the experimental classes showed not only higher performance on content exams but were also observed to have a higher level of enthusiasm, morale, and motivation as well as less tardiness and absenteeism.

Situational Leadership may provide some insights into problems that have developed in the innovative self-paced learning curricula that have sprung up across the country at many educational levels, particularly in elementary and secondary schools.[17] These programs have been developed in an attempt to individualize instruction and are premised on maximum freedom for the student. For example, in learning basic chemistry, students are given a detailed outline of what they must know and must do to pass a proficiency exam in chemistry. Once this initial direction has been provided, the teacher quickly moves through the cycle to a low relationship/low task style. The intention now is for the students to initiate structure for themselves. The teacher becomes involved only at the student's request. Students often can take the exam any time they are ready.

Problems sometimes develop when this unstructured program is used universally for all students in a school. For the intellectually and emotionally mature student who has clear goals and objectives, such a curriculum has numerous advantages. These include "a savings of time which can be devoted to other areas of interest, a genuine and personal recognition of his ability, and the opportunity to be treated and behave as an adult."[18] For the immature student who lacks motivation and ability to direct his or her own work schedule, such a low relationship/low task teaching style can be detrimental. It can even encourage immaturity if the student perceives the lack of structure as permissiveness. In the case of students who look at the educational system as something that must be tolerated but is not well integrated with their own personal goals, higher task behavior and a somewhat lower relationship style would seem more appropriate until the students begin to show signs of maturing and the teacher can vary his or her style accordingly.

Administrator-Governing Board Relationship. An important area for the top administrator (college president or superintendent) in an educational institution is the relationship this person maintains with the governing board. Since these boards have the ultimate power to remove college presidents or superintendents when they lose confidence in their leadership, these administrators often tend to use a high relationship style (S3), providing only a limited amount of structure for these decision-making groups.[19] In fact, they sometimes seem to shy away from directing the activities of their board for fear of arousing their criticism. Situational Leadership questions this behavior.

Although the members of the governing board are often responsible, well-educated individuals, they tend to have little work experience in an educational setting. For example, in a survey of college trustees in New York State, it was found that less than 10 percent of the trustees serving on these boards had any teaching or administrative experience in an educational institution.[20] In fact, the large majority of the 1,269 trustees sampled were occupied primarily in industry, insurance and banking, merchandising and transportation, and medicine and law. Virtually half acted as corporation officials with the rank of treasurer, director, or above. In addition to their involvement in other than educational institutions, these trustees tended to be overcommitted and were probably unable to give the time to university problems that they would have liked to give. In fact, the most frequent dissatisfaction expressed by trustees was the lack of time to devote to the board.

The relative inexperience of the trustees and the heavy commitment elsewhere suggest that it may be appropriate for college presidents to combine with their high relationship behavior an increase of task behavior in working with their trustees. In fact, the responsibility for defining the role of trustees and organizing their work should fall on the college president. Henry Wriston, former president of Brown University, has said it well:

> It may seem strange, at first thought, that this should be a president's duty. A moment's reflection makes it clear that it can evolve on no other person. Trustees are unpaid; they have no method of analyzing talents and making assignments. The president is in a position to do so.[21]

Administrator-Faculty Relationship. In working with experienced faculty, the low relationship/low task style (S4) characterized by a decentralized organization structure and delegation of responsibility to individuals may be appropriate. The level of education and maturity of these people is often such that they do not need their principal or department chairperson to initiate much structure. Sometimes they tend to resent it. In addition, some teachers desire or need only a limited amount of socioemotional support (relationship behavior).

Often an effective leader style in working with faculty tends to be low relationship/low task, but certain deviations may be necessary. For example, during the early stages of a school year or curriculum change, a certain amount of structure as to the specific areas to be taught, by whom, when, and where must be established. Once these requirements and limitations are understood by the faculty, the administrator may move rapidly back to low relationship/low task style appropriate for working with mature, responsible, self-motivated personnel.

Other deviations may be necessary. For example, a new, inexperienced teacher might need more direction and socioemotional support until gaining experience in the classroom.

UNDERSTANDING EARLIER RESEARCH

One of the major contributions of Situational Leadership is that it provides a way of understanding much of the research findings that prior to a situational approach seemed to be incompatible with each other. Examples can be cited.

At first glance, the extensive research that Likert[22] did in industrial sections of the United States in the 1950s and a similar study that Hersey[23] conducted in western Africa in the 1960s seem to be in conflict. Likert found in his studies that the tendency is for employee-centered supervisors who provide general supervision to have high producing sections, while the low producing sections tend to have job-centered supervisors who provide close supervision. Hersey's findings were almost the exact opposite of the results generated by Likert. In emerging industrial settings in western Africa, he found the more effective style to be job-centered close supervision. By examining these different results using Situational Leadership, one may gain some insights into why these differing results are predictable.

As indicated, the population for Likert's research was drawn from industrial sections of the United States. This is particularly relevant when one considers what we have come to call "cultural maturity" or "work force maturity." We have found that three phenomena—level of education, standard of living, and industrial experience—can have a pronounced effect on the task-relevant maturity level of the work force from which an organization is attempting to draw its employees.

In terms of Likert's research, the work force maturity of his sample upon examination appears to be quite mature. The level of education, standard of living, and industrial experiences of people in industrial sections of the United States in the 1950s were probably moderate to high. This is not surprising when one examines the research in terms of Situational Leadership. Likert found that moderate to low task behavior and relatively high relationship behavior (S3) tended to be the most effective leadership styles—that is, they had the highest probability of being effective given the cultural maturity involved. At the same time, it is not surprising to see the results Hersey found. In the middle 1960s emerging countries in Africa seemed to have labor forces characterized for many by very little formal education, a subsistence standard of living, and little or no industrial experience. Considering this low level of work force maturity at that time, one could predict from Situational Leadership that the highly structured, close supervision style that Hersey found would have the highest probability of being effective in that environment.

The same kind of analysis can be made in comparing the results of the classical participation study done by Coch and French[24] in an American factory in the Northeast and a replication of their study by French, Israel and Ås [25] in a Norwegian factory. In the industrial setting in the United States, it was found that involving employees in decision making tends to be effective, but in Norway there was no significant difference in productivity between work groups in which participative management was used and those in which it was *not* used. Once again these two studies support Situational Leadership and suggest that maturity levels and/or cultural work force differences in the followers and the situation are important in determining the appropriate leadership style.

Determining the Effectiveness of Participation

An analysis of studies in participation[26] in terms of Situational Leadership also suggests some interesting things about the appropriate use of participation. Situational Leadership suggests that the higher the level of task-relevant maturity of an individual or group, the higher the probability that participation will be an effective management technology. The less task-relevant maturity, the lower the probability that participation will be a useful management practice.

Involvement and participation in decision making with people at extremely low levels of maturity might be characterized by a pooling of ignorance or the blind leading the blind, and, therefore, directive leadership might have a higher probability of success. At the other end of the maturity continuum (extremely high levels of task-relevant maturity), some of these people tend to resist engaging in "group think." They would prefer the individual with the highest level of expertise in an area to make the decisions there. "Bill, how do you think we should go on this? It's your area." Thus, according to Situational Leadership, participation as a management technique has a higher probability of success as one moves from low to moderate levels of maturity, and then begins to plateau in potential effectiveness as one's followers become high in task-relevant maturity, as illustrated in Figure 7-5.

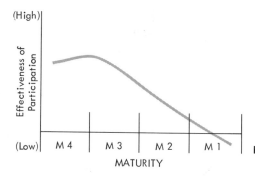

FIGURE 7-5   Participation as an effective management technique

One further point about participation. Although participation tends to satisfy affiliation and esteem needs by giving people a chance to feel in on things and be recognized as important in the decision-making process, it should be remembered that self-actualization may not result from participation. This high level need satisfaction most often occurs in a work environment where people are given a job that allows them an opportunity for achievement, growth and development, and challenge.

The Influence of Cultural Change[27]

The scientific and technical advancements in United States society since the turn of the century almost stagger the imagination. As a result, we have become a dynamic, industrial society with a higher level of education and standard of living than ever thought possible. This phenomenon is beginning to have a pronounced effect on much of the work force utilized by organizations.

Today many employees enjoy a higher standard of living and tend to be better educated and more sophisticated than ever before. As a result, these workers have increased potential for self-direction and self-control. Consistent with these changes in maturity, a large majority of our population, in Maslow's terms, now have their basic physiological and safety-security needs fairly well satisfied. Management can no longer depend on the satisfaction of these needs—through pay, incentive plans, hospitalization, and so on—as primary motivating factors that influence industrial employees. In our society today, there is almost a built-in expectation in people that physiological and safety needs will be fulfilled. In fact, most people do not generally have to worry about where their next meal will come from or whether they will be protected from the elements of physical danger. They are now more susceptible to motivation from other needs: people want to belong, be recognized as "somebody," and have a chance to develop to their fullest potential. As William H. Haney has said:

> The managerial practice, therefore, should be geared to the subordinate's *current level of maturity with the overall goal of helping him to develop, to require progressively less external control, and to gain more and more self-control.* And why would a man want this? Because under these conditions he achieves satisfaction on the job at the levels, primarily the ego and self-fulfillment levels, at which he is the most motivatable.[28]

This concept is illustrated in Figure 7-6.

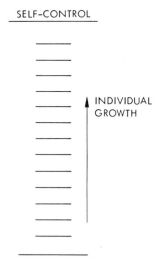

SELF-CONTROL

INDIVIDUAL
GROWTH

EXTERNAL CONTROL

FIGURE 7-6   External control versus self-control

This shift in the maturity level and need disposition of our general population helps us to understand why the findings of many studies of the relationship between leadership styles and productivity, like those conducted by Likert and Halpin, seem to cluster around styles 2 and 3 but not at the extremes (1 and 4).

DOES SITUATIONAL LEADERSHIP WORK?

The widespread acceptance of Situational Leadership as a concept with face validity is well documented. Practicing managers throughout the world say that it gives them some helpful handles to determine what they should do in what situation. It has been a major training component for such Fortune 500 companies as Bank of America, Caterpillar, IBM, Mobil Oil, Union 76, and Xerox. It has been widely accepted in all the military services and numerous fast-growing entrepreneurial companies. Respresentatives from the Center for Leadership Studies are doing Situational Leadership training in the four corners of the world.

Despite this widespread acceptance, Situational Leadership has only recently begun to be studied to any great extent. We have already discussed the studies of Stinson and Johnson[29] on the relationship between leader behavior and task structure and the study by Angelini, Hersey and Carcushansky[30] applying Situational Leadership to teaching. A number of graduate dissertations and theses[31] have attempted to study various aspects of Situational Leadership.

While these studies have attempted to validate Situational Leadership from various directions, the real question that practitioners ask is: Does Situational Leadership work? A recent study at Xerox Corporation, conducted by Raymond A. Gumpert and Ronald K. Hambleton,[32] attempts to answer that question.

In 1974 the Information Systems Group (ISG) of Xerox, responsible for copier/duplicator products, made a major commitment to Situational Leadership as a training concept. Situational Leadership now is a cornerstone of ISG's building-block training strategy, and is taught to middle-level as well as new first-level managers. As Gumpert and Hambleton indicate:

> Despite the model's intuitive appeal and quick acceptance by our managers, because of the training resources required, ISG management development had to answer a critical question: Are managers who use the model correctly in their interactions with employees more effective than those who do not? After all, if they are no more effective, there would be no point to training in situational leadership.[33]

Sixty-five managers in sales, service, administration, and staff functions participated in the study. These managers completed three types of forms:[34]

- A *manager questionnaire*, which was constructed to provide demographic data, such as age, sex, years of service, and so on. The questionnaire also asked for perceptions of the managers' job performance and use of situational leadership.
- A *professional maturity scale*, which was used to determine a subordinate's level of maturity for a set of major job objectives. Each manager assessed one to four employees.
- A *manager rating form*, which allowed the managers to assess their own leadership

styles and their subordinates' job performance for each major job objective. The following job performance rating scale, identical to Xerox's appraisal scale, was used:

Rating	Performance Description
5	Exceptional
4	Consistently exceeds expected level
3	Expected level
2	Meets minimal requirements
1	Unsatisfactory

To test the validity of Situational Leadership, data were collected for two predictions:

- Highly effective managers will indicate more knowledge and use of Situational Leadership than less effective managers.
- Employee job performance will be higher when managers apply [Situational Leadership] correctly than when they apply it incorrectly.[35]

The study led to these conclusions:

- Highly effective managers indicate greater knowledge and use of Situational Leadership than less effective ones.
- All managers in the study reported using Situational Leadership at least some of the time. This finding demonstrates that training in this area has had substantial on-the-job impact.
- On the average, managers who apply the model correctly rate their subordinates' job performance higher than managers who do not. The data in this area are highly supportive of the Hersey-Blanchard model of leadership effectiveness.[36]

Gumpert and Hambleton conclude:

Stated simply, highly effective managers knew more about Situational Leadership and used it more than less effective managers. Data supporting this came from the managers themselves. Also, there is strong evidence suggesting that when Situational Leadership was applied correctly, subordinate job performance was judged higher, and the gains in job performance were practically and statistically significant.[37]

CHANGING LEADERSHIP STYLE APPROPRIATELY

If managers are currently using a style that is appropriate for the level of maturity of their group, as Fred Finch of the University of Massachusetts suggested to the authors,[38] one of the indicators that they can use in determining when and to what degree they should shift their style is performance or results. How well is their group performing in their present activities? If performance is increasing, it would be appropriate for managers to shift their style to the left along the curvilinear function of Situational Leadership Theory. This would indicate that task-relevant maturity is increasing. If performance results are on the decline, it gives managers a clue that they may need to shift their leader behavior to the right along the curvilinear function. In the next chapter we will discuss specifically the implications and implementation of these processes.

NOTES

[1] Edgar H. Schein, *Organizational Psychology* (Englewood Cliffs, N.J.: Prentice-Hall, Inc., 1965), p. 61.

[2] *Ibid.*

[3] Situational Leadership was developed by Paul Hersey and Kenneth H. Blanchard at the Center for Leadership Studies. It was first published by those authors as "Life Cycle Theory of Leadership" in *Training and Development Journal,* May 1969. The concept has continually been refined until its present form presented in this text.

[4] A. K. Korman, " 'Consideration,' 'Initiating Structure,' and Organizational Criteria—A Review," *Personnel Psychology: A Journal of Applied Research,* XIX, No. 4 (Winter 1966), pp. 349–61.

[5] Fillmore H. Sanford, *Authoritarianism and Leadership* (Philadelphia: Institute for Research in Human Relations, 1950).

[6] David C. McClelland, J. W. Atkinson, R. A. Clark and E. L. Lowell, *The Achievement Motive* (New York: Appleton-Century-Crofts, 1953); and *The Achieving Society* (Princeton, N.J.: D. Van Nostrand Co., Inc., 1961).

[7] Chris Argyris, *Personality and Organization* (New York: Harper & Row, Publishers, 1957); *Interpersonal Competence and Organizational Effectiveness* (Homewood, Ill.: Dorsey Press, 1962); and *Integrating the Individual and the Organization* (New York: John Wiley & Sons, Inc., 1964).

[8] These two instruments were developed by Ronald K. Hambleton, Kenneth H. Blanchard and Paul Hersey through a grant from Xerox Corporation. We are grateful to Xerox Corporation not only for providing financial support for the instrument development project but also for allowing us to involve many of their managers and employees in our development and validation work. In particular, we would like to acknowledge Audian Dunham, Warren Rothman and Ray Gumpert for their assistance, encouragement and constructive criticism of our work. The instruments are available through the Center for Leadership Studies, Escondido, Calif.

[9] The Maturity Style Match instruments were developed by Paul Hersey, Kenneth H. Blanchard and Joseph Keilty. Information on these instruments is available through Center for Leadership Studies, Escondido, Calif.

[10] The integration of Situational Leadership with Contracting for Leadership Styles was first published as Paul Hersey, Kenneth H. Blanchard and Ronald K. Hambleton, "Contracting for Leadership Style: A Process and Instrumentation for Building Effective Work Relationships" in *The Proceedings of OD'78,* San Francisco, Calif., sponsored by University Associates/LRC. This presentation is available through the Center for Leadership Studies, Escondido, Calif.

[11] These leadership scales were developed by Paul Hersey, Kenneth H. Blanchard and Ronald K. Hambleton. Information on these instruments is available through the Center for Leadership Studies, Escondido, Calif.

[12] Paul Hersey and Kenneth H. Blanchard, *The Family Game* (Escondido, Calif.: Center for Leadership Studies, 1979).

[13] W. Lloyd Warner, *Social Class in America* (New York: Harper & Row, Publishers, 1960).

[14] See Paul Hersey and Kenneth H. Blanchard, "Managing Research and Development Personnel: An Application of Leadership Theory," *Research Management,* September 1969.

[15] See Kenneth H. Blanchard and Paul Hersey, "A Leadership Theory for Educational Administrators," *Education,* Spring 1970.

[16] Arrigo L. Angelini, Paul Hersey and Sofia Caracushansky, "The Situational Leadership Theory Applied to Teaching: A Research on Learning Effectiveness," an unpublished paper (being reviewed for publication), São Paulo, Brazil.

[17] Examples of self-paced learning curricula can be found at the Nova Educational Complex, Fort Lauderdale, Florida, where they are being used from elementary school through graduate study; Valley High School, Las Vegas, Nevada; and Brigham Young University and Ohio University in some undergraduate courses.

[18] Jesse H. Day and Clifford Houk, "Student-Paced Learning: A Proposal for an Experiment in the Improvement of Learning in General Chemistry," unpublished proposal (Athens: Ohio University, 1968), p. 10.

[19] Kenneth H. Blanchard, "College Boards of Trustees: A Need for Directive Leadership," *Academy of Management Journal,* December 1967.

[20] F.H. Stutz, R. G. Morrow and K. H. Blanchard, "Report of a Survey," in *College and University Trustees and Trusteeship: Recommendations and Report of a Survey* (Ithaca: New York State Regents Advisory Committee on Educational Leadership, 1966).

[21] Henry M. Wriston, *Academic Procession* (New York: Columbia University Press, 1959), p. 78.

[22] Rensis Likert, *New Patterns of Management* (New York: McGraw-Hill Book Company, 1961).

[23] Paul Hersey, an unpublished research project, 1965.

[24] L. Coch and J. R. P. French, "Overcoming Resistance to Change," in Dorwin Cartwright and Alvin Zander, eds., *Group Dynamics: Research and Theory,* 2nd ed. (Evanston, Ill.: Row, Peterson & Company, 1960).

[25] John R. P. French, Jr., Joachim Israel and Dagfinn Ås, "An Experiment on Participation in a Norwegian Factory," *Human Relations,* 13 (1960), 3–19.

[26] A classic study in the area of participation is Victor H. Vroom, *Some Personality Determinants of the Effects of Participation* (Englewood Cliffs, N.J.: Prentice-Hall, Inc., 1960).

[27] See Paul Hersey and Kenneth H. Blanchard, "Cultural Changes: Their Influence on Organizational Structure and Management Behavior," *Training and Development Journal,* October 1970.

[28] William H. Haney, *Communication and Organizational Behavior: Text and Cases,* rev. ed. (Homewood, Ill.: Richard D. Irwin Inc., 1967), p. 20.

[29] John E. Stinson and Thomas W. Johnson, "The Path-Goal Theory of Leadership: A Partial Test and Suggested Refinement," *Academy of Management Journal,* 18, No. 2 (June 1975), pp. 242–52.

[30] Arriso L. Angelini, Paul Hersey and Sofia Caracushansky, "The Situational Leadership Theory Applied to Teaching: A Research on Learning Effectiveness," an unpublished paper, São Paulo, Brazil.

[31] As examples, John D. W. Beck, "Leadership in Education: A Field Test of Hersey and Blanchard's Situational Leadership Theory," an unpublished dissertation, School of Education, University of Massachusetts, May 1978; David J. Ducharme, "The Relationship Between Maturity Level and Leader Behavior Preference Among Urban Elementary School Teachers," an unpublished thesis, Ontario Institute for Studies in Education (OISE), University of Toronto, 1970; Lee Gordon Peters, "Some Aspects of Leader Style, Adaptability and Effectiveness Among Western Massachusetts Principals," an unpublished dissertation, School of Education, University of Massachusetts, September 1974; Maryse R. Raynor, "A Study of the Relationship Among Knowledge of Leader-

ship Theory, Behavior and Effectiveness," an unpublished dissertation, School of Education, University of Massachusetts, 1976; Brian Smith and Nancy McDonald, "The Relationship Between Birth Order, Leadership Style and Effectiveness," an unpublished paper, Concordia University, Montreal, Canada, 1975; and Mary J. Smith, "Effectiveness in Urban Elementary Schools as a Function of the Interaction Between Leadership Behavior of Principals and Maturity of Followers, an unpublished dissertation, School of Education, University of Massachusetts, Amherst, Mass., December 1974.

[32] Raymond A. Gumpert and Ronald K. Hambleton, "Situational Leadership: How Xerox Managers Fine-Tune Managerial Styles to Employee Maturity and Task Needs," *Management Review,* December 1979, pp. 8–12.

[33] *Ibid.,* p. 9.

[34] *Ibid.,* p. 11.

[35] *Ibid.*

[36] *Ibid.,* p. 12.

[37] *Ibid.*

[38] Suggestion made at the Faculty Club, University of Massachusetts, Fall 1974.

chapter 8

Situational Leadership, Perception, and the Impact of Power

The concepts of leadership and power have generated lively interest, debate and occasionally confusion throughout the evolution of management thought. The concept of power is closely related to the concept of leadership, for power is one of the means by which a leader influences the behavior of followers.[1] Given this integral relationship between leadership and power, Hersey, Blanchard, and Natemeyer[2] feel leaders must not only assess their leader behavior in order to understand how they actually influence other people but they must also examine their possession and use of power.

POWER DEFINED

In spite of the widespread usage of the term "power" in the management literature, there is considerable confusion over its definition. Power and other concepts, such as influence and authority, are often definitionally indistinct among scholars.[3] Russell[4] defined power as "the production of intended effects." Bierstedt[5] defined power as "the ability to employ force." Wrong[6] limited power to the intended, successful control of others. French[7] defined the power that person A has over person B as "equal to the maximum force which A can induce on B minus the maximum force which B can mobilize in the opposing direction." For Dahl,[8] "A has power over B to the extent that A can get B to do something that B would otherwise not do."

Rogers[9] attempted to clear up the terminological confusion by defining power as "the potential for influence." Thus, power is a resource which may or may not be used. The use of power resulting in a change in the probability that a person or group will adopt the desired behavioral change is defined as "influence." Accepting Rogers' definition, we make this distinction between leadership and power. As was suggested in Chapter 4, leadership is defined as the process of influencing the activities of an individual or a group in efforts toward goal accomplishment in a given situation. Therefore, leadership is simply any attempt to influence, while power is well described as a leader's *influence potential*. It is the resource that enables a leader to induce compliance from or influence others.

POWER: AN ERODING CONCEPT

If power is defined as influence potential, how does one describe authority? Authority is a particular type of power which has its origin in the position that a leader occupies. Thus, authority is the power that is legitimatized by virtue of an individual's formal role in a social organization.

Hundreds of years ago the kings and queens had all the power; the serfs had none. After all, their positions gave them ultimate authority. For years it was almost a similar case with managers. They could make all the decisions. If they didn't like the way you looked, or the way you combed your hair, they could fire you, and workers could do very little to stop such arbitrary action. Today, that is no longer the case. What does that mean in terms of a leader's influence potential?

First of all, managers must realize that power is finite. There is only so much power around. If someone else has it, you don't. If your power is legislated or negotiated away, it is no longer there. The amount of power available does not expand in different situations. As James A. Lee argues, "Leader power is what is left after subtracting all subordinate power (i.e., collective, legal, economic independence, and expertise), power removed from their grasp by the nature of the task (i.e., a machine-paced assembly line, lack of proximity, and physical barriers), and that removed by power sources outside their organizational unit (organizational policies, intrusions from their boss, and public sentiment).[10] Thus, today's manager only has a limited amount of power.

Second, if managers have only a portion of the total power available, they must learn ways to use the power they have in realistic and meaningful ways. In addition, where managers used to rely on the power in their position, they now have to look for other bases or sources of power.

BASES OF POWER

In Chapter 5 two sources or bases of power were discussed: position power and personal power.[11] It was suggested that describing power in terms of these two sources has been popular ever since Machiavelli first raised the question in the sixteenth century whether it is better to have a relationship based on love (personal power) or on fear (position power).[12]

While position power and personal power are important and useful in examining power, they are limited because you are forced to divide "the pie" always into just two pieces.

Natemeyer cites a number of other attempts to classify bases of power. Peabody[13] classified the statements of respondents in a police department, a welfare office, and an elementary school into four categories. These were power of legitimacy (laws, rules, policies), of position, of competence (professional and technical expertise), and of person.

A study by Filley and Grimes[14] identified eleven reasons why an individual would seek a decision from another on various work-related matters in a professional organization. These reasons, from most frequently to least frequently mentioned, were: responsibility and function (the person is responsible for the particular matter); formal authority (the person is in a position to make decisions generally); control of resources (the person controls money, information, etc.); collegial (a group of peers has the right to be consulted); manipulation (the person can get the decision made in the manner desired); default or avoidance (the person is available and will deal with the problem); bureaucratic rules (the rules specify the person to consult); traditional rules (custom, tradition, or seniority specify the person to consult); equity (the person is a fair decision maker); friendship (the person is personally liked); and expertise (the person has superior knowledge of the subject).

Many other power base classification systems have been developed,[15] but the framework devised by French and Raven[16] appears to be the most widely accepted. They propose that there are five different bases of power: coercive power, expert power, legitimate power, referent power, and reward power.

Later, Raven collaborating with Kruglanski,[17] identified a sixth power base—information power. Then, in 1979, Hersey and Goldsmith proposed a seventh basis of power—connection power. These seven bases of power, identified as potential means of successfully influencing the behavior of others, are defined as follows:[18]

COERCIVE POWER is based on fear. A leader high in coercive power is seen as inducing compliance because failure to comply will lead to punishment such as undesirable work assignments, reprimands, or dismissal.

LEGITIMATE POWER is based on the position held by the leader. Normally, the higher the position, the higher the legitimate power tends to be. A leader high in legitimate power induces compliance or influences others because they feel that this person has the right, by virtue of position in the organization, to expect that suggestions will be followed.

EXPERT POWER is based on the leader's possession of expertise, skill, and knowledge, which, through respect, influence others. A leader high in expert power is seen as possessing the expertise to facilitate the work behavior of others. This respect leads to compliance with the leader's wishes.

REWARD POWER is based on the leader's ability to provide rewards for other people who believe that compliance will lead to positive incentives such as pay, promotion, or recognition.

REFERENT POWER is based on the leader's personal traits. A leader high in referent power is generally liked and admired by others because of personality. This liking for, admiration for, and identification with the leader influences others.

INFORMATION POWER is based on the leader's possession of or access to information that is perceived as valuable by others. This power base influences others because they need this information or want to be in on things.

CONNECTION POWER is based on the leader's "connections" with influential or important persons inside or outside the organization. A leader high in connection power induces compliance from others because they aim at gaining the favor or avoiding the disfavor of the powerful connection.

IS THERE A BEST TYPE OF POWER?

Even though the French and Raven initial classification system was not derived from research, it motivated a number of scholars to try to answer the following question: Given the wide variety of power bases available to the leader, which type of power should be emphasized in order to maximize effectiveness? In any attempt to answer this question, it is important to remember the definition of effectiveness. As stated in Chapter 5, organizational effectiveness, as well as leader effectiveness, is a function of both performance (output variables) and satisfaction (intervening variables). Natemeyer[19] reviewed the various studies that attempted to investigate the relationship between work group effectiveness and the degree to which a leader utilizes various power bases.

Student[20] studied forty production groups in two plants of a company manufacturing home appliances. Employees rated the extent to which they comply with their foremen due to each of the five French and Raven power bases. Legitimate power was found to be the strongest reason for compliance, followed by expert power, reward power, referent power, and last, coercive power.

Student also related the foreman's power base utilization (as perceived by the workers) to a number of measures of performance. He found that legitimate power, while most important among the reasons for compliance, was not related to the performance of the work groups. Reward and coercive power were positively related to some performance measures (suggestions submitted, supply cost performance) but negatively related to others (average earnings, maintenance cost performance). Expert and referent power were significantly and positively related to four and five measures of performance, and thus emerged as the most effective base of supervisory power. Student explains these results by suggesting that expert and referent power are qualitatively different from legitimate, reward, and coercive power. Expert and referent power are considered idiosyncratic in character and to depend on an individual's unique role behavior, while legitimate, reward, and coercive power are organizationally determined and designed to be equal for supervisors at the same hierarchical level. Implicit in Student's conclusions is the contention that subordinates are more responsive to and satisfied with a leader whose influence attempts are not based entirely on position-based power (i.e., legitimate, reward, and coercive).

Similar results were obtained in a study by Bachman, Smith and Slesinger.[21] Data were obtained from thirty-six branch offices of a national sales organization. Each office was managed by a single office supervisor. Employees were asked to rank each of the five power bases according to the extent to which it was a reason for compliance. These results were then correlated with satisfaction and performance measures. Legitimate and expert power again emerged as numbers 1 and 2 in importance, followed by reference, reward, and coercive power.

In those offices in which referent and expert power predominated, performance and satisfaction were high. In those offices in which reward power was high, performance tended to be poor and there was marked dissatisfaction. Coercive and legitimate bases of power were associated with dissatisfaction, but they were unrelated to performance.

The findings of Student and Bachman and others were included in a comparative study of five organizations by Bachman, Bowers and Marcus.[22] In addition to the appliance firm and the sales organization, other organizations examined were twelve liberal arts colleges, forty agencies of a life insurance company, and twenty-one work groups of a large Midwestern utility company. A ranking procedure was used to ascertain the strength of the supervisors' power bases in the colleges and the utility company, while an independent rating procedure for each power base was used with the life insurance agencies.

Expert and legitimate power were again the most important reasons for complying with superiors in all three organizations. Expert power was most important and legitimate second in the colleges and insurance agencies, while the order was reversed in the utility company. Referent power was third in importance in the colleges, fourth in the insurance agencies, and fifth in the utility companies. Reward power was third in importance in the utility company and the agencies, and fourth in the colleges. Finally, coercive power was least important in the colleges and the insurance agencies, and fourth in the utility company.

Expert and referent power were again strongly and positively related to satisfaction in these three additional organizations, while reward and legitimate power were not strongly related to the satisfaction measures. Coercive power was consistently related to dissatisfaction. Performance data were obtained from the insurance agencies, but not from the colleges or utility company. Expert and reward power were positively related to insurance agency performance measures, while coercive, legitimate, and referent power yielded insignificant correlations.

Ivancevich and Donnelly[23] studied salesmen's perceptions of their managers' power bases in thirty-one branches of a large firm that produces food products. The employees were asked to rank the power bases in order of importance for compliance. Expert power was most important, followed by legitimate, reward, referent, and coercive power. Referent and expert power were positively related to performance, while reward, legitimate and coercive power showed no relationship.

Burke and Wilcox[24] conducted a study of leader power bases and subordinate satisfaction in six offices of a large public utility company. Using a 1 to 5 ranking method, expert power emerged as most important, followed by legitimate, coercive, referent, and reward power. Referent and expert power were associated with greatest satisfaction; legimate and reward power were intermediate; and coercive power was associated with least satisfaction.

Jamieson and Thomas[25] recently conducted a study of power in the classroom. Data were collected from high school, undergraduate, and graduate students on their teachers' bases of power and results were correlated with several measures of student satisfaction. For the high school students, legitimate power was most important, followed by coercive, expert, referent, and reward power. The undergraduate student viewed coercive power as most important, followed by legitimate, expert, reward, and referent power. The graduate students perceived expert power as the strongest, followed by legitimate, reward, coercive, and referent power. Coercive power was strongly and negatively associated with satisfaction among all three groups, while the other four power bases yielded insignificant results.

In summarizing his review of the most important research that has been done relating supervisory power bases to subordinate satisfaction and performance, Natemeyer[26] made the following general conclusion. While expert and legitimate power bases appear to be the most important reason for compliance, and expert and referent power bases tend to be often strongly and consistently related to subordinate performance and satisfaction measures, the results are not clear enough to generalize about a *best* power base. In fact, the results suggest that the appropriate power base is largely affected by situational variables. In other words, leaders may need various power bases, depending on the situation.

Power Bases and Maturity Level

Hersey, Blanchard, and Natemeyer[27] suggest that there appears to be a direct relationship between the level of maturity[28] of individuals and groups and the kind of power bases that have a high probability of gaining compliance from those people. Situational Leadership views maturity as the ability and willingness of individuals or groups to take responsibility for directing their own behavior in a particular situation. Thus, it must be reemphasized that maturity is a task-specific concept and depends on what the leader is attempting to accomplish.

As people move from lower to higher levels of maturity, their competence and confidence to do things increase. The seven power bases appear to have significant impact on the behavior of people at various levels of maturity, as seen in Figure 8-1.

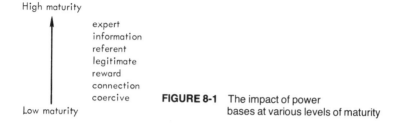

High maturity

expert
information
referent
legitimate
reward
connection
coercive

Low maturity

FIGURE 8-1 The impact of power
bases at various levels of maturity

INTEGRATING POWER BASES, MATURITY LEVEL, AND LEADERSHIP STYLE THROUGH SITUATIONAL LEADERSHIP

Situational Leadership can provide the basis for understanding the potential impact of each power base. It is our contention that the maturity of the follower not only dictates which style of leadership will have the highest probability of success, but that the maturity of the follower also determines the power base that the leader should use in order to induce compliance or influence behavior.

The Situational Use of Power

Even if the leader is using the appropriate leadership style for a given maturity level, that style may not be maximizing the leader's probability of success if it does not reflect the appropriate power base. Therefore, just as an effective leader should vary leadership style according to the maturity level of the follower, it may be appropriate to vary the use of power in a similar manner. The power bases that may influence people's behavior at various levels of maturity are pictured in Figure 8-2.

MATURITY LEVEL

High	Moderate		Low
M4	M3	M2	M1
Expert	Referent	Reward	Coercive
Information	Legitimate	Connection	

FIGURE 8-2 Power bases necessary to influence people's behavior at various levels of maturity

Figure 8-2 shows a relationship only between power bases and maturity level. There also appears to be a direct relationship between the kind of power bases a person has and the corresponding leadership style that will be effective for that person in influencing the behavior of others at various maturity levels.

Coercive power. A follower low in maturity generally needs strong directive behavior in order to become productive. To engage effectively in this *"tell-*

ing" style, coercive power is often necessary. The behavior of people at low levels of maturity seems to be influenced by the awareness that costs will be incurred if they do not learn and follow the rules of the game. Thus, if people are *unable and unwilling,* sanctions—the perceived power to fire, transfer, demote, etc.—may be an important way that a leader can induce compliance from them. The leader's coercive power may motivate the followers to avoid the punishment or "cost" by doing what the leader tells them to do.

Connection power. As a follower begins to move from *maturity level* M1 to M2, directive behavior is still needed, but increases in supportive behavior are also important. The *"telling"* and *"selling"* leadership styles appropriate for these levels of maturity may become more effective if the leader has connection power. The possession of this power base may induce compliance because a follower at this maturity level tends to aim at avoiding punishments or gaining rewards available through the powerful connection.

Reward power. A follower at a low to moderate level of maturity often needs high amounts of supportive behavior and directive behavior. This *"selling"* style is often enhanced by reward power. Since individuals at this maturity level are *willing* to "try on" new behavior, the leader needs to be perceived as having access to rewards in order to gain compliance and reinforce growth in the desired direction.

Legitimate power. The leadership styles that tend to influence effectively those at both *moderate levels of maturity* (M2 and M3) are *"selling"* and *"participating."* To engage effectively in these styles, legitimate power seems to be helpful. By the time a follower reaches these moderate levels of maturity, the power of the leader has become legitimized. That is, the leader is able to induce compliance or influence behavior by virtue of his or her position in the organizational hierarchy.

Referent power. A follower at a moderate to high level of maturity tends to need little direction but still requires a high level of communication and support from the leader. This *"participating"* style may be effectively utilized if the leader has referent power. This source of power is based on good personal relations with the follower. With people who are *able but unwilling or insecure,* this power base tends to be an important means of instilling confidence and providing encouragement, recognition, and other supportive behavior. When that occurs, followers will generally respond in a positive way, permitting the leader to influence them because they like, admire, or identify with the leader.

Information power. The leadership styles that tend to motivate followers effectively at *above-average maturity levels* (M3 and M4) are *"participating"* and *"delegating."* Information power seems to be helpful in using these two styles. People at these levels of maturity look to the leader for information to maintain or improve performance. The transition from moderate to high maturity may be facilitated if the follower knows that the leader is available to clarify or explain issues and provide access to pertinent data, reports, and correspondence when needed. Through this information power the leader is able to influence these mature people.

Expert power. A follower who develops to a high level of maturity often requires little direction or support. This follower is *able and willing* to perform the tasks required and tends to respond most readily to a *"delegating"* leadership style and expert power. Thus, a leader may gain respect from and influence most readily a person who has both competence and confidence by possessing expertise, skill, and knowledge that this follower recognizes as important.

An easy way to think about sources of power in terms of making diagnostic judgments is to draw a triangle, as shown in Figure 8-3, around the three power

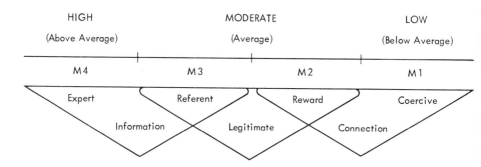

FIGURE 8-3 Power bases necessary to influence people at various maturity levels

bases necessary to influence below-average, moderate, and above-average levels of maturity. It is important to stress here that with people of below-average maturity, the emphasis is on compliance; with people of average maturity, it is on compliance and influence; and with people of above-average maturity, it is on influence.

A way to examine the high-probability power base for a specific maturity level is to draw inverted triangles, as shown in Figure 8-4. Note that M1 and M4, the extreme maturity levels, include only two power bases instead of three.

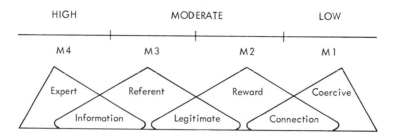

FIGURE 8-4 Power bases necessary to influence people's behavior at *specific* levels of maturity

Developing Sources of Power

Although these seven power bases are potentially available to any leader as a means of inducing compliance or influencing the behavior of others, it is important to note that there is significant variance in the powers that leaders may actually possess. Some leaders have a great deal of power while others have very little. Part of the variance in actual power is due to the organization and the leader's position in the organization (position power), and part is due to individual differences among the leaders themselves (personal power), as shown in Figure 8-5.

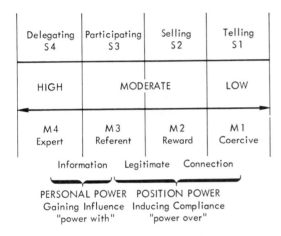

FIGURE 8-5 Summary of relationships between power bases, maturity level, and leadership style

The power bases that are most relevant at the below-average levels of maturity tend to be those that the organization or others can bestow upon the leader. The power bases that influence people who are above average in maturity must, to a large degree, be earned from the people the leader is attempting to influence. Therefore, we suggest that POSITION POWER, the word *"compliance,"* and the phrase *"power over"* are most descriptive with coercive, connection, reward, and legitimate power bases; and we suggest that PERSONAL POWER, the word *"influence,"* and the phrase *"power with"* more accurately describe the effect on behavior from referent, information, and expert power.

Sources of Power

Just as some leaders start off with little power in the beginning and gradually build and develop various power sources, other leaders gradually let their power bases erode and lose them. Why does this happen? Before we answer this question, managers need to understand where position and personal power sources come from.

As we discussed in Chapter 3, position power can be thought of simply as the authority that is delegated down in an organization. It is important to remember that just because a manager has position power today, it doesn't mean that that manager will have it tomorrow. Not only can the people above delegate the authority to provide rewards and sanctions, they can also take that authority away. So managers must remember that position power is volatile.

This is not to suggest that managers do not have some impact on how much coercive, connection, reward, and legitimate power they get. Sure they do. The extent to which they develop rapport, confidence and trust between themselves and their superiors will determine how willing those above will be to delegate power. But position power is something that a manager has to earn on a day-to-day basis.

The same can be said about personal power, except the reward, information, and expert power that managers possess depends on the confidence and trust these managers generate from the people they are attempting to influence. For example, people might think that some leaders have charisma and other leaders don't. Leaders don't have charisma; followers *give* leaders charisma. We have all seen that phenomenon with elected officials. They are often carried into office because of their charisma, but when their actions do not gain general approval, they may lose their charisma overnight. Again, this is not to say that managers do not have some impact on how much personal power they get, but it's something that they have to earn on a day-to-day basis.

It should be remembered that position power and personal power bases together constitute an interaction-influence system. That is, power does not develop in a vacuum. Each power base tends to affect each of the other power bases. Thus, it has been found that the extent to which people are willing to grant personal power to a manager depends a great deal on their perception of a leader's ability to provide rewards, punishment or sanctions (position power). At the same time, the willingness of managers above a leader to delegate position power is often determined by the extent to which they perceive that leader as being liked and respected, having information and expertise (personal power) with their people. Keep in mind that we did not say how much personal power or position power affects whether leaders will be delegated authority or treated with respect. It's the *perception* that others have of those power bases that is crucial. So, the key word, perhaps, in the whole area of the behavioral sciences is perception.

Perception of Power

It is important to remember that truth and reality do not necessarily evoke behavior. For example, when a couple has a fight, it does not matter whether the cause is real or imagined—it is just as much of a fight.

It is the perception others hold about a leader's power that gives that leader the ability to induce compliance or to influence their behavior. Therefore, power is like money in the bank. The ability of a person who has no identification to cash a check is dependent not only on the funds the person has deposited in the bank. It also depends on whether that person gives the impression of affluence. Thus, an individual's power base, like wealth, has to be known to others before it can be used effectively. Therefore, if leaders are to increase their chances of successfully influencing the behavior of others, they need information about the sources of power they are perceived as having by those people. Also, it is important for leaders to communicate to others the power they actually possess.

Eroding Sources of Power

Since leaders have only a limited amount of power available to them, one would hope for their sake that they would hold on to whatever power bases they have. And, yet, some leaders who often start off with significant power gradually lose their power bases and let them erode. The key to avoiding such erosion is using your power bases (in the eyes of others). For example, a leader could have a significant amount of coercive power but gradually lose it by threatening. If a leader continually threatens followers with some kind of punishment but never delivers the punishment, the people will start to think that the leader really does not have any coercive power. Similarly, leaders can lose their reward power if everyone gets the same reward whether they perform or not, or just because they have seniority in industry or are older in the family. Some parents establish age requirements when kids can get to do things. "When you're thirteen, you'll be able to stay out past ten o'clock. When you're sixteen, you'll be able to stay home alone." The problem with using age as a factor in determining when people can do things is that all they have to do is get older. When that is done, reward power as a parent or a leader is lost. What is happening is that people are getting rewards for being older, not for being more mature.

Connection power can be eroded when people begin to see that the sponsor or connection does not make any disciplinary interventions or provide any favors or sanctions. In other words, to be maintained, connection power needs occasional interventions from the sponsor.

Managers can lose their legitimate power by not making decisions that people think they ought to make, given their position. Erosion of this power base can also occur if a manager continually makes decisions that are not fruitful. After a while, their staff members will no longer look to them to make decisions even if they have the title of Senior Research Scientist or Department Chairman.

This process also works with referent power. When you give "strokes" to those who are performing and the same "strokes" to those who are not performing, you begin to erode your referent power. If people do not have to earn "strokes," then you no longer have referent power.

Leaders also have to be careful about eroding their information and expert power. This is particularly a concern if you give away expertise and information to people whose goals are not organizational goals. If you give away too much information and knowledge, eventually they will not need you. The only way you can get around this is to continually develop new information and new expertise so that they have to come back to the source.

If leaders let their power bases erode, they will also reduce the effectiveness of their leadership attempts. For example, an effective *"telling"* (S1) leadership style depends on having some coercive power. If leaders are not seen as being able to deliver punishments and sanctions, their use of that style is limited.

The same can be said about a *"selling"* (S2) style. Without some control over rewards, leaders are seen as not able to reinforce or reward increased performance as people grow and develop their skills.

A *"participating"* (S3) style won't work if people don't like and respect a manager. If that manager has let his reward power erode because he hasn't been good to people, then a participative/high relationship style is going to be seen not as a reward but as a punishment. It's like a manager who has ignored and left a staff member alone for a long time. Then, suddenly, when that person's family life begins to deteriorate, the manager tries to "fill the void." Since the manager has eroded his or her referent power, these supportive leadership attempts are not seen as rewards but as sanctions and punishments. Time with the boss is not seen as a positive situation.

If a manager is supervising highly competent and motivated people, that manager needs to have some expert power to make any kind of significant intervention with these people. If the manager has eroded any information and expert power that he or she had, the possibility of influencing these people in any significant way will be very limited.

In summary, it is not just style that determines whether a leader is maximizing effectiveness. Also important is whether the power bases available to the leader are consistent with the leadership style(s) appropriate to the maturity level of the individuals or groups the leader is trying to influence.

THE POWER PERCEPTION PROFILE

To provide leaders with feedback on their power bases, so that they can determine which power bases they already have and which they need to develop, Hersey and Natemeyer developed the Power Perception Profile.[29] There are two versions of this instrument: one measures self-perception of power and the other determines an individual's perception of another's power.

Development of the Power Perception Profile

The Power Perception Profile contains twenty-one forced-choice pairs of reasons often given by people when asked why they do things that a leader suggests or wants them to do. Each statement reflects one of the seven sources of power discussed above. In the following pair of statements, referent power is represented by the first statement and coercive power is depicted by the second statement.

Respondents are asked to allocate three points between each set of two alternative choices. They are asked to base their judgments on the relative importance of each alternative, judging either their perception of why people comply with their wishes (self-perception) or why they comply with a particular leader's wishes (other perception).

Respondents are asked to allocate the points between the first item and the second item based on perceived importance in any of the following fashions:

3	2	1	0
0	1	2	3

After completing the Power Perception Profile, respondents are able to obtain a score of the relative strength of each of the seven bases of power. This score represents the perception of influence for themselves or some other leader.

One of the shortcomings of most forced-choice instruments is that they provide comparisons only between items or categories, but they do not offer any perspective on the overall scope of the concepts. In other words, a leader might score high or low on a certain power base when compared with each of the other power bases, but no indication is given of how that power base score compares with the score another leader might receive. For example, even if a leader's score on coercive power is low in relation to the other six power bases, that leader may be relatively high in coercive power when compared with other leaders the respondent has known. To correct this deficiency, the Power Perception Profile goes one step farther than most forced-choice questionnaires and asks respondents to compare the leader with other leaders they have known, in reference to each of the seven power bases.

Uses of the Power Perception Profile

The Power Perception Profile can be used to gather data in actual organizational settings or any learning environment, for example, student or training groups.

In learning groups, the instrument is particularly helpful in groups that have developed some history—that is, they have spent a considerable amount of time interacting with each other analyzing or solving cases, participating in simulations or other training exercises, etc. In this kind of situation, it is recommended that the group fill out one instrument together, using a particular member as the subject and arriving at a consensus on each of the items on the instrument. During each discussion, the person whose power bases are being examined should play a nonparticipant role. That person should not ask any questions or attempt to clarify, justify, or explain his or her actions. An appropriate response might be, "Could you tell me more about that?" or "I'd like to hear more on that point." Then, at the end of the group's assessment, the person whose power bases were being examined is given an opportunity to respond to the group's discussion. This process is repeated until every participant has had a turn to get feedback from the group.

If the Power Perception Profile is being used to gather data in an organization, each organizational member from whom perceptions are desired should fill out a separate instrument. In this case, it is strongly suggested that the leaders not collect the data themselves. Instead, a third party who has the trust and confidence of all involved—such as a representative from personnel or human resource management—should administer the questionnaire. It is also important to assure respondents that only generalized data will be shared with the leader, not the scores from any particular instrument. These suggestions are important because if leaders collect their own data, even if the instruments are anonymous, there is a tendency for some respondents to answer according to what they feel the leaders do or do not want to hear. Thus, to help establish a valid data base, leaders may want to have their data gathered by a third party.

Another value of understanding power bases is important to mention. If you understand what power bases tend to influence a group of people, you have some insight into whom should be given a particular project assignment or responsibility. The person you assign to a particular task should have the power bases and be comfortable in using the appropriate leadership styles that are required in a particular setting. If someone really wants an assignment and doesn't have the appropriate power bases, it's a problem of self-development. You can work out a program to build that power base or appropriate style. What all this means is that we can increase the probability of success of a particular manager if we understand the territory—if we know what power bases and corresponding leadership styles are needed to influence the people involved in the new situation effectively. That's the whole concept of team building. We will be talking about this in much greater depth in later chapters.

CONCLUSIONS

As has been emphasized throughout this chapter, whether or not a leader is maximizing effectiveness is not a question of style alone. It is also a question of what power bases are available to that leader and whether or not these power bases are consistent with the maturity levels of the individual or group that the leader is trying to influence. As managers consider these relationships, it appears that dynamic and growing organizations gradually move away from reliance on power bases that emphasize compliance and toward the utilization of power bases that aim at gaining influence with people. It is important to keep in mind that many times this change, by necessity, will be evolutionary rather than revolutionary.

In the next chapter we will show how leaders can grow and develop their people from lower levels of maturity to higher levels. After all, the growing and developing of people is the key to the long-term effectiveness of an organization.

NOTES

[1] R. M. Stogdill, *Handbook of Leadership* (New York: The Free Press, 1974).

[2] Many of the concepts in this chapter were first published in Paul Hersey, Kenneth H. Blanchard and Walter E. Natemeyer, "Situational Leadership, Perception, and the Impact of Power," *Group and Organizational Studies,* Vol. 4, No. 4 (December 1979), pp. 418–28.

[3] This section on defining power and other concepts originated with Walter E. Natemeyer, *An Empirical Investigation of the Relationships Between Leader Behavior, Leader Power Bases, and Subordinate Performance and Satisfaction,* an unpublished dissertation, University of Houston, August 1975. See also J. J. Gibson, J. M. Ivancevich and J. H. Donnelly, *Organizations* (Dallas: Business Publications, 1973).

[4] B. Russell, *Power* (London: Allen and Unwin, 1938).

[5] R. Beirstedt, "An Analysis of Social Power," *American Sociological Review,* 15 (1950), pp. 730–36.

[6] D. H. Wrong, "Some Problems in Defining Social Power," *American Journal of Sociology,* 73 (1968), pp. 673–81.

[7] J. R. P. French, "A Formal Theory of Social Power," *Psychology Review,* 63 (1956), pp. 181–94.

[8] R. A. Dahl, "The Concept of Power," *Behavioral Science,* 2 (1957), pp. 201–15.

[9] M. F. Rogers, "Instrumental and Infra-Resources: The Bases of Power," *American Journal of Sociology,* 79, 6 (1973), 1418–33.

[10] James A. Lee, "Leader Power and Managing Change," an unpublished paper written at the College of Business Administration, Ohio University, Athens, Ohio.

[11] Amitai Etzioni, *A Comparative Analysis of Complex Organizations* (New York: The Free Press, 1961).

[12] Niccolo Machiavelli, "Of Cruelty and Clemency, Whether It Is Better to Be Loved or Feared," *The Prince and the Discourses* (New York: Random House, Inc., 1950), Chap. XVII.

[13] R. L. Peabody, "Perceptions of Organizational Authority: A Comparative Analysis," *Administrative Quarterly,* 6 (1962), pp. 463–82.

[14] A. C. Filley and A. J. Grimes, "The Bases of Power in Decision Processes" (Industrial Relations Research Institute, University of Wisconsin, Reprint Series, 104, 1967).

[15] K. D. Beene, *A Conception of Authority* (New York: Teachers College, Columbia University, 1943); H. C. Kelman, "Compliance, Identification, and Internalization: Three Processes of Attitude Change," *Journal of Conflict Resolution,* 158, 2, pp. 51–60; and G. Gilman, "An Inquiry into the Nature and Use of Authority," in M. Haire, *Organization Theory in Industrial Practice* (New York: Wiley, 1962).

[16] J. R. P. French and B. Raven, "The Bases of Social Power," in D. Cartwright, *Studies in Social Power* (Ann Arbor: University of Michigan, Institute for Social Research, 1959).

[17] B. H. Raven and W. Kruglanski, "Conflict and Power," in P. G. Swingle, ed., *The Structure of Conflict* (New York: Academic Press, 1975), pp. 177–219.

[18] Five of these descriptions of power bases (coercive, expert, legitimate, referent and reward) have been adapted from the work of French and Raven, "The Bases of Social Power." One power base (information) was introduced by Raven and Kruglanski, "Conflict and Power." In addition to modifying some of these definitions, Paul Hersey and Marshall Goldsmith added a seventh power base: connection power.

[19] Natemeyer, *An Empirical Investigation of the Relationships Between Leader Behavior.*

[20] K. R. Student, "Supervisory Influence and Work-Group Performance, *Journal of Applied Psychology,* 52, 3 (1968), pp. 188–94.

[21] J. G. Bachman, C. G. Smith and J. A. Slesinger, "Control, Performance, and Satisfaction: An Analysis of Structural and Individual Effects," *Journal of Personality and Social Psychology,* 4, 2 (1966), pp. 127–36.

[22] J. G. Bachman, D. G. Bowers and P. M. Marcus, "Bases of Supervisory Power: A Comparative Study in Five Organizational Settings," in Arnold S. Tannenbaum, *Control in Organizations* (New York: McGraw-Hill Book Company, 1968).

[23] J. M. Ivancevich and J. H. Donnelly, "Leader Influence and Performance," *Personnel Psychology,* 23, 4 (1970), 539–49.

[24] R. J. Burke and D. S. Wilcox, "Bases of Supervisory Power and Subordinate Job Satisfactions," *Canadian Journal of Behavioral Science* (1971).

[25] D. W. Jamieson and K. W. Thomas, "Power and Conflict in the Student-Teacher Relationship," *Journal of Applied Behavioral Science,* 10, 3 (1974).

[26] Natemeyer, *An Empirical Investigation of the Relationships Between Leader Behavior.*

[27] Hersey, Blanchard and Natemeyer, "Situational Leadership, Perception, and the Impact of Power."

[28] See Chapter 7, as well as extensive discussions of the concept of maturity in Chris Argyris, *Personality and Organization* (New York: Harper & Row, Publishers, 1957); *Interpersonal Competence and Organizational Effectiveness* (Homewood, Ill.: Dorsey Press, 1962); and *Integrating the Individual and the Organization* (New York: John Wiley & Sons, Inc., 1964).

[29] This instrument was developed by Paul Hersey and Walter E. Natemeyer. Published by the Center of Leadership Studies, Escondido, Calif.

chapter 9

Developing
Human Resources

In Chapter 3 we stated that in evaluating organizational performance, a manager ought to consider both output (productivity) and intervening variables (the condition of the human resources). We urged that both these factors should be examined in light of short- and long-term organizational goals. If the importance of intervening variables is accepted, then one must assume that one of the responsibilities of managers, regardless of whether they are parents' in the home or managers in a business setting, is developing the human resources for which they are responsible. Managers need to devote time to nurture the leadership potential, motivation, morale, climate, commitment to objectives, and the decision-making, communication, and problem-solving skills of their people. Thus, an important role for managers is the development of the task-relevant maturity of their followers.

We think it is vital to emphasize this developmental aspect of Situational Leadership. Without emphasizing that aspect, there is a danger that managers could use Situational Leadership to justify the use of any behavior they wanted. Since the concept contends that there is no "best" leadership style, the use of any style could be supported merely by saying "the individual or group was at such-and-such a maturity level." Thus, while close supervision and direction might be necessary initially when working with individuals who have had little experience in directing their own behavior, it should be recognized that this style is only a first step. In fact, managers should be rewarded for helping their people develop and be able to assume more and more responsibility on their own. For example, in some progressive companies in which we have worked we have been able to introduce a new policy which essentially states: No managers will be promoted in this organization unless they do at least two things: First, they have to do a good job in what they are being asked to do, i.e., good "bottom line" results (output variables). Second, they have to have a ready replacement who can take over their job tomorrow (intervening variables).

This means that, if managers are using a leadership style with a high probability of success for working with a given level of maturity (as discussed in the last chapter), this perhaps is not really enough. These managers may be getting a reasonable amount of output, but their responsibilities may not stop there. Besides maintaining an adequate level of output, managers may want to develop the ability and effectiveness of their human resources (their followers).

INCREASING EFFECTIVENESS

Likert found that employee-centered supervisors who use general supervision *tend* to have higher producing sections than job-centered supervisors who use close supervision.[1] We emphasize the word *tend* because this seems to be increasingly the case in our society; yet we must also realize that there are exceptions to this tendency, which are even evident in Likert's data. What Likert found was that subordinates generally respond well to their superior's high expectations and genuine confidence in them and try to justify their boss's expectations of them. Their resulting high performance will reinforce their superior's high trust for them; it is easy to trust and respect people who meet or exceed your expectations.

J. Sterling Livingston,[2] in discussing this phenomenon, refers to the words of Eliza Doolittle from George Bernard Shaw's play *Pygmalion* (the basis of the musical hit, *My Fair Lady*):

> You see, really and truly, apart from the things anyone can pick up (the dressing and the proper way of speaking, and so on), the difference between a lady and a flower girl is not how she behaves but how she's treated. I shall always be a flower girl to Professor Higgins, because he always treats me as a flower girl, and always will; but I know I can be a lady to you, because you always treat me as a lady, and always will.

Livingston has found from his experience and research that:

> Some managers always treat their subordinates in a way that leads to superior performance. But most managers, like Professor Higgins, unintentionally treat their subordinates in a way that leads to lower performance than they are capable of achieving. The way managers treat their subordinates is subtly influenced by what they expect of them. If a manager's expectations are high, productivity is likely to

be excellent. If his expectations are low, productivity is likely to be poor. It is as though there were a law that caused a subordinate's performance to rise or fall to meet his manager's expectations. . . .

Cases and other evidence available from scientific research now reveal:

—What a manager expects of his subordinates and the way he treats them largely determine their performance and career progress.
—A unique characteristic of superior managers is their ability to create high performance expectations that subordinates fulfill.
—Less effective managers fail to develop similar expectations, and, as a consequence, the productivity of their subordinates suffers.
—Subordinates, more often than not, appear to do what they believe they are expected to do.

When people respond to the high expectations of their managers with high performance, we call that occurrence the "effective cycle," as illustrated in Figure 9-1.

FIGURE 9-1 Effective cycle

Yet, as we have pointed out earlier, the concentration on output variables as a means of evaluating effectiveness tends to lead to short-run, task-oriented leader behavior. This style, in some cases, does not allow much room for a trusting relationship with employees. Instead, subordinates are told what to do and how to do it, with little consideration expressed for their ideas or feelings. After a while, the subordinates respond with minimal effort and resentment; low performance results in these instances. Reinforced by low expectations, it becomes a vicious cycle. Many other examples could be given that result in this all-too-common problem in organizations, as shown in Figure 9-2.

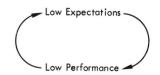

FIGURE 9-2 Ineffective cycle

These cycles are depicted as static, but in reality they are very dynamic. The situation tends to get better or worse. For example, high expectations result in high performance, which reinforces the high expectations and produces even higher productivity. It almost becomes a spiral effect, as illustrated in Figure 9-3.

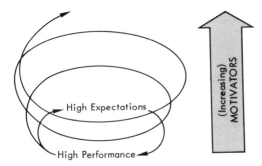

FIGURE 9-3 Spiraling effect of effective cycle

In many cases, this spiraling effect is caused by an increase in leverage created through the use of the motivators. As people perform they are given more responsibility and opportunities for achievement and growth and development.

This spiraling effect can also occur in a downward direction. Low expectations result in low performance, which reinforces the low expectations and produces even lower productivity. It becomes a spiral effect like a whirlpool, as shown in Figure 9-4.

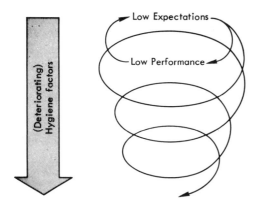

FIGURE 9-4 Spiraling effect of ineffective cycle

If this downward spiraling continues long enough, the cycle may reach a point where it cannot be turned around in a short period of time because of the large reservoir of negative past experience that has built up in the organization. Much of the focus and energy is directed toward perceived problems in the environment such as interpersonal relations and respect for supervision rather than toward the work itself. Reaction to deteriorating hygiene factors takes such form as hostility, undermining, and slowdown in work performance. When this happens, even if a manager actually changes behavior, the credibility gap based on long-term experience is such that the response is still distrust and skepticism rather than change.

One alternative that is sometimes necessary at this juncture is to bring in a new manager from the outside. The reason this has a higher probability of success is that the sum of the past experience of the people involved with the new manager is likened to a "clean slate," and thus different behaviors are on a much more believable basis. This was evident in the case of Plant Y described by Guest, which was discussed in Chapter 6. The ineffective cycle had been in a downward spiral far past the point where Stewart would have a good opportunity to make significant change. But with the introduction of a new manager, Cooley, significant changes were now possible.

Breaking the Ineffective Cycle

Although new managers may be in a better position to initiate change in a situation that has been spiraling downward, they still do not have an easy task. Essentially, they have to break the ineffective cycle. There are at least two alternatives available to managers in this situation. They can either fire the low performing personnel and hire people whom they expect to perform well or they can respond to low performance with high expectations and trust.

The first choice is not always possible because competent replacements are not readily available or the people involved have some form of job security (civil service or union tenure), which means they cannot be fired without considerable cost in time, energy, and hassle.

The latter choice for managers is difficult. In effect, the attempt is to change the expectations or behavior of their subordinates. It is especially difficult for managers to have high expectations about people who have shown no indication that they deserve to be trusted. The key, then, is to change appropriately.

From our work with Situational Leadership we have identified two different cycles that managers can use for changing or maximizing the task-relevant maturity of their followers—the developmental cycle and the regressive cycle.

In this chapter we will discuss the developmental cycle. In Chapter 10 we will present the regressive cycle.

DEVELOPMENTAL CYCLE

The role managers play in developing the maturity level of their people is extremely important. Too often managers do not take responsibility for the performance of their people, especially if they are not doing well. If they're having problems, often managers will say, "I have an example of a Peter Principle," and not take responsibility for the poor performance. It has been our experience that when managers have to fire someone or find a place to hide them (this is what Peter called a "lateral arabesque"), or when they are downright worried about someone's performance, these managers should look in the mirror. In most cases, the biggest cause of the performance problem is looking back at them. Managers are responsible for making their people "winners," and this is what the developmental cycle is all about. Managers are involved in the developmental cycle any time they attempt to increase the present maturity level of an individual or group in some aspect of their work. In other words, the developmental cycle is a growth cycle.

What Do We Want to Influence?

As we suggested in Chapter 7, the first question managers have to ask themselves when they are thinking about the development of their people is: What area of my subordinate's job do I want to influence? In other words, what are their responsibilities or goals and objectives? A foreman, for example, might want to influence his subordinates' productivity, quality, waste, absenteeism, accident rate, etc. A university department chairman might want to affect his faculty's writing and research and teaching and service.

Once the objectives or responsibilities are identified and understood, managers must clearly specify what constitutes good performance in each area, so that both they and their subordinates know when their performance is approaching the desired level. What does a good sales record mean? Does it mean number of sales made or volume of sales? What is meant by developing your people or being a good administrator? Managers have to specify what good performance *looks like*. Just telling a person, "I want you to make widgets" is not as helpful as saying, "I want you to make widgets at the rate of 200 a day." For managers and staff members to know how well someone is doing, good performance has to be clearly specified. Managers cannot change and develop their subordinates' behavior in areas that are unclear.

How Is the Person Doing Now?

Before beginning the developmental cycle with an individual in a work situation, the manager must decide how well that person is doing right now. In other words, what is the person's maturity level right now in a specific aspect of the job? How able is the person to take responsibility for his or her behavior? How willing or motivated is the person? As was discussed earlier, maturity is not a global concept. That is, people are not mature or immature in any total sense. How can we know what a person's maturity level is in a given situation?

Determining Maturity

In assessing the maturity level of an individual, we will have to make judgments about that person's ability and motivation. Where do we get the information to make these judgments? We can either *ask the person* or *observe* the person's behavior. We could ask a person such questions as, "How well do you think you are doing at such and such?" or "How do you feel about doing that?" or "Are you enthusiastic and excited about it, or not?" Obviously, with some people, asking for their own assessment of their maturity won't be productive. However, it has been surprising how even young children are able to share that kind of information. Phil and Jane learned that when they used to ask their two-year-old daughter, Lee, to do something. Often Lee would reply, "I can't want to!" When translated, what Lee was really saying (in our terms) is, "I'm both unable and unwilling to do what you want me to do." If Lee's parents still wanted her to do it, they soon learned that they had to direct and closely supervise her behavior in this area (S1—"telling"). As children get older, they can play an even more significant role in analyzing their own maturity level. In the world of work, people should play a significant role in determining their own maturity level. That process will be discussed in much more detail in Chapter 11.

You might be wondering whether people will always tell their managers the truth or just tell what is necessary to keep the manager off their backs. If managers doubt what their people tell them about their ability or willingness to do something, those managers can check out their opinion by observing staff members' behavior. Ability can be determined by examining past performance. Has the person done well in this area before, or has his or her performance been poor or nonexistent? Does the staff member have the necessary knowledge to perform well in the area, or does that person not know how to do what needs to be done?

Willingness can be determined by watching a person's behavior in a particular case. What is the person's interest level? Does the person seem enthusiastic or any less interested? What is the person's commitment to this area? Does the person appear to enjoy doing things in this area or merely anxious to get them over with? Is the person's self-confidence secure in this area or does the person lack confidence and feel insecure? Remember that people can be at any of four levels of maturity in each of their various areas of responsibility. A person's maturity level gives us a good clue to how to begin any further development of that individual. If a manager wants to influence a staff member in an area in which the person is both unable and unwilling (low maturity level), the manager must begin the developmental cycle by directing, controlling and closely supervising ("telling") the staff member's behavior. If, however, the person is willing (motivated) to do something but not able to do it (low to moderate maturity), the manager must begin the cycle by both directing and supporting ("selling") the desired behavior. If the person is able to do something without direction but is unwilling to do it, or is insecure (moderate to high maturity), the manager is faced with a motivational problem. Individuals reluctant to do what they are able to do are often insecure or lacking confidence. In this case, the manager should begin the developmental cycle by using a supportive style ("participating") to help the individual become secure enough to do what he or she already knows how to do. Finally, if staff members are both able and willing to direct their own behavor (high maturity), we can merely delegate responsibility to them and know that they will perform well. When that occurs, there is no need for beginning the developmental cycle. The person is already mature in that area.

Increasing Maturity

Managers are engaged in the developmental cycle any time they attempt to increase the task-relevant maturity of an individual or group beyond the level that individual or group has previously reached. In other words, the developmental cycle is a growth cycle.

To explain fully how the developmental cycle works, let us look at an example. Suppose a manager has been able to diagnose the environment and finds that the task-relevant maturity of one of his staff members is low (M1) in the area of developing a departmental budget. If the manager wants the staff member to perform well in this area without his supervision, the manager must determine the appropriate leadership style for starting the developmental cycle. As can be seen in Figure 9-5, once this manager has diagnosed the maturity of his follower as low, he can determine the appropriate style by constructing a right angle from a point on the maturity continuum to where it meets the curved line in the style-of-leader portion of the model. In this case, it would be appropriate to start the developmental cycle by using a directive "telling" style (S1). What would a "telling" style look like in this situation?

It would involve several things for the manager. First, he would have to tell the staff member exactly what was involved in developing a departmental budget—taking inventory, processing manpower and material requests, comparing present costs with last year's budget and so on. Second, he would begin to

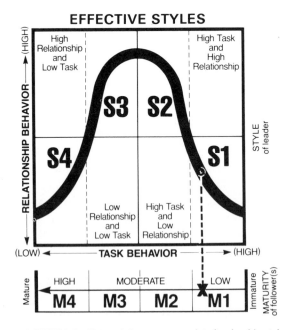

FIGURE 9-5 Determining an appropriate leadership style

show the staff member how to do each of the tasks involved. Thus, "telling" in a teaching situation involves "show and tell"; the staff member must be told what to do and then shown how to do it. Although this "telling" style is high on direction and low on support, this does not mean that the manager is not being friendly to his staff member. Low supportive behavior in this situation merely means that the manager is not patting the staff member on the back before he has earned it. Till then, the manager emphasizes explaining the what, when, where, and how of the job.

If the manager uses an S1 "telling" style in this situation, the departmental budget will probably be done fairly well, since the manager is working closely with the staff member. But if this same manager or leader assumes that one of his responsibilities is to increase the task-relevant maturity of his follower(s), then he has to be willing to *take a risk* and begin to *delegate some responsibility* to the people who work for him. This is particularly true when supervising an individual or group that has not assumed much responsibility in the past; and yet, if one is going to develop people—children in the home, employees on the job—one has to take that risk. While taking a risk is a reality in the developmental cycle, managers have to keep the degree of risk reasonable; it should not be too high. For example, suppose a mother wants to teach her eight-year-old daughter how to wash the dishes. The risk is a few broken dishes. It would be wise, then, to start the daughter off on old dishes, or even plastic dishes, rather than grandma's priceless bone china. It's not a question of whether to take a risk or not; it's a matter of taking a calculated risk.

Successive Approximations

If a manager asks a staff member to do something she has never been taught to do and expects good performance the first time, even though no help is offered the staff member, the manager has set the person up for failure and punishment. This begins the widely used "tell, leave alone and then 'zap' " approach to managing people. The manager tells the staff member what to do (without bothering to find out if the person knows how to do it), leaves the staff member alone (expecting immediate results), and then yells at and "zaps" the staff member when the desired behavior does not follow.

If the manager in our budget example used that approach with his staff member, the events might look something like this. The manager might assume that anyone could prepare the departmental budget. So he just tells his staff member to prepare the budget and have it in his office within ten days. Not bothering to analyze whether the staff member is able or willing to prepare the budget on his own, the manager gives the order and then goes about his own responsibilities. When the staff member produces the budget ten days later and the manager finds all kinds of mistakes and problems with it, he screams and yells at his staff member about the poor quality of the work.

Managers should remember that no one (including themselves!) learns how to do anything all at once. We learn a little bit at a time. As a result, if a manager wants someone to do something completely new, the manager should reward the slightest progress the person makes in the desired direction.

Many parents use this process without really being aware of it. For example, how do you think we teach a child to walk? Imagine if we stood a child up and said, "Walk," and then when he fell down we spanked him for not walking. Sound ridiculous? Of course. But it's not really any different from the manager's anger with his staff member about the poorly prepared budget. A child spanked for falling down will soon not try to walk because the child knows this leads to punishment. At this point he's not even sure what his legs are for. Therefore parents usually first teach a child how to stand up. If the child stays up even for a second or two, his parents get excited and hug and kiss him, call his grandmother, and the like. Next, when the child can stand and hold onto a table, his parents again hug and kiss him. The same happens when he takes his first step, even if he falls down. Whether or not his parents know it, they are positively rewarding the child for small accomplishments as he moves closer and closer to the desired behavior—walking.

Thus, in attempting to help an individual or group mature—to get them to take more and more responsibility for performing a specific task—a leader must first tell and show the follower(s) what to do; second, delegate *some* responsibility (not too much or failure might result); and, third, reward as soon as possible any behavior in the desired direction. This process should continue as the individual's behavior comes closer and closer to the leader's expectations of good performance. What would relationship behavior look like in this situation?

Relationship behavior would involve providing "positive strokes" and reinforcement. Positive reinforcement or strokes are anything that is desired or needed by an individual whose behavior is being reinforced. While task behavior precedes the desired behavior, relationship behavior or positive reinforcement follows the desired behavior and increases the likelihood of it recurring. It is important to remember that reinforcement must immediately follow any behavior in the desired direction. Reinforcement at a later time will be of less help in getting the individual or group to do something they've never done before on their own.

This three-step process of (1) initiating structure or providing direction (task behavior), (2) reducing the amount of direction and supervision, and (3) after adequate performance follows, increasing socioemotional support (relationship behavior) is known as *positively reinforcing successive approximations.* This concept is associated with behavior modification and reinforcement theory,[3] and more recently, in industrial circles it has been called performance management.[4] This field will be discussed in more depth later in this chapter and in Chapter 10. Let us look at an example to illustrate this concept. Suppose a manager wanted to change her leadership style with an individual from Point A to Point C along the curved line or curvilinear function of Situational Leadership, as illustrated in Figure 9-6. The first step of the process would be to provide some structure and direction for the individual at Point A. The next step would be to delegate some responsibility by decreasing her task behavior to Point B. This is a risky step since the manager is turning over the direction and the supervision of some of the tasks to the follower. If the follower responds well to the increased responsibility, then it is appropriate to engage in Step 3—positively reinforcing this behavior by increasing socioemotional support (relationship behavior) to the higher level Point C, as shown in Figure 9-6.

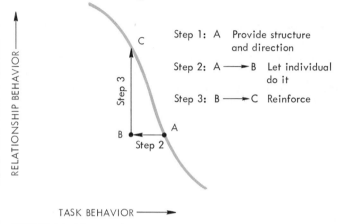

FIGURE 9-6   Three-step process of the developmental cycle

It is important to remember that a leader must be careful not to delegate too much responsibility too rapidly. This is a common error that many managers make. If this is done before the follower can handle it, the leader may be setting the follower up for failure and frustration that could prevent that person from wanting to take any additional responsibility in the future. The process is often started off by good intentions. The manager provides direction and structure but then moves too quickly to a "leave-alone" leadership style. This abrupt movement from "telling" to "delegating" often sets the person up for failure and punishment, since it assumes that telling is learning. Later, when the manager realizes that the job is not getting done, he is likely to return to Style 1 rapidly in a punitive way.

In addition, a manager should be warned not to increase socioemotional support (relationship behavior) without first getting the desired performance. In positively reinforcing nonperformance, this manager may be viewed as a soft touch. That is why the manager in our example does not immediately move from Point A to Point C along the curved line in Figure 9-6. If she moved from Point A to Point C without some evidence that the individual could assume responsibility at Point B, it would be like giving the reward before the person has earned it. It would be like paying a person twenty dollars an hour right now who at present is only worth three dollars an hour. For many people, if you gave them twenty dollars an hour up front, there would be very little incentive to improve their performance. Thus, the leader should develop the maturity of followers slowly on each task that they must perform, using less task behavior and more relationship behavior as they mature and become more willing and able to take responsibility. When an individual's performance is low on a specific task, one must not expect drastic changes overnight.

If the manager (in our example) finds that the follower is unable to handle that much added responsibility when she decreases her task behavior to Point B, she might have to return to a moderate level of direction (where the follower is able to take responsibility) somewhere between Point A and Point B. This new level of task behavior is indicated by Point B^1 in Figure 9-7. If the subordinate is now able to be effective at that level, then the manager can appropriately increase her socioemotional support (relationship behavior) to Point C^1. Although this level of socioemotional support is less than depicted at Point C, it is appropriate to the amount of task behavior that the follower, at that time, is able to assume.

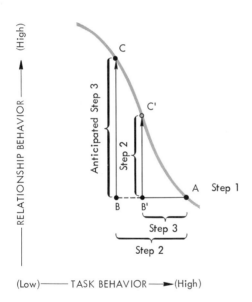

FIGURE 9-7 Adjustment when growth expectation is too high

As shown in Figure 9-8, this three-step process—telling and showing, cutting back structure and then increasing socioemotional support if the follower can respond to the additional responsibility—tends to continue in small increments until the individual is assuming moderate levels of maturity. This continual decreasing of task behavior does not mean the individual will have less structure but, rather than being externally imposed by the leader, the structure can now be internally provided by the follower.

An interesting phenomenon occurs in the developmental cycle when the high point of the curvilinear function in the leadership style portion of the model

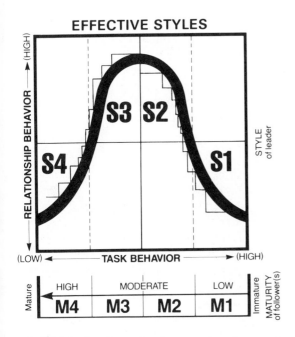

EFFECTIVE STYLES

RELATIONSHIP BEHAVIOR ——▲—— (HIGH)

S3 S2

S4 S1

STYLE of leader

(LOW) ◄———— TASK BEHAVIOR ————► (HIGH)

Mature ◄	HIGH	MODERATE		LOW	Immature ►	MATURITY of follower(s)
	M4	M3	M2	M1		

FIGURE 9-8 Development cycle as people mature over time

is reached. This is where the function crosses the mean or average of task behavior. Past this point, a leader who is appropriately using leadership style 3 or style 4 is supervising people at moderate to high levels of maturity (M3 and M4). At that time, the process changes and becomes one whereby the leader not only reduces structure (task behavior), but, when the followers can handle their responsibility, reduces socioemotional support as well. This continuation of the successive approximation process is illustrated by the downward steps in Figure 9-8.

Sometimes the following question is raised: Doesn't the reduction of socioemotional support mean that there is a lack of confidence and trust between manager and follower(s)? In reality, when a manager reduces the amount of socioemotional support and structure appropriately, this indicates that there is more mutual trust and confidence between the leader and the follower(s). This suggests that as people change, their motives and needs hierarchy often change too. For example, people who are immature tend to view increased socioemotional support and facilitating behavior as positive reinforcement. In fact, if the leader left them too much on their own, this behavior would create insecurities and help reinforce fear and anxiety on the part of the follower(s). As a result, this low relationship behavior could be perceived as punishment rather than reward.

On the other hand, as people move to high levels of maturity, they do not require as much head patting or psychological "stroking." As people become high on task-relevant maturity, one way the leader can demonstrate confidence and trust in the follower(s) is to leave them more and more on their own. Just as socioemotional support from the leader tends to be positive reinforcement for immature people, too much socioemotional support or relationship behavior for people at high levels of maturity is not seen as a reward. In fact, this supportive behavior is often seen as dysfunctional and can be interpreted by these mature people as lack of confidence and trust on the part of the leader.

Time and the Developmental Cycle

There is no set blueprint in terms of the amount of time necessary to mature an individual or group. A manager may be doing very well to move a group from maturity level 1 to maturity level 2 over a period of eighteen months to two years. On the other hand, within that group there may be an individual or several individuals who will mature much more rapidly than the group as a whole. Thus, time is a function of the complexity of the job being performed and the performance potential of the individual or group. For example, one might take someone on a specific task through the total cycle—from low maturity to extremely high maturity—in a matter of minutes. And yet, in other tasks with that same individual, the maturing process may take a much greater amount of time. In fact, it could take weeks, months, or even years to move through the complete cycle in terms of appropriate leadership style from telling (S1) to delegating (S4). To illustrate a short maturing process, an example of teaching a child to tie her shoe may be helpful.

If the child has not made any attempt on her own to learn to tie her shoes, this fact may, in a sense, become a problem to the parent. In that case, the parent needs to provide some high task behavior for the child. Since the child has not been any more mature than she presently is on this task, the parent should explain what to do, how to do it, when to do it, and where to do it. In essence, the parent must move into the early stages of coaching and counseling by providing the child with a "hands-on experience." As the child begins to show the ability to do some of those functions, the parent reduces the amount of telling behavior and increases, to some extent, supportive behavior. "That's fine! Good! You're getting it!" And perhaps in a matter of minutes, the behavior of the parent may change from a "hands-on" highly structured style to just being in close proximity, where this adult can provide a moderate amount of structure but also high levels of both verbal and nonverbal supportive and facilitative behavior. In another few minutes the parent may leave the child to practice on her own while staying close enough to make an intervention if there should be some regression. Thus, in a matter of ten to fifteen minutes, the parent has taken the child in that specific task of shoe tying from style 1 through styles 2 and 3 to almost a complete delegation of that function to the child in a manner characteristic of style 4. This does not mean that the parent's style with that child should now always be style 4. It just means that in that specific task (shoe tying), the most appropriate style to use with that child is style 4.

CHANGING MATURITY THROUGH BEHAVIOR MODIFICATION

In our discussion of the developmental cycle we made reference to behavior modification and, in particular, the concept of positively reinforcing successive approximations. This section will elaborate on some other concepts from this behavioral science field and attempt to show how these concepts provide guidelines for changing one's leadership style with shifts in maturity.[5]

Behavior modification is a useful tool for managers and leaders because it can be applied in almost all environments. Although it may involve a reassessment of customary methods for obtaining compliance and cooperation, it has relevance for persons interested in accomplishing objectives through other people. This may not be the case with some psychotherapy.

For example, some psychotherapy is based on the assumption that to change behavior one must start with the feelings and attitudes within an individual. Although the introduction of transactional analysis (TA) has helped, the problem with psychotherapy from a practitioner's viewpoint is that it tends to be too expensive and is appropriate for use only by professionals. One way of illustrating the main difference between these two approaches is to go back to a portion of the basic motivating situation model as illustrated in Figure 9-9.

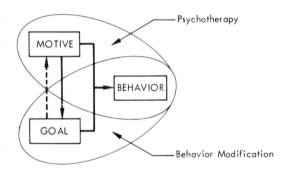

FIGURE 9-9   Comparison of psychotherapy and behavior modification

Figure 9-9 shows that both psychotherapy and behavior modification are interested in affecting behavior. The emphasis in psychotherapy is on analyzing the reasons underlying behavior that are often the result of early experience in life. Behavior modification concentrates on observed behavior and uses goals or rewards outside the individual to modify and shape behavior toward the desired performance.

Behavior modification theory is based on observed behavior and not on internal unobserved emotions, attitudes or feelings. Its basic premise is that *behavior is controlled by its immediate consequences*. Behavior can be increased, suppressed, or decreased by what happens immediately after it occurs. Because probabilities are difficult to work with, we use observations of the future frequency of the behavior as a measure of the effectiveness of a consequence. Five of the major concepts of reinforcement that help one to make behavioral changes are: positive reinforcement, punishment, negative reinforcement, extinction, and schedule of reinforcement. In our discussions in this chapter we have and will continue to emphasize positive reinforcement and schedule of reinforcement. In the next chapter, "Constructive Discipline," we will examine punishment, negative reinforcement, and extinction.

Positive Reinforcement

Positive reinforcement, as mentioned earlier, can be anything that is desired or needed by the individual whose behavior is being reinforced. A positive reinforcer tends to strengthen the response it follows and make that response more likely to recur.

To increase the probability that desirable behavior will occur, reinforcement should *immediately* follow the response. Reinforcement at a later time may be of less help in making the desired behavioral change.

Individualizing Reinforcement

When thinking about this concept of positive reinforcement, managers should remember that reinforcement depends on the individual. What is reinforcing to one person may not be reinforcing to another. Money may motivate some people to work harder. But to others money may not be a positive reinforcer; the challenge of the job might be the most rewarding aspect of the situation. In addition, the same individual at different times will be motivated by different things, depending on present need satisfaction. Thus, at one time an individual might respond to praise as a reinforcer, but at another time that same individual might not respond to praise but be eager for more responsibility. Managers must recognize the dangers of overgeneralizing and not only look for unique differences in their people but also be aware of the various fluctuations in need satisfaction within a person.

For a desirable behavior to be obtained, the slightest appropriate behavior exhibited by the individual in that direction must be rewarded as soon as possible. This is the basic premise for the concept of *reinforcing positively successive approximations* of a certain response. For example, when an individual's performance is low, one cannot expect drastic changes overnight, regardless of changes in expectations for the individual or the type of reinforcers (rewards) used.

A child learning some new behavior is not expected to give a polished performance at the outset. So, as parent, teacher, or supervisor, we use positive reinforcement as the behavior approaches the desired level of performance. Managers must be aware of any progress of their subordinates so as to be in a position to reinforce this change appropriately.

This strategy is compatible with the concept of setting short-term goals rather than final performance criteria and then reinforcing appropriate progress toward the final goal as interim goals are accomplished. In setting these goals it is important that they be programmed to be difficult but obtainable so that the individual proceeds along a path of gradual and systematic development. Eventually this individual will reach the point of a polished performance.

The type of consequence individuals experience as a result of their behavior will determine the speed with which they approach the final performance. Behavior consequences can be either positive (money, praise, award, promotion), negative (scolding, fines, layoffs, embarrassment), or neutral. The difference between positive and negative consequences is important to reiterate. Positive consequences tend to result in an increase in the rewarded behavior in the future. Negative consequences, as you will discover in the discussion of punishment, merely disrupt and suppress on-going behavior. Negative consequences tend to have neither a lasting nor sure effect on future behavior.

Schedule of Reinforcement

Once a manager has someone engaging in a new behavior, it is important that the new behavior is not extinguished over time. To ensure this not happening, reinforcement must be scheduled in an effective way. Most experts agree that there are two main reinforcement schedules: continuous and intermittent.[6] Continuous reinforcement means that the individuals being changed are reinforced each time they engage in the desired new pattern. With intermittent reinforcement, on the other hand, not every desired response is reinforced. Reinforcement either can be completely random or can be scheduled according to a prescribed number of responses occurring or a particular interval of time elapsing before reinforcement is given. With continuous reinforcement, the individual learns the new behavior faster; but if the environment for that individual changes to one of nonreinforcement, extinction can be expected to take place relatively soon. With intermittent reinforcement, extinction is much slower because the individual has been conditioned to go for periods of time without any reinforcement. Thus, for fast learning, a continuous reinforcement schedule should be used. But once the individual has learned the new pattern, a switch to intermittent reinforcement should insure a long-lasting change.

How does the concept of reinforcement relate to Situational Leadership? In the early stages of a developmental cycle, whenever a manager delegates some responsibility to a person at a low level of maturity and that person responds well, the manager should provide reinforcement. That is, every time the manager cuts back on task behavior and the staff member responds well, the manager should immediately increase relationship behavior appropriately. This kind of reinforcement should continue until the manager's style is between "selling" and "participating" and the maturity of the person shifts toward higher levels (M3 and M4). At that time, the manager should begin periodically to reinforce, so that the manager's decreased support and direction will not be seen by the staff member as punishment. When the style of a manager moves toward the "delegating" style, the person's behavior is self-reinforcing and external "strokes" from the manager are no longer necessary. In sum, the developmental cycle moves from continuous reinforcement to periodic reinforcement to self-reinforcement.

Consistency in Reinforcement

In Chapter 4 consistency was defined as behaving the same way in similar circumstances. This is very important when it comes to reinforcement. Many managers are reinforcing or supportive of their people only when they feel like it. While that's probably more convenient for leaders, it is not helpful if they want to have an impact on *other* people's behavior. Managers should know when they are being supportive and should be careful not to be supportive when their people are performing poorly. Be consistent! Only good behavior or improvement—not just any behavior—should be rewarded.

Isn't All This Reinforcement a Form of Bribery?

The ultimate goal of the developmental process discussed in this chapter is to shift people toward self-management so that they can eventually assume responsibility for motivating their own behavior. This ultimate goal is mentioned to reassure people who have some real doubts about the use of reinforcement. Some readers may ask, "People should be motivated by a desire to succeed or the desire to please people around them, not by a hoped-for reward," or "This sounds like bribery to me," or "If I use positive reinforcement with people, won't they always expect rewards for every little thing they do?"

Although we have shared similar concerns in the past, our experience in observing people in organizations has been reassuring. It has been found that people who are reinforced when they are first learning new behaviors and performance areas and then gradually allowed to be more and more on their own turn out to be happy, eager to help, self-motivated people who can be left alone without productivity dropping significantly.

In this chapter we have discussed how managers increase the maturity level of their followers in a developmental process that emphasizes the use of positive reinforcement. In the next chapter we will discuss the regressive cycle and will consider what has to be done when followers begin, for whatever reason, to decrease in their task-relevant maturity.

NOTES

[1] Rensis Likert, *New Patterns of Management* (New York: McGraw-Hill Book Company, 1961), p. 7.

[2] J. Sterling Livingston, "Pygmalion in Management," *Harvard Business Review* (July–August 1969), pp. 81–82.

[3] The most classic discussions of behavior modification, reinforcement theory, or operant conditioning have been done by B. F. Skinner. See Skinner, *Science and Human Behavior* (New York: The

Macmillan Company, 1953). See also A. Bandura, *Principles of Behavior Modification* (New York: Holt, Rinehart & Winston, 1969) and C. M. Franks, *Behavior Therapy: Appraisal & Status* (New York: McGraw-Hill Book Company, 1969).

[4] One of the first applications of behavior modification and reinforcement theory to organizations was done by Fred Luthans and Robert Creitner. See Luthans and Creitner, *Organizational Behavior Modification* (Glenview, Ill.: Scott, Foresman & Co., 1975). See also Thomas K. Connellan, *How to Improve Human Performance: Behaviorism in Business and in Industry* (New York: Harper & Row, 1978) and Lawrence M. Miller, *Behavior Management: The New Science of Managing People at Work* (New York: John Wiley & Sons, 1978).

[5] Helpful resources in developing this section in addition to those mentioned above were provided by Glenna Holsinger, *Motivating the Reluctant Learner* (Lexington, Mass.: Motivity, Inc., 1970); Madeline Hunter, *Reinforcement Theory for Teachers* (El Segundo, Calif., TIP Publications, 1967); and Lawrence M. Miller *Behavior Management: New Skills for Business and Industry* (Atlanta: Behavioral Systems, Inc., 1976). Discussions with friend and colleague Bob Lorber, President of Performance Systems, International (PSI), a division of Continuing Education Corp. in Tustin, Calif., were also extremely helpful.

[6] See C. B. Ferster and B. F. Skinner, *Schedules of Reinforcement* (New York: Appleton-Century-Crofts, 1957).

chapter 10

Constructive
Discipline

In the last chapter we discussed how to develop the maturity and independence of people through the use of positive reinforcement and changing leadership styles. In this chapter we will attempt to help managers determine what needs to be done when their people begin to regress and behave less maturely than in the past.

THE REGRESSIVE CYCLE

Managers may need to make a regressive intervention when their followers are beginning to behave less maturely than they have in the past. Thus, in a developmental cycle, managers are attempting to increase the task-relevant maturity of an individual or group beyond where it has been in the past. The regressive cycle involves an intervention that leaders need to make when an individual or a group is becoming less effective. Thus, in a regressive cycle, managers must use a leadership style appropriate to the present level of maturity rather than the style that might have been effective when the individual or group was at a higher level of maturity.

Decreases in maturity are often the result of what might be called "high strength competing responses" in the environment. Other things are competing with the goals of the leader or the organization and, therefore, have become higher strength needs to the followers in terms of their behavior. Let's look at some examples to get a better idea of how this cycle works.

While consulting with a large research and development laboratory, one of the authors worked with a manager who was responsible for supervising one of the most motivated scientists on the staff. This scientist was so committed to his job that even if the manager went into the laboratory at eight o'clock in the evening, it was not unusual to see a light under his laboratory door. Even on weekends, this scientist was often found working in the laboratory. He probably had more patents and more contributions to the overall program than any other person in the laboratory.

From the author's observations, this manager was behaving appropriately in using a low relationship/low task style (S4) for the high maturity level (M4) of this scientist. Thus, rather than operating as that staff member's supervisor, the manager was behaving more as a representative of the scientist to higher levels in the organization. His manager was attempting to maximize the potential of this staff member by engaging in such "linking pin" activities as acquiring necessary resources and coordinating his activities with the activities of other staff members.

Although this staff member was extremely mature in this organizational setting, we learned that his behavior was seen in a different light in his interactions with another organization—his family. In that organizational setting, his wife saw his behavior of long hours and weekends at work as an indication that he no longer cared about her and their young daughter. So in his wife's eyes, he was behaving quite immaturely. As a result, the scientist went home one evening and found a note from his wife in which she told him that she had packed her bags and taken their daughter away to start a new life. The scientist was shocked by his wife's action since he had perceived his own behavior quite differently than she did. He felt that he was attempting to provide for his wife and child all those things he was not able to have as a youngster.

What happened on the job was that now, with these family problems on his mind, the effectiveness of this scientist began to decrease. It has been said many times that you should leave your family problems at home and your job problems at work, but in reality we tend to carry problems both ways. Problems at home affect our behavior in the work environment and problems at work affect our home environment. This was certainly true in the scientist's case. As his concerns for his family began to take effect, the performance and corresponding maturity level of the scientist began to shift from maturity level 4 into maturity level 3, as shown in Figure 10-1. Although his work emphasized technical competency, his declining psychological maturity was now affecting his performance. He did not seem to be able to cope with these problems at home. This meant that to maximize performance, his manager had to shift behavior from style 4 to style 3 to deal with this lowering maturity level of a follower (Figure 10-1). As a result, a moderate increase in direction and structure as well as significant increases in socioemotional support, two-way communication, and the

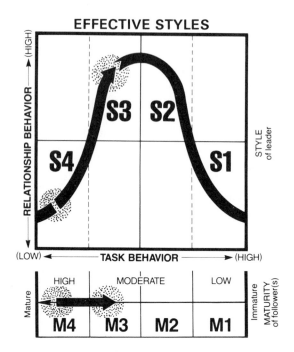

EFFECTIVE STYLES

RELATIONSHIP BEHAVIOR ──── (HIGH)

(HIGH)

S3 S2

S4　　　　**S1**

STYLE of leader

(LOW) ◀──── TASK BEHAVIOR ────▶ (HIGH)

HIGH	MODERATE	LOW	
M4	**M3**	**M2**	**M1**

Mature ← → Immature

MATURITY of follower(s)

FIGURE 10.1 An example of a regressive cycle intervention

willingness to listen actively and be supportive (relationship behavior) were necessary. At this point, the situation was still more of a problem to the follower than the leader. However, the high relationship intervention by the manager seemed to help the situation.

Once the technical staff member was able to cope with his problem and put it in perspective, it was possible for his manager to move directly back to style 4 with this person. This illustrates one of the basic differences between a developmental cycle and a regressive cycle. In a regressive cycle, once an appropriate intervention has been made, the leader may often move back to his or her former leadership style without going through the process of positively reinforcing successive approximations. This is because the follower had previously demonstrated an ability to function at that level.

However, it should be pointed out in this example that if the performance of the scientist had continued to decline, the situation clearly would have become a problem to both leader and follower and would have demanded an eventual shift by the manager to a high task/high relationship style (S2).

In another example, a construction engineer was operating as a project consultant; that is, he had a special expertise that was useful for a variety of projects. As a result, rather than being assigned to a specific project, he worked with a half-dozen projects at different construction sites. Since his maturity level was extremely high, his boss was also treating him appropriately in a style 4 manner. His supervisor was acting more as a linking pin with the rest of the organization than as his supervisor.

This style was effective until our engineer began to take an active interest in golf. As a result of this new high strength, competing response, no longer was anybody able to get in touch with this project consultant after two o'clock in the afternoon. It took several months for his boss to make this discovery, since his coworkers just assumed that he was at one of the other construction sites. The supervisor finally became aware of the engineer's behavior and discovered that his activity on the golf course was causing problems with the construction progress at some of the sites. As a result, the maturity level of the project consultant in terms of the accomplishment of organizational goals had moved from maturity level 4 to maturity level 1, particularly from 2 to 5 in the afternoon. Thus, it became appropriate for the supervisor to shift his leadership style from S4 to S1 to deal with this drastic change in maturity. What might be called a disciplinary intervention was necessary to redefine roles and expectations for the project consultant. Once this was done, if the manager was able to unfreeze this new pattern of the subordinate, he might be able to shift his style back to S4. This is possible, once again, because this subordinate had been highly mature before. Thus, it may not be necessary for the manager to positively reinforce successive approximations before he moves back to the previous appropriate style used with this consultant. This is much like the story about the mule and the two-by-four. Often in a disciplinary intervention, all managers have to do is get the attention of their followers to get them moving back in the right direction.

The regressive cycle should be taken one step at a time. Thus, if we are letting individuals operate on their own ("delegating") and performance declines, we should move to "participating" and support their problem solving. If we are being supportive but not directive with individuals (S3) and performance declines, we should move to "selling" and continue to engage in two-way communication, but we should also be more directive. If we are providing both task and relationship behavior (S2) and performance declines, we should move to "telling" and reduce some of our supportive behavior and increase direction and supervision. In both the regressive and developmental cycles, we should be careful not to jump from "delegating" (S4) to "selling" (S2) or "telling" (S1) or from "telling" to "participating" or "delegating." Making a drastic shift backward in leadership styles is one of the common mistakes managers make with their people. It sets up the "leave alone and zap" (punish) style of management—an approach that is not only disruptive to the relationship a manager has with a staff member but is also disruptive to that person's growth and maturity.

The Importance of Timing Interventions

The key to avoiding the disruptive "leave alone and zap" management style is the timing of interventions. Experience has shown that the longer managers wait to make an intervention to correct inappropriate behavior, the further back through the cycle of leadership style they will have to move. Thus, there is a higher probability that an S1 intervention will have to be made. Take our example of the construction engineer working as a project consultant. If his supervisor had discovered his golfing pattern earlier, he could have possibly intervened with leadership style 3 or 2. But the mere fact that it took months to discover this new behavior on the part of the project consultant forced the supervisor to use a highly structured, style 1 intervention when he finally did find out.

This phenomenon of delaying one's intervention probably happens most often in the family, where there is a high emotional attachment between the parent and the child. Because they care about their children and want them to have fun and enjoy themselves, parents often "look the other way" when the child's behavior is inappropriate. Hoping the problem will terminate somehow on its own, they often wait months before making an intervention. When the intervention is finally made, the parents tend to be angry and "at the end of their rope." Since they can no longer tolerate the situation, it is predictable that they will make a much harder intervention than would have been necessary or appropriate much earlier. One of the residual problems that can occur from this kind of intervention is the creation of anxiety, frustration, and resentment, which are difficult to overcome.

Let's look at an example. Suppose that when Nancy's parents first noticed that she was spending a lot of time on the phone and not doing her chores, they decided not to say anything. They were happy that Nancy was so popular and convinced themselves that it was only a phase and that she would grow out of it and the problem would solve itself.

As a result, weeks and months went by and they still didn't intervene, even though the situation continued to get worse. Now, not only was Nancy letting her chores slip, but she didn't seem to have time to give her mother a hand with anything. Boys, dates, clothes, and makeup seemed to occupy her mind exclusively. Then, one night months after the problem had begun, her father's car broke down as he was heading home from an evening meeting. After walking a mile to the nearest phone, he tried to call home for his wife to come to get him. Of course, the phone was busy and stayed busy for over an hour. Finally, in desperation, Nancy's father attempted to hitchhike, but to no avail. He began the long walk home stopping at available phones to call. The line was still busy.

Over three hours from the time he left his office, Nancy's father entered the house, ripped the phone from the wall, and angrily told Nancy she would never be permitted to make or receive a phone call on a school night again. Since Nancy's parents had never given her a hint that her behavior was "poor," Nancy perceived her father's ravings as unreasonable and totally out of control.

After a shouting match, she ran off crying to her room and slammed the door.

Her father couldn't understand why Nancy was so angry at him, for he saw her as the cause of the problem. And yet, to go from a hands-off "delegating" style to an angrily screaming "telling" style is the ultimate in a "leave alone and zap" child-rearing style. For the phone problem to be solved, Nancy's parents will probably have to enforce rules that Nancy is not committed to and feels are unfair. While movement to a more directive "telling" style may change her phone behavior, it could kindle feelings of hatred in Nancy for her parents.

This whole confrontation could have been avoided if only Nancy's mother and father had intervened in the beginning, as we described earlier, when the issue could have been settled in a reasonable manner acceptable to all. We have found that as a general rule "giving birth" is a lot easier than "resurrection." If we would only take the time in the beginning to make sure everything is going right, we wouldn't have to face the difficult task of "rescue and salvage" when things get off course. A sudden movement from "delegating" (or in this case "abdicating") to "telling" can only lead to a breakdown in parent-child communication and make things tough for Nancy's parents.

Avoiding quick style shifts is consistent with a concept that we have undoubtedly heard many times before: "It is easier to loosen up than tighten up." In other words, if we're going to be tough with children in some aspect of their lives, it's better to be tough in the beginning and then, after we see they can handle themselves in that area, loosen up. Children see loosening up as rewarding, but when parents tighten up, they are likely to regard it as punishment. An old fable about an emperor and his prime minister illustrates this rather vividly.

When the emperor assumed power, he appointed a prime minister. One day he called the prime minister in and said, "Why don't we divide up the tasks? Why don't you pass out all the punishments and I'll pass out all the rewards?" The prime minister, glad to be prime minister, agreed to this. So they did. After a while, the emperor noticed that when he asked someone to do something, the person did it sometimes, but more often didn't. But when the prime minister spoke, people moved. So the emperor called the prime minister to him and said, "Why don't we switch roles for a while? Since you've been doing all the punishing, why don't you do all the rewarding and I'll do all the punishing?" The prime minister agreed, and they switched roles. Within a month, the prime minister was emperor and the emperor was out on his ear. It seems people didn't take kindly to the "nice guy" turning nasty, and they began to look for a replacement. The logical choice? The prime minister, of course. He seemed to be coming around now and was an "all right" guy after all.

The Emotional Level of an Intervention

In making an intervention with one's followers, it is important for managers to consider how emotional they should be. If managers are making a developmental intervention (in other words, they are attempting leadership with people who have never been any more mature on a particular task than they are now), they should try to control their emotions and be fairly "low key." One of the problems that people have in understanding Situational Leadership Theory is their assumption that whenever leaders are making a high task/low relationship intervention (S1), they need to raise their voice, holler, scream, and yell. That behavior is often unnecessary. Managers can do a lot of telling what to do, where to do, and how to do it without losing control of their emotions. And this is appropriate when they are attempting to engage in a developmental cycle. If they intervene with too much emotion, they often frighten insecure people to the extent that these people become less and less willing to try on new behavior. They may withdraw into themselves psychologically, and then it becomes more difficult to draw them out.

For example, in coaching basketball, if you had a big awkward kid who had trouble catching the ball, much less putting it in the basket, a high emotional reaction to mistakes by this boy would not help him develop since he does not know how to play yet. If you began screaming and yelling at him, when you put him back in the game, he would avoid the ball or do anything not to put himself in a situation in which he could make a mistake. He does need a lot of direction and supervision, but it should be presented in a manner that can begin to help develop his confidence and not increase his insecurities.

On the other hand, if you were coaching a youngster who has already proven ability, who was just goofing off and not performing, you might want to make a disciplinary intervention (the most common form of the regressive cycle). With this kind of intervention, it sometimes becomes appropriate to be more emotional, and even display anger to a moderate level. This kind of intervention may be appropriate with this boy because if you can motivate him enough he could go back in the game and start performing well without any further direction from you. Although in a disciplinary intervention a leader wants to get people's attention, we say use a "moderate level" of emotion or anger because in many cases there is a tendency for too much emotion to become dysfunctional even in a disciplinary cycle.

In another example, suppose a young girl in the second grade has good skills in math and relatively good skills in sciences but has a real problem in reading. Although she has a reading problem, she is promoted to the third grade because of her other skills. When the third-grade teacher begins to see that Alice is not able to read at the level of the other kids, he may become frustrated. He assumes that because Alice is in the third grade she can read at that grade level. Thus, the teacher often attempts to deal with her reading problem by making a disciplinary intervention—"What's the matter with you, Alice? You're not reading the way you can. It looks to me like you're lazy!" This disciplinary intervention is quite emotional. Since Alice never has been at any higher level of maturity in terms of reading, this kind of intervention may actually increase the probability that she will withdraw further into herself and lose interest in reading and be less and less willing to grow and develop her skills. Reading now represents higher levels of anxiety; it begins to be less probable that the teacher will be able to motivate Alice in this area. An appropriate intervention would have been a developmental cycle in which the teacher increased structure but with little emotion.

This increased structure might take the form of attentional reading periods, closer supervision in terms of making sure that Alice is using the reading period appropriately, and periodic follow-up to audit her progress. All these activities should be characterized by a low emotional level that will not frighten Alice or provide an environment in which her anxieties become high. Thus, a leader should be careful not to be too emotional when the individual or group being disciplined really does not have the motivation or ability to do the task in the first place. Making an emotional disciplinary intervention when a developmental intervention is required may have damaging results.

Some Things to Remember When Disciplining an Individual

If a disciplinary intervention is called for, how can it be carried out effectively? Here are a few helpful guidelines.[1]

1. *Don't blow your cool.* As was suggested above, even when making a disciplinary intervention, managers should remain relatively calm and use only a moderate level of emotion. Keep the emotional level only high enough to get the person's attention; make it obvious that a problem exists, but don't get carried away.

2. *Don't attack personalities.* When disciplining an individual, don't attack the person's worth as a human being. Separate the individual as a person from his or her behavior. The individual is OK, but his or her behavior is not. Zero in on that behavior and not on the person.

3. *Be specific.* It is not very helpful to an individual to say, "I don't like the way you've been performing lately." That kind of feedback is too general. For disciplinary intervention to be effective, we must tell the individual specifically what he or she has done wrong, for example, "Your productivity is down 20% from last month. Two out of the last four reports you have handed in have had to be redone."

4. *Be timely.* We have already emphasized the importance of timing your interventions. Unless discipline occurs as close to the misbehavior or the poor performance as possible, it won't be helpful in influencing future behavior. Some managers are gunnysack discipliners. That is, they store up observations of poor behavior and then one day when the bag is full, they charge in and "dump everything on the table." Often, managers wait until the yearly performance review. That is why some people call an annual performance review program an "NIHYYSOB"—"Now I have you, you S.O.B." Managers using the "NIHYYSOB" performance review tell their people all the bad things they have done over the last months of year. Manager and employee usually end up arguing about the "facts," and the employee doesn't really hear what he or she has done wrong. This is a version of the "leave alone and zap" form of discipline. If managers would only intervene early, they could calmly deal with one behavior in time, and the person could "hear" the feedback.

5. *Be consistent.* Managers should avoid inconsistency in disciplining their people. The same behavior should always be met with the same response. People will become confused if they are reprimanded for poor performance one week and ignored when they engage in the same poor performance the next week. We must also be careful to treat one staff member the same as another. Be careful not to have favorites. Positive reinforcement should be given for performance, not because of who a person is.

6. *Don't threaten.* So many managers announce in ominous tones that they are going to do such and such if a person continues to behave or perform in a certain way, and then never follow through. If our people realize we are bluffing, they won't pay any attention to our threats. Then, when we finally do follow through on a threat, we are usually so out of control that we come down excessively hard. So, very simply, we must say what we mean and mean what we say.

7. *Be fair.* Managers should be careful not to make a punishment greater than the problem, and vice versa. Many managers come down harder on people for little things than for more major performance problems. If individuals know what is expected of them and they don't do it, they will readily accept discipline (in fact, they sometimes are confused if they don't receive it). But if the punishment is way out of proportion to the poor performance, they will justifiably resent their manager's response.

8. *Be careful that discipline does not reinforce poor behavior.* As was discussed earlier, sometimes the only way people can get their manager's attention is by misbehaving or by poor performance. If that's true and attention from their manager is important enough to them, they may behave inappropriately just to be recognized, even if they get disciplined and have to pay a price in the bargain. Remember, given a choice between no strokes or negative strokes, people will tend to take negative strokes every time.

Punishment and Negative Reinforcement

Punishment, as we discussed earlier, is a negative consequence. A negative consequence tends to weaken the response it immediately follows; that is, it prevents the recurrence of that behavior. It is a stimulus that an individual "will reject, if given a choice between the punishment and no stimulus at all."[2] As punishment suppresses the behavior that brought it (the punishment) on, *negative reinforcement* strengthens the response(s) that eliminate the punishment.

An example of both punishment and negative reinforcement may be helpful. Suppose whenever a manager brings her work group together to share some new information with them, Bill, one of her subordinates, usually pays little attention and often talks to people around him. As a result he is uninformed and his manager is irritated. The manager decides to punish Bill's whispering behavior by stopping in the middle of a sentence and looking at Bill whenever she sees him talk. The unexpected silence (a negative consequence) causes the whole work group to focus on what stopped the manager's sharing of information (Bill's talking). The silence from the manager and all eyes on him are uncomfortable to Bill (punishment). He stops talking and starts listening to his manager resume sharing information. His manager's use of a negative consequence or punishment (silence and look) has weakened and suppressed his whispering behavior. At the same time it has operated as negative reinforcement in strengthening his listening, the behavior that took the punishment away (his manager stops looking at him and starts talking).

It is important to remember that a manager has to be careful in using punishment because he or she does not always know what a person will do when punished. For example, suppose a manager reprimands Al, one of his subordinates, for sloppy work. If Al settles down, figures out what he has done wrong, and begins working carefully (negative reinforcement), the punishment has been helpful. After having this good experience in "shaping up" Al, the manager might try the same technique with Mary, another employee who is doing sloppy work. But rather than the punishment (reprimand) getting Mary to behave more carefully, her work becomes worse, and she begins to become disruptive in other areas. Thus, while Al shaped up with a reprimand, Mary became more troublesome after the same intervention from her manager.

Another important point to keep in mind when using punishment is that punishment shows one what *not* to do but does not show one what *to* do. This was vividly pointed out by John Huberman in a case study[3] about a Douglas fir plywood mill in which the management had continually used punitive measures to deal with sloppy workmanship and discipline problems. Although punishment seemed to stop the inappropriate behavior for the moment, it had little long-term effect. When top management finally analyzed the system during the preparation for the doubling of its capacity, they were amazed that:

> . . . *not a single desirable result* could be detected.
> The people who had been disciplined were generally still among the poorest workers; their attitude was sulky, if not openly hostile. And they seemed to be spreading this feeling among the rest of the crew.[4]

This reality and the findings that "85 percent of all those who entered the local prison returned there within three years of their release . . ."[5] made management seriously question their system. Eventually they worked out a new and highly effective system, which Huberman called "discipline *without* punishment." One of the main ingredients of the new method was that rather than a punitive approach to unsatisfactory work or a discipline problem, a six-step process was initiated that clearly spelled out appropriate behavior and placed "on the employee the onus" of deciding whether he or she wished (or was able) "to conform to the requirements of a particular work situation."[6]

As this illustrates, it is essential when making a disciplinary intervention that task behavior follows immediately. That is, once an intervention has been made, the manager must identify the new behavior that is to replace the unde-sired behavior. Only when that occurs can positive reinforcement be used to increase the likelihood of the new behavior recurring.

Extinction

When reinforcement is withheld after a behavior occurs, the behavior is said to be on extinction. Punishment tends only to suppress behavior; extinction tends to make it disappear. To extinguish a response, nothing must happen as a result of behavior. For example, suppose a child finds that whenever she stomps up and down and cries, she gets the attention of her parents and usually receives something that she wants, say a cookie. Now, if her parents don't want that kind of behavior, they could extinguish it by not responding to the child (either in a positive or negative way) whenever she engages in that behavior. After a while, when the child sees that her stomping and crying behavior does not get her anything, this behavior will tend to decrease. People seldom continue to do things that do not provide positive reinforcement.

Although extinction can help to eliminate undesirable behavior, one should be careful not to use it when it is not intended. Let's look at our example of Al again.

Imagine that Al has adjusted pretty well to his setting. He works carefully and neatly because that is what pays off. But, suddenly, the boss stops rewarding Al for neat work. Al goes for perhaps a week or two weeks working neatly with no reward. He may not be able to tell us what is different but gradually his behavior gives us a clue. He soon begins to try other behaviors. He becomes less careful and neat. If the former negative consequences (punishment) are also with-held, we see that within days he has reverted to his earlier behavior pattern. In essence, neatness and carefulness have been extinguished. As stated earlier, peo-ple seldom continue to do things that do not provide positive reinforcement, either through external reward or internal satisfaction. In Al's case, he does not yet find working carefully or neatly as rewarding in itself. The intervention by his manager helped his task maturity, but Al is not psychologically mature enough in this job (and he may never become so if it is a boring and unsatisfying job) to be left alone and not periodically reinforced for his neatness and careful-ness.

In addition to its effect on the continuation of a particular behavior, extinc-tion also can sometimes have an emotional impact on that behavior. We could predict, for example, with an excellent chance of being correct, that Al will likely become surly, may complain more than before, or may have problems getting along with his coworkers. Emotional behavior usually accompanies extinction in performance when expected reinforcement or former punishment is withheld.

Parents often have problems with extinction when they do not realize what they are doing and tend to pay attention to their children only when they are behaving poorly. When the children are behaving appropriately, they may pay little or no attention to them, which in a sense puts that behavior on extinction.

If a child wants attention from his parents (it is rewarding to him), he may be willing to endure what the parents think is punishment for that attention. So, in the long run, the parents might be reinforcing the very behavior they do not want and extinguishing more appropriate behavior.

Leaders in all kinds of settings must be careful of the possibility of positively reinforcing inappropriate behavior, and yet it happens all the time. Have you ever given a crying child a piece of candy? *"Don't cry, dear. Here's some candy."* It works. The child eats the candy and stops crying. But does it really work? Behavior Modification Theory suggests that the next time the child wants a piece of candy (or your attention), he knows exactly how to get it—by crying. You have made the mistake of positively reinforcing inappropriate behavior.[7]

This phenomenon does not just happen at home but is very common in the world of work. For example, a manager's work group had responded well to her high task/low relationship behavior of always spelling out tasks specifically and dealing firmly with anyone who did not demonstrate appropriate behavior. Now suddenly this behavior is not achieving results, and her followers are being disruptive and making unreasonable demands on her. What should the manager do? The first impulse of most managers is to think "maybe I've been too hard on them" and begin to give in to their demands. Although perhaps she should have increased her relationship behavior earlier and moved to a high task/high relationship leadership style, if she does it now she may be positively reinforcing behavior that she does not want—every time her people want something, they will become disruptive. Positively reinforcing inappropriate behavior generally results in more unwanted behavior.

When to Use Punishment or Extinction

In essence, what we are saying is that leaders must think before they behave because they never know what they may or may not be reinforcing. This is particularly true when it comes to using punishment and extinction. And yet, these can be useful concepts that managers can learn to use effectively for unfreezing inappropriate behavior so that they can begin to reinforce positively more desirable behavior. It should be remembered, however, in using punishment or extinction that it is important to know what behavior you want to change and communicate that in some way to the person(s) with whom you are working. To determine when to use punishment and when to ignore (extinguish by withholding reinforcement), managers need to estimate how long the undesirable behavior has been occurring. If the behavior is new, ignoring it (extinction) may get results and cause a person to abandon an inappropriate behavior. But if the behavior has been occurring for some time, it may be necessary to suppress this behavior through some form of punishment until some desirable behavior has a chance to become strong enough as a result of positive reinforcement to replace the undesirable behavior. As we discussed in Chapter 2, the larger the reservoir of past experience that a person has in a particular behavior, the tendency is that the more difficult the behavior will be to change, and, thus, the harder the initial intervention may have to be before positive reinforcement can be used effectively to strengthen a new behavior.

An Example of Using Behavior Modification

Consider the behavior of Tony, a new employee right out of high school, who can be described as a very aggressive and competitive individual. During his first day on the job he argues over tools with another young employee. To make certain that a manager would not be unsure about what to do with Tony's behavior and to summarize our discussion of Behavior Modification, some steps that managers can use in attempting to change employee behavior are presented here.[8]

> *Step 1:* Identify (for yourself and then with Tony) the behavior to be changed and the new behavior that is to replace the old and discover what Tony would consider to be positive reinforcement and punishment. Devise a strategy to get the new behavior and determine the way you will positively reinforce it.
>
> *Step 2:* Attempt to find out whether the old behavior (arguing over tools) is such a strong behavior that you need to suppress it through punishment or whether it is a new enough behavior that a lack of any kind of reinforcement will extinguish it. If you decide to use punishment, determine what it will be. Remember, this punishment could operate as negative reinforcement and thus strengthen the behavior that removes the punishment. So be careful!
>
> *Step 3:* Develop a strategy to get Tony to practice the new behavior and positively reinforce it on a regular schedule. As soon as Tony has practiced the new behavior so that it is more likely to occur than the old behavior, change to an intermittent schedule of reinforcing the new behavior (make the intervals between reinforcement increasingly long) so that new behavior will resist extinction.

In examining these steps, one could get the impression that the manager is dominating the process with little if any involvement from Tony. According to Situational Leadership Theory, this may be appropriate in working with people at low levels of maturity, such as a new and inexperienced employee like Tony. But, as the maturity level of the people that a manager supervises begins to increase, this process of change becomes much more of a collaborative process. As we will discuss in Chapter 11, the extent of involvement of subordinates in the change process will vary from situation to situation.

PROBLEMS AND THEIR OWNERSHIP— WHO'S GOT THE MONKEY?

As we have been suggesting in this chapter, effective managers are not only able to develop the maturity and independence of their people, they are also able to spot "slippage" in maturity and intervene early enough to turn the situation around. How can managers know when to intervene? What should they look for?

As a simple guideline, whenever managers receive feedback, either verbal (one of their people tells them) or nonverbal (they observe the performance of one of their people), indicating that that person is having a problem in some area, it's time to think about stepping in. A *problem* exists when there is a difference between what someone is doing and what that person's manager and (or) that individual thinks he or she should be doing. Thus, detecting problems is all-important in determining what areas of a person's job require attention.

Thomas Gordon, in his book *P.E.T. Parent Effectiveness Training*,[9] contends that one of the most important steps in becoming more effective in rearing responsible self-motivated children is determining whether their behavior is acceptable or unacceptable to their parents as well as to themselves. Once the acceptance question has been answered, then "who owns the problem" in terms of a child's behavior can be identified. Although the work of Gordon originated from observations of parents and teachers, the concepts behind the ownership of problems seem to apply to any organizational setting in which a leader is trying to influence the behavior of others.

Combining this concept of "who owns the monkey?" with William Oncken's helpful "monkey-on-the-back" analogy,[10] we arrive at four potential "monkey business" (problem) situations.

1. *The leader has a "monkey."* The follower's behavior is a problem to the leader but not to the follower. Thus, the "monkey" is on the leader's back.
2. *Both leader and follower have a "monkey."* The follower's behavior is a problem to both the leader and the follower. Thus, both have a "monkey."
3. *The follower has a "monkey."* The follower's behavior is a problem to the follower but not to the leader. Thus, the "monkey" is on the follower's back.
4. *Neither leader nor follower has a "monkey."* The follower's behavior is a problem to neither leader nor follower. There is no problem; the "monkey" is gone.

If managers can identify who has the monkey, then they are in a position to determine which leadership style has the best chance of success and thus when and how to intervene with followers in each of the four problem situations.

If the behavior of a follower is acceptable to a leader, it represents moderate to high levels of maturity (M3 and M4), and thus a leader can use a "participating" (S3) or "delegating" (S4) style. However, if the behavior of a follower is unacceptable to a leader, it represents low to moderate levels of maturity (M1 and M2), and thus a "telling" (S1) or "selling" (S2) leadership style is appropriate.

To differentiate further between "telling" and "selling" or "participating" and "delegating," leaders need to determine who has the monkey. Imagine that a leader is confronted with a problem that he does not know how to handle. As the leader looks at who has the monkey, he can begin to determine whether to take action and, if so, what leadership style would be appropriate with each of the four problem situations:

1. If the leader owns the problem and the follower sees no issue, the appropriate leadership style for the leader would be high task/low relationship (S1), similar to what Gordon would refer to as "you or I messages," that is, statements of

role definition and clarification. In this situation, since the follower sees no problem, the leader must initiate some structure to make any change in the follower's behavior.

2. If both leader and follower own the problem, the appropriate leadership style for the leader would be high on both task and relationship behavior (S2), since the follower needs some direction. Yet because the follower also sees the behavior as a problem, some relationship behavior in terms of two-way communication and facilitating behavior is also necessary.

3. If the follower owns the problem, but the leader sees no problem in the follower's behavior, the leader needs to make an intervention that is high on relationship behavior and low on task behavior (S3), similar to what Gordon would refer to as "active listening." Thus, the leader needs to provide the follower with supportive behavior to facilitate two-way communication. The tragedy is that managers often treat this problem situation as if it were a problem to neither. If a supportive intervention is not made here, there is a high probability that the situation will become a problem to both.

4. If neither the leader nor the follower owns the problem, the most appropriate leadership style for the leader is low relationship/low task behavior (S4), since no intervention is necessary.

Let's look at some examples of how this concept might be used as a diagnostic tool. A junior in high school is avoiding the use of drugs. Since she is not using drugs, her behavior is not a problem to her parents. However, her behavior may be a problem to the girl herself, since all her friends are involved with drugs and are putting pressure on her. If her parents treat this situation as if it was a problem to neither and leave their daughter alone, this situation can quickly become a problem to both. Because of the competing pressures at school, no socioemotional support or active listening at home could lean the girl toward the drugs and acceptance by her peers. Thus, by not making a high relationship intervention at the appropriate time, the parents have helped to create a problem for all involved.

If the situation is one in which the behavior of the child is a problem to the parent but not to the child, the parent does not have to provide socioemotional support or facilitating behaviors. The parent merely needs to provide the child with an understanding of where the limits are (an S1 intervention). The child wants to know what are the barriers, what are the parent's expectations. Since the situation is not a problem to the child, the child does not want to spend fifteen or twenty minutes discussing why he or she cannot do it. The child just wants to know what the rules are, so he or she can behave accordingly. For example, a teacher who is making an assignment for the next day may ask the class to read fifteen, twenty, or twenty-five pages. That doesn't really matter to the students; any of those reading assignments are okay. All the students want to know is the expectations of the teacher; they don't want to sit around and talk about it. But if the teacher says the assignment is one hundred pages, the situation might quickly become a problem to both the students and the teacher. Now that the situation is also a problem to the students, the teacher has to engage in "selling" behavior rather than "telling." He or she has to open up channels of communication and discussion, and engage in facilitating and "stroking" behaviors. He or she has to get the students to understand the why of the large assignment and have them "buy in" psychologically to the decision. The teacher might say, "There is a top lecturer coming this week and, for that reason, a heavy assignment is being made for tomorrow; but later in the week we'll have no reading assignment." In other words, the teacher attempts to make some trades to facilitate interaction, but he or she is still trying to get the students to buy into the decision.

As the discussion and examples suggest, it is felt that this integration of Situational Leadership with problem ownership (Gordon) and monkey business (Oncken) can be helpful in determining the appropriate leadership style in various situations. Remember, even if the follower's behavior is acceptable to the leader, the leader may still have to take action if the follower needs support and encouragement to keep up the good work. If the follower's behavior is unacceptable to the leader, a more directive intervention is needed to turn the situation around. How direct the intervention must be ("telling" or just "selling") depends on whether the follower also sees this behavior as a problem and "owns the monkey" too.

As is being suggested, one of the key factors in determining maturity is problem solving—or the care and feeding of monkeys. If leaders are going to help their people grow and develop into mature self-motivated individuals, they must gradually let them think for themselves and solve their own problems. Many managers have trouble dealing with people when they have a problem.

Inappropriate Responses to People with a Monkey

In transactional analysis (TA), a concept known as the Karpman triangle[11] is helpful in recognizing some dysfunctional reactions when a follower or staff member has a problem. As Figure 10-2 indicates, there are three basic roles in the triangle: victim, persecutor, and rescuer.

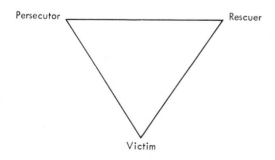

FIGURE 10-2 The Karpman triangle

If we adapt Karpman's concept to problem solving in an organization, we see that the victim would be a person with a monkey. A manager could respond to a monkey on a staff member's back from either the persecutor or the rescuer role. If a manager responds from the persecutor role, the manager puts the person down for having a problem. For example, a staff member, Carlos, might tell his boss that he has not been getting along lately with a coworker, Ted, and his boss might respond by saying, "That's ridiculous. You and Ted have worked together for years. You've never fought before and I can't believe you are having trouble getting along now." The manager doesn't even want to recognize that a problem exists for his staff member.

If a manager responds from the rescuer role, the manager tries to solve the problem for the person. In our example with Carlos and Ted, the manager may respond by saying, "That's too bad, Carlos. Why don't you contact Ted and ask him to come over here this afternoon and maybe the three of us could talk this out. I was always able to iron things out with my coworkers and I would be happy to talk with you and Ted." In TA and Situational Leadership terms, the persecutor and rescuer tend to both be coming from a Critical Parent ego state with the Critical Parent using an ineffective directive leadership style (Q1) and the rescuer using an ineffective supportive leadership style as Q3. Both roles are considered Critical Parent roles because in both instances messages are sent to the victim that he or she is not OK. The persecutor denies that a monkey exists and tells the person to forget it; the rescuer takes the monkey on his or her back and tends to let the victim (the staff member with the monkey) "off the hook." Neither of these responses teaches people to solve their own problems.

The triangle gets really interesting when a drama develops and people start to change roles. In our example of Carlos and Ted, if the manager responds to Carlos' problem with Ted from the persecutor role and puts Carlos down for having a problem, and if Carlos does a good job as the victim (mumbles to himself about Ted, looks downcast and thoroughly victimized), his boss may begin to feel guilty and realize that maybe Carlos really has a monkey. When this happens, the manager usually moves from the persecutor role to the rescuer role and attempts to rescue the victim (Carlos, in this case) and take the monkey on his back. "I'm sorry, Carlos, for yelling at you. I didn't realize how serious your disagreements with Ted were to you. Maybe I can help out."

At this point, the plot can thicken (as it often does) if Carlos moves quickly from victim to persecutor and attacks his boss (now the rescuer) for not being more understanding earlier. "You never listen to me when I try to tell you something. All I want from you is support, but you always jump to your own conclusions and start yelling." Now the persecutor turned rescuer (Carlos' boss) is the new victim.

The drama can also start when the manager initially tries to rescue the victim—the person with a monkey. What we often find is that most victims don't really want to be rescued. Either they want support or they only want to complain. So when the rescuing manager starts to make suggestions, the victimized staff member "yes buts" every suggestion. "Sounds like a good idea having a talk with Ted this afternoon, *but* he has another appointment." Then when the rescuing manager runs out of good suggestions (that the staff member didn't want to use anyway), the person moves quickly from victim to persecutor and "pounds" his or her manager for not being more helpful. "I thought you said you were good at working things out with coworkers. Not one of your solutions will work for Ted and me." So, once again, the manager ends up as the victim.

The drama gets even more exciting when there are three actors instead of just two. The drama usually unfolds when one manager responds to the person with the monkey from either the persecutor or rescuer role and another manager plays the unfulfilled role. Suppose that when Carlos' manager is persecuting him for having a problem with Ted, his boss' assistant jumps in to rescue Carlos. "Don't be so hard on Carlos. His relationship with Ted is very important to him." The rescue attempt makes Carlos' manager so angry that he stops persecuting Carlos and attacks the assistant as if she were the victim. "Why don't you stay out of this? It's between Carlos and me." When that happens, the victim escapes unharmed and the two managers battle it out.

The drama does not always start with the staff member, follower or child (in the family) as the victim. Sometimes the triangle starts off with the manager or parent being persecuted. Jongeward and Seyer give a beautiful family example of this kind of situation.[12]

Son: (as persecutor, yells angrily at mother) "You know I hate blue. Here you went and bought me another blue shirt!"

Mother: (as victim) "I never do anything right as far as you're concerned."

Father: (rescues mother, persecutes son) "Don't you dare yell at your mother like that, young man. Go to your room and no dinner!"

Son: (now as victim sulking in his room) "They tell me to be honest, and when I tell them what I don't like, they put me down. How can you satisfy people like that?"

Mother: (now rescuer, sneaks him a tray of food) "Now don't tell your father! We shouldn't get so upset over a shirt."

Mother: (returning to father as persecutor) "John, you're so tough with our son. I'll bet he's sitting in his room right now hating you."

Father: (as victim) "Gee, honey, I was only trying to help you, and you kick me where it hurts the most."

Son: (calling out as rescuer) "Hey, Mom, lay off, will ya? Dad's just tired."

How can managers stop games like this and the drama of the triangle? As discussed in Chapter 3, managers are best able to use theories and concepts when they have their Adult ego state in the executive position, that is, when they are able to think before they act.

The way to avoid the role of persecutor is to listen to your people before you begin to evaluate what they are saying. Active listening helps managers gather information so that their intervention will be effective, and it helps their staff members begin to identify and solve their own problems. How about the rescuer? How do managers avoid playing that role?

Keep the Monkey Where It Belongs

William Oncken, Jr., who developed the monkey-on-the-back analogy, warns us not to take on other people's monkeys.[13] In terms of the TA triangle, rescuing is letting a monkey jump from another person's back onto our own back. For example, suppose a son comes home and says to his parents that he has made the club's junior tennis team but practices are on Tuesdays and Thursdays at three–thirty and he doesn't know how he will get there. Most parents would immediately say, "I think I can drive you." If, however, they normally have something planned on Tuesday and Thursday afternoons and cannot make an immediate commitment, they might tell their son, "We'll try to work something out."

Now let's analyze what has just happened. Before the son entered the house, on whose back was the monkey (how he was going to get to tennis practice)? The child's. After he and his parents talked about it, on whose back was the monkey? The parents'. Now who is in the superior position? The child. And in case the parents forget who's in charge, the child periodically checks in to see how the parents are doing in terms of rearranging their Tuesday and Thursday afternoons. In essence, the parents are working for the child.

That's what often happens in organizations. Managers are exhausted from trying to solve all their subordinates' problems. This all occurs as if managers did not have their own responsibilities to handle. Subordinate-imposed time begins the moment a monkey successfully executes a leap from the back of the subordinate to the back of the subordinate's manager and does not end until the monkey is returned to its proper owner for care and feeding.[14]

What leaders need to do is get rid of their follower's monkey as the follower begins to mature. The first step, as suggested earlier, is for the leader to determine who owns the monkey. Let's look again at the four problem situations.

1. If a follower's behavior is unacceptable but is only a problem to the leader, then the leader owns the monkey and should do the initial care and feeding. But once the leader and follower know the monkey exists, the follower should take over its care and feeding. Staying with a "telling" (S1) style will guarantee only that the monkey will stay on the leader's back.

2. If a follower's behavior is unacceptable and a problem to both the leader and the follower, then the monkey is astride both backs. The follower needs some direction on how to feed this monkey, but the leader should be careful not to use a "selling" style too long, but as soon as possible get the developmental cycle going and move to a "participating" style in which the monkey and its care and feeding are now on the follower's back. A "selling" style (S2) can be a rescuing style, which sometimes is acceptable in the short run, but it could lead to full-time caring and feeding if it becomes a status quo.

3. If a follower's behavior is acceptable to the leader but is a problem to the follower, the leader should only be supportive of the follower's efforts to solve his or her own problem. The leader must be careful in this process that the monkey does not leap onto his or her back. The leader should be supportive but should not rescue the follower and take over the care and feeding of the follower's monkey.

4. If a follower's behavior is acceptable and neither the leader nor the follower owns a problem, then no leadership intervention is needed (use of a "delegating" style), since there is no monkey in need of care and feeding. Some leaders get nervous, however, when everything is going well with their people and start "hunting down monkeys and feeding them on a catch-as-catch-can basis."[15] This is a useless activity that may grow large monkeys where none really existed before.

The purpose of this chapter has been to help leaders develop strategies for turning around a decrease in maturity. The hope was to make leaders realize why it is important to work their way out of their traditional job of directing, controlling, and supervising their followers so that these people can learn to stand on their own feet and be effective in a world that is full of monkeys (problems).

NOTES

[1] These guidelines are expanded and adapted from some "rules of effective punishment" developed by Lawrence M. Miller, *Behavior Management: New Skills for Business and Industry* (Atlanta: Behavioral Systems, Inc., 1976).

[2] R. L. Solomon, "Punishment," *American Psychologist,* 19 (1964), p. 239.

[3] John Huberman, "Discipline Without Punishment," *Harvard Business Review,* May 1967, pp. 62–68.

[4] *Ibid.,* pp. 64–65.

[5] *Ibid.,* p. 65.

[6] *Ibid.*

[7] Taken from an enjoyable popular article on this subject by Alice Lake, "How to Teach Your Child Good Habits," *Redbook Magazine,* June 1971, pp. 74, 186, 188, 190.

[8] These steps were adapted from seven steps identified by Madeline Hunter, *Reinforcement Theory for Teachers* (El Segundo, Calif., TIP Publications, 1967), pp. 47–48.

[9] Thomas Gordon, *P.E.T. Parent Effectiveness Training* (New York: Peter H. Wyden, Inc., 1970).

[10] William Oncken, Jr., and Donald L. Wass, "Management Time: Who's Got the Monkey?" *Harvard Business Review,* November-December 1974, pp. 75–80.

[11] Stephen B. Karpman, *"Fairy Tales and Script Drama Analysis,"* *Transactional Analysis Bulletin* VII, No. 26 (April 1968), pp. 39–43.

[12] Dorothy Jongeward and Philip C. Seyer, *Choosing Success: Transactional Analysis on the Job* (New York: John Wiley & Sons, Inc., 1978).

[13] Oncken, *Management Time.*

[14] *Ibid.,* p. 76.

[15] *Ibid.,* p. 80.

chapter 11

Building
Effective
Relationships

In the last two chapters the emphasis was on helping leaders to develop people to their fullest potential. This involves shifting their leadership style forward and backward (according to Situational Leadership) and thus utilizing various degrees of direction and support as followers increase or decrease in maturity or development levels. This continual shifting of leadership style seems to require leaders to be flexible, i.e., to be able to use a variety of leadership styles depending on the situation. That raises two questions: (1) Are most leaders able to be that flexible or do they tend to be limited only to one or two leadership styles? (2) If leaders continually change their leadership styles, how will that affect their follower's perception of their intentions?

The first question is something that has been examined at the Center for Leadership Studies for more than a decade through the use of Leader Effectiveness and Adaptability Description (LEAD) instruments.[1] Answering the second question was an important impetus in the development of the Contracting for Leadership Style[2] process developed by Hersey and Blanchard to increase the effectiveness of management by objectives (MBO), a widely used formal superior-subordinate negotiation system.[3]

LEAD INSTRUMENTATION

The LEAD instrument developed by Hersey and Blanchard was designed to measure three aspects of leader behavior: (1) style, (2) style range, and (3) style adaptability.

The *leadership style* of an individual is the behavior pattern that person exhibits when attempting to influence the activities of others—as perceived by those others. This may be very different from the leader's perception of his or her own behavior, which we will define as *self-perception* rather than style. Comparing one's self-perception of leadership style with the perceptions of others can be very useful, particularly since one's self-perception may or may not reflect actual leadership style, depending on how close a person's perceptions are to the perceptions of others. For this reason, two LEAD instruments were developed: LEAD-Self and LEAD-Other. The LEAD-Self measures self-perception of how an individual behaves as a leader; the LEAD-Other reflects the perceptions of a leader's subordinates, superiors, and peers or associates. [4]

Leadership Style

Research at the Center for Leadership Studies has discovered that most leaders have a *primary* leadership style and a *secondary* leadership style. A leader's primary style is defined as the behavior pattern used most often when attempting to influence the activities of others. In other words, most leaders tend to have a favorite leadership style.

A leader's supporting style(s) is a leadership style that person tends to use on occasions. It is important to note that all leaders have a primary leadership style, that is, they tend to use one of the four basic leadership styles described in Situational Leadership more often than not in leadership situations. However, they may *not* have any secondary leadership style. Therefore, a leader could have no secondary styles or up to three secondary styles, but a leader would always have at least one primary style.

Style Range or Flexibility

An individual's *style range* is the extent to which that person is able to vary his or her leadership style. Leaders differ in their ability to vary their style in different situations. Some leaders seem to be limited to one basic style: these rigid people tend to be effective only in situations in which their styles are compatible with the environment. Other leaders are able to modify their behavior to fit any of the four basic styles; still others can utilize two or three styles. Flexible leaders have the *potential* to be effective in a number of situations.

The style range of a leader can be illustrated in terms of task and relationship behavior, as shown in Figure 11-1. The area of the circle indicates the range

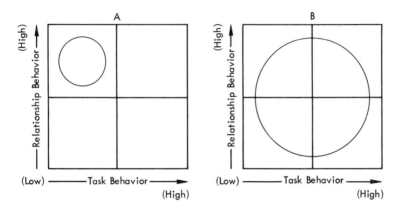

FIGURE 11-1 Style range in terms of task behavior and relationship behavior

of style. If the area is small as in A, then the range of behavior of the leader is limited; if the area is large as in B, the leader has a wide range of behavior.

Leadership situations vary in the extent to which they make demands on flexibility. Reddin has cited some of the conditions that demand, in his terms, low and high flexibility. These conditions are listed in Table 11-1[5]

TABLE 11-1 Low and high flexibility demands

Low Flexibility Demands	High Flexibility Demands
Low level managerial jobs	High level managerial jobs
Simple managerial jobs	Complex managerial jobs
Established goals	Emerging goals
Tight procedures	Fluid procedures
Established tasks	Unstructured tasks
Routine, automated decision making	Nonroutine decision making
Little environmental change	Rapid environmental change
Manager has complete power	Manager does not have complete power
Following plans essential	Using initiative essential
Manager accepted or rejected by subordinates	Subordinates neutral to manager
Few interconnecting jobs	Many interconnecting jobs

Style Adaptability

Style range indicates the extent to which leaders are able to vary their style; style *adaptability* is the degree to which they are able to vary their style appropriately to the demands of a given situation according to Situational Leadership. People who have a narrow style range can be effective over a long period of time if they remain in situations in which their style has a high probability of success. Conversely, people who have a wide range of styles may be ineffective if these behaviors are not consistent with the demands of the situation.

Thus, style range is not as relevant to effectiveness as style adaptability; a wide style range will not guarantee effectiveness. For example, in A in Figure 11-1, the leader has a dominant relationship style with no flexibility; in B, the leader has a wide range of leadership style because the leader is able to use all four leadership styles on various occasions. In this example, A may be effective in situations that demand a relationship-oriented style, such as in coaching or counseling situations. In B, however, the potential exists to be effective in a wide variety of instances. It should be remembered, however, that the B style range will not guarantee effectiveness. The B style will be effective only if the leader makes style changes appropriate to the situation.

Flexibility: A Question of Willingness

The importance of a leader's *diagnostic ability* cannot be overemphasized. It is the key to adaptability. However, most leaders are more concerned about flexibility than when to use which leadership style. That gets us back to one of the questions raised at the beginning of the chapter: Are most leaders able to be that flexible or do they tend to be limited to only one or two leadership styles?

It has been our experience at the Center for Leadership Studies that there are few, if any, leaders who cannot learn to use all four basic leadership styles. In fact, people use those behaviors almost every day. At least once a day don't you tell somebody what to do and watch them closely (Style S1), explain what you want somebody to do and permit them to ask clarifying questions (Style S2), share ideas with people and support their efforts (Style S3), and turn over responsibility to someone to "run with the ball" (Style S4)?

Learning to use the four basic styles is not the issue; the question is one of willingness. Anyone has the ability, but if the person does not want to learn, then there is not much that you can do. It is like the old saying, "You can lead a horse to water but you can't make him drink."

When people are willing to learn to use all the leadership styles, we have found an interesting phenomenon. When people learn to use the leadership style that previously was not even considered a secondary style, these compensating styles often become their most effective styles. While these styles may never become comfortable, they can become the most effective, in many cases, because they've been learned. Therefore, such leaders know a lot more about these styles because they have practiced them consciously. People often use their comfortable or primary leadership styles by the "seat of their pants." This is true not only in terms of leadership styles but also in many other areas of their lives.

For example, suppose you are a golfer who enjoys and excels at hitting a drive; yet you realize that the "drive is for show but the putt is for the dough," so you decide to take lessons in putting. If you consciously make an effort and take lessons and practice to become a good putter, very often it is this part of the game that becomes your most effective weapon. That does not mean that you would not still be more comfortable hitting the ball off the tee, but since you have studied putting in considerable detail you now know much more about that particular part of the game.

The same goes for leaders. Your primary style is often one that you do not have to think about using. But once you learn other styles through conscientious study, these compensating styles can be your most effective. Thus, we find willingness—not ability—is the main issue in terms of style flexibility.

Is There Only One Appropriate Style?

The concept of adaptability implies that the effective leader is able to use the right style at the right time. What if a leader makes a good diagnosis and then realizes that he or she does not want want to use the "best" style? Is that leader doomed to failure? As we discussed in Chapter 7, it's all a matter of degree. Situational Leadership not only suggests the high probability leadership styles for various maturity levels, but also indicates the probability of success of the other styles if the leader is unwilling or unable to use the "desired" style. The probability of success of each style for the four maturity levels is shown in Table 11-2.

TABLE 11-2   Matching maturity level with the leadership style most likely to work well

Maturity	"Best" Style	Second "Best" Style	Third "Best" Style	Least Effective Style
M1 Low	S1 Telling	S2 Selling	S3 Participating	S4 Delegating
M2 Low to Moderate	S2 Selling	S1 Telling or S3 Participating		S4 Delegating
M3 Moderate to High	S3 Participating	S2 Selling or S4 Delegating		S1 Telling
M4 High	S4 Delegating	S3 Participating	S2 Selling	S1 Telling

As Table 11-2 indicates, the "desired" style always has a second "best" style choice, that is, a style that would probably be effective if the highest probability style could not be used. In attempting to influence people at the low to moderate (M2) and moderate to high (M3) maturity levels, you will notice that there are two second "best" style choices: which one should be used depends on whether the maturity of the individual is getting better, indicating that the leaders should be involved in a developmental cycle (Chapter 9), or getting worse, revealing that a regressive cycle is occurring (Chapter 10). If the situation is improving, "participating" and "delegating" would be the "best" second choices, but if things are deteriorating, "telling" and "selling" would be the most appropriate backup choices.

Table 11-2 also suggests that "telling" and "delegating" are the risky styles because one of them is always the lowest probability style. However, even though this appears to be true, later in this chapter we will discuss why it is so important for leaders to learn to use these styles effectively.

Use of LEAD Instrumentation

When staff members at the Center for Leadership Studies diagnose an organization, part of that diagnosis often involves use of the LEAD instruments. The process consists of having managers throughout the organization complete the LEAD-Self instrument (how they perceive their own leadership style). At the same time each of these managers' subordinates, superior, and several associates or peers fill out the LEAD-Other instrument. All the instruments are sent directly to the Center for Leadership Studies for analysis. Once the data have been analyzed, a LEAD-Profile is prepared for each individual manager. On that profile the managers are given an opportunity to see if there is any significant difference between how they perceive their own leadership style and how others in the environment perceive their style.

The purpose of distributing and analyzing the LEAD-Self and LEAD-Other data is to determine if there is any discrepancy between self-perception and the perception of others. In analyzing that data and feeding it back to participating managers, a useful framework developed by Joseph Luft and Harry Ingham[6] is used.

JOHARI WINDOW

The framework developed by Luft and Ingham is called the *Johari window* (taken from the first names of its authors). The Johari window is used by Hersey and Blanchard to depict leadership personality, not overall personality as it is sometimes used. The difference between leadership personality and leadership style in this context is that leadership personality includes self-perception and the perception of others; leadership style consists only of an individual's leader behavior as perceived by others, that is, superior, subordinate(s), associates, and so on. Thus, leadership personality equals self-perception plus other perception (style).

According to this framework, there are some attitudes or behaviors engaged in by leaders that they know about themselves. This *known to self* area includes their knowledge of the way they are coming across, the impact they are having with the people they are trying to influence. At the same time, part of the leader's personality is *unknown to self;* that is, in some areas leaders are unaware of how they are coming across to others. It may be that their followers have not given them feedback or it may be that a leader has not been alert enough to pick up some of the verbal or nonverbal feedback that actually exists within the environment.

We can also look at leadership personality including behaviors and attitudes that are *known to others* in a leader's organizational setting, as well as areas *unknown to others.* In terms of what is known and unknown to self and known and unknown to others, we can create four areas that comprise the total window, as depicted in Figure 11-2.

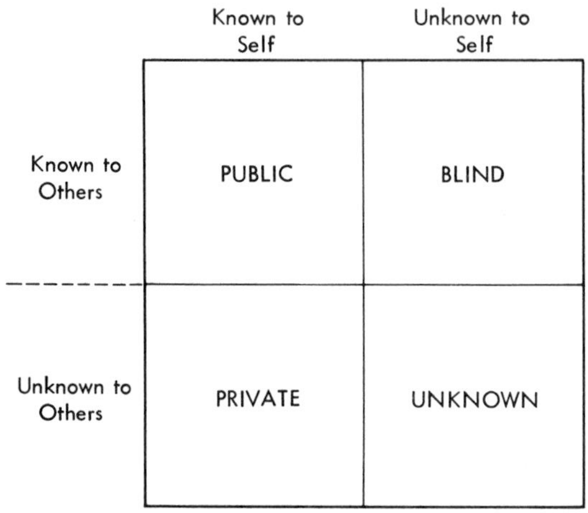

	Known to Self	Unknown to Self
Known to Others	PUBLIC	BLIND
Unknown to Others	PRIVATE	UNKNOWN

FIGURE 11-2 The Johari window

The arena that is known to self and also known to others in any specific organizational setting is called the *public* arena—it is known to all (the leader and others, that is, superior, subordinate(s), and peers) within that organizational setting.

The arena that is unknown to self (the leader) but is known to others is referred to as the *blind* arena. It is unknown to the leader either because followers have been unwilling to share feedback with or communication ("level") to that leader on how he or she is coming across; or it may be that the data are there in terms of verbal and nonverbal behavior, but the leader is not able or does not care to "see" them.

The arena that is known to self but unknown to others is referred to as the *private* arena since it is only known to the leader. Again, it may be private because the leader has been unwilling to share or disclose this to others in the organizational setting; or it may be private because the others in the system are not picking up the nonverbal and verbal responses that are available from the leader in the system.

The last arena, unknown to self and unknown to others, is called the *unknown.* In Freudian psychology this would be referred to as the subconscious or unconscious.[7] As you will recall from Chapter 2, Freud describes personality much like an iceberg. There is a certain portion of a leader's personality that is above the surface—that is, it is very graphic. Anyone who looks in that direction can hardly help but see the basic size, consistency, makeup, and configuration. But much of this iceberg exists beneath the surface and unless we make conscious efforts to probe and understand, we will really never have any insight into its consistency. And yet much of that part of a leader's personality referred to as unknown may be having a relevent impact in terms of the kinds of behaviors in which a leader engages when he or she is trying to influence the behavior of others.

Feedback

There are two processes that affect the shape of the Johari window (the configuration of the four arenas). The first, which operates in the direction illustrated in Figure 11-3, is called *feedback*. This is the extent to which others in the organizational setting are willing to share with the leader on how he or she is coming across. It is the willingness of others to be open and level and to give relevant feedback to the leader. But again you have to look at it from both perspectives. It is also the extent to which the leader is attempting to perceive the verbal and nonverbal feedback that exists in the system.

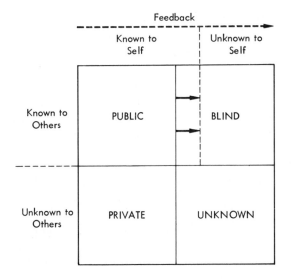

FIGURE 11-3   Effect of feedback on the Johari window

Many managers cut off and eventually stifle feedback from their people by arguing with them about their feelings and perceptions. The late Haim Ginott, author of the well-known book, *Between Parent and Child,*[8] and his wife, Alice Ginott,[9] who has been carrying on some of his work, believe that people should be allowed to have any feelings they want. Feelings are to be heard and accepted;

it's only behavior that should be limited. In other words, *everyone* is an expert on his or her own feelings and perceptions. Managers should never say to their people, "You don't really feel that way" or "That's not true" because, obviously, these people do know how they feel about things.

To illustrate this point, let's look at an example. A mother is walking through a department store with her young son when the child notices a beautiful bicycle. He says, "Boy, would I like to have a bike like that!" His mother, rather than hearing his feelings, replies harshly, "You're such an ungrateful child. We just got you a new bike for Christmas and already you want a new one. I've had enough of your spoiled attitude. See if you get anything new again for a long time." Now, what exactly has this child learned from this experience? He has learned that he should never tell his mother how he feels about anything; he will only get punished. If this scene is repeated often enough, the mother may soon lose any chance of ever receiving feedback from her son again—which is certainly a high price to pay!

What should the mother do in this situation? Alice Ginott suggests that she should recognize her son's wish and rephrase it in simple words; for example, "I bet you wish you could get a new bike any time you wanted." The child undoubtedly would agree. Then the mother should follow up with a statement or question like, "Why don't you think you can get that new bike?" The boy knows and will probably say, "Because I just got a new one for Christmas." After agreeing, the mother could conclude the conversation on a supportive note: "When you've gotten good use out of your bike and it starts to get too small for you, then you probably can get a new one." With this kind of interaction, the child won't be afraid to share his feelings with his mother again.

This same situation occurs day after day in every organization. For example, a staff member tells her boss, "Those staff meetings we have on Thursday run too long and I think generally are a waste of time." Her boss, rather than listening to her feelings and trying to find out why she feels that way about the meetings, responds quickly and harshly. "What do you mean those meetings are a waste of time? I'm sick and tired of your attitude around here. I think those meetings are the most productive sessions that we've had around here for a long time. And I'm sick and tired of this kind of ridiculous comment." Will this manager get much more feedback from the staff member? Probably not. The staff member has learned that with her boss "feelings are not allowed" unless they are "company line." That is unfortunate because in many ways "feedback is the breakfast of champions." Without feedback from their people, managers will develop significant blind areas that will eventually damage their effectiveness.

Another suggestion can give managers an additional clue to how they can encourage their people to share their feelings and perceptions with them. Why treat your people differently from the way you would treat a stranger, acquaintance, or a friend? For example, suppose a guest at a party in your home forgets his hat and you discover it just after he has headed out to his car. Would you run out the door waving the hat and yelling, "How stupid can you be to leave your hat behind? How many times have I had to run after you with something you left? If your head wasn't glued on your shoulders, you'd probably forget that, too!" Of course you wouldn't. You would probably just say, "I'm glad I caught you. You left your hat!" And that's how staff members deserve to be treated as well.

Treating staff members with respect will lead to a relationship in which they feel free to share and talk. As can be seen in Figure 11-3, the more relative feedback that takes place within an organization, the more the public arena of a leader begins to extend into and displace the blind arena and thus the smaller blind arena that leader has.

Disclosure

The other process that affects the shape of the Johari window is *disclosure*. This is the extent to which leaders are willing to share with others in their organizational setting data about themselves.

The way we use the term disclosure is different from the way others in the field often use it. First, the most relevant disclosure is not what people say about themselves but rather their behavior. It is not words that mean, it is people that mean. And if you want to understand people better, you really have to look at the behavior those people engage in to gain relevant insights into their values and what this behavior represents.

For example, over the past few years we have had an opportunity to work with various feminist groups concerned about women's liberation. This experience has provided us with an insight into something that is characteristic of many organizations. What happens is that people start to focus on words rather than behavior. We have seen individuals come in to work with feminist groups who really cared about giving women an opportunity to reach significant management positions within the organization. But because the words they used did not correspond to the jargon of the movement, the mental doors were immediately closed and the women no longer listened. We have also seen people come to work with these groups who in reality were attempting to hold back the progress of women within the organizational hierarchy but used all the appropriate jargon (used all the "buzz" words). They were accepted and looked at positively because of their language. The same has been true of blacks, students, and other groups fighting for their rights. This is just an example to emphasize once again that we must be very careful of words—it is not words that mean; much more important is the behavior that people engage in.

Second, we think disclosure is appropriate in organizations only when such disclosure is organizationally relevant. This is a different way of viewing disclosure than urged by some people in the sensitivity training and personal growth field, who feel all disclosure is appropriate. In fact, some contend that it is appropriate for a leader or manager in an organizational setting to be open and disclose as much as possible and that the organization should process that data. Our experience from numerous organizational development interventions suggests that two of the scarcest resources in any organizational setting are time and energy. Therefore, if people disclosed almost everything about themselves within the organizational setting and people took time to process these various agenda, there would not be much time left to accomplish other organizational goals and objectives. We feel disclosure is important and helpful in organizations as long as it is relevant to the operation of the organization. For example, suppose a manager is having an affair with a neighbor down the street and it does not affect the manager's work environment. It might be inappropriate to disclose and process that situation in that work setting. But it might be very appropriate to disclose, discuss, and process it at home if the situation is causing problems in that environment. Therefore, what may be organizationally relevant in one setting might be inappropriate in another.

In the process of disclosure, the more and more organizationally relevant information that leaders disclose about the way they think or behave, the more the public arena opens into the private arena and the smaller and smaller that arena becomes, as shown in Figure 11-4. An interesting phenomenon occurs in settings where there is simultaneous feedback and disclosure between leaders and the people with whom they work. Not only does the public arena of these leaders begin to extend itself into the blind and the private arenas, but there is also a high probability that some of what was previously unknown (not known to either the leaders or other people in the organization) will begin to surface into the public arena.

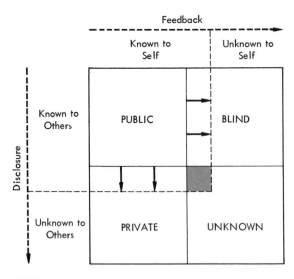

FIGURE 11-4   Effect of feedback and disclosure on the Johari window

A psychiatrist working with a patient in psychotherapy hopes to create an environment in which this process of simultaneous feedback and disclosure occurs. If that happens, the doctor can begin to release and understand some of the phenomena that have been evoking behavior in the patient that was unknown to the patient as well as the psychiatrist. This is also the same process that Carl Rogers[10] refers to in his work on coaching and counseling.

Self-Perception versus Style

When we do an organizational diagnosis, the data from the LEAD-Self, as we explained, denote self-perception. In terms of the Johari window, the self-perception of leaders would represent what is known to them about their leadership style and would include both their public and private arenas. This self-perception of leadership style can be measured using the LEAD-Self. On the other hand, an individual's leadership style would represent what is known to others and would include on the Johari window both that person's public and blind arenas. Leadership style can be measured using the LEAD-Other. The relationship between self-perception, leadership style, and the Johari window is presented in Figure 11-5.

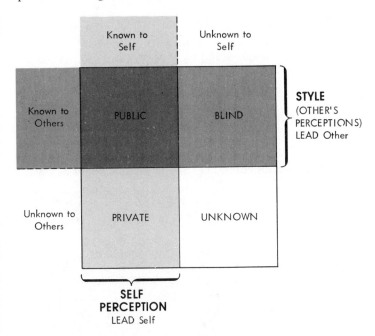

FIGURE 11-5 Self-perception and other perception (style)

One of the interesting phenomena that we have discovered at the Center for Leadership Studies is that we can predict the shape of the public arena within the Johari framework. For instance, if there is a great discrepancy between self-perception and the way others perceive a manager (style), the public arena in that manager's Johari window would tend to be very small, as illustrated in Figure 11-6.

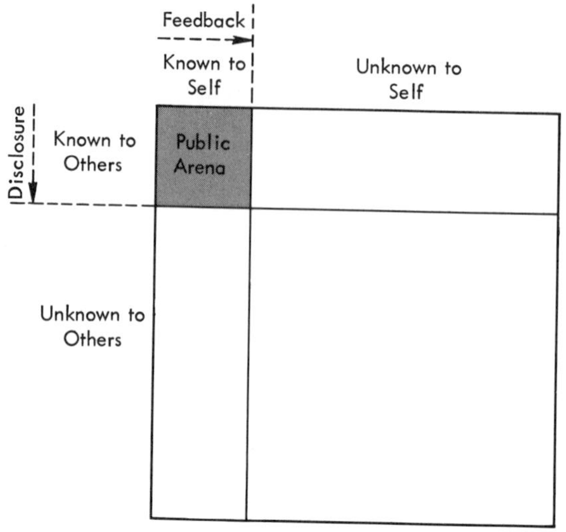

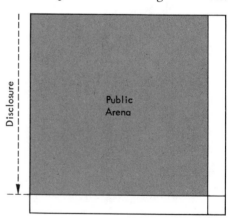

Feedback
- - - - →
Known to Self | Unknown to Self

Disclosure

Known to Others — **Public Arena**

Unknown to Others

FIGURE 11-6   Public arena when there is a large discrepancy

But if there is no significant difference between self-perception and the perception of others within a leader's organization setting, the public arena in that person's leadership Johari window would be large, as illustrated in Figure 11-7. LEAD data can actually measure the shape of the arenas in a person's leadership Johari window in each of the organizational settings in which that person operates.

For example, if a manager is responsible for three departments, she may find that in Department A in which she has good feedback and disclosure her public window is very open. In Department B in which she has very little contact, and thus infrequent feedback and disclosure, her public window might be small.

Disclosure

Public Arena

FIGURE 11-7   Public arena when there is a small discrepancy

And, finally, in Department C in which she has average interaction her public arena might be moderate in size.

Another interesting result of our work at the Center for Leadership Studies is a realization that there tends to be a high correlation between the openness of a leader's public arena and that person's effectiveness within that specific organizational setting. Since people often have different configurations for their leadership Johari window depending on the organizational setting in which they are operating, these people could vary in their effectiveness in these various settings. This is why some managers who have a very open public arena on the job and are very effective there are not as effective at home. It is often the case of managers coming home, picking up the paper, and having a drink. They are tired and don't want to be bothered by children or any problems of the home. Therefore, in their home environment there tends to exist far less feedback and disclosure. We could predict that these managers would not be as effective in their interactions at home as at work. And yet they have trouble understanding why they are not having an effective impact on the development of their children because they see themselves as effective leaders in terms of the feedback they get on the job. On the other hand, there are individuals who are quite effective in the home and wonder why they are not effective on the job. We have to recognize that each organizational setting in which we are involved is unique, and if we want to have an impact on that setting we have to be willing to engage in relevant·feedback and disclosure.

Another thing managers must recognize is that within a given organizational setting they need to be effective on both individual and group levels, and both levels involve separate Johari windows. Thus, we have found it helpful in a family, for example, for the parents to get together with each of their children individually as well as with all the children as a family. One might begin something like taking each child out to dinner once a month, giving the child a chance to choose where and what he or she wants to eat. The important thing is to create a situation in which the focus is on the child and the child's problems. You would be surprised how willing the child will be to open up and engage in feedback and disclosure when alone with the parent(s) than when brothers and sisters are there to create many competing responses in that environment. This process over time will help to develop an open public arena between children individually with their parents, as well as developing feedback and disclosure within the family as a total group. We need to build into our domestic environment, as well as our work setting, opportunities to work with groups as a whole, at the same time developing openness with individuals within that system.

Is It Too Late?

In reading about communication problems, managers might be feeling discouraged or even guilty. Maybe they have a problem employee or child or two and are thinking they really have done a poor job as a manager or a parent. Yet, as Wayne Dyer so aptly argues in his book *Your Erroneous Zones,* [11] guilt is a useless feeling.

It is by far the greatest waste of emotional energy. Why? Because, by definition, you are feeling immobilized in the present over something that has already taken place, and no amount of guilt can ever change history. [12]

Today managers can never do what they should have done at an earlier time. Maybe you have made some mistakes. But that was yesterday; what are you going to do today? Today is the beginning of the rest of your life as a leader, manager or parent. It is never too late to turn a situation around, as long as there is enough time. We mention time because it is a key factor. Why? Let us try to explain from a child-rearing point of view.

The earlier in a child's life a parent attempts to have an impact the greater will be that parent's potential influence on the child's future behavior. During the early years, an intervention by a parent represents a substantial portion of the child's sum experience in that area of his or her life; the same intervention later can never carry the same weight. In addition, the longer the behavior is reinforced the more patterned it becomes and the more difficult it is to change. That's why, as a child gets older, it takes more time and more new experiences to bring about a change in behavior. Think of it this way: one drop of red food coloring in a half-pint bottle of clear liquid may be enough to change drastically the appearance of the total contents. But the same drop in a gallon jug may make little, if any, noticeable difference.

If our children are now teenagers—young adults—it is still possible, though difficult, to bring about some change in their behavior. Now it becomes a matter of economics: how much time are we willing to invest in implementing such a change.

Let's take an extreme case. Suppose a teenage son is discovered by his parents to be into drugs and in trouble with the law. What can his parents do now? One choice is to feel guilty and try to make up for past mistakes by putting all kinds of time in with the son now. But the son might resent all this attention from his parents after having been left on his own for so long. If the son doesn't resent the sudden attention from his parents, then it becomes an economic question: our children have unlimited needs, but we have limited time. Where can we put in the most effective time with the biggest payoff?

If the parents have plenty of time and decide to attempt to change their son's behavior (even though it's an old pattern), the concepts presented in this book should provide some helpful hints as to where and how to begin. Probably they will have to do some "telling" (S1) and "selling" (S2), both of which are time-consuming styles. But with some concentrated effort, the parents can probably have an impact on this boy's behavior.

Before parents throw themselves into a change effort with one of their kids, it's a wise idea to consider what impact this attention will have on the other children in the family. By devoting all their time and energy to one problem, the parents may unwittingly create other problems. If all of the parents' time is spent on this teenage son, the other children still at home may get the impression that the only way to get time with mom and dad is by getting into trouble (in effect, the parents have put all their good behavior on "extinction"). And soon one problem child has mushroomed into other problem children. Therefore, it's important always to look at the big picture and allot time accordingly.

The lesson to be learned in this example as a manager is to "get your shots in early" with your people. As we stated in Chapter 10, loosening up is much easier than tightening up. Rescue and salvage work is tough and time-consuming and often comes too late to do much good.

LEAD PROFILES

As was indicated earlier, LEAD data are gathered in organizations to give managers feedback on how they perceive their own leadership style as compared with how others see their style. Once a manager has learned that his people think that he tends to use one style or another most of the time with them, what does it all mean?

Sample

In this section we will examine and interpret some of the common profiles that we have found from analysis of LEAD-Self and LEAD-Other data accumulated at the Center for Leadership Studies.[13] The information was generated from a LEAD sample of over twenty thousand leadership events from fourteen different cultures. A "leadership event" occurs when we have data not only in terms of self-perception (LEAD-Self) but also the perception of others (LEAD-Other) in that leadership environment. Of these respondents, we have interviewed some two thousand middle managers from industry and education; of that number, we have conducted over five hundred in-depth interviews. The interviews have not only included the leaders in terms of self-perception but also a sample of the leader's followers and their perceptions of the style of the leader.

What Is a Two-Style Profile?

In our in-depth interviews the emphasis has been on what we call "two-style profiles." A two-style profile includes either (1) a basic style that encompasses two of the four possible style configurations or (2) a basic style and a supporting style.

It is suggested that as feedback is given on the specific two-style profiles you keep in mind what you know about your own leadership style. If you think you have a one-style profile (you tend to use only one primary leadership style with little flexibility), then you need to remember that your profile represents only a portion of the two-style profile. If you think you have a three- or four-style profile (you have more than one supporting style in addition to your primary style), you may have to integrate the feedback that will be given to you into several of the two-style profiles. It must be pointed out that unless you have gathered specific data on how your leadership style is perceived by others, your perception of your own leadership style is only that—your perception.

Wide Flexibility

We have found that in working with people who have a wide range of styles, even though their effectiveness score may be low, a shorter period of time is needed to increase their effectiveness than is needed with people who have a smaller range of behavior. If people are engaging in a wide range of behavior, all you have to do to make a significant change in their effectiveness is to change their knowledge and attitude structure—in other words, teach them diagnostic skills. On the other hand, for people who have had no experience in using a variety of styles, much more time is necessary for them to become comfortable in using different styles.

Reference to Situational Leadership

Since we will be referring to Situational Leadership throughout the discussion of the two-style profiles, the basic framework is reproduced for your use in Figure 11-8.

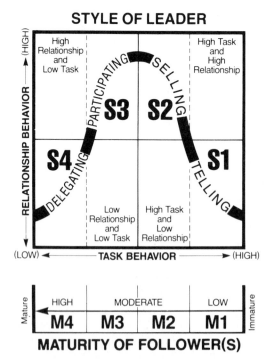

FIGURE 11-8 Situational leadership

Style Profile 1-3

People who are perceived as using predominately styles 1 and 3 fall into what is called the "Theory X–Theory Y profile." What we have found is that people who have a style profile 1–3, with little flexibility to styles 2 and 4, generally view their subordinates with either Theory X or Theory Y assumptions about human nature. They see some people as lazy, unreliable, and irresponsible. The only way to get anything out of these people is to coerce, reward and punish, and closely supervise them. Other people they see very positively as creative and self-motivated; the only thing they have to do with these people is to provide socioemotional support. In fact, in interviewing managers with this profile, it has been found that they talk about individuals they supervise as "good people" or "bad people," "with me" or "against me." Their subordinates, when interviewed, tend to agree. They see their managers as labeling people, and thus being very supportive (Q3) with people they see in their "camp," but closely supervising, controlling (Q1) and even punishing people they see against them.

One of the interesting things that occurs with this style profile is that it often becomes a self-fulfilling prophecy. A manager with this style takes people who are at moderate maturity levels (M2) and either moves them up to moderate to high (M3) or moves them down to low levels of maturity (M1). Thus, this manager tends to be effective working with low levels of maturity or moderate to high levels.

A problem with this style is that the leaders who adopt it often are doing little to develop the potential of the people they don't like; they keep them locked into immature states by always relying on Q1 (high task/low relationship behavior) with them. They lack the interim behaviors between style 1 and style 3 to operate effectively in the developmental cycle. At the same time, their style 3 (high relationship/low task behavior) with moderately mature people might keep

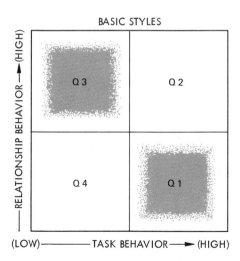

BASIC STYLES

FIGURE 11-9 Style profile 1–3   (LOW) ————— TASK BEHAVIOR ——► (HIGH)

these people psychologically dependent on them too long. These kinds of leaders do not seem to allow people to develop fully through delegation.

It is also interesting that people who work for leaders with this style profile claim that if there is any change in their leader's style with them, it usually occurs in a movement from style 3 to style 1. In other words, it is very difficult if you are being treated in a style 1 fashion by these leaders ever to receive style 3 types of behavior from them. But it is not too difficult to move from receiving style 3 behaviors to receiving style 1 behaviors. All you have to do is make some mistakes and these leaders tend to respond with highly structured behavior.

Style Profile 1-4

People who are perceived as using mainly styles Q1 and 4 have some similarity to the "Theory X–Theory Y profile" of style 1–3 leaders. But rather than assessing people on whether they are good or bad in terms of personal attachment to them, the sorting mechanism for this kind of leader often becomes competency. When interviewed, these managers suggest that if you are competent you will be left alone, but if you are incompetent they will "ride you" and closely supervise your activities. Their style is either "telling" or "delegating." A leader with this style is effective at crisis interventions. This is the kind of style we might look for to make an intervention into an organization with severe problems where there are short-time restrictions to solve them. This kind of leader is quite capable of making disciplinary interventions, going in and turning around a situation, and hopefully moving people back to a higher level of maturity. But again, much like the style 1–4 profile, this type of leader lacks the developmental skills to take people from low levels of maturity and develop them into higher levels of maturity.

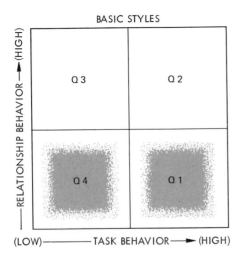

FIGURE 11-10 Style profile 1–4

An interesting thing occurs when leaders with this type of profile are introduced into a group with a normal distribution of maturity. What tends to happen is that the leader treats people in such a way that they either progress in their maturity or they regress, so that now, rather than a normal distribution of maturity levels, followers are clustered at the high end (M4) or low end (M1) of the maturity continuum. Once again, this becomes a self-fulfilling prophecy.

Style Profile 2-3

People who are perceived as using predominately styles Q2 and Q3 tend to do well working with people of average levels of maturity but find it difficult handling discipline problems and immature work groups (M1), as well as "delegating" with competent people to maximize their development. This style tends to be the most frequently identified style in the United States and other countries that have a high level of education and extensive industrial experience. Managers in some of the emerging cultures tend to have a more structured style profile (Q1 and Q2).

This style leader tends to be effective more often than not, because most people in work settings usually fall in maturity levels M2 and M3. We find far fewer people on the whole at maturity levels M1 and M4.

If styles Q2 and Q3 are considered "safe styles," then we would have to say that styles Q1 and Q4 are the "risky styles." We say "risky" because if they are used inappropriately, they can result in a great deal of crisis. For instance, if someone is supervising a very low level of maturity and uses style Q4, leaving people on their own, there is a high probability that the environment is going to deteriorate and serious problems will result. On the other hand, if you have an extremely high level of maturity among your followers and you are attempting

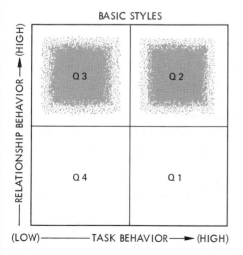

FIGURE 11-11 Style profile 2–3

to use style Q1 interventions, you are likely to generate much resentment, anxiety, and resistance, which may lead to what Machiavelli refers to as attempts to undermine, overthrow, or get out from under the leader, that is, hatred rather than fear. Although styles Q1 and Q4 are risky styles, if you are going to maximize your role as leader, you have to be willing to take the risk and use these styles when the situation is appropriate. One caution is that if you feel style 1 or style 4 is needed in a situation, you should be more careful in your diagnostic judgments before you make these kinds of interventions.

You need to learn to make style Q1 interventions for the following reasons: First, they are effective interventions when beginning the process of developing the task-relevant maturity of people with low maturity levels. Second, this style is often necessary in making disciplinary interventions. On the other hand, style S4 is often necessary if you are going to allow people to reach self-actualization by satisfying their need for achievement and desire to maximize their potential.

Learning to use style Q4 is also important to leaders themselves. In many of the organizations for which we work, there are at least two prerequisites for promotion. The first is that managers have to do an outstanding job in their present position. In other words, their output in terms of that organization has to be high. The second prerequisite is that they have to have a ready replacement, someone who is ready and able to take over their responsibilities. To have this kind of ready replacement, managers must have at least one of several key subordinates with whom they are able to use style Q4 and delegate significant responsibilities. If this is not so, the probability of these managers having a ready replacement is very low. In summary, the style profile Q2–Q3 is an excellent style for working with moderately mature individuals, but if leaders with this profile are going to maximize their potential as leaders, they need to learn to use styles Q1 and Q4 when necessary.

Style Profile 1-2

People who are perceived as using predominately styles Q1 and Q2 tend to be able to raise and lower their socioemotional support or relationship behavior, but they often feel uncomfortable unless they are "calling the shots," that is, when they are providing the structure and direction. In our sample, we found that this style profile tends to be characteristic of engineers who have become supervisors of other engineers but tend to be reluctant to give up their engineering; salespersons who have become sales managers and yet still love to sell themselves; and teachers who have become administrators but who still want to be directing the activities of children. These leaders often project in interviews that "no one can do things as well as I can," and this often becomes a self-fulfilling prophecy.

The style profile Q1–Q2 tends to be effective with low to moderate levels of maturity. It is often an extremely effective style for people engaged in manufacturing and production where managers have real pressures to produce, as well as with leaders in crisis situations where time is an extremely scarce resource. But

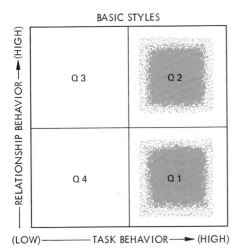

BASIC STYLES

RELATIONSHIP BEHAVIOR ──▶ (HIGH)

Q 3   Q 2

Q 4   Q 1

(LOW) ──────── TASK BEHAVIOR ──▶ (HIGH)

FIGURE 11-12   Style profile 1–2

leaders with this style, when the crisis or time pressure is over, often are not able to develop people to their fullest potential. And this remains true until they learn to use style S3 and S4 appropriately.

Style Profile 2-4

People who are perceived as using mainly styles Q2 and Q4 usually have a primary style of Q2 and a secondary style of Q4. This style seems to be characteristic of managers who do not feel secure unless they are providing much of the direction, as well as developing a personal relationship with people in an environment characterized by two-way communication and socioemotional support (high relationship behavior). Only occasionally do these people find a person to whom they feel comfortable delegating. And when they do delegate, their choice may not be able to handle the project. Thus, such a person may not be able to complete the task or may come to the manager for help because he or she is used to the leader's providing direction and socioemotional support. The reason that style profile Q2—4 leaders tend not to be successful in delegating is that they generally move from style Q2 to style Q4 without moving through style Q3. Let's look at an example.

Suppose your supervisor usually directs and closely supervises (high task behavior) your activities, but you also have a good rapport with this supervisor and open communication and you receive socioemotional support from these interactions (high relationship behavior). One day the supervisor puts a couple of projects on your desk and tells you that they must be completed in a couple of weeks. You don't see the supervisor during that time. You would probably respond to that behavior from your manager as if it were a punishment rather than a reward. You might respond by saying, "What's he giving me all this work

BASIC STYLES

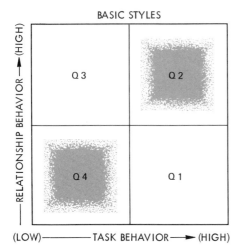

RELATIONSHIP BEHAVIOR ——→ (HIGH)

(HIGH)

Q 3

Q 2

Q 4

Q 1

(LOW) ——————— TASK BEHAVIOR ——► (HIGH)

FIGURE 11-13 Style profile 2–4

for?" and "He must not care about me much anymore because I never see him now!" So rather than suddenly shifting from style Q2 to Q4, managers with this style, if they are going to be effective in delegating, have to learn to move from "selling" (S2) through "participating" (S3) and then to "delegating" (S4).

In the previous example, if this strategy were followed by your supervisor, he should provide you with some socioemotional support, telling you that you have been doing a good job, that he has confidence in you, and that he feels that you will be able to take on some additional responsibility. Then he might give you a choice of several projects so that you could then participate in choosing which of the projects you would be interested in taking over. So your supervisor would be moving from style S2 into style S3 (participation and supportive behavior). Then he might say, "Look, I think you can run with this project on your own. If you get into some problems, give me a call." Now, because your supervisor has moved from style S2 through the supportive relationship behaviors (S3) to delegation (S4), you would tend to see this behavior as a reward rather than a punishment.

Style Profile 3-4

People who are perceived as using predominately styles 3 and 4 tend to be able to raise and lower their socioemotional support or relationship, but they often feel uncomfortable if they have to initiate structure or provide direction for people. Thus, while this style profile is appropriate for working with moderate to high levels of maturity, it tends to create problems with people who are becoming less mature and need a regressive intervention or with inexperienced people who require more direction during the early phases of the developmental cycle.

We have found style profile Q3–Q4 to be characteristic of certain types of

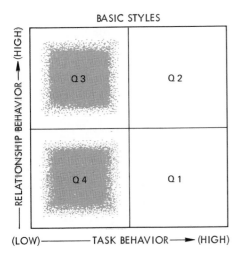

BASIC STYLES

RELATIONSHIP BEHAVIOR ──▶ (HIGH)

Q 3   Q 2

Q 4   Q 1

(LOW) ──────── TASK BEHAVIOR ──▶ (HIGH)

FIGURE 11-14   Style profile 3–4

individuals or groups. It tends to be representative of very effective top managers in organizational settings where they have a mature, competent staff that needs little direction from the top. It has also been found to be characteristic of managers who have been very deeply involved in sensitivity training, personal growth groups, or laboratory training. These managers sometimes become more interested in how people feel and the process of interpersonal relationships than what people do in terms of organizational goals. We also have found this profile among people who have studied or are practicing in the area of humanistic education. For example, teachers with this kind of profile tend to be comfortable in "student-centered" environments where the norm is not for teachers to direct, control, and closely supervise the learning activities of children. However, because many youngsters are not yet ready to assume direction of their own learning, this style universally applied can lead to problems. In fact, some parents complain today that although youngsters seem to be much more willing to level, share, and be open about their feelings with adults—teachers in school and parents in the home—they often seem to lack the solid technical skills of reading, writing, and arithmetic, which tend to require for development in the initial stage more directive teacher behavior with an emphasis on the technical as well as the human skills.

   Another group we have found, in several dozen cases, to have style profile 3–4 is women who have recently been promoted into significant middle-management positions. In interviewing these women, it has been noted that prior to their promotion, top management had not given them opportunities to engage in much "telling" (S1) or "selling" (S2) leader behavior; that is, they had little practice in initiating structure within the organizational setting. As a result, the only way they had an impact in the past was by raising or lowering socioemotional support. In terms of training experience, we found that with very little training these women respond quickly to trying on some of the other styles. It is just a matter of exposing them to concepts such as the Situational Leadership Theory to get them to feel comfortable trying these new behaviors. The tragedy is that women and other minorities restricted from management positions often have not received this training prior to promotion. And yet, they may find that they are dealing with people who need direction and supervision. When they initially use a high relationship (Q3) style, it is much more difficult to use other styles later, even though they now understand that they are appropriate.

Implications for Growth and Development

If we look at an organizational hierarchy from very low levels of supervision to what we might call top management, we find that effective managers at each level require different profiles, as shown in Figure 11-15.

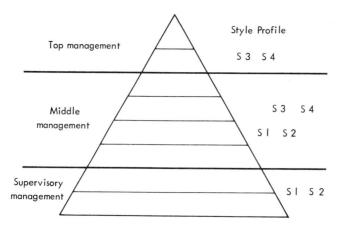

FIGURE 11-15 Style needs for different levels of management

We have found that effective managers at the lower levels tend to have style profile S1–S2. The reason is that at these lower levels of management (in industry, the general foremen and first- and second-line supervisors), there is an emphasis on productivity—getting the work out. At the other end of the management hierarchy, however, effective top managers tend to engage in more "participating" and "delegating." The reason seems to be that as you move up in an organizational hierarchy, the greater and greater the probability that the subordinates who report directly to you will have a high level of task-relevant maturity. So you can see that as you progress through an organization, you learn to engage in styles 3 and 4, as well as those styles that might be effective at lower ends of the hierarchy (styles S1 and S2). Thus, we have found in working with manufacturing organizations that while it may be appropriate for first-line supervisors to have a basic style of S1 and a supporting style of S2, when those people get promoted, it would be more appropriate if they had a basic style of S2 with supporting styles in S1 and S3. At this new supervisory level, they are no longer managers of hourly employees but have now become managers of managers.

Another interesting observation in terms of the management hierarchy is that it is the middle managers who really have to wear "both hats"—they need the most flexibility. They have to be able to provide the structured style S1 and style S2 interventions when appropriate but they also must be able to use "participating" and "delegating" styles when necessary. It is interesting to think of this phenomenon in terms of the Peter Principle.

As you will recall, the Peter Principle states: "In a hierarchy every employee tends to rise to his level of incompetence.[14] What we find in our work at the Center for Leadership Studies is that this is *not* a principle. In other words, it does not hold as a universal truth. In fact, as we suggested in Chapter 6, one might think of the Anti-Peter Principle vaccine as being the appropriate training and development or experience prior to moving up to the next level of the hierarchy. Better than training and development *after* being appointed to the new position is having worked for a boss who is willing to delegate responsibilities and provide on-the-job experience for future higher level positions. Another interesting observation is that although the Peter Principle is not really a principle, it occurs often enough to merit some attention. There certainly is a tendency for people to reach their level of incompetency. So often when we have interviewed people who are in a position they are having trouble handling, it turns out that they have the technical skills and conceptual skills required. In most cases, their incompetence is a result of not having the human skills. Many times they are not able to adapt their leadership style to the new environment.

Although this lack of flexibility does occur, we have found in working with managers in a variety of settings and cultures that, given some training in Situational Leadership Theory, they seem willing and able, almost without exception, to expand their adaptability. They are able to take on new leadership styles effectively. The most important criterion here is motivation—people have to want to do this. But if they want to, we feel strongly that most people have the capacity to increase their style range and adaptability provided they think through the appropriate leadership style needed and then seriously try to use a new style if it is appropriate for a particular situation. This assumption is an important difference between our approach and the thinking of some other people in the field, such as Fiedler,[15] who contend that if a leader's style is not appropriate to a given situation, what really needs to be done is either change the leader or change the job demands to fit the style of the leader. We feel that approach implies Theory X assumptions about human nature; and yet our work suggests strongly that the potential of people to operate under Theory Y assumptions is there to be tapped. Although this lack of flexibility does occur, as we indicated earlier, we have found that managers in a variety of settings and cultures, once exposed to training in Situational Leadership, seem willing and able almost without exception to expand their adaptability.

Team Building

If managers have a narrow range of behavior, one way that they can expand their flexibility (without changing their own behavior) is by carefully choosing the people they gather around them. If leaders are careful to bring into the organization key subordinates who complement their leadership style rather than replicate it, the organization may develop a wider range of potential styles that can be brought to bear on the contingencies they face. As we cautioned in Chapter 6, to avoid personality conflict and to increase the likelihood of building on the strength of others, it is important to select subordinates who understand each others' roles and have the same goals and objectives, even though their styles might be somewhat different.

Who Determines the Leadership Style of a Manager?

In the beginning of the chapter we raised the following question: If leaders continually change their leadership styles, how will that affect their followers' perception of their intentions?

From our experience, the sooner managers begin to share Situational Leadership with their key subordinates and clarify what is expected of them, this question no longer becomes an issue. When that occurs, managers no longer are the sole determiners of the style they use with their people. Their key staff now play a vital role. If their managers are not practicing situational leaders, they start to realize that it is *their behavior* (not their managers) that determines the leadership style to be used with them. Thus, if everyone in a management team knows Situational Leadership, the key staff realize how they can keep their boss "off their backs." All they have to do is perform in mature, responsible ways, ways that everyone has agreed are appropriate, and their manager will be supportive (S3) or leave them alone (S4). But if they do not produce and perform in responsible ways, they know their boss will be "all over them." They know why they are getting that kind of treatment from their manager and they know how they can get their boss to treat them in a more supportive way again—by getting back on track. It must be remembered though that this is effective only if managers are consistent (that is, they treat their people the same way in similar circumstances), even when it is inconvenient and/or unpopular with their people.

Thus, Situational Leadership is a vehicle to help managers and their staff understand and share expectations in their organizational setting. If people know what is expected of them, they can gradually learn to supervise their own behavior and become responsible, self-motivated individuals.

CONTRACTING FOR LEADERSHIP STYLE[16]

The process that was developed at the Center for Leadership Studies for sharing Situational Leadership with key staff and helping to open everyone's public window (in Johari window terms) is called "Contracting for Leadership Style." This process is a helpful addition to a management by objectives (MBO) program.

Of all the management concepts and techniques developed over the past several decades, few have received such widespread attention as management by objectives. Theoretically, MBO, discussed in Chapter 5, offers tremendous potential as a participatory management approach, but problems have developed in implementation. Consequently, although many attempts have been made to utilize MBO, ineffective implementations have occurred. As a result, success stories do not occur as often as anticipated by theorists who have written about MBO or practitioners who have applied it. One reason is that often the role of the leader in helping his or her subordinates accomplish objectives is not clearly defined in MBO.

What often happens in the MBO process is that once a superior and subordinate have negotiated and agreed upon goals and objectives for the subordinate, the superior may or may not engage in the appropriate leader behavior that will facilitate goal accomplishment for the subordinate. For example, if the superior leaves the subordinate completely alone, and the superior will be unaware until the next interim check period that this low relationship/low task leadership style is appropriate for accomplishing objectives in areas where the subordinate has had significant experience but inappropriate when the subordinate lacks sufficient technical skill and know-how in a particular area. Conversely, if, after negotiating goals and objectives, a leader continually hovers over and directs the activities of the subordinates, this high task/low relationship style might alienate subordinates working in areas where they are competent and capable of working alone. Problems may occur when a superior uses too much of any one style.

Adding the Contracting Process

In terms of Situational Leadership, once a superior and subordinate have agreed upon and contracted certain goals and objectives for the subordinate, the next logical step would be a negotiation and agreement about the appropriate leadership style that the superior should use in helping the subordinate accomplish each one of the objectives. For example, an individual and his boss may agree on five objectives for him for the year. After this agreement, the next step would be the negotiation of leadership style. In areas where he is experienced and has been successful in accomplishing similar objectives over a period of time, the negotiated leadership contract might be for his boss to leave him on his own. In this case, rather than directing and closely supervising his behavior, the role of the boss would be to make sure that the resources necessary for goal accomplishment are available and to coordinate the results of this project with other projects under her supervision. With another goal, the subordinate might be working on a new project where he has very little experience, while the boss does have some expertise in this area. In this case, the subordinate and superior might negotiate significant structure, direction, and supervision from the boss until the subordinate is familiar with the task. To accomplish all the goals, a variety of leadership styles may be appropriate at any given time, depending on the subordinate maturity in relation to the specific task(s) involved.

Two things should be emphasized in discussing the negotiation of leadership style. First, it should be an open contract. Once style has been negotiated for accomplishing a particular goal, it can be opened for renegotiation by either party. For example, an individual may find on a particular task that working without supervision is not realistic. At this point, the subordinate may contact her boss and set up a meeting to negotiate for more direction from the boss. The superior, at the time, may gather some data that suggest the style being used with an individual on a particular task is not producing results. The boss in this case can ask for a renegotiation of style.

Second, when a boss-subordinate negotiation over leadership style occurs, it implies a shared responsibility if goals are not met. For example, if a subordinate has not accomplished the agreed-upon goals and the leader or boss has not provided the contracted leadership style or support, the data then become part of the evaluation of both people. This means that if a boss has contracted for close supervision, he cannot withhold help from a subordinate (even though the boss may be busy on another project) without sharing some of the responsibiity for lack of accomplishment of that goal.

MAKING THE PROCESS WORK

Initially, as people were exposed to Situational Leadership concepts and began to apply them in daily superior and subordinate interactions, they sought some general ways to judge similarities and differences between leadership styles and subordinate expectations.

An Example—Contracting for Leadership Styles in a School

Some interesting results of the Contracting for Leadership Style process occurred in an elementary school in eastern Massachusetts. In many school systems, the principal of a school is required by school policy to visit each of his or her classrooms a certain number of times each year. This visitation policy is dysfunctional for principals who recognize that their teachers vary in their experience and competence, and therefore have varying needs for supervision from the principal. If a principal decides to schedule visitations according to her perception of the competence of the teachers, problems often occur with teachers at either end of the extreme. As we discussed earlier, left alone, a highly experienced teacher may be confused by the lack of contact with the principal and may even interpret it as a lack of interest. At the same time, an inexperienced teacher may interpret the frequent visits of the principal as a sign of lack of trust and confidence. In both cases, what the principal does may be interpreted as negative by the teachers.

These problems were eliminated in this elementary school when the principal shared Situational Leadership Theory with the staff and then attempted to negotiate what the principal's leadership style should be with each of the teachers. It was found that when low relationship/low task, "hands-off" leadership style was negotiated between the principal and teachers, because both agreed that these teachers were capable of working on their own, infrequent visits from the principal were perceived by the teachers as a reward rather than a punishment.

The same thing held true at the other end of the continuum. It was found that when negotiation for leadership style took place with inexperienced teachers, who realized that the system was designed to help teachers learn to work on their own, these teachers were less reluctant to share anxieties about certain aspects of their teaching. If the negotiation led to initial close supervision and direction, the teachers were able to view this interaction as positive not punitive, because it was a temporary style and demonstrated the principal's interest in helping them to operate on their own.

Using the Maturity Style Match

Since those early days, a valuable instrument has been developed by Hersey, Blanchard and Keilty at the Center for Leadership Studies. The instrument formalizes the process of implementing Contracting for Leadership Style between superior and subordinate. It's called the Maturity Style Match.[17] As discussed in Chapter 7, the Maturity Style Match measures maturity using two dimensions: (1) *ability* or job maturity and (2) *willingness* or psychological maturity. The rating form also describes precisely the four basic leadership styles. The description of those styles and the two maturity scales are depicted in Figure 11-16.

As indicated in Figure 11-16, a person's ability (knowledge and skill) is thought of as a matter of degree. That is, an individual's ability does not change drastically from one moment to the next. At any given moment, an individual has a little, some, quite a bit or a great deal of ability. Willingness (competence and motivation), however, is different. A person's maturity can, and often does, fluctuate from one moment to another. Therefore, a person is seldom, on occasion, often or usually willing to take responsibility in a particular area.

Combining establishing objectives and reaching consensus on performance criteria in a traditional MBO program with a similar process for negotiating the appropriate leadership style that a manager should use to facilitate goal accomplishment in a specific task area can be accomplished through the following steps: (1) Manager and staff member independently establish objectives and performance criteria for the staff member. (2) Manager and staff member come together to reach agreement on objectives and performance criteria. (3) Both manager and staff member are introduced to Situational Leadership, if they have not already been exposed to the concept (which can be accomplished by reading Chapter 7 of this text). (4) Manager and staff member independently complete a Maturity Style Match rating form. The staff member indicates what he or she thinks the primary and secondary leadership styles are that the manager has been using with him or her on each of the agreed upon goals and objectives. The manager does

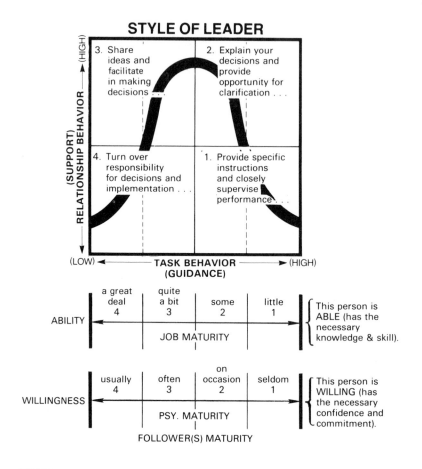

STYLE OF LEADER

RELATIONSHIP BEHAVIOR (SUPPORT) (HIGH) →

3. Share ideas and facilitate in making decisions . . .

2. Explain your decisions and provide opportunity for clarification . . .

4. Turn over responsibility for decisions and implementation . . .

1. Provide specific instructions and closely supervise performance . . .

(LOW) ← **TASK BEHAVIOR** → (HIGH)
(GUIDANCE)

	a great deal 4	quite a bit 3	some 2	little 1	
ABILITY					This person is ABLE (has the necessary knowledge & skill).
		JOB MATURITY			

	usually 4	often 3	on occasion 2	seldom 1	
WILLINGNESS					This person is WILLING (has the necessary confidence and commitment).
		PSY. MATURITY			

FOLLOWER(S) MATURITY

FIGURE 11-16 Defining maturity and the four basic leadership styles

the same, indicating what leadership style has been used with the staff member on each of the agreed upon goals and objectives. If the staff member has never had a particular objective area before, no past leadership style can be diagnosed. After analyzing leadership style, both the staff member and manager make judgments on the ability and the willingness of the staff member to accomplish each of the goals and objectives established at the desired performance level without any supervision. In other words, the staff member participating in this process would analyze the leadership style that the boss has been using with him or her as well as self-assessment judgments of his or her own maturity level. At the same time, the manager would be analyzing the maturity level of the staff member as well as making self-assessment judgments of his or her own leadership style. (5) Manager and staff member meet together and share the data from their Maturity Style Match rating forms. It is recommended that they consider one objective or responsibility at a time. The purpose of sharing data is to agree upon the maturity level and appropriate leadership style that can be utilized with the staff member to maximize performance. During this process both manager and staff member should bring their calendars. Once they have determined the appropriate leadership style to make this commitment and turn it into behavior, they will require scheduled meetings. For example, in a particular objective area, any one of the four leadership styles may have been agreed upon as appropriate. If the staff member is inexperienced and insecure about performing in a particular area, a "telling" (S1) style would be appropriate for the manager to use. If this is the case, they should schedule frequent meetings so that the manager can work closely with the staff member.

If the staff member is willing but inexperienced in a particular area, the manager should utilize a "selling" (S2) style. This would involve scheduling meetings to work with the staff member but not as frequently as under S1 supervision.

If the staff member is able in a particular area but is a little insecure about working completely on his or her own, a participating (S3) leadership style would be appropriate. That may involve meeting periodically over lunch so that the staff member can show the manager what has been accomplished and the proper support and encouragement can be given.

If the staff member is able and willing to perform at the desired level in a particular objective area, no meetings are necessary unless called by the staff member. In this case, performance review can occur on an infrequent basis.

If the Contracting for Leadership Style process is utilized, the frequency of performance review will change depending on the ability and the motivation of the staff member to perform at the desired level without supervision. As stated earlier, if this process is used, the negotiation of leadership style should be an open contract and imply shared responsibility if goals are not met. In particular, if a staff member is improving in a particular area, there should be a renegotiation of leadership style to a less directive leadership style. At the same time, if a staff member's performance is not being maximized utilizing a particular leadership style, that will signal the need to move back to a more directive style. The process has to be give and take between superior and subordinate.

One warning should be given in using the Contracting for Leadership style process and the Maturity Style Match rating forms. When managers go through that process, their public arena in the Johari window becomes wide open. Very little about what these managers think and feel about the staff member is unknown to that staff member, and vice versa. Feedback and disclosure become an ongoing process. If managers do not want their people to know what they think and feel about them, then they should be careful about using the described process. With some people they might want to remain tight-lipped and aloof. When managers make that choice, they must remember that the blind and private arenas in their Johari window with those people will be large. In some cases, that may very well be appropriate.

In summary, combining the establishment of goals and objectives and criteria performance with appropriate leadership style may help to make MBO more of a developmental process, which can be effective in working with all levels of maturity. Establishing such a program may be a significant change for an organization and its managers. In the next chapter we will discuss how to implement change in an effective way.

NOTES

[1] The development of LEAD (formerly known as the Leader Adaptability and Style Inventory (LASI) is based on Situational Leadership discussed earlier. The first publication on this LEAD instrument appeared as Paul Hersey and Kenneth H. Blanchard, "So You Want to Know Your Leadership Style?" *Training and Development Journal,* February 1974. Copies of the LEAD-Self and LEAD-Others can be ordered from the Center for Leadership Studies, Escondido, Calif.

[2] This contracting process first appeared as Paul Hersey and Kenneth H. Blanchard, "What's Missing in MBO?" *Management Review,* October 1974. Much of the discussion that follows was taken from that article.

[3] See George S. Odiorne, *Management by Objectives: A System of Managerial Leadership* (New York: Pitman Publishing Corp., 1965); John W. Humble, *Management by Objectives* (London: Industrial Education and Research Foundation, 1967); J. D. Batten, *Beyond Management by Objectives* (New York: American Management Association, 1966); Ernest C. Miller, *Objectives and Standards Approach to Planning and Control,* AMA Research Study '74 (New York: American Management Association, 1966); and William J. Reddin, *Effective Management by Objectives: The 3-D Method of MBO* (New York: McGraw-Hill Book Company, 1971).

 [4] The LEAD-Other is the same instrument as the LEAD-Self but written so a subordinate, superior or peer could fill it out on a leader.

[5] William J. Reddin, *The 3-D Management Style Theory,* Theory Paper #6—Style Flex (Fredericton, N.B., Canada: Social Science Systems, 1967), p. 6.

[6] Joseph Luft and Harry Ingham, "The Johari Window, A Graphic Model of Interpersonal Awareness," *Proceedings of the Western Training Laboratory in Group Development* (Los Angeles: UCLA, Extension Office, 1955). A more up-to-date version of the framework is presented in Joseph Luft, *Group Processes: An Introduction to Group Dynamics,* 2nd ed. (Palo Alto, Calif.: National Press Book, 1970).

[7] Sigmund Freud, *The Ego and the Id* (London: Hogarth Press, 1927).

[8] Haim Ginott, *Between Parent and Child: New Solution to Old Problems* (New York: Avon Books, 1965).

[9] Kenneth Blanchard was a faculty resource with Alice Ginott at the February 1977 YPO (Young Presidents' Organization) University in Honolulu, Hawaii. The discussions of what she said at a session entitled "Between Parent and Child" are taken from Blanchard's notes and do not represent her exact words.

[10] Carl R. Rogers, *Client-centered Therapy* (Boston: Houghton Mifflin, 1951); see also *Freedom to Learn* (Columbus, Ohio: Merrill, 1969).

[11] Wayne W. Dyer, *Your Erroneous Zones* (New York: Funk & Wagnalls, 1976).

[12] This sentence is adapted from a quotation by Dorothy Canfield Fisher that Wayne Dyer referred to in *Your Erroneous Zones,* p. 195.

[13] The analysis of LEAD data was first published in Paul Hersey, *Situational Leadership: Some Aspects of Its Influence on Organizational Development,* an unpublished dissertation, University of Massachusetts, 1975.

[14] Laurence J. Peter and Raymond Hull, *The Peter Principle: Why Things Always Go Wrong* (New York: William Morrow & Co., Inc., 1969).

[15] Fred E. Fiedler, "Engineer the Job to Fit the Manager," *Harvard Business Review,* 51 (1965), pp. 115–122.

[16] This contracting process first appeared as Paul Hersey and Kenneth H. Blanchard, "What's Missing in MBO?" *Management Review,* October 1974. Much of the discussion that follows was taken from that article.

[17] Maturity Style Match instruments were developed by Paul Hersey, Kenneth H. Blanchard and Joseph Keilty. Information on these instruments is available through the Center for Leadership Studies, Escondido, Calif.

chapter 12

Planning and Implementing Change

In the dynamic society surrounding today's organizations, the question of whether change will occur is no longer relevant. Instead, the issue is how do managers and leaders cope with the inevitable barrage of changes that confront them daily in attempting to keep their organizations viable and current? Although change is a fact of life, if managers are to be effective, they can no longer be content to let change occur as it will. They must be able to develop strategies to plan, direct, and control change.

To be effective managers of change, leaders must have more than good *diagnostic skills.* Once they have analyzed the demands of their environment, they must be able to *adapt* their leadership style to fit these demands and develop the means to *change* some or all of the other situational variables. Recognizing that sometimes the only avenue to effectiveness is through change, in this chapter we will concentrate on the processes and strategies for planning and implementing change.

GENERAL FRAMEWORK FOR UNDERSTANDING CHANGE

Managers who are interested in implementing some change in their group or organization should have (or be able to obtain people with) skills, knowledge, and training in at least two areas:

1. *Diagnosis.* The first, and in some ways the most important, stage of any change effort is diagnosis. Broadly defined, the skills of diagnosis involve techniques for asking the right questions, sensing the environment of the organization, establishing effective patterns of observation and data collection, and developing ways to process and interpret data. In diagnosing for change, managers should attempt to find out: (a) what is *actually* happening now in a particular situation; (b) what is *likely* to be happening in the future if no change effort is made; (c) what would people *ideally* like to be happening in this situation; and (d) what are the blocks or restraints stopping movement from the actual to the ideal.

2. *Implementation.* This stage of the change process is simply the translation of diagnostic data into change goals and plans, strategies and procedures. Such questions must be asked as: How can change be effected in a work group or organization and how will it be received? What is adaptive and what is resistant to change within the environment?

DIAGNOSIS

There are at least three steps in the diagnostic process: point of view, identification of problem(s), and analysis.

Point of View

Before beginning to diagnose in an organization, you should be clear through whose eyes you will be observing the situation—your own, those of your boss, your associates, your subordinates, an outside consultant, or others. Ideally, to get the full picture you should look at the situation from the points of view of as many as possible of the people who will be affected by any changes. Reality, however, sometimes restricts such a broad perspective. At any rate, you should be clear about your frame of reference from the start.

Identification of Problem(s)

Any change effort begins with the identification of the problem(s). A problem in a situation exists when there is a discrepancy between what is actually happening (the *real*) and what you or someone who hired you (point of view) would like to be happening (the *ideal*). For example, in a given situation, there might be tremendous conflict occurring among individuals in a work group. If this kind of conflict is not detrimental, there may be no problem. Until you can explain precisely what you would like to be occurring and unless that set of conditions is different from the present situation, no problem exists. On the other hand, if in the above example, you would ideally like this work group to be harmonious and cooperative, then you have a problem—there is a discrepancy between the real and the ideal. *Change efforts involve attempting to reduce discrepancies between the real (actual) and the ideal.* It should be pointed out that change efforts should not always involve attempting to move the real closer to the ideal. Sometimes after diagnosis you might realize that your ideal is unrealistic and should be brought more in line with what is actually happening.

It is in problem identification that the concepts and theoretical frameworks presented in this text begin to come into play. For example, two important potential areas for discrepancy are, in Likert's terms, output/end-result variables and intervening variables.

In examining *end-result variables,* the question becomes: Is the organization, work group, or individual doing an effective job in what it was asked to do, that is, production, sales, teach the 3 Rs, and so on? Are short-term goals being accomplished? How does the long-term picture look? If performance is not what it should be, there is an obvious discrepancy.

If performance is a problem, you might want to look for discrepancies in the *intervening variables* or condition of the human resources. For example, is there much turnover, absenteeism, or tardiness? How about grievances, accident rate, and such? The theories and frameworks of people that you have been reading can generate all kinds of diagnostic questions for the change situation you are examining, such as:

- What leadership, decision-making, and problem-solving skills are available? What is the motivation, communication, commitment to objectives, and climate (morale)? (Likert)
- What is the maturity level of the people involved? Are they willing and able to take significant responsibility for their own performance? (Hersey and Blanchard)
- What need level seems to be most important for people right now? (Maslow)
- How are the hygiene factors and motivators? Are people getting paid enough? How are the working conditions? Is job security an issue? How are interpersonal relations? Do people complain about the manager? Are people able to get recognition for their accomplishments? Is there much challenge in the work? Are there opportunities for growth and development? Are people given much responsibility? (Herzberg)

The questions and the theorists they represent point out that the material you have read was meant to be used. Good theory is just common sense organized. So use the theories presented to help you to sort out what is happening in your situation and what might need to be changed.

Analysis—An Outgrowth of Problem Identification

Problem identification flows almost immediately into analysis. Once a discrepancy (problem) has been identified, the goal of analysis is to determine why the problem exists. The separation between problem identification and analysis is not always that clear, however, for identifying areas of discrepancy is often a part of analysis.

Once a discrepancy has been identified in the end-result variables or intervening variables, the most natural strategy is to begin to examine what Likert calls "causal variables"—the independent variables that can be altered or changed by the organization and its management, such as leadership or management style, organizational structure, organizational objectives. In other words, can you identify what in the environment might have caused the discrepancy? Again, different theorists come to mind and stimulate various questions.

- What is the dominant leadership style being used? How does it fit with the maturity level of the people involved? (Hersey and Blanchard)
- What are the prevailing assumptions about human nature adhered to by management? How well do those assumptions match the capabilities and potential of the people involved? (McGregor)
- Are people able to satisfy a variety of needs in this environment? How do the opportunities for need satisfaction compare with high strength needs of the people involved? (Maslow)
- How do the expectations of the various situational variables compare with the leadership style being used by management? (Hersey and Blanchard)

Again, these theories and questions are presented to suggest how the concepts studied can help you to analyze problems that exist in your environment and provide guidelines for developing strategies for implementing change.

IMPLEMENTATION

The implementation process involves the following: identifying alternative solutions and appropriate implementation strategies to use in attempting to reduce the discrepancy between what is actually happening and what you would like to be happening; anticipating the probable consequences of using each of the alternative strategies; and choosing a specific strategy and implementing it.

Once your analysis is completed, the next step is to determine alternative solutions to the problem(s). Hand in hand with developing alternative solutions is determining appropriate implementation strategies. Three theories seem helpful in designing change strategies.

Force Field Analysis

In Chapter 5 force field analysis was examined as a useful technique in looking at the variables involved in determining effectiveness. This technique for diagnosing situations, which was developed by Kurt Lewin,[1] also may be useful in analyzing the various change strategies that can be used in a particular situation.

Once you have determined that there is a discrepancy between what is actually happening and what you would like to be happening in a situation, and have done some analysis on why that discrepancy exists, then force field analysis becomes a helpful tool. Before embarking on any change strategy, it seems appropriate to determine what you have going for you in this change effort (driving forces) and what you have going against you (restraining forces). We have found from our experience that if managers start implementing a change strategy without doing that kind of analysis, they can get blown out of the water and not know why. An example might help.

In August, an enthusiastic superintendent of schools and his assistant took over a suburban school district outside a large urban area in the Midwest. Both men were committed to "humanizing" the schools. In particular, they wanted to change the predominant teaching approach used in the system from a teacher-centered approach in which the teachers always tell the students what to do, how to do it, when to do it, and where to do it (high task/low relationship style) to a child-centered approach in which students play a significant role in determining what they are to do (high relationship/low task or low relationship/low task style).

To implement the changes they wanted, the two administrators hired a business manager to handle the office and the paper work. They themselves essentially had no office. They put telephones in their cars and spent most of their time out in the schools with teachers and students. They spent fifteen to eighteen hours a day working with and supporting teachers and administrators who wanted to engage in new behavior. Then, suddenly, in January, only six months after they had been hired, the school board called a special meeting and fired the superintendent by a seven to two vote.

The administrators could not believe what had happened. They immediately started a court suit against the school board for due process. They charged that the board had served as both judge and jury. In addition to the court actions, the administrators became educational martyrs and began to hit the lecture tour and talk about the evils of schools. During one of their trips, the assistant superintendent was asked by one of the authors of this book to come to his graduate seminar on the management of change. The class at that time was discussing the usefulness of force field analysis. The administrator, who did not know Lewin's theory, was asked to think about the driving and restraining forces that had been present in his change situation. In thinking about the driving forces that were pushing for the change they wanted, the administrator was quick to name the enthusiasm and commitment of the top administrators, some teachers, and some students, but really could not think of any other driving forces. When asked about the number of teachers and students involved, the administrator suggested that they were a small but growing group.

In thinking about restraining forces, the assistant superintendent began to mention one thing after another. First of all, he said that they had never really had a good relationship with the mayor, chief of police, or editor of the town paper. These people felt that the two administrators were encouraging permissiveness in the schools. In fact, the town paper printed several editorials against their efforts. In addition, the teachers' association had expressed concern that the programs being pushed were asking the teachers to assume responsibilities outside their contract. Even the Parent-Teachers Association (PTA) had held several meetings because of parent concerns about discipline in the schools. The administrator also reported the fact that the superintendent had been hired by a five to four vote of the board and that some of his supporters had been defeated in the November election. In general, he implied that the town had been traditionally very conservative in educational matters, and on and on.

Figure 12-1 suggests the relationship between driving and restraining forces in this change situation. As can be seen, even with adding some board members as driving forces and not mentioning some teachers and students as restraining forces, the restraining forces for changing this school system from a teacher-centered approach to a child-centered approach not only outnumbered but easily outweighed the driving forces. As a result, the restraining forces eventually overpowered the driving forces and pushed the equilibrium even more in the direction of a teacher-centered approach.

In utilizing force field analysis for developing a change strategy, there are a few guidelines that can be used: (1) If the driving forces far outweigh the restraining forces in power and frequency in a change situation, managers interested in driving for change can often push on and overpower the restraining forces. (2) If the reverse is true and the restraining forces are much stronger than the driving forces, managers interested in driving for change have several choices. First, they can give up the change effort, realizing that it will be too difficult to implement. Second, they can pursue the change effort but concentrate on maintaining the driving forces in the situation while attempting, one by one, either to change each of the restraining forces into driving forces or somehow immobi-

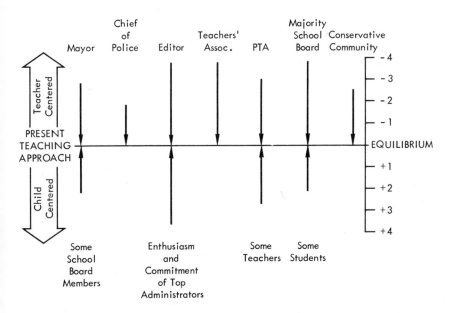

FIGURE 12-1 Driving and restraining forces in an educational change example

lize each of the restraining forces so that they are no longer factors in the situation. The second choice is possible but very time-consuming. (3) If the driving forces and restraining forces are fairly equal in a change situation, managers probably will have to begin pushing the driving forces, at the same time attempting to convert or immobilize some or all of the restraining forces.

In this school example, the situation obviously represented an imbalance in favor of restraining forces, and yet the administrators acted as if the driving forces were clearly on their side. If they had used force field analysis to diagnose their situation, they would have seen that their change strategy was doomed until they took some time to try to work on the restraining forces.

Once force field analysis has been completed and managers have decided whether to increase the driving forces, work on the restraining forces, or both, some understanding of the levels of change and the change cycles available might be useful.

Change Cycles

Levels of Change. In Chapter 1 four levels of change were discussed: knowledge changes, attitudinal changes, individual behavior changes, and group or organizational performance changes.

Changes in knowledge tend to be the easiest to make; they can occur as a result of reading a book or an article or hearing something new from a respected person. Attitude structures differ from knowledge structures in that they are emotionally charged in a positive or negative way. The addition of emotion often makes attitudes more difficult to change than knowledge.

Changes in individual behavior seem to be significantly more difficult and time-consuming than either of the two previous levels. For example, managers may have knowledge about the advantages of increased follower involvement and participation in decision making and may even feel that such participation would improve their performance, and, yet, they may be unable to delegate or share decision-making responsibilities significantly with subordinates. This discrepancy between knowledge, attitude, and behavior may be a result of their own authoritarian management-subordinate upbringing. This past experience has led to a habit pattern that feels comfortable.

While individual behavior is difficult enough to change, it becomes even more complicated when you try to implement change within groups or organizations. The leadership styles of one or two managers might be effectively altered, but drastically changing the level of follower participation throughout an entire organization might be a very time-consuming process. At this level you are trying to alter customs, mores, and traditions that have developed over many years.

Levels of change become very significant when you examine two different change cycles—the participative change cycle and the directive change cycle.[2]

Participative Change. A participative change cycle is implemented when new knowledge is made available to the individual or group. It is hoped that the group will accept the data and will develop a positive attitude and commitment in the direction of the desired change. At this level an effective strategy may be to involve the individual or group directly in helping to select or formalize the new methods for obtaining the desired goals. This is group participation in problem solving.

The next step will be to attempt to translate this commitment into actual behavior. This step is significantly more difficult to achieve. For example, it is one thing to be concerned about increased follower participation in decision making (attitude) but another thing to be willing actually to get involved in doing something (behavior) about the issue. An effective strategy may be to identify the informal and formal leaders among the work group(s) and concentrate on gaining their behavioral support for the desired change. Once this is accomplished, organizational change may be effected by getting other people to begin to pattern their behavior after those persons whom they respect and perceive in leadership roles. This participative change cycle is illustrated in Figure 12-2.

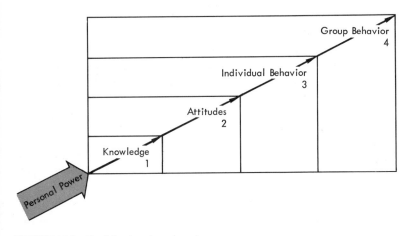

FIGURE 12-2 Participative change cycle

Directive Change. We have all probably been faced with a situation similar to the one in which there is an announcement on Monday morning that "as of today all members of this organization will begin to operate in accordance with Form 10125." This is an example of a directive change cycle. It is through this change cycle that many managers in the past have attempted to implement such innovative ideas as management by objectives, job enrichment, and the like.

This change cycle begins by change being imposed on the total organization by some external force, such as higher management, the community, new laws.

This will tend to affect the interaction network system at the individual level. The new contacts and modes of behavior create new knowledge, which tends to develop predispositions toward or against the change. The directive change cycle is illustrated in Figure 12-3.

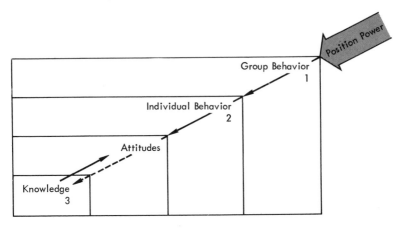

FIGURE 12-3 Directive change cycle

In some cases where change is forced, the new behavior engaged in creates the kind of knowledge that develops commitment to the change, and, therefore, begins to approximate a participative change as it reinforces the individual and group behavior. The hope is that "if people will only have a chance to see how the new system works, they will support it."

Is There a "Best" Strategy for Change? Given a choice between the polarities of directive and participative change, most people would tend to give the "nod" in our society to the participative change cycle. But just as we have argued that there is no "best" leadership style, there also is no best strategy for implementing change. Effective change agents are identified as those who can adapt their strategies to the demands of their unique environment. Thus, the participative change cycle is not a better change strategy than the directive change cycle, and vice versa. The appropriate strategy depends on the situation, and there are advantages and disadvantages to each.

Advantages/Disadvantages of Change Cycles. The participative change cycle tends to be more appropriate for working with individuals and groups who are achievement motivated, seek responsibility, and have a degree of knowledge and experience that may be useful in developing new ways of operating—in other words, people with task-relevant maturity. Once the change starts, these people are much more capable of assuming responsibilities for implementation of the desired change. Although these people may welcome change and the need to improve, they may become very rigid and opposed to change if it is implemented in a directive (high task/low relationship) manner. A directive change style is inconsistent with their perceptions of themselves as mature, responsible, self-motivated people who should be consulted throughout the change process. When they are not consulted, and change is implemented in an authoritarian manner, conflict often results. Examples of this occur frequently in organizations in which a manager recruits or inherits a competent, creative staff that is willing to work hard to implement new programs and then proceeds to bypass the staff completely in the change process. This style results in resistance and is inappropriate to the situation.

A coercive, directive change style might be very appropriate and more productive with individuals and groups who are less ambitious, are often dependent, and who are not willing to take new responsibilities unless forced to do so. In fact, these people *might prefer* direction and structure from their leader to being faced with decisions they are not mature or experienced enough to make. Once again, diagnosis is all-important. It is just as inappropriate for a manager to attempt to implement change in a participative manner with a staff that has never been given the opportunity to take responsibility and has become dependent on its manager for direction as it is to implement change in a coercive manner with a staff that is ready to change and willing to take responsibility for implementing it.

There are other significant differences between these two change cycles. The participative change cycle tends to be effective when induced by leaders who have personal power; that is, they have referent, information and expert power. On the other hand, the directive cycle necessitates that a leader have significant position power, that is, coercive, connection, reward, and legitimate power.

If managers decide to implement change in an authoritarian, coercive manner, they would be wise to have the support of their superiors and other sources of power or they may be effectively blocked by their staff.

With the participative change cycle, a significant advantage is that once the change is accepted it tends to be long lasting. Since everyone has been involved in the development of the change, each person tends to be more highly committed to its implementation. The disadvantage of participative change is that it tends to be slow and evolutionary—it may take years to implement a significant change. An advantage of directive change, on the other hand, is speed. Using position power, leaders can often impose change immediately. A disadvantage of this change strategy is that it tends to be volatile. It can be maintained only as long as the leader has position power to make it stick. It often results in animosity, hostility, and, in some cases, overt and covert behavior to undermine and overthrow.

In terms of force field analysis discussed earlier, the directive change cycle could be utilized if the power of the driving forces pushing for change far outweighed the restraining forces resisting change. On the other hand, a directive change cycle would be doomed to failure if the power of the restraining forces working against the change was more frequent and powerful than the power of the driving forces pushing for the change.

A participative change cycle that depends on personal power could be appropriate in either of the cases described above. With frequent and powerful driving forces pushing for change in a situation, a leader might not have to use a high task, directive change cycle since the driving forces are ready to run with the change already and do not have to be forced to engage in the new desired behavior. At the same time, when the restraining forces could easily overpower the driving forces, managers would be advised to begin with participative change techniques designed gradually to turn some of the restraining forces into driving forces or at least immobilize their influence in the situation. In other words, when things are stacked against you, it would seem to be more effective trying to reeducate the forces against the change than trying to force change in a situation when little power is on the side of the change effort.

These two change cycles have been described as if they were either/or positions. The use of only one of these change cycles exclusively, however, could lead to problems. For example, if managers introduce change only in a directive, high task/low relationship manner without any movement toward participative change, members of their staff, if they decide to remain, may react in one of two ways. Some may fight the managers "tooth and nail" and organize efforts to undermine them. Others may "buckle under" to their authority and become very passive, dependent staff members, always needing the manager to tell them "what to do" and "when to do it" before doing anything. These kinds of people say "yes" to anything the manager wants, and then moan and groan and "drag their feet" later. Neither of these responses makes for a very healthy organization. At the other extreme, managers who will not make a move without checking with their staff and getting full approval also can immobilize themselves. They may establish such a complicated network of "participative" committees that significant change becomes almost impossible.

Thus, in reality, it is more a question of the proper blend of the directive and participative change cycles, depending on the situation, than a forced choice between one or the other.

Patterns of Communication

One of the most important considerations in determining whether to use a participative or directive change strategy or some combination of both is how communication patterns are structured within a group or organization prior to implementing a change.[3] Two of the most widely used ways of structuring communications, illustrated in Figure 12-4, are the star and the circle.

The arrowed lines represent two-way communication channels. In the circle each person can send messages in either direction to two colleagues on either side, and, thus, the group is free to communicate all around the circle. In other words, nothing in the structure of the communication pattern favors one group member

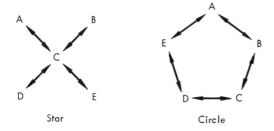

Star   Circle

FIGURE 12-4   Two ways of structuring communications

over another as leader. In essence, this depicts an open, democratic organization in which there is participation in decision making by all members. In the star communication pattern, however, one individual (C) is definitely in a leadership position; C can communicate with the other four members of the group and they can communicate with C but not with each other. This group represents an autocratic structure with C acting as the boss. Either of these groups might be analogous to groups of department heads, each having his or her own department but all reporting eventually to the same manager. In both patterns, A, B, D, and E are department heads and C is the manager.

Is There a "Best" Pattern of Communication? Once these two patterns of communication have been identified, the usual question arises about which is the "best" pattern. Some classic experiments conducted by Alex Bavelas[4] attempted to answer that question. In particular, Bavelas was interested in determining how each of these communication patterns affected the efficiency of a group's performance as well as the group's morale.

In one experiment, the two groups were put to work in the star and circle patterns. Sets of five marbles were given to each of the five group members. The marbles of each set had different colors, but one color was common to all sets. Both groups were to discover the common color. When that had been accomplished, the task was completed. In essence, it was the star or autocratic pattern against the circle or democratic pattern.

The autocratic star pattern was much faster. Its four subordinate members simply had to describe their marbles to the leader. After noting the common color, the designated leader sent correct information back. In trial after trial, the star group arrived at correct answers in an average of about thirty to forty seconds. The circle group took sixty to ninety seconds. The star group was not only faster but used fewer messages and developed more efficient ways of solving problems. In addition, group members respected their communication pattern.

The star pattern, although fast, tended to have a negative effect on morale. While group members had a high opinion of their communication pattern or organization, they had a low opinion of themselves except for the leader (C). With each ensuing trial they felt less important and more dissatisfied. In fact, on one occasion the leader received a message, "To hell with this game; let's play tick-tack-toe." On other occasions, messages were torn up or written in French and Spanish; yet, on the whole, the group still was faster and more productive than the circle group.

The circle could be described as "slow, inaccurate, but happy." It developed no system for working on problems and no one leader seemed to emerge. While members were openly critical of the organization's productivity, they seemed to enjoy the tasks. No one attempted to sabotage.

In terms of performance, everything seemed to be in favor of the autocratic groups, until Bavelas created a so-called emergency. He changed the marbles. Instead of simple solid colors, each group was given odd-colored marbles that were difficult to describe. The task, as before, was to find out which marble all members of the group had in common. The new marbles required close observation to tell one from another. In fact, two group members could be looking at identical marbles and describe them quite differently.

Since morale and the condition of the human resources were good in the circle group, members pulled together in the "emergency" and were able to solve the problem by utilizing all the available resources. On the other hand, the star pattern was a leader-dominated system; so group members looked to the leader in the emergency to solve the problem with little commitment from them.

The new task confused both groups. Errors mounted, and it took ten minutes or more to solve the problem. Yet, eventually, the circle seemed to adapt to the crisis and after a number of trials had restored its efficiency completely. On the other hand, the star could not seem to cope with it, taking twice as much time and committing three to four times as many errors.

Why was the star communication pattern faster? Essentially, because it was a one-way communication system dominated by a single leader. With this communication pattern, an orderliness was imposed on the group that eliminated extra messages. In the circle, no such clear organization existed. Group members could communicate with two people. Since they had this kind of mobility, they seemed to get around more and thus spend more time. However, since the members of a circle group sent more messages, they also could take advantage of more checkpoints and, thus, could locate and correct more of their errors.

Members of the circle group had more chance to participate and take responsibility. They were less dependent on one person since they could check with another member. Thus, they were more satisfied and happy. The leader (C) in the star also felt quite happy and satisfied, probably for the same reasons as the members of the circle pattern—C was given responsibility and had several sources of information and checkpoints. In essence, C was independent and powerful.

In summary, these experiments suggest that the mere structure of communication patterns can influence how people feel and act in terms of independence, security, and responsibility. This same structure also can influence the total operational efficiency of a group in terms of speed, accuracy, and adaptability. In essence, the structure seems to influence the way people feel in one direction and their speed and accuracy in another. Although the two communication patterns discussed have been described as if they were either/or structures, in reality, the design for an effective organization may need to incorporate both. For example, with the professional teaching staff, a school principal might find it most appropriate to structure the communication pattern in a democratic, free-wheeling manner as in the circle. However, with the nonprofessional service personnel, the principal might find it appropriate to operate in a more autocratic manner as in the star pattern. These groups may be at different levels of commitment, motivation, and ability to take responsibility, and therefore different kinds of communication patterns are needed.

Relationship Between Communication Patterns and Change Strategies. The structure of communication patterns seems to have two significant relationships with the participative and directive change strategies discussed earlier. First, in implementing a change strategy, managers or leaders have to incorporate into the strategy the development of an appropriate communication pattern. In that sense, the unstructured democratic wheel pattern seems very compatible with the participative change cycle, while the structured, autocratic star pattern seems appropriate for the directive change cycle. In fact, the results of Bavelas' experiments with the circle and star patterns of communication seem to support the suggested advantages and disadvantages of the participative and directive change cycles; that is, the participative change cycle is slow but tends to develop involvement and commitment; the directive change cycle is fast but can create resentment and hostility.

Second, before implementing a change strategy in an organization or group, it is important for the change agent to know the present communication structure in operation. For example, if an organization has been run in a democratic manner in which the communication pattern did not favor the manager as a leader over any of the subordinates, a new manager should probably think twice before implementing a directive, coercive change. The structure of communication required of a directive change strategy would be alien to the already established communication pattern. The same warning applies to a manager attempting to implement change in a participative manner in an organization that for years has been organized with the manager in a strong leadership position. In such a situation, supervisors and staff members often learn to be more dependent and less responsible because the manager always seems to assume leadership. As a result, they may not be ready for a more open, democratic system at this time.

In conclusion, there is no one "best" strategy for implementing change in organizations. The strategy used, whether participative, directive, or some combination of both, depends on the situation. One variable that seems important to analyze in developing an appropriate change strategy is the present structure of communication patterns within the target group or organization.

Change Process

In examining change, Lewin identified three phases of the change process—unfreezing, changing, and refreezing.[5]

Unfreezing

The aim of unfreezing is to motivate and make the individual or the group ready to change. It is a thawing out process in which the forces acting on individuals are rearranged so that now they see the need for change. According to Edgar H. Schein, when drastic unfreezing is necessary, the following common elements seem to be present: (1) the physical removal of the individuals being changed from their accustomed routines, sources of information, and social relationships; (2) the undermining and destruction of all social supports; (3) demeaning and humiliating experience to help individuals being changed to see their old attitudes or behavior as unworthy and thus to be motivated to change; (4) the consistent linking of reward with willingness to change and of punishment with unwillingness to change.[6]

In brief, unfreezing is the breaking down of the mores, customs and traditions of individuals—the old ways of doing things—so that they are ready to accept new alternatives. In terms of force field analysis, unfreezing may occur when either the driving forces are increased or the restraining forces that are resisting change are reduced.

Changing

Once individuals have become motivated to change, they are ready to be provided with new patterns of behavior. This process is most likely to occur by one of two mechanisms: identification and internalization.[7] *Identification* occurs when one or more models are provided in the environment, models from whom individuals can learn new behavior patterns by identifying with them and trying to become like them. *Internalization* occurs when individuals are placed in a situation in which new behaviors are demanded of them if they are to operate successfully in that situation. They learn these new behavior patterns not only because they are necessary to survive but because of new high strength needs induced by coping behavior.

> Internalization is a more common outcome in those influence settings where the direction of change is left more to the individual. The influence that occurs in programs such as Alcoholics Anonymous, in psychotherapy or counseling for hospitalized or incarcerated populations, in religious retreats, in human relations training of the kind pursued by the National Training Laboratories (1953), and in certain kinds of progressive education programs is more likely to occur through internalization or, at least, to lead ultimately to more internalization.[8]

Identification and internalization are not either/or courses of action, but effective change is often the result of combining the two into a strategy for change.

Force or compliance is sometimes discussed as another mechanism for inducing change.[9] It occurs when an individual is forced to change by the direct manipulation of rewards and punishment by someone in a power position. In this case, behavior appears to have changed when the change agent is present, but it is often dropped when supervision is removed. Thus, rather than discuss force as a mechanism of changing, we should think of it as a tool for unfreezing.

Refreezing

The process by which the newly acquired behavior comes to be integrated as patterned behavior into the individual's personality and/or ongoing significant emotional relationships is referred to as *refreezing*. As Schein contends, if the new behavior has been internalized while being learned, "this has automatically facilitated refreezing because it has been fitted naturally into the individual's personality. If it has been learned through identification, it will persist only so long as the target's relationship with the original influence model persists unless new surrogate models are found or social support and reinforcement is obtained for expressions of the new attitudes."[10]

This highlights how important it is for an individual engaged in a change process to be in an environment that is continually reinforcing the desired change. The effect of many a training program has been short-lived when the person returns to an environment that does not reinforce the new patterns or, even worse, is hostile toward them.

What we are concerned about in refreezing is that the new behavior does not get extinguished over time. To keep this from happening, reinforcement must be scheduled in an effective way. There seem to be two main reinforcement schedules: continuous and intermittent.[11] As we discussed in Chapter 9, with continuous reinforcement, the individuals learn the new behavior quickly, but if their environment changes to one of nonreinforcement, extinction can be expected to take place relatively soon. With intermittent reinforcement, extinction is much slower because the individuals have been conditioned to go for periods of time without any reinforcement. Thus, for fast learning, a continuous reinforcement schedule should be used. But once the individual has learned the new pattern, a switch to intermittent reinforcement should insure a long-lasting change.

Change Process—Some Examples

To see the change process in operation, several examples can be cited.

A college basketball coach recruited Bob Anderson, a six-foot, four-inch center from a small town in a rural area where six feet four inches was a good height for a center. This fact, combined with his deadly turnaround jump shot, made Anderson the rage of his league and enabled him to average close to thirty points a game.

Recognizing that six feet four inches is small for a college center, the coach hoped that he could make Anderson a forward, moving him inside only when they were playing a double pivot. One of the things the coach was concerned about, however, was how Anderson, when used in the pivot, could get his jump shot off when he came up against other players ranging in height from six feet eight inches to seven feet. He felt that Anderson would have to learn to shoot a hook shot, which is much harder to block, if he was going to have scoring potential against this kind of competition. The approach that many coaches would use to solve this problem would probably be as follows: On the first day of practice the coach would welcome Anderson and then explain the problem to him as he had analyzed it. As a solution, he would probably ask Anderson to start to work with the varsity center, Steve Cram, who was six feet ten inches tall and had an excellent hook. "Steve can help you start working on that new shot, Bob," the coach would say. Anderson's reaction to this interchange might be one of resentment, and he would go over and work with Cram only because of the coach's position power. After all, he might think to himself, "Who does he think he is? I've been averaging close to thirty points a game for three years now and the first day I show up here the coach wants me to learn a new shot." So he may start to work with Cram reluctantly, concentrating on the hook shot only when the coach is looking but taking his favorite jump shot when not being observed. Anderson is by no means unfrozen or ready to learn to shoot another way.

Let us look at another approach the coach could have used to solve this problem. Suppose that on the first day of practice he sets up a scrimmage between the varsity and the freshmen. Before he starts the scrimmage he takes big Steve Cram, the varsity center, aside and tells him, "Steve, we have this new freshman named Anderson who has real potential to be a fine ball player. What I'd like you to do today, though, is not to worry about scoring or rebounding—just make sure every time Anderson goes up for a shot you make him eat it. I want him to see that he will have to learn to shoot some other shots if he is to survive against guys like you." So when the scrimmage starts, the first time Anderson gets the ball and turns around to shoot, Cram leaps up and stuffs the ball right down his throat. Time after time this occurs. Soon Anderson starts to engage in some coping behavior, trying to fall away from the basket, shooting from the side of his head rather than from the front in an attempt to get his shot off. After the scrimmage, Anderson comes off the court dejected. The coach says, "What's wrong, Bob?" Bob replies, "I don't know, coach, I just can't seem to get my shot off against a man as big as Cram. What do you think I should do, Coach?" he asks. "Well, Bob, why don't you go over and start working with Steve on a hook shot. I think you'll find it much harder to block. And with your shooting eye I don't think it will take long for you to learn." How do you think Anderson feels about working with Cram now? He is enthusiastic and ready to learn. Having been placed in a situation in which he learns for himself that he has a problem has gone a long way in unfreezing Anderson from his past patterns of behavior and preparing him for making the attempt at identification. Now he is ready for identification. He has had an opportunity to internalize his problem and is ready to work with Steve Cram.

So often the leader who has knowledge of an existing problem forgets that until the people involved recognize the problem as their own, it is going to be much more difficult to produce change in their behavior. Internalization and identification are not either/or alternatives, but they can be parts of developing specific change strategies appropriate to the situation.

Another example of the change processes in operation can be seen in the military, particularly in the induction phase. There are probably few organizations that have entering their ranks people who are less motivated and committed to the organization than the recruits the military gets. And yet in a few short months they are able to mold these recruits into a relatively effective combat team. This is not an accident. Let us look at some of the processes that help accomplish this.

The most dramatic and harsh aspects of the training are the unfreezing phase. All four of the elements that Schein claims drastic unfreezing situations have in common are present. Let us look at some specific examples of these elements in operation.

1. The recruits are *physically removed from their accustomed routines, sources of information, and social relationships* in the isolation of Parris Island (Marine training base in South Carolina).

   During the first week of training at Parris Island, the recruit is . . . hermetically sealed in a hostile environment, required to rise at 4:55 a.m., do exhausting exercises, attend classes on strange subjects, drill for hours in the hot sun, eat meals in silence and stand at rigid attention the rest of the time; he has no television, no radio, no candy, no coke, no beer, no telephone—and can write letters only during one hour of free time a day.[12]

2. *The undermining and destruction of social supports* is one of the DI's (drill instructor's) tasks. "Using their voices and the threat of extra PT (physical training), the DI . . . must shock the recruit out of the emotional stability of home, pool hall, street corner, girl friend, or school."[13]

3. *Demeaning and humiliating experiences* are commonplace during the first two weeks of the training as the DIs help the recruits *see themselves as unworthy and thus motivated to change* into what they want a marine to be. "It's a total shock . . . Carrying full seabags, 80 terrified privates are herded into their "barn," a barracks floor with 40 doubledecker bunks. Sixteen hours a day, for two weeks, they will do nothing right.[14]

4. Throughout the training there is *consistent linking of reward with willingness to change and of punishment with unwillingness to change.*

> Rebels or laggards are sent to the Motivation Platoon to get "squared away." A day at Motivation combines constant harassment and PT (physical training), ending the day with the infiltration course. This hot, 225-yard ordeal of crawling, jumping, and screaming through ditches and obstacles is climaxed by the recruit dragging two 30-pound ammo boxes 60 yards in mud and water. If he falters, he starts again. At the end, the privates are lined up and asked if they are ready to go back to their home platoons . . . almost all go back for good.[15]

While the recruits go through a severe unfreezing process, they quickly move to the changing phase, first identifying with the DI and then emulating informal leaders as they develop. "Toward the end of the third week a break occurs. What one DI calls 'that five per cent—the slow, fat, dumb, or difficult' have been dropped. The remaining recruits have emerged from their first week vacuum with one passionate desire—to stay with their platoon at all costs."[16]

Internalization takes place when the recruits through their forced interactions develop different high strength needs. "Fear of the DI gives way to respect, and survival evolves into achievement toward the end of training. 'I learned I had more guts than I imagined' is a typical comment."[17]

Since the group tends to stay together throughout the entire program, it serves as a positive reinforcer, which can help to refreeze the new behavior.

The three theories discussed—force field analysis, change cycles and change process—should help a person interested in change determine some alternative solutions to the identified problem(s) and suggest appropriate implementation strategies. For example, let us reexamine the case of our enthusiastic school administrators who wanted to humanize the schools in their system and change the predominant teaching approach from teacher-centered to child-centered. As we suggested, if they had done a force field analysis, they would have realized that the restraining forces working against this change far outweighed the driving forces in power and frequency. The analysis would have suggested that a directive, coercive change strategy would have been ineffective for implementing change since significant unfreezing had to occur before the restraining forces against the change could have been immobilized or turned into driving forces. Thus, a participative change effort probably would have been appropriately aimed at reeducating the restraining forces by exposing them in a nonthreatening way (through two-way communication patterns) to new knowledge directed at changing their attitudes and eventually their behavior.

While this participative, reeducative approach might be appropriate, it also must be recognized that it will be time-consuming (four to seven years). The superintendent and his assistant just might not be willing to devote that kind of time and effort to this change project. If they are not, then they could decide not to enter that school system, charge on in a coercive, directive manner, and be ready for the consequences. Or they could choose their action from a number of other alternatives that may have been generated at this time.

Recommended Action

After suggesting various alternative solutions and appropriate implementation strategies, a leader/manager interested in change should anticipate the probable consequences (both positive and negative) of taking each of the alternative actions. *Remember:* (1) Unless there is a high probability that a desired consequence will occur and that consequence will be the same as the conditions that would exist if the problem was not present, then you have not solved the problem or changed the situation. (2) The ultimate solution to a problem (the change effort) may not be possible overnight, and, therefore, interim goals must be set along the path to the final goal (the solving of the problem).

The end-result of analysis (which includes determining alternative solutions) should be some recommended action that hopefully will decrease the discrepancy between the actual and the ideal. Although action is the end-result, you must remember that action based on superficial analysis may be worse than taking no action at all. Too frequently, people want to hurry on to the action phase of a problem before they have adequately analyzed the situation. The importance of the analysis part cannot be given too much emphasis—a good analysis frequently makes the action obvious.

MANAGING INTERGROUP CONFLICT

One of the problems that often occurs during a change effort is intergroup conflict. A total organization is really a composite of its various working units or groups. The important thing for organizational accomplishment, whether these groups be formal or informal, is that these groups either perceive their goals as being the same as the goals of the organization or, although different, see their own goals being satisfied as a direct result of working for the goals of the organization.

On occasion groups or parts of an organization come into conflict. The atmosphere *between* groups can affect the total productivity of the organization. According to Schein,

> this problem exists because as groups become more committed to their own goals and norms, they are likely to become competitive with one another and seek to undermine their rivals' activities, thereby becoming a liability to the organization as a whole. The overall problem, then, is how to establish high-productive, *collaborative* intergroup relations.[18]

Consequences of Group Competition

Sherif was the first to study systematically the consequences of intergroup conflict.[19] His original studies and more recent replications have found the effects of competition on individuals consistent to the extent that they can readily be described.[20] As Schein reports, some interesting phenomena occur both *within* and *between* each competing group.[21]

During competition, each group becomes more cohesive; internal differences are forgotten for the moment as increased loyalty takes over. The group atmosphere becomes more task-oriented as group accomplishment becomes paramount. The leadership shifts more toward an autocratic style as the group becomes more tolerant of someone's taking the lead. The group becomes more organized and highly structured, and with this demands more loyalty and conformity from its members in order to present a "solid front."

At the same time that these phenomena are occurring *within* the group, the relationship *between* the groups has some common characteristic. Each group starts to see the other as the enemy and distorts perceptions of reality—recognizing only their own strengths and the weaknesses of the other group. Hostility toward the other group increases, while communication decreases. This makes it easier to maintain negative feelings and more difficult to correct false perceptions. If the groups are forced to interact, as at a bargaining table, neither one really listens to the other, but only listens for cues that support its arguments.

Schein stresses that while competition and the responses it generates may be very useful to a group in making it more effective and achievement-motivated, "the same factors which improve intragroup effectiveness may have negative consequences for intergroup effectiveness."[22] Labor-management disputes are cases in point because the more these parties perceive themselves as competitors, the more difficult they find it to resolve their differences.

When win-lose confrontations occur between two groups or teams, even though there eventually is a winner, the loser (if it is not a clear-cut win) is not convinced that it lost, and intergroup tension is higher than before the competition began. If the win is clear-cut, the winner often loses its edge, becomes complacent, and is less interested in goal accomplishment. The loser in this case often develops internal conflict while trying to discover the cause of the loss or someone to blame. If reevaluation takes place, however, the group may reorganize and become more cohesive and effective.[23]

When the negative consequences of intergroup conflict outweigh the gains, management seeks ways to reduce this intergroup tension. As Schein suggests, "the basic strategy of reducing conflict, therefore, is to find goals upon which groups can agree and to reestablish valid communication between the group."[24] He contends that this strategy can be implemented by any combination of the following: *locating a common enemy, inventing a negotiation strategy which brings subgroups of the competing groups into interaction with each other,* and *locating a superordinate goal.*

Preventing Intergroup Conflict

Since it is difficult to reduce intergroup conflict once it has developed, it may be desirable to prevent its occurrence in the first place. This might be done in several ways. First of all, management should emphasize the contributions to total goals rather than the accomplishment of subgroup goals. Second, an attempt should be made to increase the frequency of communication and interaction between groups and develop a reward system for groups who help each other. Third, whenever possible individuals should be given experiences in a wide range of departments to broaden their base for empathy and understanding of intergroup problems.[25]

Collaborative organizations often appear to have an abundance of task-relevant conflict, which improves overall effectiveness. This may occur because under these conditions individuals trust each other and are frank and open in sharing information and ideas. In competitive situations characterized by win-lose confrontations, observations may suggest lower levels of open conflict, since total interaction is significantly less and each group is committed to withholding its resources and information from the other groups, thus lowering the potential for overall organizational effectiveness.

Blake, Shepard, and Mouton Model

According to Blake, Shepard, and Mouton,[26] there are three attitudinal sets or basic assumptions that people can have toward intergroup conflict: (1) conflict is inevitable, agreement is impossible; (2) conflict is not inevitable, yet agreement is impossible; and (3) although there is conflict, agreement is possible. These attitudinal sets will lead to predictable behavior depending on the way the people involved see the "stakes," that is, the extent to which they see what the conflict is over as important or having value.

As illustrated in Figure 12-5, if people think that conflict is inevitable, agreement is impossible, their behavior will range from being passive to very active. When the stakes are low, they will tend to be passive and willing to let fate (like a flip of a coin) decide the conflict. When the stakes are moderate, they

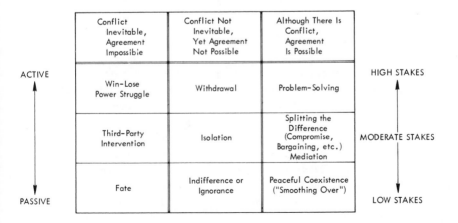

	Conflict Inevitable, Agreement Impossible	Conflict Not Inevitable, Yet Agreement Not Possible	Although There Is Conflict, Agreement Is Possible	
ACTIVE				HIGH STAKES
	Win-Lose Power Struggle	Withdrawal	Problem-Solving	
	Third-Party Intervention	Isolation	Splitting the Difference (Compromise, Bargaining, etc.) Mediation	MODERATE STAKES
PASSIVE	Fate	Indifference or Ignorance	Peaceful Coexistence ("Smoothing Over")	LOW STAKES

FIGURE 12-5 Three basic attitudes toward conflict and the behavior each evokes as involvement ("stakes") increase and decrease[27]

will permit a third-party judgment to decide the conflict. And, finally, when the stakes are high, they will actively engage in a win-lose confrontation or power struggle.

If people think that conflict is not inevitable, yet if it occurs, agreement is impossible, they will be passive and indifferent if the stakes are low. When the stakes are moderate, they will isolate themselves from such a conflict situation. And when the stakes are high and they find themselves actively involved, they will eventually withdraw.

If people think that although there is conflict, agreement is possible, they will be passive and attempt to smooth over the situation when the stakes are low. When the stakes are moderate, they will engage in bargaining or some form of negotiation. And if the stakes are high, they will actively engage in problem solving.

In using this model in consulting, we contend that if you have some knowledge of the attitudes people have about a potential conflict and what the "stakes" are for them, you can predict their behavior, and vice versa. If you observe the behavior of people during a conflict, you can usually predict their assumptions about conflict in this situation. For example, if you see people actively engaging in a win-lose power struggle, you can predict that the stakes in this conflict are high and that they think agreement is impossible. At the same time, if you learn that people think that a certain conflict is inevitable, but agreement is impossible and the stakes are high in this situation, you can predict that if the conflict occurs the situation will deteriorate to a win-lose power struggle. If such a win-lose power struggle occurs, one possible intervention might be to attempt initially to lower the stakes so that the conflicting parties will at least permit a third-party intervention. When that intervention is made, efforts can be directed toward changing the assumptions of the people involved to "although there is conflict, agreement is possible." When that is done, an attempt to increase commitment again will tend to move them into an active problem-solving mode.

ORGANIZATIONAL GROWTH

Our discussions in this chapter have focused on changing or working on problems in organizations that are already established. How different are the issues in new or emerging organizations? A developmental theory developed by Larry E. Greiner[28] is helpful in examining growing organizations.

Greiner argues that growing organizations move through five relatively calm periods of *evolution,* each of which ends with a period of crisis and revolution. According to Greiner, "each evolutionary period is characterized by the dominant *management* style used to achieve growth, while each revolutionary period is characterized by the dominant *management* problem that must be solved before growth will continue."[29]

As illustrated in Figure 12-6, the first stage of organizational growth is called *creativity.* This stage is dominated by the founders of the organization, and the emphasis is on creating both a product and a market. These "founders are

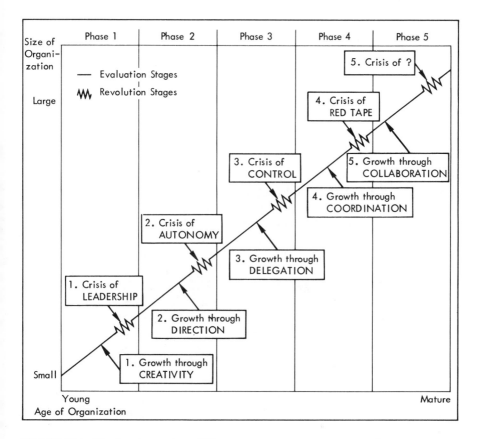

Size of Organization	Phase 1	Phase 2	Phase 3	Phase 4	Phase 5

— Evaluation Stages

ᴧᴧ Revolution Stages

5. Crisis of ?

4. Crisis of RED TAPE

3. Crisis of CONTROL

5. Growth through COLLABORATION

4. Growth through COORDINATION

2. Crisis of AUTONOMY

3. Growth through DELEGATION

1. Crisis of LEADERSHIP

2. Growth through DIRECTION

1. Growth through CREATIVITY

Large

Small

Young   Mature
Age of Organization

FIGURE 12-6 The five stages of growth[30]

usually technically or entrepreneurially oriented, and they disdain management activities; their physical and mental energies are absorbed entirely in making and selling a new product."[31] But as the organization grows, management problems occur that cannot be handled through informal communication and dedication. "Thus the founders find themselves burdened with unwanted management responsibilities . . . and conflicts between the harried leaders grow more intense."[32]

It is at this point that the *crisis of leadership* occurs and the first revolutionary period begins. "Who is going to lead the organization out of confusion and solve the management problems confronting the organization?" The solution is to locate and install a strong manager "who is acceptable to the founders and who can pull the organization together."[33] This leads to the next evolutionary period—growth through *direction.*

During this phase the new manager and key staff "take most of the responsibility for instituting direction, while lower level supervisors are treated more as functional specialists than autonomous decision-making managers."[34] As lower level managers demand more autonomy, this eventually leads to the next revolutionary period—the *crisis of autonomy*. The solution to this crisis is usually greater delegation.

> Yet it is difficult for top managers who were previously successful at being directive to give up responsibility. Moreover, lower level managers are not accustomed to making decisions for themselves. As a result numerous [organizations] flounder during this revolutionary period, adhering to centralized methods, while lower level employees grow more disenchanted and leave the organization.[35]

When an organization gets to the growth stage of *delegation,* it usually begins to develop a decentralized organization structure, which heightens motivation at the lower levels. Yet, eventually, the next crisis begins to evolve as the top managers "sense that they are losing control over a highly diversified field operation . . . freedom breeds a parochial attitude."[36]

The *crisis of control* often results in a return to centralization, which is now inappropriate and creates resentment and hostility among those who had been given freedom. A more effective solution tends to initiate the next evolutionary period—the *coordination* stage. This period is characterized by the use of formal systems for achieving greater coordination with top management as the "watchdog." Yet most coordination systems eventually get carried away and result in the next revolutionary period—the *crisis of red tape*. This crisis most often occurs when "the organization has become too large and complex to be managed through formal programs and rigid systems."[37]

If the crisis of red tape is to be overcome, the organization must move to the next evolutionary period—the phase of *collaboration*. While the coordination phase was managed through formal systems and procedures, the collaboration phase "emphasizes greater spontaneity in management action through teams and the skillful confrontation of interpersonal differences. Social control and self-discipline take over from formal control."[38]

Greiner is not certain what the next revolution will be, but he anticipates that it will "center around the 'psychological saturation' of employees who grow emotionally and physically exhausted by the intensity of teamwork and the heavy pressure for innovative solutions."[39]

It is felt that to overcome and even avoid the various crises managers could attempt to move through the evolutionary periods more consistently with the sequencing that Situational Leadership Theory would suggest—direction to coordination to collaboration to delegation—rather than the ordering depicted by Greiner.

ORGANIZATIONAL DEVELOPMENT

Throughout this chapter we have been discussing various frameworks that managers may find useful in helping them initiate change in their organizations. The need for managers to be able to plan and implement change in the future is a given, particularly as people begin to demand more and more that organizations be more than just a place to "pick up a pay check." As Richard Beckhard views it,[40] the challenge of change facing managers is

> How can we optimally mobilize human resources and energy to achieve the organization's mission and, at the same time, maintain a viable, growing organization of people whose personal needs for self-worth, growth and satisfaction are significantly met at work?

An attempted response to this dilemma and the corresponding need for changes in the way organizations operate has been the growing field of organizational development (O.D.).

Organizational Effectiveness and O.D.

In defining O.D. from our perspective, it is important to remember, as we discussed in Chapter 5, that the effectiveness of a particular organization depends on its goals and objectives. Thus, we do not accept a set of normative goals that are right for all organizations as many O.D. theorists and practitioners seem to do.[41] As Bennis suggests, the philosophy and values of O.D. change agents provide the "guidelines and directions for *what* will be undertaken in an organization development effort and *how* the program will evolve and be sustained."[42] With the humanistic values that are communicated by O.D. practitioners and theorists, it is not hard to understand why the goals of organizational development are generally reported as aiming toward an open, trusting type of organization and O.D. interventions seem to stress the use of collaborative or interpersonal strategies for change. As Bennis argues:[43]

> I have yet to see an organization development program that uses an intervention strategy other than an interpersonal one, and this is serious when one considers that the most pivotal strategies of change in our society are political, legal and technological.

A Problem with Organizational Development

If it is true that most O.D. consultants and practitioners use collaborative or interpersonal strategies of change and thus almost always concentrate on the "people variable" in helping organizations, it becomes clear why there are more O.D. intervention failures than successes. First, as we have suggested throughout this chapter, using the same strategy for change all the time will lead to effective change in some situations but in many others might be ineffective. Thus, there is no one best strategy of change. Effective O.D. interventions depend on diagnosing the situation and determining the highest probability success approach for the particular environment.

Second, if one analyzes the interpersonal change strategy so often used in O.D. interventions, one can see that it tends to be related to high relationship/

low task(Q3). According to Situational Leadership Theory, this interpersonal change strategy would be most appropriate in organizations in which members tend to have moderate to high levels of maturity; that is, they are able to take responsibility for implementing the desired change but just need someone to help facilitate it. Such an organization, as we discussed in Chapter 3, would probably be classified by Argyris as a YB organization. And yet as Argyris[44] contends, most organizations are not operating in YB patterns but are more typically XA organizations. These organizations, in terms of Situational Leadership Theory, would be at low levels of maturity since they are not only unable to direct their own change but are often even unwilling. Thus, one of the greatest challenges facing the field of organizational development is developing strategies to move organizations from XA to YB and from immature (in terms of implementing their own change) to more mature states. As a result, O.D. practitioners and change agents need to develop their skills in structural, directive change strategies as well as maintain their skills in interpersonal, participative change strategies so that the movement toward "self-renewing" organizations can begin with some hope of success.

IMPACT OF CHANGE ON THE TOTAL SYSTEM

In Chapter 1 the importance of combining the social and the technical into a unified social systems concept was stressed. As Robert H. Guest argues:

> On his part the social scientist often makes the error of concentrating on human motivation and group behavior without fully accounting for the technical environment which circumscribes, even determines, the roles which the actors play. Motivation, group structure, interaction processes, authority—none of these abstractions of behavior takes place in a technological vacuum.[45]

A dramatic example of the consequences of introducing technical change and ignoring its consequences on the social system is the case of the introduction of the steel axe to a group of Australian aborigines.[46]

This tribe remained considerably isolated, both geographically and socially, from the influence of Western cultures. In fact, their only contact was an Anglican mission established in the adjacent territory. The polished stone axe was traditionally a basic part of the tribe's technology. Used by men, women, and children, the stone axe was vital to the subsistence economy. But more than that, it was actually a key to the smooth running of the social system; it defined interpersonal relationships and was a symbol of masculinity and male superiority. "Only an adult male could make and own a stone axe; a woman or a child had to ask his permission to obtain one."[47]

The Anglican mission, in an effort to help improve the situation of the aborigines, introduced the steel axe, a product of European technology. It was given indiscriminately to men, women, and children. Because the tool was more efficient than the stone axe it was readily accepted, but it produced severe reper- cussions unforeseen by the missionaries or the tribe. As Stephen R. Cain reports:

> The adult male was unable to make the steel axe and no longer had to make the stone axe. Consequently, his exclusive axe-making ability was no longer a necessary or desirable skill, and his status as sole possessor and dispenser of a vital element of technology was lost. The most drastic overall result was that traditional values, beliefs, and attitudes were unintentionally undermined. [48]

The focus in this book has been on the management of human resources, and as a result we have spent little time on how technical change can have an impact on the total system. Our attempt in this example was to reiterate that an organization is an "open social system," that is, all aspects of an organization are interrelated; a change in any part of an organization may have an impact on other parts or on the organization itself. Thus, a proposed change in one part of an organization must be carefully assessed in terms of its likely impact on the rest of the organization.

NOTES

[1] Kurt Lewin, *Field Theory in Social Science,* D. Cartwright, ed. (New York: Harper & Brothers, 1951).

[2] Paul Hersey and Kenneth H. Blanchard, "Change and the Use of Power," *Training and Development Journal,* January 1972.

[3] Kenneth H. Blanchard and Paul Hersey, "The Importance of Communication Patterns in Implementing Change Strategies," *Journal of Research and Development in Education,* 6, No. 4 (Summer 1973), pp. 66–75.

[4] Alex Bavelas, "Communication Patterns in Task-Oriented Groups" in Dowin Cartwright and Alvin Zander, eds., *Group Dynamics: Research and Theory* (Evanston, Ill.: Row, Peterson & Company, 1953).

[5] Kurt Lewin, "Frontiers in Group Dynamics: Concept, Method, and Reality in Social Science; Social Equilibria and Social Change," *Human Relations,* I, No. 1 (June 1947), pp. 5–41.

[6] Edgar H. Schein, "Management Development as a Process of Influence," in David R. Hampton, *Behavioral Concepts in Management* (Belmont, Calif.: Dickinson Publishing Co., Inc., 1968), p. 110. Reprinted from *Industrial Management Review,* II, No. 2 (May 1961) pp. 59–77.

[7] The mechanisms are taken from H. C. Kelman, "Compliance, Identification and Internalization: Three Processes of Attitude Change," *Conflict Resolution,* II (1958) pp. 51–60.

[8] Schein, "Management Development," p. 112.

[9] Kelman discussed compliance as a third mechanism for attitude change.

[10] Schein, "Management Development," p. 112.

[11] See C. B. Ferster and B. F. Skinner, *Schedules of Reinforcement* (New York: Appleton-Century-Crofts, 1957).

[12] "Marine Machine," *Look Magazine,* August 12, 1969.

[13] *Ibid.*

[14] *Ibid.*

[15] *Ibid.*

[16] *Ibid.*

[17] *Ibid.*

[18] Edgar H. Schein, *Organizational Psychology* (Englewood Cliffs, N.J.: Prentice-Hall, Inc., 1965), p. 80.

[19] M. Sherif, O. J. Harvey, B. J. White, W. R. Hood and Carolyn Sherif, *Intergroup Conflict and Cooperation: The Robbers Cave Experiment* (Norman, Okla.: Book Exchange, 1961).

[20] Robert R. Blake and Jane S. Mouton, "Reactions to Intergroup Competition under Win-Lose Conditions," *Management Science*, 7 (1961), pp. 420–35.

[21] Schein, *Organizational Psychology*, p. 81.

[22] *Ibid.*

[23] *Ibid.*, p. 82.

[24] *Ibid.*, p. 83.

[25] *Ibid.*, p. 85.

[26] Robert R. Blake, Herbert Shepard and Jane S. Mouton, *Managing Intergroup Conflict in Industry* (Houston: Gulf Publishing Co., 1964).

[27] *Ibid.*, p. 13. Minor changes made in the figure but major change in the figure title so it is more consistent with the way we use the model in consulting.

[28] Larry E. Greiner, "Evolution and Revolution as Organizations Grow," *Harvard Business Review*, July–August 1972, pp. 37–46.

[29] *Ibid.*, p. 40.

[30] *Ibid.*, p. 41.

[31] *Ibid.*, p. 42.

[32] *Ibid.*

[33] *Ibid.*

[34] *Ibid.*

[35] *Ibid.*, p. 43.

[36] *Ibid.*

[37] *Ibid.*

[38] *Ibid.*

[39] *Ibid.*, p. 44.

[40] Richard Beckhard, *Organization Development: Strategies and Models* (Reading, Mass.: Addison-Wesley Publishing Company, 1969), p. 3.

[41] Warren G. Bennis, *Organization Development: Its Nature, Origins, and Prospects* (Reading, Mass.: Addison-Wesley Publishing Company, 1969) p. 13.

[42] *Ibid.*

[43] Bennis, "Editorial," *Journal of Applied Behavioral Science*, 4, No. 2 (1968), p. 228.

[44] Chris Argyris, *Management and Organization Development: The Path From XA to YB* (New York: McGraw-Hill Book Company, 1971).

[45] Robert H. Guest, *Organizational Change: The Effect of Successful Leadership* (Homewood, Ill.: Dorsey Press and Richard D. Irwin, Inc., 1964), p. 4.

[46] Lauriston Sharp, "Steel Axes for Stone Age Australians," in *Human Problems in Technology Changes*, ed. Edward H. Spicer (New York: Russell Sage Foundation, 1952), pp. 69–94.

[47] Stephen R. Cain, "Anthropology and Change," taken from *Growth and Change*, University of Kentucky, I, No. 3 (July 1970).

[48] *Ibid.*

chapter 13

Synthesizing Management Theory: A Holistic Approach

All the theories, concepts and empirical research presented in earlier chapters have made a contribution to the field of management. They seem to have some relevance in diagnosing an environment, in making some predictions and in planning for changes in behavior. These viewpoints have often appeared to be like threads, each thread unique to itself.

Our attempt in this book has been to weave these independent viewpoints into a holistic fabric to increase significantly the usefulness of each in diagnosis and prediction. In this last chapter we will attempt to integrate these theories, using Situational Leadership (discussed in Chapter 7) as a synthesizing framework to portray their compatibilities rather than their differences.

SITUATIONAL LEADERSHIP AND MOTIVATION

In developing the model of the motivating situation (Chapter 2) it was contended that motives directed toward goals result in behavior. One way of classifying high strength motives is Maslow's hierarchy of needs[1] (Chapter 2); goals that tend to satisfy these needs can be described by Herzberg's hygiene factors and motivators[2] (Chapter 3). Both these frameworks can be integrated in Situational

Leadership in terms of their relation to various maturity levels and the appropriate leadership styles that have a high probability of satisfying
these needs or providing the corresponding goals, as illustrated in Figure 13-1.

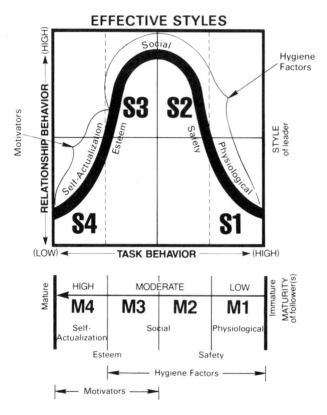

FIGURE 13-1   Relationship between situational leadership and Maslow's hierarchy
of needs and Herzberg's motivation-hygiene theory

It should be stressed that the relationship of theories (Maslow and Herzberg) to maturity levels in Situational Leadership are not necessarily absolute,
direct correlations: they are integrative bench marks for practitioners to use in
attempting to make better decisions for managing human resources. As a result,
styles suggested as appropriate for one concept might not be exclusively for that
concept; other styles may also satisfy these needs or goals to some degree. This
caution will hold true throughout our discussions in this chapter.

Upon examining Figure 13-1, one can begin to plot the styles that tend to
be appropriate for working with people motivated by the various high strength
needs described by Maslow. At the same time, leadership styles S1, S2, and S3

tend to provide goals consistent with satisfying hygiene factors, whereas styles S3 and S4 seem to facilitate the occurrence of the motivators.

SITUATIONAL LEADERSHIP, MANAGEMENT STYLES, AND HUMAN NATURE

McGregor's Theory X and Theory Y,[3] Likert's management systems,[4] and Argyris' immaturity-maturity[5] continuum (Chapter 3) blend easily into Situational Leadership, as illustrated in Figure 13-2.

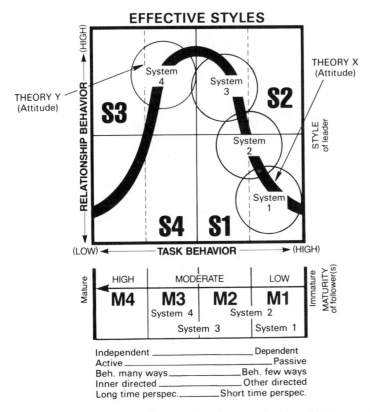

FIGURE 13-2   Relationship between Situational Leadership and McGregor's Theory X and Theory Y, Argyris' maturity-immaturity continuum, and Likert's management systems

In essence, Likert's System 1 describes behaviors that have often been associated with Theory X assumptions. According to these assumptions, most people prefer to be directed, are not interested in assuming responsibility, and want security above all. These assumptions and the corresponding System 1 behaviors seem to be consistent with the immature end of Argyris' continuum. System 4 illustrates behaviors that have often been associated with Theory Y assumptions. A Theory Y manager assumes that people are *not* lazy and unreliable by nature, and thus can be self-directed and creative at work if properly motivated. These assumptions and the corresponding System 4 behaviors seem to relate to the mature end of Argyris' continuum. System 1 is a task-oriented, highly structured authoritarian management style. System 4 is based on teamwork, mutual trust, and confidence. Systems 2 and 3 are intermediate stages between these two extremes.

In general, the tendency among people is to consider Theory X managers as engaging primarily with task behaviors in highly structured ways, and Theory Y managers primarily as using relationship behaviors. This is not always accurate. Theory X and Theory Y are managers' *assumptions* about the nature of people and do not necessarily translate directly into leader *behaviors*. There are examples of both Theory X and Theory Y managers who use all of the four leadership styles.

In one example, a Theory X manager calls a staff meeting and asks for participative (Q3) solutions to a problem. In reality, though, he may keep everyone at the table until they agree with his own *predetermined* ideas for a solution. His behavior is participative in nature, but his assumptions are that only his own answer is acceptable.

In another instance, a Theory X manager with a wide span of control does not have sufficient time to supervise closely all the people who report to him. Therefore he uses close supervision (Q1) with those people he perceives as major problems, and by necessity leaves the others on their own (Q4).

In a third example, a Theory X manager may demonstrate Quadrant 2 behaviors in explaining his decisions to his subordinates. However, his behavior may be manipulative rather than "selling," and may be related more closely to his personal objectives than to the goals of the organization or his subordinates.

On the other hand, a Theory Y manager who has learned to diagnose subordinate levels of readiness may be found using all four leadership styles effectively. With people at below-average levels of maturity, he provides the necessary guidance and close supervision (Q1). He gives support to people whose abilities are improving but who still need encouragement (Q2 and Q3). And he delegates appropriately to confident and competent employees who are capable of functioning on their own (Q4).

As illustrated in Figure 13-3, Argyris' concept of examining A behavior (structured) and B behavior (unstructured) patterns with Theory X and Theory Y,[6] Schein's four assumptions about human nature and their implied managerial styles,[7] and McClelland's achievement motive[8] can also be integrated into Situational Leadership Theory.

Argyris contends that most often structured, controlling A behavior patterns are associated with Theory X assumptions about human nature and that

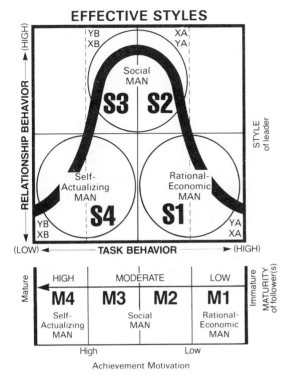

EFFECTIVE STYLES

FIGURE 13-3 Relationship between Situational Leadership and Argyris' A and B behavior patterns, McGregor's Theory X and Theory Y, Schein's four assumptions about people and their implied managerial strategies, and McClelland's achievement motive

unstructured, nondirective B behavior patterns are associated with Theory Y assumptions. But, as discussed in Chapter 3, there is an important difference between attitude and behavior, and therefore the relationship between Theory X and Theory Y assumptions and A behavior and B behavior patterns is not necessarily a one-to-one relationship. Thus, as Argyris points out, you can find a number of managers who have the predictable XA combination, but there are also some YA managers. Although both types of manager will tend to use styles Q1 and Q2, their assumptions or attitudes are not the same. The same holds true for YB and XB managers. Their behavior is similar (Q3 and Q4), but their assumptions are different.

In his book *Organizational Psychology*, Schein discusses four assumptions about people and their implied managerial styles: (1) rational-economic man, (2) social man, (3) self-actualizing man, and (4) complex man. These assumptions can help us further to integrate the work of Argyris, Likert, and McGregor into Situational Leadership, as seen in Figure 13-3.

The assumptions underlying *rational-economic* people are very similar to those depicted by McGregor's Theory X. In essence, people are seen as primarily motivated by economic incentives; passive beings to be manipulated, motivated, and controlled by the organization; irrational beings whose feelings must be neutralized and controlled. These assumptions imply a managerial strategy that places emphasis on efficient task performance and would be consistent with styles Q1 and Q2.

With *social* people come the assumptions that human beings are basically motivated by social needs; they seek meaning in the social relationships on the job and are more responsive to these than to the incentives and the controls of the organization. The managerial strategy implied for social people suggests that managers should not limit their attention to the task to be performed but should give more attention to the needs of the people. Managers should be concerned with the feelings of their subordinates, and in doing so, must often act as the communication link between the employees and higher management. In this situation, the initiative for work begins to shift from leader to follower, with the leader tending to engage in behaviors related to styles Q2 and Q3.

Self-actualizing people are seen as seeking meaning and accomplishment in their work as their other needs become fairly well satisfied. As a result, these people tend to be primarily self-motivated, capable of being mature on the job, and willing to integrate their own goals with those of the organization. With self-actualizing people, managers need to worry less about being considerate to them and more about how to enrich their jobs and make them more challenging and meaningful. Managers attempt to determine what will challenge particular workers—managers become catalysts and facilitators rather than motivators and controllers. They delegate as much responsibility as they feel people can handle. Managers are now able to leave people alone to structure their own jobs and to provide their own socioemotional support through task accomplishment. This strategy is consistent with an S4 style appropriate for working with people of high levels of maturity (M4).

According to Schein, people are really more complex than rational-economic, social, or self-actualizing. In fact, people are highly viable, are capable of learning new motives, are motivated on the basis of many different kinds of needs, and can respond to numerous different leadership styles. Complex individuals tax the diagnostic skills of managers, and as Situational Leadership implies, effective managers must change their style appropriately to meet various contingencies.

According to McClelland, achievement-motivated people have certain characteristics in common. They like to set their own goals, especially moderately difficult but potentially achievable ("stretching") goals. In addition, they seem to be more concerned with personal achievement than with the rewards of success. As a result, they like concrete task-relevant feedback. They want to know the score. As illustrated in Figure 13-3, high achievement motivation tends to be associated with maturity levels M3 and M4 and low achievement motivation tends to be associated with maturity levels M1 and M2.

SITUATIONAL LEADERSHIP
AND TRANSACTIONAL ANALYSIS

As discussed in Chapter 3, two concepts from transactional analysis (TA) and the work of Berne[9] and Harris[10] are ego states and life positons. As illustrated in Figure 13-4, these concepts can be integrated into Situational Leadership.

The three ego states in TA are Parent; Adult and Child. An individual whose behavior is being evoked from the child ego state can be either a destructive

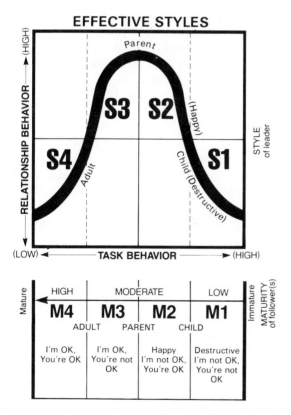

FIGURE 13-4   Relationship between Situational Leadership
and ego states and life positions
associated with transactional analysis

child or a happy child. The destructive child seems to be associated with maturity M1 and, therefore, the leadership style that is necessary with that child ego state is S1. Low "strokes" are appropriate because too much socioemotional support along with the high structure may be viewed as permissiveness and support for the destructive behavior. If you are interacting with a happy child, movement is toward maturity M2, and thus the style that seems to be most effective is S2. Now there is a need for more two-way communication, socioemotional support and facilitating behavior along with the structure.

An individual whose behavior is being evoked from the parent ego state can be either a nurturing parent or critical parent. The nurturing parent seems to be associated with M2, and, therefore, the leadership style that is necessary with that parent ego state, as illustrated in Figure 13-4 is S2. Any role defining or structuring has to be done in a supportive way. Too much task behavior without corresponding relationship behavior might suggest to nurturing parents that the person trying to influence them does not care for them, and this might move their ego state more toward a critical parent. That form of parent ego state tends to be associated with maturity level M3 because style S3 tends to work best when trying to work with a critical parent ego state. If leaders use a high task style with critical parents, it just tends to evoke more critical parent "tapes," and soon these leaders may find themselves in a win-lose, parent/parent-power struggle. To work with individuals with a critical parent, leaders first must try to develop a good personal relationship with them before being able to use effectively either of the high task styles (S1 and S2).

In working with people whose behavior is being evoked from their adult ego state, leaders can use an S4 style and leave them alone. These people are already thinking in rational, problem-solving ways and, provided they have the competence to do their jobs, tend to prefer to be left alone.

As illustrated in Figure 13-4, individuals with an "I'm not OK, you're not OK" life position tend to be associated with maturity level M1 and thus need high direction and close supervision. People who feel "I'm not OK, you're OK" are related to maturity level M2 and thus need both direction and socioemotional support. They will appreciate direction from leaders because they think these people are "OK" but also need high relationship behavior to help increase their "OK" feelings about themselves. People who feel "I'm OK, you're not OK" tend to be associated with maturity level M3. (Remember we are talking about normal people with this ego state and not mentally disturbed people, to whom psychiatrists like Berne would be referring in their discussions of transactional analysis.) Since people with this life position are often covering up "not OK" feelings about themselves, they tend to require high relationship behavior from others before feeling "OK" about them or themselves. People with life positions of "I'm OK, you're OK" seem to relate to maturity level M4 because they can be given responsibility and be left alone and still feel good about themselves and other people.

SITUATIONAL LEADERSHIP
AND CONTROL SYSTEMS

In Chapter 6 we discussed three fundamental control systems: Type I is the most structured and like an assembly line; Type II involves job enlargement but still requires manager control; and Type III is the least structured and involves job enrichment and little manager control. The impact that these various control systems have on leadership style is illustrated in Figure 13-5.

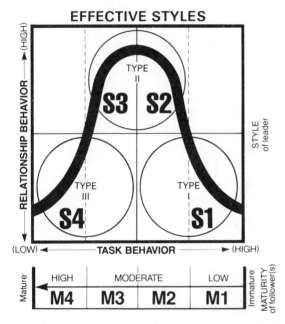

FIGURE 13-5 Structural impact of control system on leadership style

As is evident in Figure 13-5, the appropriate style to use with a Type I control system is high task/low relationship; Type II needs a high task/high relationship or high relationship/low task style; and Type III requires a low relationship/low task style. Relationships between control systems and appropriate leadership style are supported by the research of Stinson and Johnson.[11]

SITUATIONAL LEADERSHIP
AND POWER BASES

In Chapter 8 we discussed seven power bases: coercive, connection, reward, legitimate, referent, information and expert. As illustrated in Figure 13-6 and supported by the work of Hersey, Blanchard and Natemeyer,[12] Situational Leadership can provide the basis for understanding the potential impact of each power base. In fact, in Chapter 8 it was argued that the maturity of the follower not only dictates which style of leadership will have the highest probability of success, but that the maturity of the follower also determines the power base that the leader should have in order to induce compliance or influence behavior.

As is suggested in Figure 13-6, a follower low in maturity (M1) generally needs strong directive behavior in order to become productive. To engage effec-

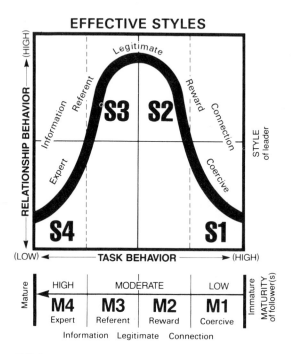

FIGURE 13-6   Relationship between Situational Leadership and power bases

tively in this S1 style, coercive power is often needed. As a follower begins to move from maturity level M1 to M2, directive behavior is still needed and increases in supportive behavior are also important. The S1 and S2 leadership styles appropriate for these levels of maturity may become more effective if the leader has connection power and reward power. Legitimate power seems to be helpful to the S2 and S3 leadership styles that tend to influence moderate levels of maturity (M2 and M3). Referent power enhances the high supportive but low directive S3 style required to influence a moderate to high level of maturity. Information and expert power seem to be helpful in using the S3 and S4 styles that tend to motivate followers effectively at above average maturity levels (M3 and M4).

SITUATIONAL LEADERSHIP
AND PROBLEM OWNERSHIP

As discussed in Chapter 11, the work of Thomas Gordon[13] on parent effectiveness training (translated into leader/follower terminology) and the William Oncken, Jr., and Donald L. Wass[14] "monkey-on-the-back" analogy integrate well into Situational Leadership, as illustrated in Figure 13-7.

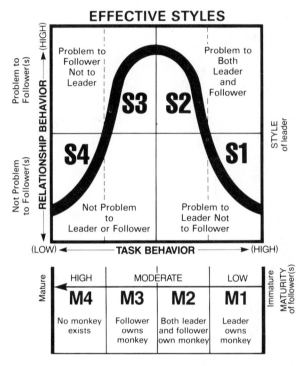

FIGURE 13-7   Situational Leadership Theory and its relationship to concepts associated with parent effectiveness training

In working with people, Gordon suggests that people's behavior can either be acceptable or unacceptable to leaders. If the behavior of the follower is acceptable to the leader, the leader can use an S3 or S4 style. If the behavior of the follower is unacceptable to the leader, an S1 or S2 leadership style is appropriate. To differentiate further among S1 and S2 and S3 and S4 styles, a leader needs to determine who owns the problem, or in Oncken and Wass' terms, "who owns the monkey." As Figure 13-7 illustrates, if the behavior of the follower is acceptable and not a problem to either the leader or the follower (no monkey exists), then an S4 style is appropriate. If that same acceptable behavior is a problem to the follower—that is, the follower lacks understanding or motivation to continue the acceptable behavior for long periods of time but not the leader (the follower owns the monkey) — the appropriate leadership style to be used with that follower is S3. If a follower's behavior is unacceptable and a monkey to both follower and the leader, then an S2 style should be used. And, finally, when the follower's behavior is unacceptable and a problem to the leader but not a problem to the follower (the leader owns the monkey), an S1 leadership style has the highest probability of changing that behavior.

SITUATIONAL LEADERSHIP AND ORGANIZATIONAL GROWTH

As suggested in Chapter 12, organizations might be able to grow and develop over time without the crisis or revolutionary phases discussed by Greiner.[15] This could occur if after the phase of creativity managers moved their organization through the growth phases in an order consistent with Situational Leadership.

As illustrated in Figure 13-8, the crisis of leadership might be averted by

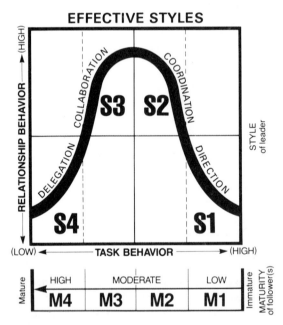

FIGURE 13-8 Situational Leadership Theory and the evolutionary and growth phases of organizations discussed by Greiner

moving from the phase of creativity right into the phase of direction; the crisis of autonomy, control, and red tape might be averted by moving from the direction phase right into the coordination phase, then into the collaboration phase, and finally into delegation.

SITUATIONAL LEADERSHIP
AND CHANGE

Whenever you talk about initiating change (Chapter 12), a first step is determining the maturity level of the people with whom you are working. If they are low in maturity—dependent and unwilling to take responsibility for the change—they will tend to require more unfreezing (Lewin[16]) than if you are working with people who are moderate or high on maturity. As illustrated in Figure 13-9, leadership styles S1 and S2 tend to play a major role in terms of unfreezing; the emphasis in S2 and S3 styles is on the change process; and S3 and S4 stress the refreezing process.

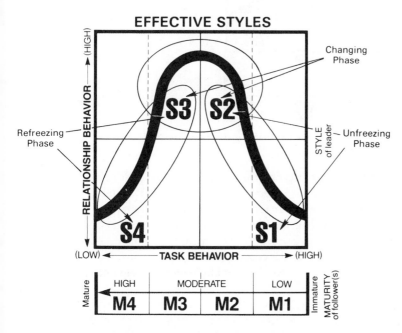

FIGURE 13-9 Relationship between Situational Leadership Theory and the process of change

One of the techniques used to increase maturity is behavior modification[17] (Chapter 9), as illustrated in Figure 13-10. When working with immature people, at first leaders tend to cut back on structure, giving individuals an opportunity to take some responsibility. When leaders get the smallest approximation of mature behavior, they must immediately increase the socioemotional support as positive reinforcement. This stairlike process (cut back on structure and then increase socioemotional support) continues until the change or changes start to become a habit as the people mature. At that point, leaders tend also to cut back on reinforcement as they move toward S4 and a low relationship/low task style. If done earlier, this cutback on socioemotional support would have appeared as

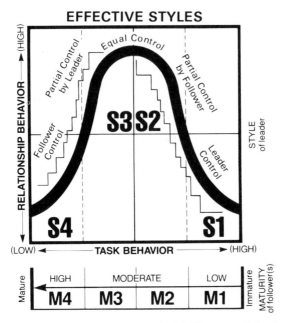

EFFECTIVE STYLES

RELATIONSHIP BEHAVIOR ⟶ (HIGH)

Partial Control by Leader

Equal Control

Partial Control by Follower

Follower Control

S3 | S2

Leader Control

STYLE of leader

S4

S1

(LOW) ⟵ TASK BEHAVIOR ⟶ (HIGH)

Mature	HIGH	MODERATE		LOW	Immature / MATURITY of follower(s)
	M4	**M3**	**M2**	**M1**	

FIGURE 13-10   Situational Leadership Theory and behavior modification

punishment to low or moderately mature people. But to people of high maturity, the fact that their leader tends to leave them alone is positive reinforcement not only in terms of the task but also in terms of socioemotional support. As discussed in Chapter 9 and depicted in Figure 13-10, Homme's concept of contingency contracting[18] illustrates the gradual developmental movement (associated with behavior modification) from leader control (S1) to partial control by follower (S2) to equal control (S2 and S3) to partial control by leader (S3) and finally to follower control (S4).

As illustrated in Figure 13-11, S1 and S2 styles seem to be consistent with the behaviors associated with a directive change cycle, while S3 and S4 are more representative of a participative change cycle (Chapter 2).[19] In a participative change cycle, the change begins at the knowledge level and eventually moves to the organization level, while the directive change cycle starts with changes in the organization and gradually moves toward changes in knowledge and attitudes.

As also shown in Figure 13-11, S1 and S2 styles tend to be appropriate for building on strong driving forces; S3 and S4 styles seem appropriate for attempting to overcome restraining forces (Chapters 5 and 12).[20] In increasing the driving forces, the emphasis seems to be on short-term output; when attempting to eliminate restraining forces, the concern is more with building intervening variables and concentrating on long-term goals. It should be emphasized that these are only tendencies and bench marks, and it should be recognized that under certain conditions other styles might be appropriate.

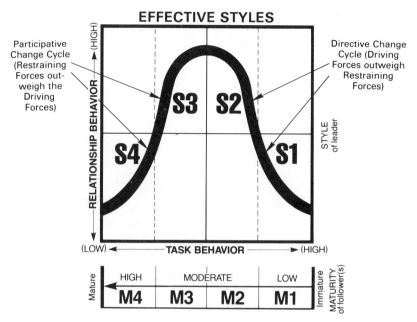

EFFECTIVE STYLES

Participative Change Cycle (Restraining Forces outweigh the Driving Forces)

Directive Change Cycle (Driving Forces outweigh Restraining Forces)

RELATIONSHIP BEHAVIOR (HIGH)

S3 S2

S4 S1

STYLE of leader

(LOW) ◄─── TASK BEHAVIOR ───► (HIGH)

Mature	HIGH	MODERATE		LOW	Immature
	M4	**M3**	**M2**	**M1**	MATURITY of follower(s)

FIGURE 13-11 Relationship between Situational Leadership, change cycles, and force field analysis

SUMMARY

Table 13-1 integrates the summary material presented in this chapter. The table indicates how many of the theories discussed throughout this book are related to the various maturity levels and their corresponding appropriate leadership style.

TABLE 13-1 Relationship between leadership styles, maturity levels, and other organizational behavior theory, concepts, and research

MATURITY of followers (therefore high probability)	STYLE of Leader
(M1) *Low Maturity* "Unable and insecure or unwilling . . ." Physiological/safety hygiene factors Rational-economic man Low achievement motivation Child (destructive) ego state	(S1) *HT/LR Telling* "Provide specific instructions and closely supervise . . ." Theory X (attitude) XA/YA System 1/System 2 Coercive and connection power Type 1 control system
I'm not OK, you're not OK Unacceptable behavior Leader "owns the monkey"	Leader control contracting Direction growth stage Unfreezing, changing (coercion) Directive change cycle

TABLE 13-1 *(continued)*

MATURITY of followers (therefore high probability)	STYLE of Leader
(M2) *Low to Moderate Maturity* "Unable but confident or willing . . ." Safety/Social hygiene factors Rational-economic man/social man Low achievement motivation Child (happy)/parent ego state I'm not OK, you're OK Unacceptable behavior Both leader and follower "own the monkey"	**(S2)** *HT/HR Selling* "Explain your decision and provide opportunity for clarification . . ." Theory X (attitude) XA/YA System 2/System 3 Connection, reward and legitimate power Type 2 control by follower/equal control contractor Coordination growth stage Unfreezing, changing (identification) Directive/participative change cycles
(M3) *Moderate to High Maturity* "Able but insecure or unwilling . . .' Social/esteem Hygiene factors and motivators Social/self-actualizing man High achievement motivation Parent and adult ego states I'm OK, you're not OK Acceptable behavior Follower "owns the monkey"	**(S3)** *HR/LT Participating* "Share ideas and facilitate in decision making . . ." Theory Y (attitude) YB/XB System 3/System 4 Legitimate, referent, information power Type 2 control system Equal control/partial control by leader contracting Collaborative growth stage Changing/refreezing (internalization) Participative/directive change cycles
(M4) *High Maturity* "Able and confident or willing . . ." Esteem/self-actualization motivators Self-actualizing man High achievement motivation Adult ego state I'm OK, you're OK Acceptable behavior No monkey exists	**(S4)** *LR/LT Delegating* "Turn over responsibility for decisions and implementation . . ." Theory Y (attitude) YB/XB System 4 Information, expert power Type 3 control system Follower control contracting Delegation growth stage Refreezing Participative change cycle

CONCLUSIONS

There is still much that is unknown about human behavior. Unanswered questions remain and further research is necessary. Knowledge about motivation, leader behavior, and change will continue to be of great concern to practitioners of management for several reasons: it can help improve the effective utilization of human resources; it can help in preventing resistance to change, restriction of output, and union disputes; and often it can lead to a more productive organization.

Our intention has been to provide a conceptual framework that may be useful to the reader in applying the conclusions of the behavioral sciences. The value that a framework of this kind has is *not* in changing one's knowledge, but it comes when it is applied in changing one's behavior in working with people. How does that process get started?

The key to starting the process of changing behavior is sharing the theories that you have read about in this book with other people in your own organization—superior(s), subordinates, and peers. Two things occur when people who work together all have a common language. First, they are able to give each other feedback and help in a very rational, unemotional way that effects behavior. For example, we once worked with a notorious autocratic manager who was noted for his Theory X memos, such as, "It has come to my attention, and, therefore, as of Monday all personnel will be required to . . ." Shortly after exposing this manager and his staff from two levels below him on the management hierarchy to Situational Leadership Theory, the manager sent out one of his "famous" Theory X memos. Several days later when we talked to him, he related that he had received a number of written (unsigned) comments on the memo. The comments included such remarks as "a little Theory X today, don't you think?" "Do you have anything else in your repertoire besides style 1?" "Are we really that immature?" This feedback had a real impact on the manager as he reexamined his memo and his approach. It was difficult for him to rationalize away the feedback, because like R. D. Laing's *Knots*[21] "he knew that they knew that he knew the theory" and "they knew that they knew that he knew the theory." As some of the managers suggested, this was one of the first times he had really "heard" feedback. As a result of this incident and use of the language in meetings, everyone started helping each other (not just the manager) make changes in their behavior so they could become a more effective working team.

Second, subordinates start to realize, if their manager is using Situational Leadership, that it is not the manager but *their* behavior that determines the leadership style to be used with them. For example, if everyone knows the theory in a family, the children (especially teenagers) realize how they can keep their parents off their backs. All they have to do is behave in mature, responsible ways, which everyone has agreed are appropriate, and their parents will be supportive (S3) or leave them alone (S4). But if they want to get hassled and closely supervised by their parents, all they have to do is misbehave and be irresponsible.

Thus, theory is a vehicle to help people understand and share expectations in their environment so that they can gradually learn to supervise their own behavior and become responsible, self-motivated individuals. An observation on leadership by the Chinese philosopher Lao-Tse[22] sums it up well: "Of the best leaders, when their task is accomplished, the people all remark, 'We have done it ourselves.' "

NOTES

[1] Abraham Maslow, *Motivation and Personality* (New York: Harper & Row, Publishers, 1954).

[2] Frederick Herzberg, *Work and the Nature of Man* (New York: World Publishing Co., 1966).

[3] Douglas McGregor, *The Human Side of Enterprise* (New York: McGraw-Hill Book Company, 1960).

[4] Rensis Likert, *The Human Organization* (New York: McGraw-Hill Book Company, 1967).

[5] Chris Argyris, *Personality and Organization* (New York: Harper & Row, Publishers, 1957).

[6] Chris Argyris, *Management and Organizational Development: The Path From XA to YB* (New York: McGraw-Hill Book Company, 1971).

[7] Edgar H. Schein, *Organizational Psychology,* 2nd ed. (Englewood Cliffs, N.J.: Prentice-Hall, Inc., 1970), pp. 50–72.

[8] David C. McClelland, J. W. Atkinson, R. A. Clark and E. L. Lowell, *The Achievement Motive* (New York: Appleton-Century-Crofts, 1953); and *The Achieving Society* (Princeton, N.J.: D. Van Nostrand Co., Inc., 1961).

[9] Eric Berne, *Games People Play* (New York: Grove Press, 1964).

[10] Thomas Harris, *I'm OK—You're OK: A Practical Guide to Transactional Analysis* (New York: Harper & Row, Publishers, 1969).

[11] John E. Stinson and Thomas W. Johnson "The Path-Goal Theory of Leadership: A Partial Test and Suggested Refinement," *Academy of Management,* 18, No. 2 (June 1975), pp. 242–52.

[12] Paul Hersey, Kenneth H. Blanchard and Walter E. Natemeyer, "Situational Leadership, Perception, and the Impact of Power," *Group and Organizational Studies,* Vol. 4, No. 4 (December 1979), pp. 418–28.

[13] Thomas Gordon, *P.E.T. (Parent Effectiveness Training)* (Peter H. Wyden, Inc., 1970).

[14] William Oncken, Jr., and Donald L. Wass, "Management Time: Who's Got the Monkey?" *Harvard Business Review,* November-December 1974, pp. 75–80.

[15] Larry E. Greiner, "Evolution and Revolution as Organizations Grow," *Harvard Business Review,* July-August 1972, pp. 37–46.

[16] Kurt Lewin, "Frontiers in Group Dynamics: Concept Method, and Reality in Social Science; Social Equilibria and Social Change," *Human Relations,* I, No. 1 (June 1947), pp. 5–41.

[17] B. F. Skinner, *Science and Human Behavior* (New York: The MacMillan Company, 1953). See also A. Bandura, *Principles of Behavior Modification* (New York: Holt, Rinehart & Winston, 1969).

[18] Lloyd Homme, *How to Use Contingency Contracting in the Classroom* (Champaign, Ill.: Research Press, 1970).

[19] Paul Hersey and Kenneth H. Blanchard, "Change and the Use of Power," *Training and Development Journal,* January 1972.

[20] Lewin, "Frontiers."

[21] R. D. Laing, *Knots* (New York: Pantheon Books, 1970).

[22] We do not have a source for this quote from Lao-Tse.

Recommended Supplementary Reading

ARGYRIS, CHRIS, *Integrating the Individual and the Organization*. New York: John Wiley & Sons, Inc., 1964.

BENNIS, WARREN G., *Changing Organizations*. New York: McGraw-Hill Book Company, 1966.

BERELSON, BERNARD, and GARY A. STEINER, *Human Behavior: An Inventory of Scientific Findings*. New York: Harcourt, Brace & World, Inc., 1964.

CARTWRIGHT, DORWIN, and ALVIN ZANDER, eds.: *Group Dynamics: Research and Theory* (2nd ed.). Evanston, Ill.: Row, Peterson & Company, 1960.

DRUCKER, PETER F., *The Practice of Management*. New York: Harper & Row, Publishers, 1954.

FILLEY, ALAN C., and ROBERT J. HOUSE, *Managerial Process and Organizational Behavior*. Glenview, Ill.: Scott, Foresman & Company, 1969.

FINCH, FREDERIC E., HALSEY JONES, and JOSEPH A. LITTERER, *Managing for Organizational Effectiveness: An Experiential Approach*. New York: McGraw-Hill Book Company, 1975.

GUEST, ROBERT H., PAUL HERSEY, and KENNETH H. BLANCHARD, *Organizational Change through Effective Leadership*. Englewood Cliffs, N.J.: Prentice-Hall, Inc., 1977.

HERZBERG, FREDERICK, *Work and the Nature of Man*. New York: World Publishing Co., 1966.

JAMES, MURIEL and DOROTHY JONGEWARD, *Born to Win: Transactional Analysis with Gestalt Experiments*. Reading, Mass.: Addison-Wesley Publishing Company, 1971.

KEPNER, C. H. and B. B. TREGOE, *The Rational Manager*. New York: McGraw-Hill Book Company, 1965.

KOLB, DAVID A., IRWIN M. RUBIN, and JAMES M. MCINTYRE, *Organizational Psychology: A Book of Readings*. Englewood Cliffs, N.J.: Prentice-Hall, Inc., 1971.

LIKERT, RENSIS, *New Patterns of Management*. New York: McGraw-Hill Book Company, 1961.

MACHIAVELLI, NICCOLÒ, *The Prince*. New York: Mentor Classic—New American Library, 1952.

MACKENZIE, R. ALEX, *Time Trap*. New York: McGraw-Hill Book Company, 1975.

313

MARROW, ALFRED J., *Practical Theorist: The Life and Work of Kurt Lewin*. New York: Basic Books, Inc., Publishers, 1969.

MASLOW, ABRAHAM H., *Motivation and Personality*. New York: Harper & Row, Publishers, 1954.

MAYO, ELTON, *The Social Problems of an Industrial Civilization*. Boston: Harvard Business School, 1945.

MCCLELLAND, DAVID C., et al., *The Achieving Society*. Princeton, N.J.: D. Van Nostrand Co., Inc., 1961.

MCGREGOR, DOUGLAS, *The Human Side of Enterprise*. New York: McGraw-Hill Book Company, 1960.

REDDIN, WILLIAM, *Effective Management by Objectives: The 3-D Method of MBO*. New York: McGraw-Hill Book Company, 1971.

SCHEIN, EDGAR H., *Organizational Psychology*. Englewood Cliffs, N.J.: Prentice-Hall, Inc., 1972.

WARNER, W. LLOYD, and NORMAN H. MARTIN, eds., *Industrial Man*. New York: Harper & Brothers, 1959.

Selected Bibliography

ADLER, ALFRED. *Social Interest*. London: Faber & Faber, Ltd., 1938.

ALDERFER, C. P. *Existence, Relatedness, and Growth: Human Needs in Organizational Settings*. New York: Free Press, 1972.

———. "Group and Intergroup Relations," in *Improving Life at Work*, J. R. Hackman and J. L. Suttle, eds. Santa Monica, Calif.: Goodyear, 1977.

ALLEN, T. J. *Managing the Flow of Technology*. Cambridge, Mass.: MIT Press, 1977.

ALLISON, G. T. *Essence of Decision*. Boston: Little-Brown, 1971.

ANGELINI, ARRIGO L., PAUL HERSEY, and SOFIA CARACUSHANSKY. "The Situational Leadership Theory Applied to Teaching: A Research on Learning Effectiveness" (unpublished paper being reviewed for publication), São Paulo, Brazil.

ANSBACHER, K. L., and R. R. ANSBACHER, eds. *The Individual Psychology of Alfred Adler*. New York: Basic Books, Inc., Publishers, 1956.

APPLEWHITE, PHILLIP. *Organizational Behavior*. Englewood Cliffs, N.J.: Prentice-Hall, Inc., 1965.

ARENDT, HANNAH. *The Human Condition*. Chicago: University of Chicago Press, 1958.

ARENSBURG, C. M., and D. McGREGOR. "Determination of Morale in an Industrial Company," *Applied Anthropology*, I, No. 2 (1942), 12–34.

ARENSBURG, CONRAD M. "Behavior and Organization: Industrial Studies," in *Social Psychology at the Crossroads*, John H. Rohrer and Muzafer Sherif, eds. New York: Harper & Bros., 1951.

ARGYRIS, CHRIS. *Executive Leadership: An Appraisal of a Manager in Action*. Hamden, Conn.: Shoe String Press, Inc., 1953.

———. *Integrating the Individual and the Organization*. New York: John Wiley & Sons, Inc., 1964.

———. "Interpersonal Barriers to Decision-Making," *Harvard Business Review*, 22, No. 2 (1966), 84–97.

———. *Interpersonal Competence and Organizational Effectiveness*. Homewood, Ill.: Dorsey Press and Richard D. Irwin, Inc., 1962.

_____. *Intervention Theory and Method: A Behavioral Science View*. Reading, Mass.: Addision-Wesley Publishing Company, 1970.

_____. "Leadership, Learning, and Changing the Status Quo, *Organizational Dynamics* (Winter 1976), 29–43.

_____. *Management and Organizational Development: The Path From XA to YB*. New York: McGraw-Hill Book Company, 1971.

_____. *Organization and Innovation*. Homewood, Ill.: Dorsey Press and Richard D. Irwin, Inc., 1965.

_____. *Personality and Organization*. New York: Harper & Row, Publishers, 1957.

_____. "T-Groups for Organization Effectiveness," *Harvard Business Review*, 42. 1964.

_____. *Understanding Organizational Behavior*. Homewood, Ill.: Dorsey, 1960.

_____. "We Must Make Work Worthwhile," *Life*, May 5, 1967, p. 66.

_____, and D. Schon. *Organizational Learning: A Theory of Action Perspective*. Reading, Mass.: Addison-Wesley, 1978.

_____. *Theory in Practice: Increasing Professional Effectiveness*. San Francisco: Jossey-Bass, 1974.

ASCH, S. E., "Effects of Group Pressure upon the Modification and Distortion of Judgments," in *Group Dynamics* (2nd ed.), Dorwin Cartwright and Alvin Zander, eds., pp. 189–200. Evanston, Ill.: Row, Peterson & Company, 1960.

_____. *Social Psychology*. Englewood Cliffs, N.J.: Prentice-Hall, Inc., 1952.

ATHOS, ANTHONY G., and ROBERT E. COFFEY. *Behavior in Organizations: A Multidimensional View*. Englewood Cliffs, N.J.: Prentice-Hall, Inc., 1968.

ATKINSON, JOHN W. "Motivational Determinants of Risk-Taking Behavior," *Psychological Review*, 64 No. 6 (1957), 365.

BACHMAN, J. G., D. G. BOWERS, and P. M. M ARCUS. "Bases of Supervisory Power: A Comparative Study in Five Organizational Settings," in Arnold S. Tannenbaum, *Control in Organizations*. New York: McGraw-Hill Book Company, 1968.

BACHMAN, J. G., C. G. SMITH, and J. A. SLESINGER. "Control Performance, and Satisfaction: An Analysis of Structural and Individual Effects," *Journal of Personality and Social Psychology*, 4, No. 2 (1966), 127–36.

BAILYN, L., and E. H. SCHEIN. "Life/Career Considerations as Indicators of Quality of Employment," in A. D. Biderman and T. F. Drury, *Measuring Work Quality for Social Reporting*. New York: Wiley (Sage Publications), 1976.

_____. *Living with Technology: Issues at Mid-careers*. Cambridge, Mass.: MIT Press, 1980.

_____. "Where Are They Now and How Are They Doing?" *Technology Review*, 74 (1972), 3–11.

BALDRIDGE, J. V. *Power and Conflict in the University*. New York: Wiley, 1971.

BALES, R. F. "Task Roles and Social Roles in Problem-Solving Groups," in *Readings in Social Psychology* (3rd ed.), N. Maccoby et al. New York: Holt, Rinehart, & Winston, Inc., 1958.

BANDURA, A. *Principles of Behavior Modification*. New York: Holt, Rinehart & Winston, 1969.

BARKER, H., T. DEMBO, and K. LEWIN, *Frustration and Aggression*. Iowa City: University of Iowa Press, 1942.

BARNARD, CHESTER I., *The Functions of the Executive*. Cambridge: Harvard University Press, 1938.

BARASH, D. P. *Sociobiology and Behavior*. New York: Elsevier, 1977.

BASS, B. M. *Organizational Psychology*. Boston: Allyn & Bacon, 1965.

BASS, B ERNARD M. *Leadership, Psychology, and Organizational Behavior. New York: Harper & Row* Publishers, 1960.

_____. *Organization and Management*. Cambridge: Harvard University Press, 1948.

_____. MARGARET W. PRYER, EUGENE L. G AIER, and AUSTIN W. FLIT. "Interacting Effects of Control, Motivation, Group Practice, and Problem Difficulty on Attempted Leadership," *Journal of Abnormal and Social Psychology*, 56 (1958), 352–58.

BATESON, G. *Steps to an Ecology of Mind*. New York: Ballantine, 1972.

BATTEN, J. D. *Beyond Management by Objectives*. New York: American Management Association, 1966.

BAUMGARTEL, H. J., J R. "Leadership Motivation and Attitudes in Research Laboratories," *Journal of Social Issues*, XII, No. 2 (1956), 24–31.

BAVELAS, A. "Communication Patterns in Task-Oriented Groups," in *Group Dynamics*, D. Cartwright and A. Zander, eds. Evanston, Ill.: Row, Peterson & Company, 1953.

————, and G. STRAUSS. "Group Dynamics and Intergroup Relations, in K. Benne and R. Chin, eds. *The Planning of Change*. New York: Holt, Rinehart, & Winston, 1962.

BECKHARD, R. *Organization Development: Strategies and Models*. Reading, Mass.: Addison-Wesley, 1969.

————, and HARRIS, R. T. *Organizational Transitions: Managing Complex Change*. Reading, Mass.: Addison-Wesley Publishing Company, 1977.

BEER, MICHAEL, ROBERT BUCKHOUT, MILTON W. HOROWITZ, and SEYMOUR LEVY. "Some Perceived Properties of the Difference between Leaders and Non-Leaders," *The Journal of Psychology*, 47 (1959), 49–56.

BEIRSTEDT, R. "An Analysis of Social Power," *American Sociological Review*, 15 (1950), 730–36.

BELL, GRAHAM B., and ROBERT L. FRENCH. "Consistency of Individual Leadership Position in Small Groups of Varying Membership," *Journal of Abnormal and Social Psychology*, 45 (1950), 764–67.

BENDIX, R. *Work and Authority in Industry*. New York: John Wiley & Sons, Inc., 1956.

BENNE, KENNETH D., and PAUL SHEATS. "Functional Roles of Group Members," *Journal of Social Issues, IV*, No. 2 (1948), 41–49.

BENNIS, WARREN G. *Beyond Bureaucracy: Essays on the Development and Evolution of Human Organizations*. New York: McGraw-Hill Book Company, 1973.

————. *Changing Organizations*. New York: McGraw-Hill Book Company, 1966.

————. "Leadership Theory and Administrative Behavior: The Problem of Authority," *Administrative Science Quarterly, IV*, No. 3 (December 1959), 259–301.

————. *Organization Development: Its Nature, Origins and Prospects*. Reading, Mass.: Addison-Wesley Publishing Company, 1969.

————. "Revisionist Theory of Leadership," *Harvard Business Review*, 39 (1961), 26ff.

————. *The Unconscious Conspiracy: Why Leaders Can't Lead*. New York: AMACON, 1976.

————. "Toward a Truly Scientific Management: The Concept of Organizational Health," *General Systems Yearbook*, 7 (1962), 269–82.

————, K. D. BENNE, and R. CHIN. *The Planning of Change* (2nd ed.). New York: Holt, Rinehart, & Winston, 1969.

BERELSON, BERNARD, and GARY A. STEINER. *Human Behavior: An Inventory of Scientific Findings*. New York: Harcourt, Brace & World, Inc., 1964.

BERGEN, GARRET L., and WILLIAM V. HANEY. *Organizational Relations and Management Action*. New York: McGraw-Hill Book Company, 1966.

BERNE, ERIC. *Games People Play*. New York: Grove Press, 1964.

————. *Principles of Group Treatment*. New York: Oxford University Press, 1964.

BLAKE, R. R., and J. S. MOUTON. *Consultation*. Reading, Mass.: Addison-Wesley Publishing Company, 1976.

————. "Headquarters-field Team Training for Organizational Improvements," *Journal of the American Society of Training Directors* (1962), 16.

————. *The Managerial Grid*. Houston, Texas: Gulf Publishing, 1964.

BLAKE, ROBERT R., et al., "Breakthrough in Organizational Development," *Harvard Business Review* (November-December 1964).

BLAKE, ROBERT R., HERBERT SHEPARD, and JANE S. MOUTON, *Managing Inter-group Conflict in Industry*. Houston: Gulf Publishing, 1964.

BLAKE, ROBERT R., and JANE S. MOUTON. *The Managerial Grid*. Houston, Tex.: Gulf Publishing, 1964.

————. "Reactions to Intergroup Competition under Win-Lose Conditions," *Management Science*, 7 (1961), 420–35.

BLANCHARD, KENNETH H. "College Boards of Trustees: A Need for Directive Leadership," *Academy of Management Journal*, December 1967.

BLAU, PETER M. *The Dynamics of Bureaucracy*. Chicago: University of Chicago Press, 1955.

————, and SCOTT, W. R. *Formal Organizations*. San Francisco: Chandler, 1962.

BLAUNER, R. *Alienation and Freedom*. Chicago: University of Chicago Press, 1964.

BLUM, F. H. *Toward a Democratic Work Process*. New York: Harper & Row, Publishers, 1953.

BORG, WALTER R. "The Behavior of Emergent and Designated Leaders in Situational Tests," *Sociometry*, 20 (1957), 95–104.

————, and ERNEST C. TUPES. "Personality Characteristics Related to Leadership Behavior in Two Types of Small Group Situational Problems," *Journal of Applied Psychology*, 42 (1958), 252–56.

BORGATTA, EDGAR F., ROBERT F. BALES, and ARTHUR S. COUCH. "Some Findings Relevant to the Great Man Theory of Leadership," *American Sociological Review*, 19 (1954), 755–59.

BOWERS, D. G., and S. E. SEASHORE. "Predicting Organizational Effectiveness with a Four-Factor Theory of Leadership," *Administrative Science Quarterly*, XI, No. 2 (1966), 238–63.

BRADFORD, L. P. *National Training Laboratories: Its History 1947–1970*. Bethel, Maine: National Training Laboratories, 1974.

BRADFORD, LELAND P., JACK R. GIBB, and KENNETH D. BENNE. *T-Group Theory and Laboratory Method*. New York: John Wiley & Sons, Inc., 1964.

BREMAN, N. *The Making of a Moron*. New York: Sheed & Ward, 1953.

BROOKS, E. "What Successful Executives Do," *Personnel*, XXXII, No. 3 (1955), 210–25.

BROWN, J. A. C. *The Social Psychology of Industry*. London: Penguin Books, 1954.

BROWNE, C. G., and B. J. NEITZEL. "Communication, Supervision and Morale," *Journal of Applied Psychology*, 36 (1952), 86–91.

BROWNE, C. G., and RICHARD P. SHORE. "Leadership and Predictive Abstracting," *Journal of Applied Psychology*, 40 (1956), 112–16.

BURKE, R. J., and D. S. WILCOX. "Bases of Supervisory Power and Subordinate Job Satisfactions," *Candian Journal of Behavioral Science* (1971).

BURNS, T., and G. M. STALKER. *The Management of Innovation*. London: Tavistock Publications, 1961.

CARLSON, RICHARD O. *Executive Succession and Organizational Change*. Chicago: Midwest Administration Center, University of Chicago, 1962.

CARP, FRANCIS M., BART M. VITOLA, and FRANK L. MCLANATHAN. "Human Relations Knowledge and Social Distance Set in Supervisors," *Journal of Applied Psychology*, 47 (1963), 78–90.

CARTER, LAUHOR, WILLIAM HAYTHORN, and MARGARET HOWELL. "A Further Investigation of the Criteria of Leadership," *Journal of Abnormal and Social Psychology*, 45 (1950), 350–58.

CARTWRIGHT, D. "Achieving Change in People: Some Applications of Group Dynamics Theory," *Human Relations*, 4 (1951) 381–92.

————, ed. *Studies in Social Power*. Ann Arbor, Mich.: University of Michigan Press, 1959.

————. "The Potential Contribution of Graph Theory to Organization Theory," in *Modern Organization Theory*, M. Haire, ed. New York: John Wiley & Sons, Inc., 1959.

————, and R. Lippitt. "Group Dynamics and the Individual," *International Journal of Group Psychotherapy*, VII, No. 1 (1957), 86–102.

————, and A. ZANDER, eds. *Group Dynamics: Research and Theory* (2nd ed.). Evanston, Ill.: Row, Peterson & Company, 1960.

CARVELL, FRED J. *Human Relations in Business*. Toronto: The MacMillan Company, 1970.

CATTELL, RAYMOND B. "New Concepts for Measuring Leadership in Terms of Group Syntality," *Human Relations*, 4 (1951), 161–84.

CHANDER, A. D., JR. *Strategy and Structure*. Cambridge, Mass.: MIT Press, 1962.

CHAPPLE, ELIOTT D., and CARLETON COON. *Principles of Anthropology*. New York: Henry Holt and Co., 1942.

CHOWDHRY, KAMLA, and THEODORE M. NEWCOMB. "The Relative Abilities of Leaders and Non-Leaders to Estimate Opinions of Their Own Groups," *Journal of Abnormal and Social Psychology*, 47 (1952), 51–57.

CHRISTNER, CHARLOTTE A., and JOHN K. HEMPHILL. "Leader Behavior of B-29 Commanders and Changes in Crew Members' Attitudes toward the Crew," *Sociometry*, 18 (1955), 82–87.

CLARK, J. V., and C. G. KRONE. "Towards an Overall View of Organization Development in the Early Seventies," in J. Thomas and W. C. Bennis, eds. *Management of Change and Conflict*. Baltimore: Penguin Books, 1972.

COATES, CHARLES H., and ROLAND J. PELLEGRIN. "Executives and Supervisors: Informal Factors in Differential Bureaucratic Promotion," *Administrative Science Quarterly*, 2 (1957), 200–215.

———. "Executives and Supervisors: Contrasting Self-Conceptions of Each Other," *American Sociological Review*, 22 (1957), 217–20.

COCH, L., and J. R. P. FRENCH, JR. "Overcoming Resistance to Change," *Human Relations*, I, No. 4 (1948), 512–32.

COMREY, A. L., W. S. HIGH, and R. C. WILSON. "Factors Influencing Organizational Effectiveness," VII. *Personnel Psychology*, VIII, No. 2 (1955), 245–57.

COOLEY, C. H. *Human Nature and the Social Order*. New York: Scribners, 1922.

———. *Social Organization*. New York: Scribners, 1909.

COOPER, WILLIAM W., HAROLD J. LEAVITT, and MAYNARD W. SHELLY II, eds. *New Perspectives in Organization Research*. New York: John Wiley & Sons, Inc., 1964.

COWLEY, W. H. "The Traits of Face-to-Face Leaders," *Journal of Abnormal and Social Psychology*, 26 (1931), 304–13.

CROCKETT, WALTER H. "Emergent Leadership in Small Decision-Making Groups," *Journal of Abnormal and Social Psychology*, 51 (1955), 378–83.

CROZIER, MICHAEL. *The Bureaucratic Phenomenon*. Chicago: University of Chicago Press, 1964.

CUMMINGS, T. G., and S. SRIVASTVA. *Management of Work: A Sociotechnical Systems Approach*. Kent, Ohio: Kent State University Press, 1977.

CYERT, RICHARD M., W. R. DILL, and JAMES G. MARCH. "The Role of Expectations in Business Decision Making," *Administrative Science Quarterly*, 3 (December 1958), 307–40.

CYERT, RICHARD M., and JAMES G. MARCH. *A Behavioral Theory of the Firm*. Englewood Cliffs, N.J.: Prentice-Hall, Inc., 1963.

DAHL, R. A. "The Concept of Power," *Behavioral Science*, 2 (1957), 201–218.

DALE, ERNEST. *The Great Organizers*. New York: McGraw-Hill Book Company, 1960.

DALTON, G. W., P. H. THOMPSON, and R. PRICE. "Career Stages: A model of Professional Careers in Organizations," *Organizational Dynamics*, 6 (1977), 19–42.

DALTON, GENE W. "Influence and Organizational Change," reprinted in David A. Kolb, Irwin M. Rubin and James M. McIntyre, *Organizational Psychology: A Book of Readings*. Englewood Cliffs, N.J.: Prentice-Hall, Inc.; 1970, pp. 401–425.

DALTON, M. *Men Who Manage*. New York: John Wiley & Sons, Inc., 1959.

DAVIS, J. H., P. R. LAUGHLIN and S. S. KOMORITA. "The Social Psychology of Small Groups: Cooperative and Mixed Motive Interactions," *Annual Review of Psychology*, 27 (1976), 501–541.

DAVIS, L. E. "The Design of Jobs," *Industrial Relations*, 6 (1966), 21–45.

———. "Toward a Theory of Job Design," *Journal of Industrial Engineering*, 8 (1957), 305–309.

———, and A. B. CHERNS. *The Quality of Working Life, 2 vols*. New York: Free Press, 1975.

DAVIS, S. M. *Comparative Management*. Englewood Cliffs, N.J.: Prentice-Hall, Inc., 1971.

———. and P. R. LAWRENCE. *Matrix*. Reading, Mass.: Addison-Wesley Publishing Company, 1977.

DAY, JESSE H., and CLIFFORD HOUK. "Student-Paced Learning: A Proposal for an Experiment in the Improvement of Learning in General Chemistry," unpublished proposal, p. 10. Athens: Ohio University, 1968.

DAY, ROBERT C., and ROBERT L. HAMBLIN. "Some Effects of Close and Punitive Styles of Supervision," *The American Journal of Sociology*. 69 (1964), 499–510.

DENT, J. K. "Managerial Leadership Styles: Some Dimensions, Determinants, and Behavioral Correlates," unpublished doctoral dissertation, University of Michigan, 1957.

DEUTSCH, MORTON, "An Experimental Study of the Effects of Cooperation and Competition upon Group Process," *Human Relations*, 2 (1949), 199–231.

DILL, WILLIAM R. "Environment as an Influence of Managerial Autonomy," *Administrative Science Quarterly,* 2 (March 1958), 409–443.

————. THOMAS L. HINTON and WALTER R. REITMAN. *The New Managers.* Englewood Cliffs, N.J.: Prentice-Hall, Inc., 1962.

DITTES, JAMES E. "Attractiveness of Group as Function of Self-Esteem and Acceptance by Group," Journal of Abnormal and Social Psychology, 59 (1959), 77–82.

DRUCKER, PETER F. *Effective Executive.* New York: Harper & Row, Publishers, 1967.

————. "How to Be an Employee," *Psychology Today* (March 1968), reprint from *Fortune* magazine.

————. *Landmarks of Tomorrow.* New York: Harper & Row, Publishers, 1959.

————. *Managing for Results.* New York: Harper & Row, Publishers, 1964.

————. *The Practice of Management.* New York: Harper & Row, Publishers, 1954.

DUBIN, R. *Human Relations in Administration. Englewood Cliffs,* N.J.: Prentice-Hall, Inc., 1951.

DUBLIN, R. "Industrial Workers' Worlds," *Social Problems,* 3 (1956), 131–42.

————. "Work in Modern Society." in *Handbook of Work, Organization, and Society,* R. Dublin, ed. Chicago: Rand-McNally, 1976.

————, et al. *Leadership and Productivity.* San Francisco, Calif.: Chandler Publishing Co., 1965.

DUNCAN, R. B. "Multiple Decision-making Structures in Adapting to Environmental Uncertainty: The Impact on Organizational Effectiveness, *Human Relations,* 26 (1973), 273–91.

————. "The Characteristics of Organizational Environments and Perceived Environmental Uncertainty," *Administrative Science Quarterly,* 17 (1972), 313–27.

DYER, W. G. *Team Building.* Reading, Mass.: Addison-Wesley Publishing Company, 1977.

EMERY, F. E. "Some Characteristics of Socio-Technical Systems," doc. no. 527, *The Tavistock Institute of Human Relations* (January 1959).

EMERY, F. E., and E. THORSRUD. *Form and Content in Industrial Democracy.* London: Tavistock Publications, 1969.

EMERY,F. E., and E. L. TRIST. "The Casual Texture of Organizational Environments," *Human Relations, 18 (1965), 21–32.*

ETZIONI, AMITAI. *A Comparative Analysis of Complex Organizations on Power, Involvement and Their Correlates.* New York: The Free Press, 1961.

————. *Complex Organizations.* New York: Holt, Rinehart & Winston, 1961.

EVAN, W. M. ed. *Inter-organizational Relations.* Philadelphia: University of Pennsylvania Press, 1978.

EVAN, WILLIAM M. "The Organization-Set: Toward a Theory of InterOrganizational Relations," *Approaches to Organizational Design,* James D. Thompson, ed. Pittsburgh, Pa.: The University of Pittsburgh Press, 1966.

EVANS, C. E. "Supervisory Responsibility and Authority," *American Management Association, Reserve Report,* 30 (1957).

FARRIS, G. "Organizational Factors and Individual Performance: A Longitudinal Study," *Journal of Applied Psychology,* 53 (1969), 87–92.

FAYOL, HENRI. *Industrial and General Administration.* Paris: Dunod, 1925.

FERSTER, C. B., and B. F. SKINNER. *Schedules of Reinforcement.* New York: Appleton-Century-Crofts, 1957.

FESTINGER, LEON. *A Theory of Cognitive Dissonance.* Stanford, Calif.: Stanford University Press, 1957.

————, STANLEY SCHACHTER and KURT BACK. *Social Pressures in Informal Groups.* New York: Harper & Row, Publishers, 1950.

FIEDLER, FRED E. "Engineer the Job to Fit the Manager," *Harvard Business Review,* 51 (1965), 115–22.

————. *Leader Attitudes and Group Effectiveness.* Urbana: University of Illinois Press, 1958.

————. "Leadership and Leadership Effectiveness Traits: A Reconceptualization of the Leadership Trait Problem," in *Leadership and Interpersonal Behavior,* Luigi Petrullo and Bernard M. Bass, eds. New York: Holt, Rinehart & Winston, Inc., 1961.

_____. *A Theory of Leadership Effectiveness*. New York: McGraw-Hill Book Company, 1967.

_____. "Validation and Extension of the Contingency Model of Leadership Effectiveness: A Review of Empirical Findings," *Psychological Bulletin*, 76 (1971) 128–48.

_____, M. M. CHEMERS and L. MAHAR. *Improving Leadership Effectiveness: The Leader Match Concept*. New York: John Wiley & Sons, Inc., 1976.

FILLEY, A. C., and A. N. GRIMES. "The Bases of Power in Decision Processes." Industrial Relations Research Institute, University of Wisconsin, Reprint Series, 104, 1967.

FILLEY, ALAN C., and ROBERT J. HOUSE. *Managerial Process and Organizational Behavior*. Glenview, Ill.: Scott, Foresman & Company, 1969.

FLEISHMAN, E. A. "Twenty Years of Consideration and Structure," in E. A. Fleishman and J. G. Hunt, eds. *Current Developments in the Study of Leadership*. Carbondale, Ill.: Southern Illinois University Press, 1973.

_____, E. F. HARRIS and H. E. BURTT. "Leadership and Supervison in Industry," *Ohio State Business Education Reserve Monograph*, 33 (1955).

FLEISHMAN, E. A., and EDWIN HARRIS. "Patterns of Leadership Behavior Related to Employee Grievances and Turnover," *Personnel Psychology*, 15 (1962), 43–56.

FLEISHMAN, E. A., and DAVID R. PETERS. "Interpersonal Values, Leadership Attitudes, and Managerial 'Success,' " *Personnel Psychology*, 15 (1962), 127–43.

FLEISHMAN, EDWIN A. "Leadership Climate, Human Relations Training, and Supervisory Behvior," *Personnel Psychology*, 6 (1953), 205–22.

_____. "The Measurement of Leadership Attitudes in Industry," *Journal of Applied Psychology*, 37 (1953), 153–58.

FOA, URIEL G. "Relation of Worker's Expectations to Satisfaction with the Supervisor," *Personnel Psychology*, 10 (1957), 161–68.

FORD, R. N. "Job Enrichment Lessons from AT&T," *Harvard Business Review* (January-February 1973), 96–106.

Foundation for Research on Human Behavior. *An Action Research Program for Organization Improvement*. Ann Arbor, Mich., 1960.

_____. *Assessing Managerial Potential*. Ann Arbor, Mich., 1958.

_____. *Communication Problems in Superior-Subordinate Relationships*. Ann Arbor, Mich., 1960.

_____. *Creativity and Conformity: A Problem for Organizations*. Ann Arbor, Mich., 1958.

_____. *Managing Major Change in Organizations*. Ann Arbor, Mich., 1960.

FRANK, ANDREW G. "Goal Ambiguity and Conflicting Standards," *Human Organization*, 17 (Winter 1958), 8–13.

FRANKS, C. M. *Behavior Therapy: Appraisal and Status*. New York: McGraw-Hill Book Company, 1969.

FRENCH, J. R. P., JR. "A Formal Theory of Social Power," *Psychological Review*, LXIII, No. 3 (1956), 181–94.

_____, JOACHIM ISRAEL and DAGFINN ÅS. "An Experiment on Participation in a Norwegian Factory," *Human Relations*, XIII, No. 1 (1960), 3–19.

FRENCH, J. R. P., and B. RAVEN. "The Bases of Social Power," in D. Cartwright, *Studies in Social Power*. Ann Arbor: University of Michigan, Institute for Social Research, 1959.

_____, J. C. ROSS, S. KIRBY, J. R. NELSON and P. SMYTH. "Employee Participation in a Program of Industrial Change," *Personnel* (November-December 1958), 16–29.

FRENCH, WENDELL L., and CECIL H. BELL, JR. *Organizational Development: Behavioral Science Intervention for Organizational Improvement*. Englewood Cliffs, N.J.: Prentice-Hall, Inc., 1973.

FREUD, SIGMUND. *The Ego and the Id*. London: Hogarth Press, 1927.

_____. *New Introductory Lectures on Psychoanalysis*. New York: W. W. Norton & Company, Inc., 1933.

FRIEDMANN, G. *Industrial Society: The Emergency of Human Problems of Automation*. Glencoe, Ill.: The Free Press, 1948.

FROMM, ERIC. *The Sane Society*. New York: Rinehart, 1955.

FROST, C., J. H. WAKELEY, and R. A. RUH. *The Scanlon Plan for Organization Development*. East Lansing, Mich.: Michigan State University Press, 1974.

GALBRAITH, J. *Designing Complex Organizations.* Reading, Mass.: Addison-Wesley Publishing Company, 1973.

———. *Organization Design.* Reading, Mass.: Addison-Wesley Publishing Company, 1977.

GARDNER, JOHN W. "The Antileadership Vaccine" (reprinted from the 1965 *Annual Report*, Carnegie Corporation of New York). See also "Executive Trends Beat the Management Shortage," *Nation's Business*, LII, No. 9 (September 1964).

GAUDET, FREDERICK J., and A. RALPH CARLI. "Why Executives Fail," *Personnel Psychology*, 10 (1957), 7–21.

GELLERMAN, SAUL W. *Leadership Style and Employee Morale.* New York: General Electric Company, Public and Employee Relations Services, 1959.

———. *Management by Motivation.* New York: American Management Association, 1968.

———. *Motivation and Productivity.* New York: American Management Association, 1963.

GERTH, HANS H., and C. WRIGHT MILLS, eds. *From Max Weber.* Oxford: Oxford University Press, 1946.

GETZELS, JACOB W., and EGON E. GUBA. "Social Behavior and the Administrative Process," *The School Review*, LXV, No. 4 (Winter 1957), 423–41.

GHISELLI, E. E. *Explorations in Managerial Talent.* Pacific Palisades, Calif.: Goodyear, 1971.

GHISELLI, EDWIN E. "Individuality as a Factor in the Success of Management Personnel," *Personnel Psychology*, 13 (1960), 1–10.

———, and R. BARTHOL. "Role Perceptions of Successful and Unsuccessful Supervisors," *Journal of Applied Psychology*, 40 (1956), 241–44.

GIBB, CECIL A. "Leadership," in *Handbook of Social Psychology*, Gardner Lindzey, ed. Cambridge, Mass.: Addison-Wesley Publishing Company, 1954.

———. "The Principles and Traits of Leadership," *Journal of Abnormal and Social Psychology*, 42 (1947), 267–84.

———. "The Sociometry of Leadership in Temporary Groups," *Sociometry*, 13 (1950), 226–43.

GILMAN, G. "An Inquiry into the Nature and Use of Authority," in *Organization Theory in Industrial Practice*, M. Haire, ed. New York: John Wiley & Sons, Inc., 1962.

GOFFMAN, E. *Behavior in Public Places.* New York: Free Press, 1963.

———. *Interaction Ritual.* Chicago: Aldine, 1967.

———. *The Presentation of Self in Everyday Life.* New York: Doubleday, 1959.

GOODACRE, D. M. "Group Characteristics of Good and Poor Performing Combat Units," *Sociometry*, XVI, No. 2 (1953), 168–79.

———. "Stimulating Improved Man Management," *Personnel Psychology*, 16 (1963), 133–43.

GORDON, OAKLEY, J. "A Factor Analysis of Human Needs and Industrial Morale," *Personnel Psychology*, 8 (1955), 1–18.

GORDON, T. *Group-centered Leadership.* Boston: Houghton Mifflin Company, 1955.

GORDON, THOMAS. *P.E.T. Parent Effectiveness Training.* New York: Peter H. Wyden, Inc., 1970.

GORE, WILLIAM J. *Administrative Decision-making.* New York: John Wiley & Sons, Inc., 1964.

GRAVES, CLARE W. "Human Nature Prepares for a Momentous Leap," *The Futurist* (April 1974), 72–87.

GREEN, B. "Attitude Measurement," in *Handbook of Social Psychology*, G. Lindzey, ed. Cambridge, Mass.: Addison-Wesley Publishing Company, 1954.

GREER, F. LOYAL. "Leader Indulgence and Group Performance," *Psychological Monographs*, 75, no. 12, whole no. 516 (1961).

GREINER, LARRY E. "Evolution and Revolution as Organizations Grow," *Harvard Business Review* (July-August 1972), 37–46.

GROSS, N., W. S. MASON and A. MCEACHERN. *Explorations in Role Analysis.* New York: John Wiley & Sons, Inc., 1958.

GROSS, NEAL, and WILLIAM E. MARTIN. "On Group Cohesiveness," *American Journal of Sociology*, 57 (1952), 546–54.

GRUSKY, O. "Authoritarianism and Effective Indoctrination: A Case Study," *Administrative Science Quarterly*, 7 (1962), 79–95.

GUEST, ROBERT H. "Of Time and the Foreman," *Personnel*, 32, No. 6 (May 1956), 478–96.
———. *Organizational Change: The Effect of Successful Leadership*. Homewood, Ill.: Dorsey Press and Richard D. Irwin, Inc., 1964.
GULICK, LUTHER, and L. URWICK, eds. *Papers on the Science of Administration*. New York: Institute of Public Administration, 1937.
HABERMAN, JOHN. "Discipline Without Punishment," *Harvard Business Review* (May 1967), 62–68.
HACKMAN, J. R. Work Design," in *Improving Life at Work*, J. R. Hackman and J. L. Suttle, eds. Santa Monica, Calif.: Goodyear, 1977.
HACKMAN, J. R., and E. E. LAWLER. "Employee Reactions to Job Characteristics," *Journal of Applied Psychology Monograph* (1971), 259–86.
HACKMAN J. R., and G. R. OLDHAM. "Development of the Job Diagnostic Survey," *Journal of Applied Psychology*, 60 (1975), 159–70.
———. *Work Design*. Reading, Mass.: Addison-Wesley Publishing Company, 1979.
HAIRE, M. "Psychological Problems Relevant to Business and Industry," *Psychological Bulletin*, 56 (1959), 169–94.
———. *Psychology in Management*. New York: McGraw-Hill Book Company, 1956.
HALL, D. T. *Careers in Organizations*. Santa Monica, Calif.: Goodyear, 1976.
HALL, E. *Beyond Culture*. New York: Anchor, 1977.
———. *The Hidden Dimension*. New York: Doubleday, 1966.
———. *The Silent Language*. New York: Doubleday, 1959.
HALPIN, ANDREW W. *The Leadership Behavior of School Superintendents*. Chicago: Midwest Administration Center, The University of Chicago, 1959.
———, and BEN J. WINER. *The Leadership Behavior of Airplane Commanders*. Columbus: The Ohio State University Research Foundation, 1952.
HAMBLIN, ROBERT L. "Leadership and Crises," in *Group Dynamics: Research and Theory* (2nd ed.), Dorwin Cartwright and Alvin Zander, eds. Evanston, Ill.: Row, Peterson & Company, 1960. Also in *Sociometry*, 21 (1958), 322–35.
HAMMOND, LEO K., and MORTON GOLDMAN. "Competition and Non-competition and Its Relationship to Individual and Group Productivity," *Sociometry*, 24 (1961), 46–60.
HAMPTON, DAVID R. *Behavioral Concepts in Management*. Belmont, Calif.: Dickinson Publishing Co., Inc., 1968.
HANEY, WILLIAM H. *Communication and Organizational Behavior: Text and Cases* (rev. ed.). Homewood, Ill.: Richard D. Irwin, Inc., 1967.
HARARY, F., and R. NORMAN. *Graph Theory as a Mathematical Model in the Social Sciences*. Ann Arbor, Mich.: Institute for Social Research, 1953.
HARBISON, F., and C. A. MYERS. *Management in the Industrial World*. New York: McGraw-Hill Book Company, 1959.
HARE, A. PAUL. *Handbook of Small Group Research*. New York: The Free Press, 1962.
———, E. F. BORGATTA, and R. F. BALES. *Small Group*. New York: Alfred A. Knopf, Inc., 1955.
HARRELL, T. W., and M. S. HARRELL. "The Personality of MBA's Who Reach General Management Early," *Personal Psychology*, 26 (1973), 127–34.
HARRIS, F. G., and R. W. LITTLE. "Military Organization and Social Psychiatry," *Symposium on Preventive and Social Psychiatry*. Washington, D.C.: Walter Reed Army Institute of Research, 1957.
HARRIS, T. *I'm OK—You're OK: A Practical Guide to Transactional Analysis*. New York: Harper & Row, Publishers, 1969.
HEALY, JAMES H. "Coordination and Control of Executive Functions," *Personnel*, 33 (1956), 106–17.
HELMREICH, R., R. BAKEMAN, and L. SCHERWITZ. "The Study of Small Groups," *Annual Review of Psychology*, 24 (1973) 337–54.
HEMPHILL, J. K. *Leader Behavior Description*. Columbus, Ohio: Ohio State University, 1950.

HEMPHILL, JOHN K. "Relations between the Size of the Group and the Behavior of 'Superior' Leaders," *The Journal of Social Psychology*, 32 (1950), 11–32.

————. *Situational Factors in Leadership*, Monograph No. 32. Columbus: Bureau of Educational Research, Ohio State University, 1949.

————. "Why People Attempt to Lead," in *Leadership and Interpersonal Behavior*, Luigi Petrullo and Bernard M. Bass, eds. New York: Holt, Rinehart & Winston, Inc., 1961.

————, and ALVIN E. COONS. "Development of the Leader Behavior Description and Questionnaire," in *Leader Behavior: Its Description and Measurement*, Monograph No. 88, Ralph M. Stogdill and Alvin E. Coons, eds. Columbus: Bureau of Business Research, Ohio State University, 1957.

HENRY, WILLIAM E. "The Business Executive: The Psychodynamics of a Social Role," *The American Journal of Sociology*, LIV, No. 4 (January 1949), 286–91.

HERBST, P. G. *Autonomous Group Functioning*. London: Tavistock Publications, 1962.

HERSEY, P., BLANCHARD K. H., and W. E. NATEMEYER. "Situational Leadership, Perception, and the Impact of Power," *Group and Organizational Studies*, Vol. 4, No. 4 (December 1979), 418–28.

HERSEY, PAUL, and KENNETH H. BLANCHARD. "Cultural Changes: Their Influence on Organizational Structure and Management Behavior," *Training and Development Journal* (October 1970).

————. "Life Cycle Theory of Leadership," *Training and Development Journal* (May 1969).

————. "So You Want to Know Your Leadership Style?" *Training and Development Journal* (February 1974).

————. "What's Missing in MBO?" *Management Review* (October 1974).

HERSEY, PAUL, and DOUGLAS SCOTT. "A Systems Approach to Educational Organizations: Do We Manage or Administer?" *OCLEA*, A Publication of the Ontario Council for Leadership in Educational Administration, Toronto, Canada, pp. 3–5.

HERZBERG, FREDERICK, "One More Time: How Do You Motivate Employees?" *Harvard Business Review*, 46, 1 (January-February 1968), 53–62.

————. *Work and the Nature of Man*. New York: World Publishing Co., 1966.

————. B. MAUSNER and BARBARA SNYDERMAN. *The Motivation to Work* (2nd ed.). New York: John Wiley & Sons, Inc., 1959.

HICKSON, D. J., R. J. BUTLER, R. AXELSON and D. WILSON. "Decision Coalitions," *Managerial Control and Organizational Democracy*, B. King, S. Streufert and F. E. Fiedler, eds. New York: Wiley, 1978.

HICKSON, D. J., D. S. PUGH and D. C. PHEYSEY. "Operations Technology and Organizational Structure: An Empirical Re-appraisal," *Administrative Science Quarterly*, 14 (1969), 378–97.

HOLLAND, J. L. *Making Vocational Choices: A Theory of Careers*. Englewood Cliffs, N.J.: Prentice-Hall, Inc., 1973.

————. *The Psychology of Vocational Choice*. Waltham, Mass.: Blaisdell, 1966.

HOLLANDER, E. P. "Emergent Leadership and Social Influence," in *Leadership and Interpersonal Behavior*, Luigi Petrullo and Bernard M. Bass, eds. New York: Holt, Rinehart & Winston, Inc., 1961.

HOLSINGER, GLENNA G. *Motivating the Reluctant Learner*. Lexington, Mass.: Motivity, Inc., 1970.

HOMANS, G. *Social Behavior: Its Elementary Forms*. New York: Harcourt, Brace, 1961.

HOMANS, G. C. *The Human Group*. New York: Harcourt, Brace & World, Inc., 1950.

HOMME, LLOYD. *How to Use Contingency Contracting in the Classroom*. Champaign, Ill.: Research Press, 1970.

HOPPOCK, R. *Job Satisfaction*. New York: Harper & Brothers, Publishers, 1935.

HORNSTEIN, H. A., B. B. BUNKER, W. W. BURKE, M. GINDES, and R. J. LEWICKI. *Social Intervention*. New York: Free Press, 1971.

HORSFALL, A. B., and C. M. ARENSBERG. "Teamwork and Productivity in a Shoe Factory," *Human Organization*, 8 (1949), 13–25.

HOSKING, D., and C. SCHRIESHEIM. "Review of Fielder et al.," *Improving Leadership Effectiveness: The Leader Match Concept* (New York: Wiley, 1976). *Administrative Science Quarterly*, 23 (1978), 496–504.

HOUSE, ROBERT J. *Management Development: Design, Implementation and Evaluation.* Ann Arbor: Bureau of Industrial Relations, University of Michigan, 1967.

———. "A Path-Goal Theory of Leader Effectiveness," *Administrative Science Quarterly*, 16 (1971), 321–38.

HOUSER, J. D. *What People Want from Business.* New York: McGraw-Hill Book Company, 1938.

HOVLAND, C. I., and I. L. JANIS, eds. *Personality and Persuasibility*, 2, Yale Studies in Attitude and Communication. New Haven, Conn.: Yale University Press, 1959.

HOVLAND, C. I., I. L. JANIS, and H. H. KELLEY. *Communication and Persuasion.* New Haven, Conn.: Yale University Press, 1953.

HOVLAND, C. I., and M. J. ROSENBERG. *Attitude, Organization and Change*, 3, Yale Studies in Attitude and Communication. New Haven, Conn.: Yale University Press, 1960.

HUBERMAN, JOHN. "Discipline Without Punishment," *Harvard Business Review*, 62–68.

HUGHES, EVERETT C. *Men and their Work.* New York: The Free Press, 1958.

HUMBLE, JOHN W. *Management by Objectives.* London: Industrial Education and Research Foundation, 1967.

HUNT, J. G., and L. L. LARSON, eds. *Contingency Approaches to Leadership.* Carbondale: Southern Illinois University Press, 1974.

HUNTER, MADELINE. *Reinforcement Theory for Teachers.* El Segundo, Calif.: TIP Publications, 1967.

HUSE,E., and J. BOWDITCH. *Behavior in Organization: A Systems Approach to Managing.* Reading, Mass.: Addison-Wesley Publishing Company, 1973.

HYMAN, HERBERT H. "The Psychology of Status," *Archives of Psychology*, 269 (1942).

INDIK, BERNARD P., BASIL S. GEORGOPOULOS, and STANLEY E. SEASHORE. "Superior Subordinate Relationships and Performance," *Personnel Psychology*, 14 (1961), 357–74.

Institute for Social Research. *Factors Related to Productivity.* Ann Arbor, Mich.: author, 1951.

IVANCEVICH, J. M., and J. H. DONNELLY. "Leader Influence and Performance," *Personnel Psychology*, 23, No. 4 (1970), 539–49.

JACKSON, J. M. "The Effect of Changing the Leadership of Small Work Groups," *Human Relations*, VI, No. 1 (1953), 25–44.

———, and H. D. SALTZSTEIN. *Group Membership and Group Conformity Processes.* Ann Arbor, Mich.: Institute for Social Research, 1956.

JAHODA, M. *Current Concepts of Positive Mental Health.* New York: Basic Books, 1958.

JAMES, MURIEL, and DOROTHY JONGEWARD. *Born to Win.* Reading, Mass.: Addison-Wesley Publishing Company, 1971.

JAMES, WILLIAM. *The Principles of Psychology*, vol. 1. London: Macmillan & Co., Ltd., 1890.

JAMIESON, D. W., and K. W. THOMAS. "Power and Conflict in the Student-Teacher Relationship," *Journal of Applied Behavioral Science*, 10, No. 3 (1974).

JANIS, I. L. *Victims of Group Think.* Boston: Houghton-Mifflin, 1972.

JANIS, I. L., and B. T. KING. "The Influence of Role Playing on Opinion Change," *Journal of Abnormal and Social Psychology*, 69 (1954), 211–18.

JANIS, I. L., and L. MANN. *Decision Making.* New York: Free Press, 1977.

JANOWITZ, MORRIS. "Changing Patterns of Organizational Authority: The Military Establishment," *Administrative Science Quarterly*, 3 (March 1959), 473–93.

JAQUES, E. *The Changing Culture of a Factory.* London: Tavistock Publications, 1951.

———. *Measurement of Responsibility.* London: Tavistock Publications, 1956.

JASINSKI, F. J. "Technological Delimitations of Reciprocal Relationships: A Study of Interaction Patterns in Industry," *Human Organization*, 15, No. 2 (1956).

———, and R. H. GUEST, "Redesigning the Supervisor's Job," *Factory Management and Maintenance*, 115, No. 12 (December 1957).

JENKINS, W. O. "A Review of Leadership Studies with Particular Reference to Military Problems," *Psychological Bulletin*, XLIV, No. 1 (1947), 54–79.
JENNINGS, EUGENE E. "The Anatomy of Leadership," *Management of Personnel Quarterly*, 1 No. 1 (Autumn, 1961).
JENNINGS, H. H. *Leadership and Isolation* (2nd ed.). New York: Longmans Green, 1950.
JOHNSON, DEWEY E. *Concepts of Air Force Leadership*. Washington, D.C.: Air Force ROTC, 1970.
JONGEWARD, D., and P. C. SEYER. *Choosing Success: Transactional Analysis on the Job*. New York: John Wiley & Sons, Inc.,\1978.
JONGEWARD DOROTHY. *Everybody Wins: Transactional Analysis Applied to Organizations*. Reading, Mass.: Addison-Wesley Publishing Company, 1974.

KAHN, R. L. "Human Relations on the Shop Floor," *Human Relations and Modern Management*, E. M. Hugh-Jones, ed., pp. 43–74. Amsterdam: North-Holland Publishing Co., 1958.
———. "The Prediction of Productivity," *Journal of Social Issues*, XII, No. 2 (1956), 41–49.
———. "Productivity and Job Satisfaction," *Personnel Psychology*, XIII, No. 3 (1960), 275–78.
KAHN, R. L., and D. KATZ. "Leadership Practices in Relation to Productivity and Morale," *Group Dynamics: Research and Theory* (2nd ed.), D. Cartwright and A. Zander, eds., pp. 554–71. Evanston, Ill.: Row, Peterson & Company, 1960.
KAHN, R. L., D. M. WOLFE, R. P. QUINN, J. D. SNOCK, and R. A. ROSENTHAL. *Organizational Stress: Studies in Role Conflict and Ambiguity*. New York: John Wiley and Sons, Inc., 1964.
KATZ, D. "Morale and Motivation in Industry," in *Current Trends in Industrial Psychology*, W. Dennis, ed., pp. 145–71. Pittsburgh: University of Pittsburgh, 1949.
KATZ, D. and ROBERT L. KAHN. *The Social Psychology of Organization*. New York: John Wiley and Sons, Inc., 1966.
KATZ, D., N. MACCOBY, G. GURIN and L. G. FLOOR. *Productivity, Supervision and Morale among Railroad Workers*. Ann Arbor, Mich.: Institute for Social Research, 1951.
KATZ. D., N. MACCOBY, and NANCY C. MORSE. *Productivity, Supervision, and Morale in an Office Situation*. Ann Arbor, Mich.: Institute for Social Research, 1950.
KATZ, E., and P. F. LAZARSFELD. *Personal Influence*. Glencoe, Ill.: Free Press, 1955.
KATZ, R. "Job Longevity as a Situational Factor in Job Satisfaction," *Administrative Science Quarterly*, 23 (1978), 204–23.
———. "The Influence of Group Conflict on Leadership Effectiveness," *Organizational Behavior and Human Performance*, 20 (1977), 265–86.
———, and J. VAN MAANEN. "The Loci of Work Satisfaction," *Human Relations*, 30 (1977), 469–86.
KATZ, ROBERT L. "Skills of an Effective Administrator," *Harvard Business Review* (January-February 1955), 33–42.
KEEN, P. G. W., and M. S. SCOTT-MORTON. *Decision Support Systems: An Organizational Perspective*. Reading, Mass.: Addison-Wesley, Publishing Company, 1978.
KELMAN, H. C. "Compliance, Identification and Internalization: Three Processes of Attitude Change," *Conflict Resolution*, II (1958), 51–60.
KEPNER, C. H., and B. B. TREGOE. *The Rational Manager*, New York: McGraw-Hill Book Company, 1965.
KNICKERBOCKER, IRVING. "Leadership: A Conception and Some Implications," *The Journal of Social Issues*, IV, No. 3 (1948), 23–40.
KNOWLES, HENRY P., and BORJE O. SAXBERG. *Personality and Leadership Behavior*. Reading, Mass.: Addison-Wesley Publishing Company, 1970.
KOLB, DAVID A., IRWIN M. RUBIN, and JAMES M. MCINTYRE. *Organizational Psychology: A Book of Readings*, Englewood Cliffs, N.J.: Prentice-Hall, Inc., 1971.
KOONTZ, HAROLD, and CYRIL O'DONNELL. *Principles of Management* (5th ed.). New York: McGraw-Hill Book Company, 1972.
KORMAN, A. K. " 'Consideration,' 'Initiating Structure,' and Organizational Criteria—A Review," *Personnel Psychology: A Journal of Applied Research*, XIX, No. 4 (1966), 349–61.

KOTTER, J. P. *Organizational Dynamics: Diagnosis and Intervention.* Reading, Mass.: Addison-Wesley Publishing Company, 1978.
————. "The Psychological Contract," *California Management Review,* 15 (1973), 91–99.
K RONE, C. G. "Open Systems Redesign," in J. D. Adams, ed. *Theory and Method in Organization Development: An Evolutionary Process.* Arlington, Va.: NTL Institute for Applied Behavioral Science, 1974.
KRULEE, G. K. "The Scanlon Plan: Co-operation through Participation," *Journal of Business,* University of Chicago, XXVIII, No. 2 (1955), 100–13.
LADD, E. C., and S. M. LIPSETT. *The Divided Academy.* New York: McGraw-Hill Book Company, 1975.
LARSON, L. L., J. G. HUNT, and R. N. OSBORN. "The Great Leader Behavior Myth," *Proceedings of the Academy of Management,* 1975, pp. 170–72.
LAWLER, E. E., III. *Pay and Organizational Effectiveness.* New York: McGraw-Hill Book Company, 1971.
————. "Pay, Participation, and Organizational Change, in *Man and Work in Society,* E. L. Cass and F. G. Zimmer, eds. New York: Van Nostrand Reinhold, 1975.
LAWRENCE, P. R., and J. W. LORSCH. *Developing Organization: Diagnosis and Action.* Reading, Mass.: Addison-Wesley Publishing Company, 1969.
LAWRENCE, P. R., and J. W. LORSCH. *Organization and Environment: Managing Differentiation and Integration.* Boston: Harvard Graduate School of Business Administration, 1967.
LEAVITT, H. J. "Applied Organizational Change in Industry: Structural, Technological and Humanistic Approaches," in *Handbook of Organizations,* James G. March, ed. New York: Rand McNally and Co., 1965.
————. *Managerial Psychology.* Chicago: University of Chicago Press, 1958.
————. "Some Effects of Certain Communication Patterns on Group Performance," *Journal of Abnormal and Social Psychology,* 46 (1951), 38–50.
————. "Suppose We Took Groups Seriously?" in *Man and Work in Society,* E. L. Cass and F. G. Zimmer, eds. New York: Van Nostrand Reinhold, 1975.
————. *The Social Science of Organizations: Four Perspectives.* Englewood Cliffs, N.J.: Prentice-Hall, Inc., 1963.
LESIEUR, F. *The Scanlon Plan.* New York: John Wiley and Sons, Inc., 1958.
LEVINSON, H. *Men, Management, and Mental Health.* Cambridge, Mass.: Harvard University Press, 1962.
————. *The Exceptional Executive: A Psychological Conception.* Cambridge, Mass.: Harvard University Press, 1968.
LEWIN, K. *Field Theory in Social Science,* D. Cartwright, ed. New York: Harper & Brothers, 1951.
————. "Frontiers in Group Dynamics," *Human Relations,* 1 (1947), 5–41.
————. "Group Decision and Social Change," *Readings in Social Psychology* (3rd ed.), E. E. Maccoby, T. M. Newcomb and E. L. Hartley, eds., pp. 197–211. New York: Holt, Rinehart & Winston, Inc., 1958.
————. "Psychology of Success and Failure," *Occupations,* 14 (June 1936), 926–30.
————. *Resolving Social Conflict,* Gertrude Lewin, ed. New York: Harper & Brothers, 1948.
————, R. LIPPETT and R. WHITE. "Leader Behavior and Member Reaction in Three 'Social Climates,' " in *Group Dynamics: Research and Theory* (2nd ed.), D. Cartwright and A. Zander, eds. Evanston, Ill.: Row, Peterson & Company, 1960.
LIEBERMAN, S. "The Effects of Changes in Roles on the Attitudes of Role Occupants," *Human Relations,* IX, No. 4 (1956), 385–402.
LIKERT, RENSIS. "Effective Supervision: An Adaptive and Relative Process," *Personnel Psychology,* II, No. 3 (1958), 317–52.
————. *The Human Organization.* New York: McGraw-Hill Book Company, 1967.
————. "Measuring Organizational Performance," *Harvard Business Review,* XXXVI, No. 2 (1958), 41–50.

_____. "Motivation: The Core of Management," American Management Association, *Personnel Series* (155), 3–21.

_____. "Motivational Approach to Management Development," *Harvard Business Review,* XXXVII, No. 4, (1959), 75–82.

_____. *New Patterns of Management.* New York: McGraw-Hill Book Company, 1961.

_____, and D. KATZ. "Supervisory Practices and Organizational Structures as They Affect Employee Productivity and Morale," American Management Association, *Personnel Series* (120), 1948, 14–24.

LINDAHL, LAWRENCE. "What Makes a Good Job," *Personnel,* 25 (January 1949).

LINDBLOM, C. E. *The Intelligence of Democracy.* New York: Free Press, 1965.

_____. "The Science of Muddling Through," *Public Administration Review,* 19 (1959) 79–99.

LINDHOLM, R., and J. NORSTEDT. *The Volvo Report.* Stockholm: Swedish Employers' Confederation, 1975.

LIPPETT, GORDON. *Organizational Renewal.* New York: Appleton-Century-Crofts, 1969.

_____, JEANNE WATSON and B. WESTLEY. *The Dynamics of Planned Change: A Comparative Study of Principles and Techniques.* New York: Harcourt, Brace & World, Inc., 1958.

LITTERER, J. A. *Analysis of Organizations.* New York: John Wiley & Sons, Inc., 1965.

LIVINGSTON, J. STERLING. "Pygmalion in Management," *Harvard Business Review* (July-August 1969), 81–89.

LORENZ, K., and P. LEYHAUSEN. *Motivation of Human and Animal Behavior.* New York: Van Nostrand Reinhold, 1973.

LOWIN, A., and J. R. CRAIG. "The Influence of Level of Performance on Managerial Style," *Organizational Behavior and Human Performance,* 3 (1968), 440–58.

LUTHANS, F. *Introduction to Management: A Contingency Approach.* New York: McGraw-Hill Book Company, 1976.

MACHIAVELLI, NICCOLO. *The Prince.* New York: Mentor Classic—New American Library, 1952.

_____. *The Prince and the Discourses.* New York: Random House, Inc., 1950.

MAHONEY, T., and P. FROST. "The Role of Technology in Models of Organizational Effectiveness," *Organizational Behavior and Human Performance,* 11 (1974), 122–38.

MAIER, N. R. F. *Psychology in Industrial Organizations.* Boston: Houghton-Mifflin, 1973.

MAIER, NORMAN R. F. *Frustration.* Ann Arbor: The University of Michigan Press, 1961.

_____. *Psychology in Industry* (2nd ed.). Boston: Houghton Mifflin Company, 1955.

MAILICK, SIDNEY, and EDWARD H. VAN NESS. *Concepts and Issues in Administrative Behavior.* Englewood Cliffs, N.J.: Prentice-Hall, Inc., 1962.

MANN, F. C. "Changing Superior-Subordinate Relationships," *Journal of Social Issues,* VII, No. 3 (1951), 56–63.

_____. "Putting Human Relations Research Findings to Work," *Michigan Business Review,* II, No. 2 (1950), 16–20.

_____. "Studying and Creating Change: A Means of Understanding Social Organization," *Research in Industrial Human Relations,* pp. 146–67. Madison, Wis.: Industrial Relations Research Association, 1957.

_____, and L. R. HOFFMAN. *Automation and the Worker: A Study of Social Change in Power Plants.* New York: Holt, Rinehart & Winston, Inc. 1960.

MARCH, J. G., and H. A. SIMON. *Organizations.* New York: John Wiley & Sons, Inc., 1958.

MARCUS, PHILIP M. "Supervision and Group Process," *Human Organization,* XX, No. 1 (1961), 15–19.

MARQUIS, D. G. "Individual Responsibility and Group Decisions Involving Risk," *Industrial Management Review,* 3 (1962), 8–23.

_____, H. J. REITZ. "Effects of Uncertainty on Risk Taking in Individual and Group Decisions," *Behavioral Science,* 4 (1969), 181–88.

MARROW, A. J., D. G. BOWERS, and S. E. SEASHORE. *Management by Participation.* New York: Harper & Row, Publishers, 1967.

MARROW, ALFRED J. *Behind the Executive Mask.* New York: American Management Association, 1965.

———. *Practical Theorist: The Life and Work of Kurt Lewin.* New York: Basic Books, Inc., Publishers, 1969.

MASLOW, ABRAHAM H., *Eupsychian Management.* Homewood, Ill.: Richard D. Irwin, Inc., and The Dorsey Press, 1965.

———. *Motivation and Personality.* New York: Harper & Row, Publishers, 1954.

———. *New Knowledge in Human Values* New York: Harper & Row, Publishers, 1959.

———. *Toward a Psychology of Being.* Princeton, N.J.: D. Van Nostrand Co., Inc., 1962.

MAYO, ELTON. *The Human Problems of an Industrial Civilization.* New York: The Macmillan Company, 1933.

———. *The Social Problems of an Industrial Civilization.* Boston: Harvard Business School, 1945.

MCCLELLAND, D., and D. H. BURNHAM. "Power Is the Great Motivator," *Harvard Business Review,* (March-April 1976), 100–110.

MCCLELLAND, DAVID C. *Personality.* New York: Holt, Rinehart & Winston, Inc., 1951.

———, et al. *The Achievement Motive.* New York: Appleton-Century-Crofts, 1953.

———. *The Achieving Society.* Princeton, N.J.: D. Van Nostrand Co., Inc., 1961.

MCGREGOR, DOUGLAS. "Conditions of Effective Leadership in Industrial Organization," *Journal of Consulting Psychologists,* 8 (1944), 56–63.

———. *The Human Side of Enterprise.* New York: McGraw-Hill Book Company, 1960.

———. *Leadership and Motivation.* Boston: MIT Press, 1966.

———. *Professional Manager.* New York: McGraw-Hill Book Company, 1967.

MCKELVEY, B., and R. H. KILMANN. "Organization Design: A Participative Multi-variate Approach," *Administrative Science Quarterly,* 20 (1975), 24–36.

MCMURRY, R. N. "The Case for Benevolent Autocracy," *Harvard Business Review,* 36 (1958), 82–90.

MEAD, G. H. *Mind, Self, and Society,* C. W. Morris, ed. Chicago: University of Chicago Press, 1930.

MEDALIA, NAHUM Z. "Unit Size and Leadership Perception," *Sociometry,* 17 (1954), 64–67.

——— and DELBERT C. MILLER. "Human Relations Leadership and the Association of Morale and Efficiency in Work Groups," *Social Forces,* 33 (1955), 348–52.

MELLINGER, G. D. "Interpersonal Trust as a Factor in Communication," *Journal of Abnormal and Social Psychology,* LII, No. 3 (1956), 304–309.

MELTZER, LEO, and JAMES SALTER. "Organizational Structure and Performance Job Satisfaction," *American Sociological Review,* 27 (1962), 351–62.

MEREI, F. *Group Leadership and Institutionalization. Human Relations,* 2 (1949), 23–39.

MERTON, ROBERT K. *Social Theory and Social Structure* (rev. ed.). Glencoe, Ill.: Free Press, 1957.

———, et al., eds. *Reader in Bureaucracy.* Glencoe, Ill: Free Press, 1952.

MEYERS, SCOTT M. "Who Are Your Motivated Workers," *Harvard Business Review* (January-February 1964), 73–88.

MILES, M. *Learning to Work in Groups.* New York: Teachers College, Columbia University, 1959.

MILES, RAYMOND E. "Human Relations or Human Resources," *Harvard Business Review* (July-August 1965).

MILGRAM, STANLEY. "Group Pressure and Action against a Person," *Journal of Abnormal and Social Psychology,* 69 (1964), 137–43.

MILLER, ERNEST C. *Objectives and Standards Approach to Planning and Control,* AMA Research Study, 1974.

MILLER, J. G. "Toward a General Theory for the Behavioral Sciences," *American Psychologist,* 10 (1955), 513–31.

MILLER, WALTER B. "Two Concepts of Authority," *American Anthropologist,* 57 (April 1955), 271–89.

MINER, JOHN B., and JOHN E. CULVER. "Some Aspects of the Executive Personality," *Journal of Applied Psychology,* 39 (1955). 348–53.

MINTZBERG, H. *The Nature of Managerial Work.* New York: Harper & Row, Publishers, Inc., 1973.

MOONEY, J. D., and A. C. RILEY. *The Principles of Organization.* New York: Harper & Brothers, 1939.

————. *Onward Industry.* New York: Harper & Brothers, 1931.

MORENO, J. L. *Who Shall Survive?* Washington, D.C.: Nervous and Mental Diseases Publishing Co., 1934.

MORSE, N., and E. REIMER. "The Experimental Change of a Major Organizational Variable," *Journal of Abnormal Social Psychology,* 52 (1956), 120–29.

MORSE, NANCY, and R. WEISS. "The Function and Meaning of Work and the Job," *American Social Review,* XX, No. 2 (1955), 191–98.

NAGLE, BRYANT F. "Productivity, Employee Attitude and Supervisor Sensitivity," *Personnel Psychology,* 7 (1954), 219–33.

NATEMEYER, W. E. "An Empirical Investigation of the Relationships Between Leader Behavior, Leader Power Bases, and Subordinate Performance and Satisfaction," an unpublished dissertation, University of Houston, August 1975.

NATIONAL COMMISSION ON PRODUCTIVITY AND WORK QUALITY. *A Plant-Wide Productivity Plan in Action: Three Years of Experience with the Scanlon Plan.* Washington, D.C., 1975.

NATIONAL TRAINING LABORATORIES. *Explorations in Human Relations Training.* Washington, D.C.: National Education Association, 1953.

NEWCOMB, T. M. *Social Psychology.* New York: Holt, Rinehart & Winston, Inc., 1950.

NEWMAN, WILLIAM H., CHARLES E. SUMMER and E. KIRBY WARREN. *The Process of Management* (2nd ed.), Englewood Cliffs, N.J.: Prentice-Hall, Inc., 1967.

OAKLANDER, HAROLD, and EDWIN A. FLEISHMAN. "Patterns of Leadership Related to Organizational Stress in Hospital Settings," *Administrative Science Quarterly,* 8 (1964), 520–32.

OBROCHTA, RICHARD J. "Foreman-Worker Attitude Patterns," *Journal of Applied Psychology,* 44 (1960), 88–91.

ODIORNE, GEORGE S. *Management by Objectives.* New York: Pitman Publishing Corp., 1965.

O'DONNELL, C. "The Source of Managerial Authority," *Political Science Quarterly,* 67 (1952), 573.

OSIPOW, S. H. *Theories of Career Development* (2nd ed.). New York: Appleton-Century-Crofts, 1973.

OUCHI, W. G., and A. M. JAEGER. "Social Structure and Organizational Type," in *Environments and Organizations,* M. W. Meyer and Associates, eds. San Francisco: Jossey-Bass, 1978.

OWENS, ROBERT G. *Organizational Behavior in Schools.* Englewood Cliffs, N.J.: Prentice-Hall, Inc., 1970.

PACKARD, VANCE. *The Status Seekers.* New York: David McKay Co., Inc., 1959.

PARKER, T. C. "Relationships among Measures of Supervisory Behavior, Group Behavior, and Situational Characteristics," *Personnel Psychology,* 16 (1963), 319–34.

PARKINSON, C. NORTHCOTE. *Parkinson's Law.* Boston: Houghton Mifflin, 1957.

PATCHEN, M. "The Effect of Reference Group Standards on Job Satisfactions," *Human Relations,* XI, No. 4 (1958), 303–14.

PEABODY, R. L. "Perceptions of Organizational Authority: A Comparative Analysis," *Administrative Quarterly,* 6 (1962), 463–82.

PEARLIN, L. I. "Alienation From Work," *American Sociological Review,* 27 (1962), 314–26.

PEARLIN, LEONARD I. "Sources of Resistance to Change in a Mental Hospital," *American Journal of Sociology,* 68 (1962), 325–34.

PELZ, D., and F. M. ANDREWS. "Organizational Atmosphere, Motivation, and Research Contribution," *American Behavioral Scientist,* 6 (1962), 43–47.

PELZ, D. C. "Influence: A Key to Effective Leadership in the First-Line Supervisor," *Personnel* (November 1952), 3–11.

_____. "Leadership within a Hierarchial Organization," *Journal of Social Issues*, 7 (1951), 49–55.

_____. "Motivation of the Engineering and Research Specialist," American Management Association, *General Management Series* (186), 1957, 25–46.

_____. "Some Social Factors Related to Performance in a Research Organization," *Administrative Science Quarterly*, I, No. 3 (1956), 310–25.

PERES, SHERWOOD H. "Performance Dimensions of Supervisory Positions," *Personnel Psychology*, 15 (1962), 405–10.

PERLS, F., R. HEFFERLINE and P. GOODMAN. *Gestalt Therapy*. New York: Delta, 1965.

PERROW, CHARLES. "The Analysis of Goals in Complex Organizations, *American Sociological Review*, 26 (December 1961), 854–66.

_____. *Organizational Analysis: A Sociological View*. Belmont, Calif.: Wadsworth Publishing Co., Inc., 1970.

PETER, LAWRENCE J., and RAYMOND HULL. *The Peter Principle*. New York: William Morrow & Co., Inc., 1969.

PFIFFNER, J. M. "The Effective Supervisor: An Organization Research Study," *Personnel*, 31 (1955), 530–40.

PIGORS, P., and C. A. MYERS. *Personnel Administration* (8th ed.). New York: McGraw-Hill Book Company, 1977.

PORTER, DONALD E., and PHILLIP B. APPLEWHITE. *Studies in Organizational Behavior and Mangement*. Scranton, Pa.: International Textbook Company, 1964.

PORTER, LYMAN W. "A Study of Perceived Need Satisfactions in Bottom and Middle Management Jobs," *Journal of Applied Psychology*, 45 (1961), 1–10.

PREMACK, DAVID. "Toward Empirical Behavioral Laws: 1. Positive Reinforcement," *Psychological Review*, 66 (1959), 219–33.

PRYER, MARGARET W., AUSTIN W. FLINT and BERNARD M. BASS. "Group Effectiveness and Consistency of Leadership," *Sociometry*, 25 (1962), 391–97.

PUGH, D. S. "The Measurement of Organization Structure," *Organizational Dynamics*, 1 (1973), 19–34.

RAVEN, B. H., and W. KRUGLANSKI. "Conflict and Power," in *The Structure of Conflict*, P. G. Swingle, ed. New York: Academic Press, 1975, 177–219.

REDDIN, WILLIAM J. *Effective Management by Objectives: The 3-D Method of MBO*. New York: McGraw-Hill Book Company, 1971.

_____. *Managerial Effectiveness*. New York: McGraw-Hill Book Company, 1970.

_____. "The 3-D Management Style Theory," *Training and Development Journal* (April 1967), 8–17.

REID, P. "Supervision in an Automated Plant," *Supervisory Management* (August 1960), 2–10.

REISMAN, DAVID. *The Lonely Crowd*. New Haven, Conn.: Yale University Press, 1950.

REITZ, H. J. *Behavior in Organizations*. Homewood, Ill.: Irwin, 1977.

REVANS, R. W., "The Analysis of Industrial Behavior," *Automatic Production-change and Control*. London: Institution of Production Engineering, 1957.

RICE, A. K. *The Enterprise and its Environment*. London: Tavistock Publications, 1963.

_____. *Productivity and Social Organization*. London: Tavistock Publications, 1958.

RICHARDSON, FREDERICK L. W., and CHARLES R. WALKER. *Human Relations in an Expanding Company*. New Haven: Labor and Management Center, Yale University, 1948.

ROACH, DARRELL E. "Factor Analysis of Rated Supervisory Behavior," *Personnel Psychology*, 9 (1956), 487–98.

ROE, A. *The Psychology of Occupations*. New York: John Wiley and Sons, Inc., 1956.

ROETHLISBERGER, F. J. *Management and Morale*. Cambridge: Harvard University Press, 1941.

_____, and W. J. DICKSON. *Management and the Worker*. Cambridge: Harvard University Press, 1939.

ROGERS, C. *On Becoming a Person*. Boston: Houghton-Mifflin Company, 1961.

ROGERS, C. R. *Client-centered Therapy*. Boston, Mass.: Houghton Mifflin Company, 1951.

_____. *Counseling and Psychotherapy*. Boston: Houghton Mifflin Company, 1942.

————. *Freedom to Learn*. Columbus, Ohio: Merrill, 1969.

ROGERS, M. F. "Instrumental and Infra-Resources: The Bases of Power," *American Journal of Sociology*, 79, No. 6 (1973), 1418–33.

RONKEN, H. O., and P. R. LAWRENCE. *Administrating Changes*. Boston: Harvard Graduate School of Business Administration, 1952.

ROSS, I. C. and A. ZANDER. "Need Satisfactions and Employee Turnover," *Personnel Psychology*, X, No. 3 (1957), 327–38.

RUBENSTEIN, ALBERT H., and CHADWICK J. HABERSTROH. *Some Theories of Organization*. Homewood, Ill.: Richard D. Irwin, Inc., 1960.

RUSSELL, B. *Power*. London: Allen and Unwin, 1938.

SANFORD, FILLMORE H. *Authoritarianism and Leadership*. Philadelphia: Institute for Research in Human Relations, 1950.

————. "Leadership Identification and Acceptance," *Groups, Leadership and Men*, Harold Guetzkow, ed. Pittsburgh: Carnegie Press, 1951.

SCHACHTER, S. "Deviation, Rejection, and Communication," *Journal of Abnormal and Social Psychology*, 46 (1951), 190–207.

SCHACHTER, STANLEY. *The Psychology of Affiliation*. Stanford, Calif.: Stanford University Press, 1959.

SCHAFFER, R. H. "Job Satisfaction as Related to Need Satisfaction in Work," *Psychological Monographs*, 67, No. 14 (1953).

SCHEIN, E. H. *Career Dynamics*. Reading, Mass.: Addison-Wesley Publishing Company, 1978.

————. "How 'Career Anchors' Hold Executives to Their Career Paths," *Personnel*, 52 No. 3 (1975) 11–24.

————. "How to Break in the College Graduate," *Harvard Business Review* (November-December 1964), 68–76.

————. "Organizational Socialization and the Profession of Management," *Industrial Management Review*, 9 (1968), 1–15.

————. *Process Consultation: Its Role in Organization Development*. Reading, Mass.: Addison-Wesley Publishing Company, 1969.

————. *Professional Education: Some New Directions*. New York: McGraw-Hill Book Company, 1972.

————. "The Chinese Indoctrination Program for Prisoners of War," *Psychiatry* (1956), 149–72.

————. "The Individual, the Organization, and the Career: A conceptual Scheme," *Journal of Applied Behavioral Science*, 7 (1971), 401–426.

————. "The Reluctant Professor: Implications for University Management," *Sloan Management Review*, 12, No. 1 (1970), 35–49.

————. "The Role Innovator and His Education," *Technology Review*, 72 (1970), 33–37.

————. "The Role of the Consultant: Content Expert or Process Facilitator?" *Personnel and Guidance Journal* (February 1978), 339–343.

————, and WARREN G. BENNIS. *Personal and Organizational Change through Group Methods*. New York: John Wiley & Sons, Inc., 1965.

SCHEIN, E. H., and J. S. OTT. The legitimacy of organizational influence. *American Journal of Sociology*, 1962, 67, 682–689.

SCHEIN, E. H., L. SCHNEIER and C. H. BARKER. *Coercive Persuasion*. New York: Norton, 1961.

SCHEIN, EDGAR H., *Organizational Psychology*. Englewood Cliffs, N.J.: Prentice-Hall, Inc., 1965.

————. "Management Development as a Process of Influence," *Industrial Management Review*, II, No. 2 (May 1961), 59–77.

SCHLEH, E. C. *Management by Results*. New York: McGraw-Hill Book Company, 1961.

SCHRANK, R. *Ten Thousand Working Days*. Cambridge, Mass.: MIT Press, 1978.

SEASHORE, S. F. *Group Cohesiveness in the Industrial Work Group*. Ann Arbor, Mich.: Survey Research Center, University of Michigan, 1954.

SEILER, JOHN A. *Systems Analysis in Organizational Behavior.* Homewood, Ill.: Richard D. Irwin, Inc., 1967.

SELZNICK, P. "Foundations of the Theory of Organization," *American Sociological Review,* 13 (February 1948), 25–35.

———. *Leadership in Administration.* Evanston, Ill.: Row, Peterson & Company, 1957.

SHARP, LAURISTON. "Steel Axes for Stone Age Australians," in *Human Problems in Technological Changes,* Edward H. Spicer, ed., pp. 69–94. New York: Russell Sage Foundation, 1952.

SHARTLE, C. L. *Effective Performance and Leadership.* Englewood Cliffs, N.J.: Prentice-Hall, Inc., 1956.

SHAW, M. E. *Group Dynamics: The Psychology of Small Groups.* New York: McGraw-Hill Book Company, 1971.

SHERIF, M., O. J. HARVEY, B. J. WHITE, W. R. HOOD and C. SHERIF. *Intergroup Conflict and Cooperation: The Robbers' Cave Experiment.* Norman, Okla.: University Book Exchange, 1961.

SHERIF, M., and C. SHERIF. *Social Psychology.* New York: Harper & Row, Publishers, Inc. 1969.

SHULTZ, G. P. "Worker Participation on Production Problems," American Management Association, *Personnel,* XXVIII, No. 3 (1951), 202–11.

SILBERBAUER, E. R. *Understanding and Motivating the Bantu Worker.* Johannesburg, South Africa: Personnel Management Advisory Service, 1968.

SIMON, H. A. *Administrative Behavior.* New York: The Macmillan Company, 1947.

———. *Models of Man, Social and Rational.* New York: John Wiley & Sons, Inc., 1957.

———. *The New Science of Management Decisions.* New York: Harper & Row, Publishers, Inc., 1960.

SKINNER, B. F. *Science and Human Behavior.* New York: The Macmillan Company, 1953.

———. *Analysis of Behavior.* New York: McGraw-Hill Book Company, 1961.

SOLOMON, R. L. "Punishment," *American Psychologist,* 19 (1964), 239.

SPECTOR, AARON J. "Expectations, Fulfillment, and Morale," *Journal of Abnormal and Social Psychology,* 52 (1956), 51–56.

SPEER, A. *Inside the Third Reich.* New York: The Macmillan Company, 1970.

STAGNER, ROSS. "Motivational Aspects of Industrial Morale," *Personnel Psychology,* 11 (1958), 64–70.

———. "Psychological Aspects of Industrial Conflict: Perception," *Personnel Psychology,* 1 (1948), 131–43.

STANTON, ERWIN S. "Company Policies and Supervisors' Attitudes Toward Supervision," *Journal of Applied Psychology,* 44 (1960), 22–26.

STEERS, R. M. *Organizational Effectiveness: A Behavioral View.* Santa Monica, Calif.: Goodyear, 1977.

STEINER, IVAN D., and HOMER H. JOHNSON. "Authoritarianism and Conformity," *Sociometry,* 26 (1963), 21–34.

STEWART, MICHAEL. "Resistance to Technological Change in Industry," *Human Organization,* XVI, No. 3 (1957), 36–39.

STINSON, JOHN E., and THOMAS W. JOHNSON. "The Path-Goal Theory of Leadership: A Partial Test and Suggested Refinement," *Academy of Management Journal,* 18, No. 2 (June 1975), 242–52.

STOGDILL, R. M. *Handbook of Leadership.* New York: The Free Press, 1974.

STOGDILL, R. M., *Individual Behavior and Group Achievement.* New York: Oxford University Press, 1959.

———, and ALVIN E. COONS, eds. *Leader Behavior: Its Description and Measurement,* Research Monograph No. 88. Columbus: Bureau of Business Research, The Ohio State University, 1957.

———, and C. L. SHARTLE. *Methods in the Study of Administrative Leadership.* Columbus: Ohio State University, Bureau of Business Research, 1956.

———. *Patterns of Administrative Performance.* Columbus: Ohio State University, Bureau of Business Research, 1956.

————. "Personal Factors Associated with Leadership: A Survey of the Literature," *Journal of Psychology*, 25 (1948), 35–71.

STONER, J. A. "Risky and Cautious Shifts in Group Decisions: The Influence of Widely Held Values," *Journal of Experimental Social Psychology*, 4 (1968), 442–59.

STRAUSS, G. "Workers: Attitudes and Adjustments," in *The Worker and the Job, J.* M. Rosow, ed. Englewood Cliffs, N.J.: Prentice-Hall, Inc., 1974.

STRAUSS, GEORGE. "Tactics of Lateral Relationship: The Purchasing Agent," *Administrative Science Quarterly*, U, No. 2 (September 1962), 161–86.

STRONG, E. K. *Vocational Interests of Men and Women.* Stanford, Calif.: Stanford University Press, 1943.

STUDENT, K. R. "Supervisory Influence and Work-Group Performance," *Journal of Applied Psychology*, 52, No. 3 (1968), 188–94.

STUTZ, F. H., R. G. MORROW and K. H. BLANCHARD. "Report of a Survey," in *College and University Trustees and Trusteeship: Recommendations and Report of a Survey.* Ithaca: New York State Regents Advisory Committee on Educational Leadership, 1966.

SUOJANEN, WAINO W. *The Dynamics of Management.* New York: Holt, Rinehart & Winston, Inc., 1966.

————. "The Span of Control—Fact or Fable?" *Advanced Management*, XX, No. 11 (1955), 5–13.

SUPER, D. E., and M. J. BOHN. *Occupational Psychology.* Belmont, Calif.: Wadsworth, 1970.

SUTERMEISTER, ROBERT A. *People and Productivity.* New York: McGraw-Hill Book Company, 1963.

TALACCHI, SERGIO. "Organization Size, Individual Attitudes and Behavior," *Administrative Science Quarterly*, 5 (1960), 398–420.

TANNENBAUM, A. S. "The Concept of Organizational Control," *Journal of Social Issues*, XII, No. 2 (1956), 50–60.

————. "Personality Change as a Result of an Experimental Change of Environmental Conditions," *Journal of Abnormal Social Psychology*, 52 (1957), 404–406.

————, and F. H. ALLPORT. "Personality Structure and Group Structure: An Interpretative Study of Their Relationship through an Event-Structure Hypothesis," *Journal of Abnormal Social Psychology*, LI, No. 3 (1956), 272–80.

TANNENBAUM, ROBERT, and WARREN H. SCHMIDT. "How to Choose a Leadership Pattern," *Harvard Business Review* (March-April 1958), 95–102.

————, IRVING R. WESCHLER, and FRED MASSARIK. *Leadership and Organization: A Behavioral Science Approach,* New York: McGraw-Hill Book Company, 1959.

TAYLOR, D. W., BERRY, P. C., and C. H. BLOCK. "Does Group Participation When Using Brainstorming Techniques Facilitate or Inhibit Creative Thinking?" *Administrative Science Quarterly*, 3 (1958), 23–47.

TAYLOR, FREDERICK W. *The Principles of Scientific Management.* New York: Harper & Brothers, 1911.

TERKEL, S. *Working.* New York: Random House, 1974.

TERRY, GEORGE R. *Principles of Management* (3rd ed.). Homewood, Ill.: Richard D. Irwin, Inc., 1960.

THELEN, H. A. *Dynamics of Groups at Work.* Chicago: University of Chicago Press, 1954.

THIBAUT, JOHN W., and HAROLD H. KELLEY. *The Social Psychology of Groups.* New York: John Wiley & Sons, Inc., 1959.

THOMAS, EDWIN J. "Role Concepts and Organizational Size," *American Sociological Review*, 24 (February 1959), 30–37.

THOMPSON, J. D. *Organizations in Action.* New York: McGraw-Hill Book Company, 1967.

————, and FREDERICK L. BATES. "Technology, Organization, and Administration," *Administrative Science Quarterly*, 2 (December 1957), 325–42.

————, and WILLIAM J. MCEWEN. "Organizational Goals and Environment: Goal-Setting as an Interaction Process," *American Sociological Review*, 23 (February 1958), 23–31.

THOMPSON , JAMES D. "Common and Uncommon Elements in Administration," *The Social Welfare Forum*. New York: Columbia University Press, 1962.

THOMPSON , VICTOR A. *Modern Organization*. New York: Alfred A. Knopf, Inc., 1961.

TOWNSEND, ROBERT C. *Up the Organization*. New York: Alfred A. Knopf, Inc., 1970.

TRIST, E. L., et al. *Organizational Choice*. London: Tavistock Publications, 1963.

TRIST, E. L., and K. W. B ANFORD. "Some Social and Psychological Consequences of the Long Wall Method of Goal Getting," *Human Relations,* 4, No. 1 (1951), 3–38.

TROW, DONALD B. "Autonomy and Job Satisfaction to Task Oriented Groups," *Journal of Abnormal and Social Psychology,* 54 (1957), 204–209.

TRUMBO, DON A. "Individual and Group Correlates of Attitudes Toward Work-Related Change," *Journal of Applied Psychology,* 45 (1961), 338–44.

TURNER, ARTHUR N. "Interaction and Sentiment in the Foreman-Worker Relationship," *Human Organization,* XIV, No. 1 (1955), 10–16.

U RWICK, LYNDALL F., *The Theory of Organization*. New York: American Management Association, 1952.

VAN BEINUM, H. J. J., and P. D. DE BEL. *Improving Attitudes Toward Work Especially by Participation*. London: Tavistock Publications, No. HRC 101, 1968.

VAN MAANEN, J. "Breaking in: Socialization to Work," in *Handbook of Work, Organization and Society,* R. Dublin, ed. Chicago: Rand-McNally, 1976.

————, and E. H. SCHEIN. "Improving the Quality of Work Life: Career Development," in *Improving Life at Work,* J. R. Hackman and J. L. Suttle, eds. Santa Monica, Calif.: Goodyear, 1977.

————. "Toward a Theory of Organizational Socialization," in *Research in Organizational Behavior,* Vol. I, B. Staw, ed. Greenwich, Conn.: JAI Press, Inc., 1979.

————, and L. BAILYN. "The Shape of Things to Come: A New Look at Organizational Careers," in *Perspectives on Behavior in Organizations,* J. R. Hackman, E. E. Lawler and L. W. Porter, eds. New York: McGraw-Hill Book Company, 1977.

VITELES, M. S. *Motivation and Morale in Industry*. New York: W. W. Norton & Company, Inc., 1953.

VROOM, V. H. "Can Leaders Learn to Lead?" *Organizational Dynamics* (Winter 1976), 17–28.

————. "The Effects of Attitudes on the Perception of Organizational Goals," *Human Relations,* XIII, No. 3 (1960), 229–40.

————. "Employee Attitudes," in *Frontiers of Industrial Relations,* R. Gray, ed. Pasadena, Calif.: California Institute of Technology, 1960.

————. "Leadership Revisited," *Man and Work in Society,* Man and Work in Society, in E. L. Cass and F. G. Zimmer, eds. New York: Van Nostrand Reinhold, 1975.

————. *Some Personality Determinants of the Effects of Participation*. Englewood Cliffs, N. J.: Prentice-Hall, Inc., 1960.

————, and F. C. MANN. "Leader Authoritarianism and Employee Attitudes," *Personnel Psychology,* XIII, No. 2 (1960), 125–40.

————, and PHILIP YETTON. *Leadership and Decision Making*. Pittsburgh, Pa.: University of Pittsburgh Press, 1973.

WAGNER, A. *Say It Straight or You'll Show It Crooked: Communication Skills for Employers and Employees*. Englewood Cliffs, N.J.: Prentice-Hall, Inc., 1981.

WALKER, C., and H. GUEST. *The Man on the Assembly Line*. Cambridge: Harvard University Press, 1952.

WALTON, R. E. "From Hawthorne to Topeka to Kalmar," in *Man and Work in Society,* E. I. Cass and F. G. Zimmer, eds. New York: Van Nostrand Reinhold, 1975.

————. "How to Counter Alienation in the Plant," *Harvard Business Review* (November-December 1972), 70–81.

————. "Improving the Quality of Work Life," *Harvard Business Review* (May-June 1974), 12ff.

———. *Interpersonal Peacemaking: Confrontations and Third Party Consultation.* Reading, Mass.: Addison-Wesley Publishing Company, 1969.

———. "The Diffusion of New Work Structures: Explaining Why Success Didn't Take," *Organizational Dynamics* (Winter 1975), 3–22.

WARNER, W. LLOYD. *Social Class in America.* New York: Harper & Row, Publishers, 1960.

———, and NORMAN H. MARTIN, eds. *Industrial Man.* New York: Harper & Row: Publishers, 1959.

WEBBER, ROSS A. *Management: Basic Elements of Managing Organizations.* Homewood, Ill.: Richard D. Irwin, Inc., 1975.

WEBER, MAX. *The Theory of Social and Economic Organization,* trans. A. H. Henderson, and ed. Talcott Parsons. New York: Oxford University Press, 1946.

WEITZ, JOSEPH, and ROBERT C. NUCKOLS. "Job Satisfaction and Job Survival." *Journal of Applied Psychology,* 39 (1955), 294–300.

WESTERLUND, G. *Group Leadership and Field Experiment.* Stockholm: Nordisk Rotogravyr, 1952.

WHITE, HARRISON. "Management Conflict and Sociometric Structure," *American Journal of Sociology,* 67 (September 1961), 185–99.

WHITE, ROBERT W. "Motivation Reconsidered: The Concept of Competence," *Psychological Review,* LXVI, 5 (1959).

———, and R. LIPPITT. *Autocracy and Democracy: An Experimental Inquiry.* New York: Harper & Row, Publishers, 1960.

WHITEHEAD, T. N. *The Industrial Worker* (2 vols.). Cambridge: Harvard University Press, 1939.

WHYTE, W. F. *Human Relations in the Restaurant Industry.* New York: McGraw-Hill Book Company, 1948.

———. "Human Relations Theory—A Progress Report," *Harvard Business Review,* XXXIV, No. 5 (1965), 125–34.

———. *Man and Organization.* Homewood, Ill.: Richard D. Irwin,Inc., 1959.

———, ed. *Money and Motivation.* New York: Harper & Row, Publishers, 1955.

———. *The Street Corner Society.* Chicago: University of Chicago Press, 1943.

WHYTE, W. H. JR., *The Organization Man.* New York: Simon and Schuster, Inc., 1956.

WHYTE, WILLIAM F. "Framework for the Analysis of Industrial Relations," *Industrial and Labor Relations Review,* 3, No. 3 (April 1950).

WOODWARD, J. *Industrial Organization: Theory and Practice.* London: Oxford University Press, 1965.

WRIGHTSMAN, L. S. *Assumptions about Human Nature.* Monterey, Calif.: Brooks-Cole, 1974.

———. "Measurement of Philosophies of Human Nature," *Psychological Reports,* 14 (1964), 743–51.

———. *Social Psychology.* Monterey, Calif.: Brooks-Cole, 1977.

WRISTON, HENRY M. *Academic Procession,* p. 78. New York: Columbia University Press, 1959.

WRONG, D. H. "Some Problems in Defining Social Power," *American Journal of Sociology,* 73 (1968), 673–81.

YANKELOVICH, D. "The Meaning of Work," in *The Worker and the Job,* J. M. Rosow, ed. Englewood Cliffs, N.J.: Prentice-Hall, Inc., 1974.

ZALEZNIK, A. *Worker Satisfaction and Development.* Boston: Harvard Business School, 1956.

———, C. R. CHRISTIENSEN and F. J. ROETHLISBERGER. *The Motivation, Productivity, and Satisfaction of Workers: A Prediction Study.* Boston: Division of Research, Harvard Business School, 1958.

ZANDER, A., E. J. THOMAS, and T. NATSOULAS. "Personal Goals and the Group's Goals for the Member," *Human Relations,* XIII, No. 4 (1960), 333–44.

Index

H

I

J

K

L

Transactional analysis (TA), 67–77, 227, 360–62
Transactions, 68, 72–76
Tri-Dimensional Leader Effectiveness Model, 96–99, 101–3, 308–9
Turnover, 50, 113

U

Unconscious, 238–39
Unfreezing, 280
University of Michigan, 63

V

Value systems, 53
Variables:
    causal, 111, 112, 268
    environmental, 125–39, 145
    intervening, 111, 112, 115, 194, 268
    output (end-result), 111–12, 115, 135, 194
    situational, 135–39, 143
Vroom, Victor H., 131, 137

W

Wages, 41
Wagner, Abe, 67, 70
Warner, Lloyd, 164
Wass, Donald L., 303
Weschler, Irving R., 82
Western Electric Company, 45–47
White, Robert W., 37–38
Whyte, William F., 40–41
Wilcox, D. S., 181
Winer, Ben J., 93
Work groups, 51–52
Working conditions, 41–42
Wriston, Henry, 167

Y

Your Erroneous Zones (Dyer), 245–46

Z

Zander, Alvin, 87, 92